'Finally, a book that gives dozens of examples of innovative pricing. Even one idea that grabs your attention can create a fortune.'
Philip Kotler, *S.C. Johnson & Son Distinguished Professor of International Marketing at Kellogg School of Management, Northwestern University, USA*

'Getting a fair price for a superior offer should be value based. We at SKF believe that clearly demonstrated sustainable measured value is a cornerstone of gaining competitive advantage for industry as a whole. We want our customers to be profitable and successful. This book is a must read to those who want to raise the level of performance of their enterprise to become a valuable contributor to the business sector they work in.'
Vartan Vartanian, *President, Industrial Market, Regional Sales & Service of SKF, Sweden*

'The very premise of this book, that great pricing is driven by active "innovation", not passive "optimization", is itself innovative. This book is a chronology of value-based pricing innovations that have made some companies more profitable. It is both a source of inspiration and a guide to pricing more creatively and, therefore, more profitably. I hope it will prove inspirational to those who have heretofore lagged behind.'
Tom Nagle, *Senior Advisor of Monitor and Author of* The Strategy and Tactics of Pricing, *USA*

'From historical perspectives to the latest strategies, innovations, metrics and research, *Innovation in Pricing – Contemporary Theories and Best Practices* covers a wide range of important pricing topics from leaders in industry, academia and expert content providers. It is this breadth in both subject matter and varied viewpoints that make this book a unique, valued resource for those who wish to drive results for their companies.'
Kevin Mitchell, *President of The Professional Pricing Society, USA*

'An understanding of the mechanics of pricing is one of the key weak spots in the skill sets of those responsible for revenue generation – be they marketers or salespeople. I've waited a long time for a book that successfully opens up the mysteries of innovative pricing.'
David Thorp, *Director of The Chartered Institute of Marketing, UK*

'At TrueFit, we believe that innovation is essential for people to thrive, and an essential ingredient in a thriving marketplace is a compelling value exchange. Too often, in settling for outdated or overly simplistic pricing models, we compromise the very client relationships we seek to elevate. Thank you for inspiring us to take a creative and intentional approach to our pricing and for clearly demonstrating the dramatic potential it holds to improve our client experience.'

Darrin Grove, *CEO TrueFit Solutions Inc., USA*

'A timely collection of contemporary insights about pricing's continuing evolution. An important work helping to strengthen the bridge between academia and industry. This book offers just the right mix of pricing innovation examples from industry along with modern day academic research. A great encapsulation of current thinking new ideas and a must have for every pricing book collection.'

Richard Cardot, *Simon Graduate School of Business, University of Rochester, USA*

'The brilliance of *Innovation in Pricing* is the ease with which Hinterhuber and Liozu bridge the vexing scholar–practitioner chasm by stripping complex pricing ideas down to their pragmatic utility. By introducing innovative dimensions for thinking strategically about how components of the pricing mix can be optimized, their book is an essential read for executives and consultants in search of new combinations to revitalize the pricing function as a source of competitive advantage and value creation.'

Nnaoke Ufere, *CEO of iServiceX, Inc., USA*

'Companies spend vast amount of resources in R&D, engineering and marketing while, most of the time, neglecting their pricing and value strategies. This book shows that pricing is a critical dimension of marketing strategies and that pricing innovation can bring the best out of these strategies. It also emphasizes the multi-dimensional nature of pricing which requires innovation, creativity and breakthrough thinking.'

Andreas Ising Schulze, *CEO of Advanced Polymer Technology Corp., USA*

'*Innovation in Pricing* presents a refreshing and optimistic outlook for pricing – one that is pragmatic yet creative. The book guides innovation and related best practices based on real situations facing pricing which makes it a must-have for senior managers.'

Navdeep S. Sodhi, *Sodhi Pricing and Author of* Six Sigma Pricing, *USA*

'Quite often, pricing discussions are simply a formality in strategic planning and budgeting sessions. But this book demonstrates the importance and value of strategic pricing initiatives. In today's highly competitive markets, innovative pricing strategies could very well provide companies with the edge they need to succeed.'

Al Neupaver, *President and CEO of Wabtec Corporation, USA*

'Our experience advising high tech startups has exposed us to innovation across the business spectrum – business models, products and technology. This book makes it clear that the often overlooked element of pricing is overdue for a bit of innovation as well. This book leaves no element overlooked – it addresses the organizational, strategic, tactical and psychological elements of pricing. It is a must-have resource for both scholars and practitioners.'

Martin L. Abbott & Michael T. Fisher, *AKF Partners, USA*

'Hinterhuber and Liozu represent a clear and steady voice in the movement to elevate the discipline of pricing to its rightful place ... one that is strategic, with plenty of opportunity for innovation and value creation.'

Justin McElhattan, *CEO of Industrial Scientific, USA*

'Andreas Hinterhuber's and Stephan Liozu's book *Innovation in Pricing* is a ground-breaking book on pricing theory and practice – a topic which influences each firm's bottom line but rarely is addressed as a key topic in academic research in marketing or strategy. Their collection demonstrates the unique value that practitioner oriented scholarship can offer to management theory and practice. It highlights well how the best practitioner scholars now truly create new vibrant interdisciplinary fields that demonstrate the value of problem oriented research and yet rely on rigorous academic scholarship. It represents an example of the best research we have generated in our practitioner oriented Doctor of Management program over the last years. I warmly recommend it to anyone who is interested in learning about practitioner oriented management scholarship in general and new innovative models and competencies of pricing in particular.'

Kalle Lyytinen, *Weatherhead School of Management, Case Western Reserve University, USA*

'I really enjoyed reading this book as it is one of the very few books written from a true marketing angle and giving a real attractiveness to pricing theory. Consistent with the definition of an innovation, the authors suggest to CHANGE THE RULE of pricing and display a comprehensive list of pricing strategies to align price and value. Congratulations for this revolution in pricing!'

Paul Millier, *EM Lyon, France*

'This book is full of the latest pricing strategies practicing executives and researchers on marketing have to know.'

Atsuo Utaka, *Kyoto University, Japan*

INNOVATION IN PRICING

Pricing has a substantial and immediate impact on profitability. Most companies, however, still use costs or competition as a main basis for setting prices. Product or business model innovation has a high priority for many companies whereas innovation in pricing has received scant attention. This book examines how innovation in pricing can drive profits.

The text examines innovation in pricing from four complementary perspectives. Innovation in Pricing Strategy illustrates how companies implement innovative pricing strategies, such as customer value-based pricing. Innovation in Pricing Tactics deals with innovative tools to measure and increase customer willingness to pay and to communicate value to B2B and B2C customers. Innovation in Organizing the Pricing Function looks at state-of-the art approaches to embed the pricing function in the organization. Psychological Aspects of Pricing illustrates how companies can influence customer perceptions of value and price in their quest to implement innovation in pricing.

This edited volume brings together 26 articles from academics, business practitioners and consultants. Authors are from the world's largest companies, leading research-based universities and consulting companies specialized in pricing.

This book is the only book dedicated to innovation in pricing and an essential read for business executives and pricing managers wishing to treat innovation in pricing as seriously as they treat product or business model innovation.

Andreas Hinterhuber is a Partner of Hinterhuber & Partners, a consultancy specialized in strategy, pricing and leadership. He is also a visiting professor at USI Lugano, Switzerland and at Bocconi University, Italy.

Stephan Liozu is President and CEO of ARDEX Americas, a high performance building materials company. He is also a PhD in Management candidate (2013) at Case Western Reserve University in Cleveland, OH, USA.

INNOVATION IN PRICING

Contemporary theories and best practices

Edited by Andreas Hinterhuber
and Stephan Liozu

LONDON AND NEW YORK

First published 2013
by Routledge
2 Park Square, Milton Park, Abingdon, Oxon OX14 4RN

Simultaneously published in the USA and Canada
by Routledge
711 Third Avenue, New York, NY 10017

Routledge is an imprint of the Taylor & Francis Group, an informa business

© 2013 Andreas Hinterhuber and Stephan Liozu

The right of Andreas Hinterhuber and Stephan Liozu to be identified as the authors of the editorial material, and of the authors for their individual chapters, has been asserted in accordance with sections 77 and 78 of the Copyright, Designs and Patents Act 1988.

All rights reserved. No part of this book may be reprinted or reproduced or utilised in any form or by any electronic, mechanical, or other means, now known or hereafter invented, including photocopying and recording, or in any information storage or retrieval system, without permission in writing from the publishers.

Trademark notice: Product or corporate names may be trademarks or registered trademarks, and are used only for identification and explanation without intent to infringe.

British Library Cataloguing in Publication Data
A catalogue record for this book is available from the British Library

Library of Congress Cataloging in Publication Data
Innovation in pricing: contemporary theories and best practices/
edited by Andreas Hinterhuber and Stephan Liozu.
  p. cm.
Includes bibliographical references and index.
1. Pricing. 2. Marketing–Technological innovations.
I. Hinterhuber, Andreas. II. Liozu, Stephan.
HF5416.5.I586 2012
658.8'16–dc23   2012015157

ISBN: 978-0-415-52161-1 (hbk)
ISBN: 978-0-415-52164-2 (pbk)
ISBN: 978-0-203-08568-4 (ebk)

Typeset in Bembo
by Sunrise Setting Ltd.

CONTENTS

List of illustrations   xii

List of contributors   xvii

PART I
Introduction   1

1. Innovation in pricing: Introduction   3
   Andreas Hinterhuber and Stephan M. Liozu

PART II
Innovation in organizing the pricing function   25

2. The organizational design of the pricing function in firms: a centre-led management approach   27
   Stephan M. Liozu and Kellie Ecker

3. Organizational barriers and the implementation of customer value map analysis: a case study of a global manufacturing firm in the polymer technology industry   46
   Niklas L. Hallberg and Linn Andersson

4. CEO championing of pricing and the impact on firm performance   67
   Stephan M. Liozu, Andreas Hinterhuber, Sheri Perelli and Toni M. Somers

5. Who is in charge of value? The emerging role of Chief Value Officer   99
   Ronald J. Baker and Stephan M. Liozu

6	B2B pricing systems: proving ROI *Mark Stiving*	119

PART III
Innovation in pricing strategy — 129

7	Innovation in B2B pricing *Rafael Farrés*	131
8	Why segmentation matters *Linda Trevenen*	151
9	The five fundamental value factors *Ralf Drews*	164
10	The journey to pricing excellence: the case of a mid-sized manufacturing firm *W. Michael Crouch and Greg Hunsicker*	178
11	Pricing processes in fast paced business-to-business settings *Magnus Johansson*	183
12	Pricing due diligence in the mergers and acquisition process *David Dvorin, Jered W. Haedt and Vernon E. Lennon*	197
13	Busting the four fatal myths in pricing *Nelson Hyde*	217
14	Creating and communicating customer value: how companies can set premium prices that customers are willing to pay *Todd Snelgrove*	228
15	Pricing strategies for recessionary times *Fernando Resende*	241
16	A zero-based approach to the pricing strategy *Roberto Bedotto*	245

PART IV
Innovation in pricing tactics — 253

17	Using economic value communication to bend business-to-business buyers' value perceptions *Christopher D. Provines*	255

18	Value: distilling the essence Harry Macdivitt	273
19	Innovations in determining willingness-to-pay for B2B companies Neil Biehn and Craig Zawada	288
20	Cross-functional collaboration in value-based pricing Steven Forth	298
21	Implementing effective pricing strategies: tools for tracking prices Richard Coppoolse	310
22	Winning on the margin: the B2B value imperative Mike Moorman	323
23	The thick and thin tails of pricing Darren Huxol	344

PART V
Psychological aspects of pricing   355

24	Behavioral aspects of pricing Ben Lowe, Julian Lowe and David Lynch	357
25	Research on odd prices: dead end or field of potential innovation? Carmen Balan	376
26	Applying consumer psychology to software pricing Anshu Jalora	393

PART VI
The next frontier   401

27	The next frontier of the pricing profession Kevin Mitchell	403

Index	410

ILLUSTRATIONS

Figures

1.1	Innovation in pricing strategy: price and value segmentation	4
1.2	Pricing to drive market expansion: the example for Ford's Model T	7
1.3	Overview of book contents	15
2.1	Types of pricing organizations	31
2.2	Price point definition process for value-based pricing (VBP)	35
2.3	Differences in the decision making process between firms using value-based pricing and those that did not	36
2.4	Price point definition process for cost-based pricing (CBP)	37
2.5	Evidence of role specialization in firms that use value-based pricing	37
2.6	Evidence of expertise centralization in firms that use value-based pricing	38
3.1	The moderating effect of sales force price delegation on the relationship between customer value map analysis and value-based pricing strategy	47
3.2	Graphical illustration of CVMA	49
4.1	Research model and proposed hypotheses	69
4.2a	Second-order measurement model results for pricing orientation	82
4.2b	Second-order measurement model results for relative performance	83
5.1	Sustainable value-assessment circle	105
5.2	Two options for CVO role design	114
5.3	Proposed process-oriented CVO job description	115

7.1	The price waterfall	140
7.2	The price–value map	143
7.3	Turnover build-up	144
7.4	Price floors, list prices and target prices	145
7.5	The terms and conditions (T&C) tool	146
7.6	The pricing explorer	148
7.7	Sample value chain	149
8.1	Segmentation Preparation Plan	155
8.2	Example of a medical device firm	161
9.1	Market prioritization	166
9.2	Target product value profile reflecting the needs of the most powerful buying influence	168
9.3	HPT's eight most important buying criteria and its positioning against the competition	169
9.4	Analysis of the eight most important buying criteria by means of conjoint analysis	170
9.5	The overall value equation	171
9.6	The ideal customer profile of HPT	172
9.7	Result of the "day in a life" approach	174
9.8	Unweighted relevant functions of the HPT cleaner	174
9.9	Performance of the competitors' products in all relevant functions	174
9.10	Importance of the functions from the ideal customer's point of view	175
9.11	Target profile of HPT's new cleaner	175
10.1	The ARDEX journey	182
12.1	Due diligence – existing process	199
12.2	Due diligence – improved process: 'digging deeper'	200
12.3	Strategic pricing capability assessment	203
12.4	Valuation equation	212
12.5	Price premium equation	213
13.1	US car industry profit and capacity	219
13.2	Price elasticity in the product life cycle	220
13.3	Pricing power defined	223
14.1	The priceberg	232
14.2	Price versus TCO	233
14.3	Documenting customer value	235
14.4	Quantifying customer value	237
14.5	Price versus value	239
17.1	Intersection of benefits communicated and buyer type	259
17.2	Supplier segmentation and procurement tactics	261

17.3	Summary of economic benefit communication tools	266
17.4	Economic value communication strategy framework	268
18.1	The value triad	275
18.2	Importance of value triad factors to different stakeholders	280
18.3	Extract from value calculator – lubricant company	284
19.1	Methods of WTP estimation as found in Breidert	289
19.2	Common pricing models in B2B	290
19.3	Histogram of volume versus price	295
20.1	Internal participants in the pricing conversation	299
20.2	The canonical value model	301
20.3	Conceptual blending of commodity and differentiation pricing	303
20.4	Order of conversations	307
21.1	Price–sales chart	313
21.2	Price–mix chart	314
21.3	Price change report	314
21.4	Price scatter chart	315
21.5	Price band chart	316
21.6	Price bubble chart	316
21.7	Revenue causality report	317
21.8	Target price analysis	317
21.9	Floor price analysis	318
21.10	Price index analysis	320
21.11	Pricing key performance indicators (KPIs)	321
22.1	Total cost-in-use components	325
22.2	VBS customer value management cycle	326
22.3	Sales effectiveness system	327
22.4	Sales and Marketing "three-legged race" collaboration (case example)	329
22.5	Two-dimensional B2B segmentation (case example)	330
22.6	Marketing offerings and value proposition (case example)	331
22.7	Brand positioning versus value proposition	332
22.8	Value proposition development roadmap	332
22.9	Value proposition strategy continuum	334
22.10	VBS sales process (case example)	336
22.11	Sales process benefits (case example)	336
22.12	Sales channels and sales force structure design considerations	338
22.13	VBS software tools requirements (case example)	340
22.14	VBS sales managers focus heavily on advanced coaching elements	341

23.1	Risk and benefit transfer in different industries	345
23.2	The thick and thin tail in pricing	348
23.3	The efficient frontier	348
23.4	Value comparisons for competing products	349
23.5	Price and performance corridors	350
24.1	The value pricing thermometer	367
25.1	Scope of the research on odd prices	380
26.1	Microsoft Office prices	394
26.2	Norton prices	394
26.3	McAfee prices	394
26.4	Adobe Acrobat prices	395
26.5	IBM SPSS Statistics prices	395
26.6	Microsoft Windows 7 prices	396
26.7	Options offered to test group	396
26.8	Options offered to control group	398
27.1	Framework for transformation	406

Tables

1.1	Innovation in pricing strategy – new metrics	6
2.1	Centre-led survey items	34
2.2	EFA summary statistics	39
2.3	Construct correlation scores	39
2.4	Results of the measurement model	40
2.5	Results of the structural model	41
2.6	Pricing capabilities R square decomposition	41
2.7	Qualitative survey sample characteristics	42
2.8	Quantitative survey sample characteristics	43
3.1	ManComp's pricing prior to the pricing project, actions taken, and pricing after the project	53
4.1	Descriptive statistics, reliability, correlations and discriminant validity	79
4.2	Measurement model results for first-order constructs	80
4.3	Structural model results	84
5.1	Critical function of commercially related C-level positions	110
8.1	Segment and value offering	159
8.2	Sales strategy	160
9.1	Industry attractiveness independent of the company's strengths	166

9.2	Strength of enterprise	166
9.3	Distribution of decision-making influence	167
9.4	Workflow for the installation of a cable duct	173
13.1	Capacity utilization and profitability in the US car industry	226
16.1	Brand growth matrix	247
16.2	Brand growth matrix by product category	247
16.3	Brand growth matrix by channel	248
16.4	Brand growth matrix by customer	249
17.1	Focus areas and objectives for procurement	262
17.2	Summary of decision analytic models and examples	264
18.1	Tangible and intangible drivers	277
18.2	So what analysis – warranty manager	279
18.3	So what analysis (tissue viability nurse)	281
21.1	An overview of price tracking tools	311
26.1	Results – test group	398
26.2	Results – control group	398

CONTRIBUTORS

Linn Andersson is a PhD candidate in strategic management at the Institute of Economic Research at Lund University, Sweden.

Ronald J. Baker is the founder of VeraSage Institute, a think tank dedicated to educating professionals on value-based pricing, USA.

Carmen Balan is Professor PhD at the Faculty of Marketing of the Bucharest Academy of Economic Studies in Romania.

Roberto Bedotto is Global Pricing Director for Honeywell Process Solutions, a division of Honeywell.

Neil Biehn is the Vice President of Science and Research at PROS Pricing, USA.

Richard Coppoolse is Founding Partner of ValuePricing Consultancy, The Netherlands.

W. Michael Crouch is Vice President and Chief Marketing Officer of ARDEX Americas.

Ralf Drews has been the CEO and President of Dräger Safety in North America since 2008.

David Dvorin is a Senior Operating Executive at Welsh, Carson, Anderson & Stowe, USA.

Kellie Ecker is VP, Head of Corporate Pricing at Institut Straumann AG, Basel, Switzerland.

Rafael Farrés is Head of Strategy & Pricing at Agfa Graphics in Belgium.

Steven Forth is CEO of LeveragePoint Innovations Inc, Canada.

Jered W. Haedt is Chief Scientist and a Managing Partner of The Pricing Cloud.

Niklas L. Hallberg is Associate Professor in Strategic Management at Lund University, Sweden.

Andreas Hinterhuber is a Partner of Hinterhuber & Partners, a consultancy specialized in strategy, pricing and leadership. He is also a visiting professor at USI Lugano, Switzerland and at Bocconi University, Italy.

Greg Hunsicker is the Manager of Pricing and Revenue Optimization at ARDEX Americas.

Darren Huxol is a Marketing Leader at GE Aviation located in Cincinnati, Ohio, USA.

Nelson Hyde is the Director of Price Strategy for Philips Healthcare, USA.

Anshu Jalora is Associate Professor of Pricing and Customer Relationship Management at the Narsee Monjee Institute of Management Studies, India.

Magnus Johansson holds a PhD from the School of Economics and Management at Lund University, Sweden.

Vernon E. Lennon, III is CEO and founder of The Pricing Cloud.

Stephan Liozu is President and CEO of ARDEX Americas, a high performance building materials company. He is also a PhD in Management candidate (2013) at Case Western Reserve University in Cleveland, OH, USA.

Ben Lowe is Senior Lecturer in Marketing at Kent Business School, University of Kent, England.

Julian Lowe is Conjoint Fellow at the University of Newcastle, Australia.

David Lynch is a Research Associate with the Centre for Regional Competitiveness at The Business School, University of Ballarat, Australia.

Harry Macdivitt is Director of Axia Value Solutions, a specialist consultancy firm, UK.

Kevin Mitchell is President of the Professional Pricing Society and publisher of *The Pricing Advisor* newsletter and *The Journal of Professional Pricing*.

Mike Moorman is Managing Principal Go-to-Market Strategy & Transformation for ZS Associates.

Sheri Perelli is a practitioner scholar with international corporate, government and consulting experience, and teaches in both the School of Business Administration and the School of Engineering at Wayne State University, USA.

Christopher D. Provines is Vice President, Pricing & Sales Effectiveness at Holden Advisors. He has 20-plus years of experience in executive roles at Siemens and Johnson & Johnson. In addition, he is an Adjunct Professor at the Graduate School of Business at Rutgers University.

Fernando Resende is Commercial Manager for Smart Grid Projects in Latin America at General Electric, Brazil.

Todd Snelgrove is Global Manager, Value for SKF for the design and maintenance of industrial rotating equipment, USA.

Toni M. Somers is Professor of Management & Information Systems in the School of Business Administration at Wayne State University, USA.

Mark Stiving PhD, is Director of Pricing at Maxim Integrated Products, USA.

Linda Trevenen is the Director of Marketing Excellence & Market Intelligence for Philips Home Healthcare Solutions and has been with the company since 2005. She earned her CPP (Certified Pricing Professional) in 2009.

Craig Zawada serves as Senior Vice President, Pricing Excellence, at PROS. Prior to joining PROS, he was a partner and co-leader of the Pricing Strategy Practice at McKinsey & Company.

PART I
Introduction

1

INNOVATION IN PRICING

Introduction

Andreas Hinterhuber

Stephan M. Liozu

Few companies treat innovation in pricing as seriously as they treat product or business model innovation. One key objective of this edited volume is thus to raise the importance of innovation in pricing, both in academia as well as in the industry.

A historical perspective on innovation in pricing

Nearly five decades ago, in 1968, Elizabeth Marting edited the book *Creative Pricing*. This book is a collection of papers by 19 scholars and pricing practitioners on creative pricing approaches. The book covers the following topics: the role of pricing, pricing policy and objectives, nonfinancial aspects of pricing, pricing by distribution channel, pricing by product type, the use of computers in pricing, and management of price changes. In the foreword, Elizabeth Marting comments (Marting 1968: 5): 'It is the thesis of this book that with sound planning, flexible techniques, and adequate support, pricing can be made to have a positive, productive impact on company profits; in short, that it can be creative.' We agree. Pricing can and should be a topic of innovation and creativity.

In the first chapter, Oxenfeldt suggests (Oxenfeldt 1968: 9) that 'the notion that pricing can be creative is itself quite creative and new'. For decades, research in pricing has been dominated first by economic theory and later by cost accounting. We conjecture that price strategists and price setters have the opportunity to be creative, although 'it runs counter to the writing and thinking of most economic theorists' (Oxenfeldt 1968: 10).

The questions raised 50 years ago are still valid. The answers as to what constitutes an innovation in pricing have changed.

4 Andreas Hinterhuber and Stephan M. Liozu

What is innovation in pricing?

Innovation in pricing regards instances in which companies innovate their pricing strategies, tactics, or organization, or where companies use an understanding of consumer psychology to change customer perceptions of value and price. In this section we provide an overview.

Innovation in pricing strategy
Price and value segmentation

One way to implement innovation in pricing strategy is to move from a one-size-fits-all pricing policy to a policy with multiple price and value configurations, reflecting differences in value creation for different market segments (see Figure 1.1).

Allstate, one of the most profitable auto insurance companies, is able to successfully compete against no-frills Internet competitors, through a policy of price and value segmentation: depending on the customer's brand/price sensitivity and her needs for customer support, Allstate divides customers into four distinct clusters

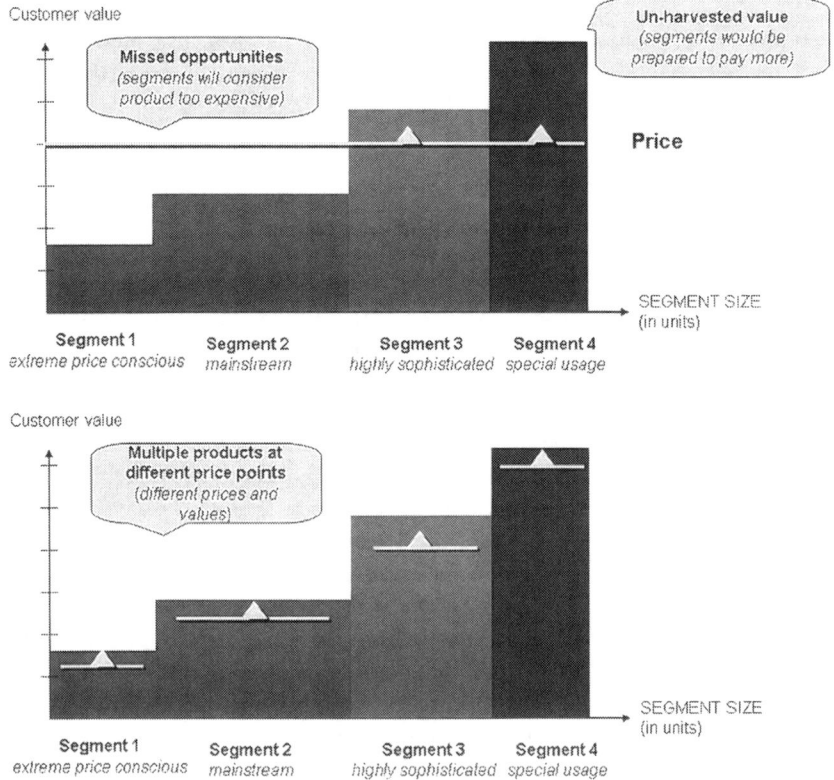

FIGURE 1.1 Innovation in pricing strategy: price and value segmentation

(high/low brand sensitivity and high/low self-service) and competes in these different market segments through four distinct brands, offering a substantially different customer experience at different price points.

Pay for performance pricing

Pay for performance pricing is an arrangement whereby the seller is paid depending on performance outcomes determined conjointly with the customer. The following example may serve as illustration: the UK, along with Sweden, Australia and Canada, is among the few countries where the reimbursement of new pharmaceutical products is closely tied to criteria reflecting the new product's incremental value over existing therapies. For new pharmaceuticals, the UK has a threshold range of £20,000 to £30,000 per QUALY (quality-adjusted life year). In this environment, Velcade (bortezomib), by Johnson and Johnson (J&J), a product for treating multiple myeloma, is considered not cost-effective, since treatment costs are approximately £3,200 per treatment cycle, or £40,000 per QUALY. Traditional pricing approaches thus would have suggested either to drop the price to reach the threshold – implying a price drop by up to 50 per cent – or to exit the UK market. J&J, however, proposes an alternative pricing approach to regulatory authorities (Hinterhuber 2012). Under the new pricing scheme, J&J links reimbursement to effectiveness. Only when patients respond fully to the new drug, do they remain on therapy and the drug is funded by the National Health System. When patients show no or a minimal response, the treatment ceases, and J&J bears the full costs. This new approach (full reimbursement by J&J in case of no response) reduces the costs for patients on therapy to approximately £22,000 per QUALY. As a result, Velcade is today the market share leader in the UK while also being the most expensive therapy in this segment. Global sales are in excess of $1 billion in a very competitive environment.

Advertising, industrial services (e.g. software, consulting, logistics and transportation), and complex engineering projects are other areas where pay for performance pricing is currently widespread. Performance-based pricing is costly: monitoring is intensive. Nevertheless, we expect to see a substantial increase in these arrangements in other areas in the future, very likely also in consumer-good markets.

New metrics

Innovative pricing strategies align pricing with customer goals. This frequently leads to new pricing metrics. Levitt, a marketing professor at Harvard Business School, famously quotes Leo McGinneva about why people buy quarter-inch drill bits: 'They don't want quarter inch bits. They want quarter inch holes' (Levitt 1986: 128). Table 1.1 provides an overview of innovative metrics.

In all these cases, companies align the basis of their own pricing policies with customer outcomes. This interest alignment enables high customer satisfaction, thus overcoming customer resistance to a change in pricing approach.

TABLE 1.1 Innovation in pricing strategy – new metrics

Company	Traditional pricing strategy	New pricing metric	Result
General Electric	Cost-based. Fixed pricing for aircraft engines; spare parts sold with substantial mark-up (+300% over costs).	'Power by the hour': value-based pricing for utilization rights of aircraft engines; usage-based, variable, pricing inclusive of maintenance and performance guarantee.	High customer satisfaction; interest alignment; increased profitability.
Salesforce.com	Traditionally, software companies sold boxes of software. Prices reflect volume.	Software as a service (SaaS). Price varies with usage.	New customers (low-usage customers); high growth and profitability.
BASF	Paint sold on a per kg basis to car manufacturers.	Outcome-based pricing. Price is set per painted car.	High customer satisfaction. Joint collaboration with customers to reduce environmental impact and paint consumption.
Michelin	Truck tyres sold at largely fixed prices.	Michelin Fleet Solutions sells mobility: pricing is based on performance (per km) and includes maintenance.	Initial difficulties (new business model), expansion across Europe at above-average margins.
Schindler	Elevators sold at cost-plus prices.	Sale of usage rights: variable pricing based on distance and number of passengers transported.	Market share growth in competitive market; access to new customer segments.

Pricing to drive market expansion

Rather than compete for market share, innovative pricing approaches expand the overall market. The pricing of Ford's Model T is an example (Figure 1.2) (adapted from Casadesús-Masanell 1998):

In his autobiography, originally published in 1922, Henry Ford states:

> Our policy is to reduce the price, extend the operations, and improve the article. You will notice that the reduction of price comes first. We have never

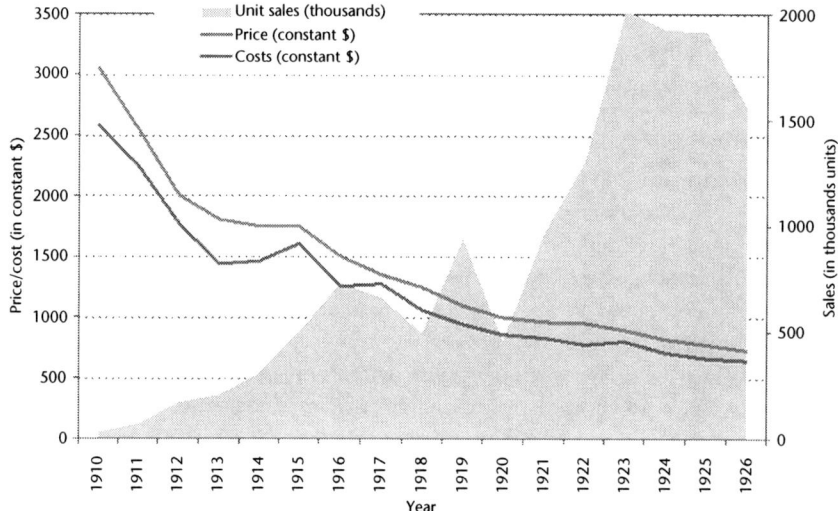

FIGURE 1.2 Pricing to drive market expansion: the example for Ford's Model T

considered any costs as fixed. Therefore we first reduce the price to a point where we believe more sales will result. Then we go ahead and try to make the price. We do not bother about the costs. The new price forces the costs down. The more usual way is to take the costs and then determine the price, and although that method may be scientific in the narrow sense, it is not scientific in the broad sense, because what earthly use is it to know the cost if it tells you that you cannot manufacture at a price at which the article can be sold? But more to the point is the fact that, although one may calculate what a cost is, and of course all of our costs are carefully calculated, no one knows what a cost ought to be.

(Ford 2007: 84)

Similar approaches where pricing strategies have expanded the overall market include Ryanair/easyJet, the pricing of wines from the New World (USA, Chile, Australia), and others.

Zero as a special price

Zero is a special price, uniquely capturing customer attention (Shampanier et al. 2007). A number of companies seem to have mastered the art of profitable growth while essentially giving away the main product. Ryanair, with average flight revenues of €40 per customer, barely breaks even on its flight operations, yet it is Europe's most profitable airline, largely as a result of the profitability of its ancillary revenues: revenues from third parties, customer penalty payments, early boarding fees, baggage fees, in-board sales (Hinterhuber 2012). Skype (Internet calls are free, fixed-line calls are sold at regular prices), Google (search is free, advertisement is sold), fast-consumption newspapers (given away for free, advertisement is sold) and open source software (standard models are free, customized versions are sold) compete using similar pricing strategies.

Name your own price

Name your own price (NYOP) mechanisms ask customers to submit a bid price for a product. The customer receives the product only if this bid price is larger than an unknown threshold price; in this case the customer pays the submitted price. In some instances, rebidding may be allowed. Priceline successfully pioneered this business model in the 1990s with very remarkable results. NYOP enables a large degree of price discrimination between customers. NYOP is more profitable than fixed prices if the seller is a monopolist; with competition, NYOP increases profitability if it allows a company to expand its current customer base with price-sensitive customers who would otherwise not purchase (Shapiro 2011). NYOP also contributes towards mitigating competition, since customers differ in their bidding costs: NYOP firms thus target customers with low bidding costs, while fixed-price sellers target customers with high bidding costs (Fay 2009). Based on these considerations we thus expect that NYOP mechanisms will gain in popularity, quite likely also in industrial markets.

Pay what you want

Pay what you want (PWYW) is a participative pricing mechanism where customers set prices. In contrast to NYOP mechanisms, sellers have to accept any price, including zero. Examples of PWYW pricing can be found in information services (e.g. Wikipedia), in museums (voluntary contributions), in the music industry (e.g. Radiohead), as well as in the hotel and restaurant industry. Fairness considerations, social norms, as well as credible threats by the seller to switch back to fixed prices (Mak et al. 2010) seem to motivate customers to pay non-zero prices. In three experimental studies involving restaurants and cinemas, PYWY pricing leads to lower average prices than previously posted fixed prices but higher revenues due to new demand (Kim et al. 2010). Thus NYOP pricing can be beneficial for sellers as well as for customers (Kim et al. 2009). We thus expect further applications of PWYW pricing, in both consumer-good as well as industrial markets.

Innovation in pricing tactics

Revenue management

Revenue management is probably the most successful pricing innovation in service industries: Successful implementation increases company revenues by 3 per cent to 7 per cent and profits by 30 per cent to 50 per cent (Skugge 2004). Revenue management varies price levels and bookable capacities conjointly to optimize profitability. Revenue management has evolved from the travel industry (airlines, then hotels, then rental cars, finally cruise lines), to leisure services (golf courses, sport clubs, restaurants), to industrial services (freight transportation, advertising time), to, finally, consumer services (equipment rental, home repair). Revenue management can be applied in industries characterized by the following features: fluctuating demand, existence of different customer segments, fixed and perishable capacity, high fixed costs, low variable costs and predictable demand. We foresee that in the future, capital-intensive industrial manufacturers will consider applying revenue management to at least part of their supply: as a testimony, Infineon, a leading chip manufacturer, is currently experimenting with dynamic pricing (Ehm 2010).

Callable revenue management

Low fare bookings frequently displace highly profitable last-minute bookings in case of higher than anticipated demand. Callable revenue management grants the supplier (e.g. the airline) the option to repurchase low-fare bookings at a predetermined price for immediate resale to high-price customers. This recall price is above the low fare and below the high-price fare (Gallego et al. 2008). Callable revenue management can be profitable for both airlines and customers: customers self-select to grant the call option if the option price is attractive and profit if the option is exercised; the supplier (e.g. airline) also profits with the resale. High-fare customers also profit, since they obtain an otherwise occupied seat. Callable revenue management thus increases profitability: it induces additional low-fare demand and reduces overbooking costs (Gallego et al. 2008). We anticipate that the use of callable revenue management will increase in the future in all industries where revenue management is currently applied. One immediate candidate is the airline industry, where bumping and re-planing raise airline costs and are a frequent cause of customer dissatisfaction.

Contingent pricing

As an alternative to a fixed high- or low-price strategy, contingent pricing is an arrangement to sell a product at a low price if the seller does not succeed in obtaining a higher price offer during a specified period (Biyalogorsky and Gerstner 2004): if a higher price is obtained, the original sale does not take place and the original buyer receives the agreed-upon compensation. Otherwise, the original buyer purchases the product at the original price. Contingent pricing mitigates the expected losses from price risks, and it benefits buyers as well as sellers. Also here we anticipate that the use of contingent pricing will increase in the future. As an example, Caterpillar sells its spare parts to dealers with the option to repurchase the product at a 10 per cent price premium in case another dealer or customer runs out of stock and has an urgent need for the product in question (Sheffi 2005).

Individualized pricing

Information technology enables service companies (e.g. insurers) to charge substantially different prices for identical products or services based on individual customer data. Price quotes reflect an estimate of customer willingness to pay and are based on the following: customer demographics, transaction history and the estimated likelihood to shop for alternative offers. SunTrust, one of the largest US banks, is implementing individualized pricing for car loans and home mortgages: the company uses software to search for instances where it undercharged customers willing to pay more for a home mortgage; the software also detects cases where the company lost business due to excessively high prices. The software finally produces an optimized, individualized price for different customers (Kadet 2008). Individualized pricing is thus likely to increase in all industries where suppliers have frequent and direct contact with known individual customers (e.g. financial services, communication, tourism, online retailing, logistics and transportation, industrial services).

Innovation in organizing the pricing function

Organizing the pricing function is a strategic activity – strategic from at least two different perspectives. First, it is strategic in the sense that pricing is an integral part of firm strategy. Second, it is strategic as encompassing a resource and activity configuration that is valuable, rare, difficult to imitate, nonsubstitutable and embedded in the firm's organization (Barney 1991) and thus enabling a firm to build a competitive advantage and to achieve superior profitability as a result (Hinterhuber and Liozu 2012). This involves the following elements:

Centralization

The literature highlights the advantages of centralization (Stephenson et al. 1979) as well as the performance benefits of decentralization (Frenzen et al. 2010). Recent research, however, suggests that centralization – that is, a central function with clearly defined decision rights on price setting and on price-negotiation latitudes for sales personnel – increases firm performance (Liozu and Hinterhuber 2012).

Championing

CEOs are powerful individuals: within any organization, the 'levers of power are uniquely concentrated in the hands of the CEO' (Nadler and Heilpern 1998: 9). CEOs themselves 'will never set a single price' (Dutta et al. 2002: 66). Current academic research, however, strongly suggests that the championing of the pricing function by the CEO has a very powerful effect on firm performance (Liozu et al. 2012c).

Capabilities

Pricing capabilities are a complex bundle of routines and activities that include acquisition of pricing-specific skills, use of pricing tools, development of pricing processes, acquisition of competitor knowledge, and acquisition of knowledge about customer needs and about customer willingness to pay (Liozu and Hinterhuber 2011). Pricing capabilities are positively linked to firm performance (Liozu et al. 2012b).

Confidence

Innovation in pricing requires organizational and individual confidence: this confidence in turn leads to superior firm performance (Liozu et al. 2012a).

Change management

Innovation in pricing finally fundamentally engages the organization in a change-management process (Liozu et al. 2012a). A new pricing approach is not 'just a change of marketing signals' but 'a new way of life' (Forbis and Mehta 1981). Engaging the organization to experiment with and implement new pricing approaches is thus fundamentally a change-management process that significantly exceeds the complexity of activities such as changing list prices: new pricing approaches frequently require new capabilities, a new organizational structure, different goal and incentive systems, new processes and tools, and new organizational priorities.

Psychological aspects of pricing and innovation

Customer preferences in business-to-consumer (B2C) and business-to-business (B2B) markets are not stable – they are constructed. Research examining behavioural and psychological aspects of pricing seeks to understand how customer perceptions of value and price are formed. Research in this area has substantially increased in the past years; for an overview, see Hinterhuber and Liozu (2013). We discuss some recent findings:

Advertised reference prices

Advertised reference prices (e.g. manufacturer-suggested retail price $299, now only $99) influence customer behaviour, even if customers themselves know that these reference prices are inflated (Suter and Burton 1996). A judicious use of advertised reference prices can thus influence customer choice towards higher margin products.

9-endings

More than 50 per cent of posted retail prices end in 9. Customers perceive prices ending in 9 as lower than they actually are; they also associate 9 endings with special offers. Thus, 9 endings have both level and image effects (Stiving and Winer 1997). Despite their widespread use and possible wear-off effects, 9 endings still seem to lead to higher sales (Anderson and Simester 2003).

Irrelevant attributes

In 2000, Shell launches V-Power, a premium fuel sold with the promise of improving engine performance and reducing fuel consumption. The product carries a price premium over regular fuel of approximately 10 per cent. A spokesperson for a large, premium car manufacturer vehemently denies that the new fuel improves engine performance (Beukert 2003). Nevertheless, premium fuels account for 25 per cent of all fuel sold by Shell five years after launch (Hinterhuber 2012). Differentiated fuels enable Shell to substantially improve downstream profitability.

In these cases, irrelevant attributes influence customer choice. Contrary to mainstream marketing theory, which argues that differentation needs to be relevant to affect customer choice, irrelevant attributes have been shown to influence customer choice in a variety of research settings (Albrecht *et al.* 2011; Carpenter *et al.* 1994). Promising avenues for future research include studies on the relevance of irrelevant attributes in industrial contexts.

Compromise effect

Brands gain market share when they become intermediate, rather than extreme, options in a choice set (Kivetz *et al.* 2004a). Customers are averse to extreme options. Pricing managers thus have the option to increase the likelihood that customers buy a premium product by adding a super-premium product to their product lines. It is well documented that companies such as Starbucks, Dell, FedEx and Amazon make heavy use of compromise effects to profitably influence customer choice.

Decoy options

The presence of a decoy – inferior option – affects customer choice: the introduction of an irrelevant option provides a strong justification for the choice of an initially unappealing option. Pricing managers thus have the possibility to steer the customer towards higher priced, thus likely more profitable, products simply by adding decoy options to the choice set (Kivetz *et al.* 2004b).

In sum, B2B and B2C customer decisions are influenced by behavioural biases. An understanding of these biases helps pricing and marketing managers influence customer choice, which in turn can facilitate the implementation of innovative pricing strategies.

Our research on innovation in pricing

In 2010, we approached the Professional Pricing Society (PPS; http://www.pricingsociety.com) with a request to conduct research on its membership base. Our goal was to gain insight on the role of innovation in pricing in US industrial firms. We interviewed CEOs, board members, business-unit heads and mid-level managers at 15 companies. In total we conducted 44 interviews.

The interviews, averaging 60+ minutes, focused on managers' experiences in making pricing decisions and in participating in their firm's pricing process. We asked them to describe their specific experience with the most recent pricing decision made in their firm or a very recent meeting during which pricing was discussed or a pricing decision was made. We also asked managers in these firms to share with us any innovation in pricing they had introduced in the past 12 to 24 months.

Our findings uncovered some interesting themes in the area of pricing decision-making processes and how pricing strategies varied by pricing orientation. Our study also revealed that pricing was indeed not perceived as a field subject to innovation by the vast majority of respondents. At first, respondents were surprised by our question related to innovation. They probed for clarification and then had to think hard about it.

> I can't think of anything we've introduced in terms of a tool. No, I can't think of anything. You know, we've done a lot more of this, the development of these value chain sort of spreadsheets, etc. But I can't say it's a tool we've introduced per se.
>
> CEO of a firm using competition-based
pricing in the advanced composites market

> I would say no. I think we've done it pretty much the same since I've been here. We have not introduced any pricing innovation.
>
> President of a firm using competition-based
pricing in the automotive interior market

> Not, not that I'm aware of here, in terms of, – no. It's not to say they're not there, I'm just not aware of them. If somebody is using some type of program, or some type of software, or something.
>
> CEO of a firm using cost-based pricing in the chemicals industry

Other respondents introduced changes to existing pricing practices. These responses were related to pricing formula and cost indexing:

> The most innovative thing we've done is come up with this indexing agreement. It's a long, tedious process to approach a Tier 1 customer with that idea, to lay out the game plan, to present it at all different levels of purchasing.
>
> Account Manager in a firm using competition-based
pricing in the automotive interior market

> It is 2005 that we launch formula pricing, because 2006 was the first year of really selling with the resin escalator/de-escalator. This quoting system, that came out – we launched that less than 18 months ago. Prior to that, price quotes were handled a lot of different ways across (company) and there was not a tremendous amount of control over what was happening.
>
> President of firm using value-based
pricing in the automotive plastic packaging market

Finally, other respondents were to clearly define and elaborate on some innovative pricing approaches or programmes introduced over the past two years. Most of these respondents worked for firms using value-based pricing and had a formalized pricing process.

> We implemented the discount review process. Because we have a very defined sales management process (SMP). And the defined process is the ongoing review and execution of our sales strategy by account.
>
> CEO of a firm using value-based pricing in the construction market

> We created a process that was a transition from raise price to give price back. It involved several steps. It involved first step to aggressively hold. Then (the second step) was to aggressively engage . . . . And then there was manage price.

14 Andreas Hinterhuber and Stephan M. Liozu

> So those were the three steps. It's nothing scientific but it was something that I think in a very short period of time we learned how to do that.
>
> Sales Manager in a firm using value-based
pricing in the speciality chemicals market

During these interviews we identified only one instance where a company had actually implemented an innovation in pricing strategy:

> We manufacture [industrial equipment]. And increasingly, more of our products are being sold into our customers as a bundled service. It's called [omitted]. Ten years ago, we just went out and sold [products]. We would compete on features and benefits of the hardware .... Now our business is driven by a service model called [omitted] where customers – it's an operating lease. Bundled into that operating lease for the equipment is a service contract on it with guaranteed turnaround times on the servicing and data – we centralize the data collection, we do diagnostics, and we provide data back to our customers about risk in the operations. So our customers – instead of getting $100,000 sale today, we would get a four-year contract that's probably $350,000 or $400,000 paid over 48 months.
>
> CEO of an industrial equipment firm

In sum: during these interviews it emerged that innovation in pricing was a rare exception. We interviewed 44 individuals at 15 industrial companies and identified only one case where an innovation in pricing strategy was actually implemented. Executives we interviewed expressed an interest in the topic of innovation in pricing but also admitted that their current knowledge on this topic was limited. The findings from this research thus provided us with a further motivation to collect recent academic findings as well as best practices from pricing executives on innovation in pricing. With this we hope to raise the awareness on innovation in pricing in both academia as well as business practice.

Book content

This book is the result of a rigorous selection process of the most insightful papers dealing with innovation in pricing. Our initial call for papers generated a high interest from both academia and pricing professionals. Ultimately, over 50 papers were submitted for review. After multiple rounds of a double-blind review process, we selected 26 papers. They are organized in four sections as shown in Figure 1.3 below.

Innovation in organizing the pricing function

Stephan Liozu and *Kellie Ecker* examine options for the organizational design of the pricing function in firms. They conduct a literature review on centralization and decentralization. Four possible designs of the pricing function are proposed: centralized, decentralized, centre-supported and centre-led. The authors conjecture

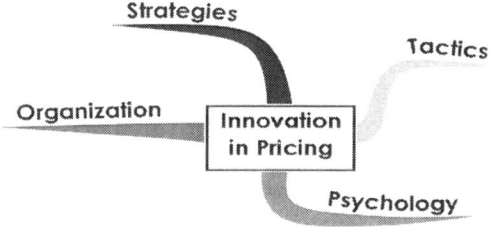

FIGURE 1.3 Overview of book contents

that centre-led pricing, which combines elements of centralization with elements of decentralization, is superior to other organizational designs. The authors also present their own research on the effectiveness of centre-led pricing. The authors hope that these research findings contribute to the ongoing debate on organizational design of pricing for performance.

Niklas Hallberg and *Linn Andersson* investigate the organizational barriers that prevent companies from implementing innovative pricing strategies, such as value-based pricing. This research, based on two case studies, identifies two main barriers: excessive decentralization and sales force incentive schemes. The authors also discuss how firms addressed these challenges: centralization of pricing authority and increased sales force control and training. The results of this study indicate that innovation in sales-force management, and, more specifically, centralization of pricing authority, is a key success factor for the implementation of value-based pricing through customer value map analysis, especially when sales force value-based pricing and value-based selling capabilities are not yet fully developed. Examining this interaction effect between decentralized pricing capabilities and the effectiveness of centralizing pricing authority is certainly worthy of future study.

Stephan Liozu, Andreas Hinterhuber, Sheri Perelli and *Toni Somers* explore the topic of the role of top executives in supporting and leading corporate pricing activities and programmes. The authors report the results of a quantitative inquiry with 557 CEOs and business owners of firms from around the globe that evaluates the levels of championing involvement of the pricing function, their perceptions on pricing and how they organize for pricing. A structural equation model is proposed which includes first- and second-order measurement models. The results suggest that the level of championing from CEO and business owners in pricing positively influences firms' decision-making rationality, pricing capabilities, level of collective mindfulness and pricing orientation, thereby leading to significantly higher firm performance. This study is thus a strong call to action for CEOs aiming to improve organizational performance. The main implication: champion the pricing function.

Ronald Baker and *Stephan Liozu* conjecture that the nature of senior management is changing. Firms face strong levels of competitiveness, and their business models are being challenged as a result. The authors suggest that value management at the organizational or corporate levels is becoming a number one priority. Although chief marketing and chief commercial officers are highly qualified to manage value processes, they do so along with performing a multitude of other functions or processes that distract their attention from the core function of value management. The authors propose that chief value officers, whether functionally or process-oriented, offer CEOs an expert and an ally dedicated to leading value strategies and processes at the organizational level. With their expertise, drive and dedication, they manage business value centrally and make sure that all firm processes and functions are aligned to create, quantify and capture value. This focused attention on value leads to a transformation of the firm's DNA and the adoption of business value as the firm's *raison d'être*.

Mark Stiving examines the difficult topic of measuring return on investment (ROI) for pricing systems investments. Pricing systems are highly underutilized partially as a result of the confusion surrounding their function and especially their ROI. The author intends to demystify these systems by explaining their three biggest capabilities (execution, analytics and science) and the types of data typically used by these systems: customer master, transaction data, waterfall data and competitor pricing. He then demonstrates a process to prove ROI by identifying the key areas where return can be found: increased margin, increased win rates, more opportunities, lower costs and reduced liabilities. Finally, attention is paid to the set of steps to incorporate all these elements in an ROI study.

Innovation in pricing strategy

Rafael Farrés further investigates the role of customer value-based pricing in industrial companies. The author makes it clear that even research-intensive, innovative companies should adopt a variety of alternative pricing strategies across their product and service portfolio. The author highlights firm and environmental conditions that make value-based pricing particularly suitable and illuminates under which conditions cost- and competition-based pricing approaches are appropriate for industrial firms. The author also presents a series of pricing tools that have enabled industrial companies to implement value-based pricing strategies: the price waterfall, the price-value map, turnover build-up, terms and conditions analyser, the pricing explorer and the price-volume scatter plot. Especially for practising executives at the beginning of the transformational journey towards value-based pricing, the discussion of these pricing tools and metrics will be useful.

Linda Trevenen proposed a grounded and practical essay on the art and science of customer segmentation, which she refers to as the heart of a profitable market strategy. In this essay, she suggests that grouping customers based on what they value enables a firm to provide distinct offerings and prices to each of these customer groups. However, too often, many firms do not make the effort to segment their customer base or simply fall back along traditional segmentation lines – demographic or geographic – because these data are available and require minimal effort to distinguish between customer types. As a result of not applying a deeper needs-based segmentation, the firm is faced with price variability, lack of adherence to contracts and a culture of 'giving in'. The author makes a few recommendations that smart firms can apply for better customer segmentation: set boundaries and fences, create pricing policies, and have a deeper level of customer understanding that leads to profitable growth. This chapter explains the importance of segmentation, and the strategies and practical activities for deploying it, and describes how to implement segmentation best practices into the organization so that a segmentation strategy realizes greater profitability.

Ralf Drews conjectures that, in many companies, the 'value-based pricing' of a new product offering is applied only after the product has passed all design stages in R&D. In addition, often the pricing approach is focused only on the offering itself. Although it seems to be common practice, the author argues that this approach has major disadvantages: first, the pricing is neither considered nor made in the context of a company's other important value contributors; second, the value of the product's features is unclear because they are not seen in the context of application; and last but not least, the new product is not tailored to the needs of a specific customer profile or to cultural buying preferences. If companies seek to create a product with superior value, it must be defined and priced before R&D even knows what it will look like. Furthermore, it is critical that the buying psychology of a specific customer be taken into account. In this unique paper, the author describes how companies can achieve this and which critical success factors are necessary for this uncommon but useful approach.

W. Michael Crouch and *Greg Hunsicker* narrate the example of the cultural transformation of the pricing orientation at ARDEX Americas. In this short case study, both authors explain the major elements of this transformation and how ARDEX Americas navigates through the journey. They explain that value-based pricing internalization requires robust initial investments in knowledge and expertise. They offer a very practical list of key lessons that allowed ARDEX Americas to make significant progress in the cultural transformation from cost to customer value.

Magnus Johansson investigates the role of pricing capabilities and processes in fast-paced B2B firms. Extant theory treats the two processes of value creation and value capture (i.e. pricing) separately. This paper suggests departing from this conceptual separation when dealing with pricing and value creation processes in fast-paced business environments, such as the semiconductor industry. In these environments value creation and value capture are iterative and intertwined, value is co-produced together with customers, and there is a high uncertainty around the total value jointly created between the supplier and the firm. This paper suggests that, in these circumstances, pricing processes have to be iterative as well and that price-setting authority has to be more localized. The contribution of this paper is thus a sketch of required pricing capabilities and processes in highly dynamic environments, which are markedly different from capabilities and processes described by extant research in static environments.

David Dvorin, Jered Haedt and *Vernon Lennon* address one of the critical elements of the mergers and acquisition process: improvements in pricing. The authors propose a robust framework for assessing opportunities of improving pricing during the mergers and acquisition process; they also highlight how to implement price increases during this process. The authors finally summarize the impact of price improvements on the enterprise value of merged or acquired businesses.

Nelson Hyde discusses four widely held pricing myths. Pricing managers seem to believe that lower prices lead to higher volumes, that customers are price-sensitive, that prices have to be set at prevailing market prices, and that lower prices increase the likelihood of closing the sale. These assumptions are, as this paper suggests, myths that prevent companies from creating and communicating customer value and from implementing value-based pricing. Overcoming these myths thus enables companies to adopt customer value-based pricing strategies.

Todd Snelgrove traces the past and present of total cost of ownership (TCO) approaches and highlights in which direction TCO could evolve. As the 'sum of purchase price plus all expenses incurred during the productive lifecycle of a product minus its salvage or resale price' (Anderson and Narus 2004), this approach is exclusively concerned with the cost side of customer value and neglects the value of customer-specific benefits (Anderson and Narus 2004). In this paper the author shows how TCO approaches can be expanded to incorporate the value of customer-specific benefits. Through case studies, this paper illustrates the difference between lowest initial purchase price, lowest TCO and an expanded view of TCO that includes the sum of all customer-specific value created. This paper also highlights the importance of communicating the price and value premium in industrial markets. The contribution of this paper is thus to illuminate that TCO can be compatible with customer value-based pricing.

Fernando Resende discusses how to optimize profitability through pricing in an environment where prices are negotiated. This paper illustrates how suppliers of complex projects can reduce their own costs through scope optimization and service-level adaptations. This paper also suggests ways to avoid price leakage through discount optimization and through a shared understanding of future required volumes, service levels and price developments.

Roberto Bedotto illustrates the benefits of a zero-based approach to pricing strategy. In many instances, path dependency and status quo bias create an environment where entrenched pricing strategies, although clearly not effective, prove hard to change. This paper suggests summarizing the company's strategy (growth, maintenance, or withdrawal) by product, application and channel. This paper then suggests analysing whether the current pricing strategy supports the company's overall strategy. This paper shows that this simple process can create an environment that is conducive to re-examining entrenched pricing practices and in which a comparison of the status quo and a strategic goal can enable the birth of new, innovative pricing strategies.

Innovation in pricing tactics

Customer value communication is an integral element of pricing tactics. *Christopher Provines* analyses a series of different value-communication tools in business markets. These tools differ by interactivity and complexity. Non-interactive tools are economic benefit claims that are developed based on observational studies or customer interviews. Interactive tools are decision-support analytical models such as ROI tools and value calculators. Complex interactive tools are workflow and business-model studies. This paper then suggests using different value communication tools depending on the degree of outcome risk and the complexity of the product offering. In sum, this paper offers an up-to-date summary of case studies and recent research on innovative ways to communicate customer value in B2B markets.

Harry Macdivitt reinforces the fact that understanding, using and communicating the value created for their customers is a challenge for many businesses. He claims that this results in an inability to respond assertively and confidently to customer demands for deep discounting. Margin erosion, premature commoditization and loss of market share follow. At the heart of the issue is the lack of a unifying framework for analysing, quantifying and communicating value. In this paper, the author introduces a framework for analysing customer value. He illustrates the application using two contemporary case studies. The author claims that the proposed tool led to new insights and the creation of deeper, richer and more focused customer value propositions. This structured approach thus facilitates the implementation of customer value-based pricing.

Neil Biehn and *Craig Zawada* examine alternative approaches to measuring customer willingness to pay. The quantification of customer willingness to pay is clearly at the centre of effective, profitable pricing strategies. The authors critically examine alternative approaches to measuring customer willingness to pay in industrial markets. The authors then illustrate the importance of measuring customer willingness to pay in five specific B2B pricing models: spot pricing, agreement or contract pricing, list or matrix pricing, subscription pricing and promotional pricing.

Steven Forth highlights the role of collaboration and conversations between stakeholders to implement innovative pricing approaches. Traditional pricing-management software is based on the analysis of transactions and its use has been limited to quantitatively oriented pricing experts. In this paper, the author describes software for quantifying customer value. The software quantifies customer value to enable collaborative processes around the pricing of B2B goods and services in negotiated markets. Collaborative approaches facilitate customer value quantification. The author suggests that in the future, pricing will need to draw on and support a more diverse group than in the past.

Richard Coppoolse presents a series of tools for tracking prices. This paper discusses price-sales charts, price-mix charts, price scatter plots, price-band charts and price waterfall reports. This paper also presents tools for analysing price realization by sales representative and by customer as well as tools for tracking sales agreements with customers. Some of these tools may thus be useful for companies engaged in improving the effectiveness of their price-realization processes.

The sales function has a fundamental role in the process of communicating and delivering value to customers. *Mike Moorman* proposes a sales-effectiveness framework composed of three parts to implement value-based selling. First, an analysis of competitors, customers and markets delivers customer insight. Then, the go-to-market-strategy is built on a segmentation strategy, a value-proposition strategy, a channel strategy and robust sales processes. Finally, operational excellence aligns sales resources, sales force capabilities, motivation, tools, marketing programmes and sales support tools to implement value-based selling vis-à-vis customers. The key feature of this paper is a structured approach blending customer, company and competitor insight (Hinterhuber 2004) to implement value-based selling.

Darren Huxol analyses tactical pricing under outcome uncertainty. In circumstances where customer received value varies widely due to exogenous factors, sellers need to conceive pricing strategies that reflect a range of different outcomes achieved. This paper proposes risk-sharing agreements and performance-based pricing as mechanisms that can align buyer and seller interest under situations of uncertainty. In line with current pricing theory – and in almost certain contrast to many prevailing pricing practices – this paper does not suggest reducing price under situations of outcome uncertainty.

Psychological aspects of pricing

Ben Lowe, Julian Lowe and *David Lynch* provide a comprehensive overview of behavioural aspects of pricing. Behavioural economics has now definitely entered the mainstream research in management: in a recent special issue in the *Strategic Management Journal* (Powell *at al.* 2011), Levinthal (2011) asks the question 'A behavioural approach to strategy – what's the alternative?' Research examining behavioural and psychological aspects of pricing seeks to understand how customer perceptions of value and price are formed. Consequentially, the paper analyses the following salient aspects of behavioural pricing: factors driving customer value perceptions; the role of internal and external reference prices, fairness perceptions in pricing, implications for price reductions (e.g. discounts, coupons, free gifts) and price increases, price endings, price quality perceptions, consumer price knowledge and, finally, price setting in nonmarket contexts. This paper emphasizes that customer willingness to pay is driven by both transaction value ('economic utility') and acquisition value ('psychological utility'). As pricing and marketing managers gain an improved understanding of factors driving psychological utility, their ability to set profitable prices also increases.

Carmen Balan specifically examines research on odd prices. Odd prices (e.g. 99 cents) have a long history: in 1965, the retailer Dave Gold discovers that charging 99 cents for all bottles of wine increases sales of all bottles, including those which previously had cost 89 cents or 79 cents. He exits the liquor business and becomes a highly successful entrepreneur after launching the 99 Cents Only chain of stores (Porter 2011). This paper summarizes current research on odd prices which points out that odd prices lead to increased demand due to both a level effect (i.e. customers underestimate prices) and an image effect (i.e. the product appears to be on sale). Odd prices still seem to work, although most of what we know stems from research in consumer-good markets. This paper suggests both an increased use of odd prices in industrial markets as well as further research examining the effects of odd prices in B2B environments.

Anshu Jalora illustrates the diffusion of two very well-documented effects of behavioural pricing in the software industry. The compromise effect, whereby brands gain share when they become the intermediate option in a choice set, is illustrated with actual examples of software pricing. The decoy effect, whereby brands gain share in the presence of an irrelevant (decoy) option that provides a compelling justification of a previously less attractive option, is illustrated through an experiment as well as through an actual example of pricing in the software industry. These examples illustrate the importance of behavioural research in order to favourably influence customer perceptions of value and price. To the robust body of research on this topic (Kivetz *et al.* 2004b) this paper thus adds some further examples. Also here, pricing managers are well advised to put some of these research findings into practice.

The next frontier in pricing

The final paper in this collection is by *Kevin Mitchell*. This paper highlights the evolution of the pricing profession over the past three decades. Pricing evolved from a clerical position to a tactical, commercial function to, finally, a C-level function deeply aligned with – and in many cases driving – company strategy. The author highlights the reflections of the Professional Pricing Society on critical elements for the future of the pricing function.

As the editors of this book, we have been honoured to work with highly talented pricing practitioners and scholars from around the world. We are blessed by the level of innovative and creative thinking that we have been able to bring to the surface by giving these experts an opportunity to share their thoughts, approaches and views. We thank all authors for their contributions to and participation in this exciting project.

It is our intention to contribute to the future evolution of the pricing profession. We are dedicated to making pricing gain the respect it deserves and to transforming the perceptions of pricing from a pure analytical and static science to a more strategic, innovative and impactful element of the marketing mix. Please join us in our journey to advance the pricing profession.

References

Albrecht, C. M., Neumann, M. M., Haber, T. E. and Bauer, H. H. (2011). The relevance of irrelevance in brand communication. *Psychology and Marketing*, 28(1): 1–28.

Anderson, E. T. and Simester, D. I. (2003). Effects of $9 price endings on retail sales: Evidence from field experiments. *Quantitative Marketing and Economics*, 1(1): 93–110.

Anderson, J. and Narus, J. (2004). *Business market management: Understanding, creating, and delivering value* (2nd ed.). Upper Saddle River, NJ: Prentice-Hall.

Barney, J. (1991). Firm resources and sustained competitive advantage. *Journal of Management*, 17(1): 99–120.

Beukert, L. (2003, 5 June). Edelsprit lockt Raser an die Zapfsäule. *Handelsblatt*.

Biyalogorsky, E. and Gerstner, E. (2004). Contingent pricing to reduce price risks. *Marketing Science*, 23(1): 146–55.

Carpenter, G. S., Glazer, R. and Nakamoto, K. (1994). Meaningful brands from meaningless differentiation: The dependence on irrelevant attributes. *Journal of Marketing Research*, 31(8): 339–50.

Casadesús-Masanell, R. (1998). Ford's model-T: Pricing over the product's life cycle. *Revista ABANTE*, 1(2): 143–65.

Dutta, S., Bergen, M., Levy, D., Ritson, M. and Zbaracki, M. (2002). Pricing as a strategic capability. *MIT Sloan Management Review*, 43(3): 61–6.

Ehm, H. (2010). *Overcoming challenges and hurdles while introducing revenue management in the semiconductor industry*. Paper presented at the Marcus Evans 2010 Strategic Pricing Conference.

Fay, S. (2009). Competitive reasons for the name-your-own-price channel. *Marketing Letters*, 20(3): 277–93.

Forbis, J. and Mehta, N. (1981). Value-based strategies for industrial products. *Business Horizons*, 24(3): 32–42.

Ford, H. (2007). *My life and work*. New York: Cosimo Inc.

Frenzen, H., Hansen, A. K., Krafft, M., Mantrala, M. K. and Schmidt, S. (2010). Delegation of pricing authority to the sales force: An agency-theoretic perspective of its determinants and impact on performance. *International Journal of Research in Marketing*, 27(1): 58–68.

Gallego, G., Kou, S. and Phillips, R. (2008). Revenue management of callable products. *Management Science*, 54(3): 550–64.

Hinterhuber, A. (2004). Towards value-based pricing – an integrative framework for decision making. *Industrial Marketing Management*, 33(8): 765–78.

Hinterhuber, A. (2012). *A primer on pricing excellence*. Hinterhuber & Partners white paper, available at http://www.hinterhuber.com.

Hinterhuber, A. and Liozu, S. M. (2012). Strategic B2B pricing. *Journal of Revenue and Pricing Management*, 11(1): 1–3.

Hinterhuber, A. and Liozu, S. (2013). Psychological aspects of pricing, PPS online course, available at http://www.pricingsociety.com.

Kadet, A. (2008). Price profiling. *Smart Money*, 17(5): 81–5.

Kim, J. Y., Natter, M. and Spann, M. (2009). Pay what you want: A new participative pricing mechanism. *Journal of Marketing*, 73(1): 44–58.

Kim, J. Y., Natter, M. and Spann, M. (2010). Pay-what-you-want–Praxisrelevanz und Konsumentenverhalten. *Zeitschrift für Betriebswirtschaft*, 80(2): 147–69.

Kivetz, R., Netzer, O. and Srinivasan, V. (2004a). Alternative models for capturing the compromise effect. *Journal of Marketing Research*, 41(8): 237–57.

Kivetz, R., Netzer, O. and Srinivasan, V. (2004b). Extending compromise effect models to complex buying situations and other context effects. *Journal of Marketing Research*, 41(8): 262–8.

Levinthal, D. A. (2011). A behavioral approach to strategy – what's the alternative? *Strategic Management Journal*, 32(13): 1517–23.

Levitt, T. (1986). *The marketing imagination*. New York: The Free Press.

Liozu, S. and Hinterhuber, A. (2011). Pricing capabilities: The design, development and validation of a scale. Working Paper: Case Western Reserve University.

Liozu, S. M. and Hinterhuber, A. (2012). Industrial product pricing: A value-based approach. *Journal of Business Strategy*, 33(4): 28–39.

Liozu, S. M., Hinterhuber, A., Perelli, S. and Boland, R. (2012a). Mindful pricing: Transforming organizations through value-based pricing. *Journal of Strategic Marketing*, 20(3): 197–209.

Liozu, S., Hinterhuber, A., Perelli, S. and Somers, T. (2012b). Organizational design for pricing and relative firm performance. Working Paper: Case Western Reserve University.

Liozu, S., Somers, T., Hinterhuber, A. and Perelli, S. (2012c). Pricing championship and firm performance: The pivotal role of the CEO. Working Paper: Case Western Reserve University.

Mak, V., Zwick, R. and Rao, A. R. (2010). *'Pay what you want' as a profitable pricing strategy: Theory and experimental evidence*. Paper presented at the Proceedings of the Management Science and Operations Seminar Series.

Marting, E. (1968). Foreword. In E. Marting (Ed.), *Creative pricing*. New York: American Management Association, Inc., pp. 5–6

Nadler, D. A. and Heilpern, J. D. (1998). The CEO in the context of discontinuous change. In D. Hambrick, D. A. Nadler and M. Tushman (Eds), *Navigating change: How CEOs, top teams, and boards steer transformation*. Boston, MA: Harvard Business School Press, pp. 3–27.

Oxenfeldt, A. (1968). Introduction: The role of price and pricing reconsidered. In E. Marting (Ed.), *Creative pricing*. New York: American Management Association, Inc., pp. 9–26.

Porter, E. (2011). *The price of everything*. London: William Heinemann.

Powell, T. C., Lovallo, D. and Fox, C. R. (2011). Behavioral strategy. *Strategic Management Journal*, 32(13): 1369–86.

Shampanier, K., Mazar, N. and Ariely, D. (2007). Zero as a special price: The true value of free products. *Marketing Science*, 26(6): 742–57.

Shapiro, D. (2011). Profitability of the name-your-own-price channel in the case of risk-averse buyers. *Marketing Science*, 30(2): 290–304.

Sheffi, Y. (2005). *The resilient enterprise: Overcoming vulnerability for competitive advantage*. Cambridge, MA: MIT Press.

Skugge, G. (2004). Growing effective revenue managers. *Journal of Revenue and Pricing Management*, 3(1): 49–61.

Stephenson, P. R., Cron, W. L. and Frazier, G. L. (1979). Delegating pricing authority to the sales force: The effects on sales and profit performance. *The Journal of Marketing*, 43(2): 21–8.

Stiving, M. and Winer, R. S. (1997). An empirical analysis of price endings with scanner data. *Journal of Consumer Research*, 24(1): 57–67.

Suter, T. A. and Burton, S. (1996). Believability and consumer perceptions of implausible reference prices in retail advertisements. *Psychology & Marketing*, 13(1): 37–54.

PART II
Innovation in organizing the pricing function

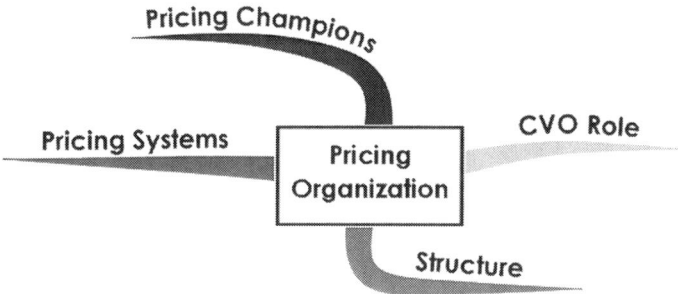

2
THE ORGANIZATIONAL DESIGN OF THE PRICING FUNCTION IN FIRMS

A centre-led management approach

Stephan M. Liozu

Kellie Ecker

Introduction

'Organizing is one of the central and inescapable tasks of top management. And the experienced executive is painfully aware of how little is known as to what constitutes effective organization' (Simon *et al.* 1954: iii). From 1954's classic management book by Simon *et al.* on centralization versus decentralization to the most recent *McKinsey Quarterly* issue on the same topic (Campbell *et al.* 2011), the debate on how to organize functional teams in firms rages on. This debate, however, has never been holistically extended to the organization of the pricing function. Traditionally, the pricing function receives limited attention in firms and in marketing literature. Data from the Professional Pricing Society, the world's largest organization dedicated to pricing, reveal that fewer than 5 per cent of Fortune 500 companies have a full-time function exclusively dedicated to pricing (Mitchell 2011) and, according to McKinsey & Company fewer than 15 per cent conduct systematic pricing research (Hinterhuber 2004). Historically, pricing has received little attention from either practitioners or marketing scholars (Hinterhuber 2004, 2008; Malhotra 1996; Noble and Gruca 1999). A review of 53 empirical pricing studies concluded that pricing literature is highly descriptive and fragmented and that theoretical understanding of firm pricing decisions is limited (Ingenbleek 2007). Pricing academic literature is silent about how organizational and behavioural characteristics of firms may affect pricing processes and how firms organize for pricing (Ingenbleek 2007). The question of centralized versus decentralized pricing organization has been debated in the pricing profession and has rarely been academically explored. To address this deficit, we conducted a literature review on the concepts of centralization and the various forms it could take in firms. Then we used the findings from a qualitative inquiry that included interviews with 44 managers in 15 companies in ten US states. The goal of this study was to explore similarities and differences in experiences related to pricing management and orientation. Results documented stark differences in how firms organize for pricing, manage the pricing process and develop internal capabilities to face uncertain and ambiguous pricing decisions. Five organizational elements associated with advanced pricing orientation and pricing maturity emerged: championing behaviours, organizational confidence, pricing capabilities, change capacity and centre-led pricing management. We also used the result of a quantitative inquiry conducted among 748 marketing, pricing, commercial and management professionals and leaders involved in managing pricing activities for their firms to measure the effect of these five characteristics on perceived firm performance.

Armed with our theoretical exploration and the findings from both our qualitative and quantitative studies, we conjecture that centre-led pricing is a critical element of the organizational design for pricing. We propose a different definition of pricing centralization which is not related to power and pricing compliance but associated with the diffusion of pricing knowledge, the support of pricing decisions and the creation of pricing intelligence and intellectual capital in firms. Our conclusions also indicate that firms using value-based pricing have adopted the centre-led management design to pursue an organizational transformation of their pricing orientation.

Theoretical foundation

Our work was informed by organization theory (March and Simon 1958; March 1994) and by the literature linking pricing and firm performance. We take organization theory to include the internal structure of the firm and the relationships between its units and departments (Grant 1996), as well as the flow of information within organizations supporting and influencing decision making processes (March 1994, 1999; Simon 1961). A critical question is how and where pricing decisions occur in organizations and what organizational factors influence processes and managerial judgement when decisions are made. For this paper, we focus on the constructs of organizational structure (Aiken *et al.* 1980; Hall 1977; Hall *et al.* 1967; Miller *et al.* 1988), centralization versus decentralization (Argyres and Silverman 2004; Fayol 1949; Simon *et al.* 1954) and finally the contemporary concept of centre-led functional management.

Organizational structure

Organizational structure, which can be variously defined and take myriad forms, relates to dimensions that 'cannot be reduced to or deduced from properties of the organization's members' (Aiken *et al.* 1980). Several reviews (Hall 1977; John and Martin 1984; Miller *et al.* 1988) have suggested that complexity (structural differentiation), formalization and centralization are the most common and consistent characteristics of structure. We focused on the characteristics of centralization of the pricing function in the hands of specialized experts. Structural differentiation 'includes differences in attitudes and behaviours on the part of the members of the differentiated departments' (Lawrence and Lorsh 1967) and is defined as the differences in occupational specialities present in the organization and their degrees of professionalism (Hage and Aiken 1967, 1970). Centralization, which reflects the hierarchical nature of the organization, is one of its most critical structural dimensions (John and Martin 1984). Van de Ven and Ferry (1980) define centralization as the 'locus of decision making authority within an organization'. However, for complex decision making that requires professional competencies, decisions are often left to experts. The notion of expertise is important in our definition of centralization. Locus of authority is highly dependent on locus of expertise. Because central positions are non-routine and highly specialized, they are likely to reflect power and influence (Pfeffer 1978) but not decision making authority.

Centralization versus decentralization

Management literature is rich in papers and studies illuminating the historical roots and drivers of the centralization debate dating from the 1920s when large multinational corporations evaluated organizational design options (Cummings 1995). Cummings defined the term centralized as indicating that 'authority to make important decisions lies towards the 'head' ... while conversely decentralization implies more autonomy' (1995: 103). Simon *et al.* (1954: 1) proposed a similar meaning on both centralization and decentralization constructs:

> an administrative organization is centralized to the extent that decisions are made at relatively high levels in the organization; decentralized to the extent that discretion and authority to make important decisions are delegated by top management to lower levels of executive authority.

Most definitions proposed by other scholars centred around the characteristics of decision making delegation (Kruisinga 1954), of levels of authority (Simon *et al.* 1954) and of hierarchical designs (Simon 1965). However, earlier in the centralization versus decentralization debate, some scholars addressed the question of balance between both approaches and started to move away from the polarized approach to centralization. Fayol (1949: 33) stated that 'the question of centralization or decentralization is simply a matter of proportion, it is a matter of finding the optimum degree for the particular concern'. Simon *et al.* (1954) concurred with this conclusion and guided their case studies towards the question of examining the degree of centralization and decentralization of the different decision making function. Others scholars conjectured that hybrid organizations and behaviours might be an appropriate intermediate design between polar forms of centralization (Argyres and Silverman 2004). Additionally, in case of required organizational change and difficult adoption and implementation of technology, several organizational configurations in the same firm might be required depending on the transformational stages they sit in (Hall 1977: 215). A more centralized approach might be more appropriate for the initial implementation stage to ensure organizational buy-in while a more decentralized approach might be better once the changes are internalized and the organization experiences high adoption levels.

More recently, authors have characterized the centralized versus decentralized phenomenon as a 'pendulum swing' in which speed is dictated by the external environment (Evaristo et al. 2005: 67) or as 'fashion that is inherently temporary' and created by management gurus (Cummings 1995: 116). The focus has now moved to the question of operating effectiveness raised at the time by Simon et al. (1954: 21), of gain versus pain analysis (Campbell et al. 2011) and of the creation of unique competitive advantage through unique organization design (Dutta et al. 2002).

Hybrid organizational design: centre-led pricing management

While the centralization versus decentralization dilemma continues to occupy the management agenda, we conjecture that there is a need to elevate the debate to a new form of organizational design. Recently centre-led management design emerged in the business world led by the procurement and supply chain management functions. The concept of centre-led management embraces the notion of hybrid organizational design by offering a centralized approach related to skills specialization, knowledge diffusion and process efficiency while encouraging a decentralization approach to decision making. This approach proposes a balance between the two centralization poles and allow firms to focus in parallel on decision making efficiency and organizational capability building. When applied to the pricing function, the presence of a centralized highly specialized team of pricing experts supporting decentralized pricing activities (Deaker and Zang 2006) can positively influence business leaders' capabilities to make better pricing decisions. These experts allow for decisions based on scientific analysis and facts rather than intuition or gut feeling. A central team of experts acts as internal consultants who can not only increase decision making rationality but also boost organizational confidence in executing pricing activities (John and Martin 1984). Central marketing and pricing teams focus on the diffusion of pricing expertise and skills across the organization. These capabilities are therefore concentrated within a few positions resulting in a 'led from the centre' pricing strategy (Ecker 2010: 13). Because these central positions are non-routine and highly specialized, their expert incumbents are likely to gain power and influence (Pfeffer 1978) while not having pricing decision making authority. The specialization of centrally grouped pricing experts in the organization is needed to perform specialized tasks supporting a broad array of pricing-related activities in marketing, sales, R&D and management.

Centralization options from a practical perspective

Pricing practitioners experience three principal variations of centralized pricing in addition to the decentralized model (Figure 2.1): centralized, centre-supported and

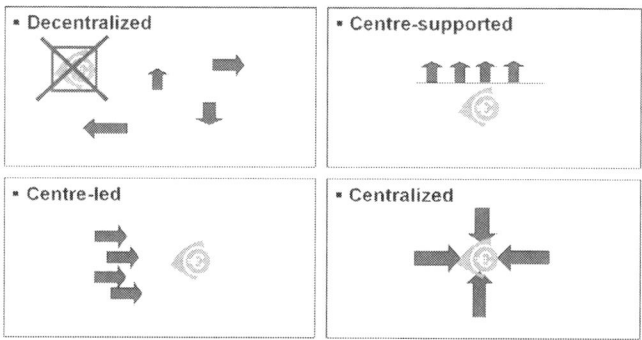

FIGURE 2.1 Types of pricing organizations

centre-led. We examined these constructs and found that while centre-led appears to be the most effective for a company employing a value-based pricing approach, the other models also have benefits in some situations.

Decentralized pricing is the de facto organizational design for most companies. It is the status quo where pricing direction is given by a headquarters function and then executed in the field based on the local conditions and situation. The key measurement of success in this environment is revenue. In other words, if customers are buying, then it must be the right price. This structure has the least control and transparency. There is also a lack of direct ownership and so when something goes wrong there is no one responsible to fix it. It does, however, give the most flexibility to the sales force who, when given the directive to increase revenue, can usually do so simply by dropping the price. Since the success of the strategy is sales driven, it is highly dependent on sales people and their relationships with the clients. This produces the danger that when a sales person leaves the company, much knowledge of the customer and their prices is lost. Companies can be surprised to learn that the best sales people in terms of revenue are rarely the best sales people in terms of profit.

Centre-supported pricing is the next level up from decentralized pricing. It is mainly used by companies that recognize they have a need for pricing, but they are not ready to give up any control or decision making authority. The key measurement of success is process improvement. The pricing function is established to support the organization in functional ways. This would include creating sales tools for evaluating business, managing SAP/Oracle pricing systems, organizing price increases, ensuring list prices are printed and enumerating pricing processes. Sometimes a company will invest in a specialized pricing system that would also be under the responsibility of the pricing team. The role of pricing is limited to supporting the decisions and direction of the management. This creates a department that is responsible officially for pricing but with no authority to influence profit management. It will lead to process improvements and still allows for flexibility of the sales force. However, it only gives the company the illusion that it has control of pricing and will not have significant impact on the bottom line. Some organizations will see this as a failure and go back to decentralized pricing rather than maintain the headcount.

Centre-led pricing establishes a pricing expertise at the strategic level of the company and then diffuses the knowledge and select responsibilities to other parts of the organization. Key measurements of success are profit and process improvement. To successfully implement centre-led pricing, change management will need to be employed to ensure that all levels are aligned to the goals of pricing and will make decisions on the local level to support those goals. The pricing experts are responsible for not only tools and processes, but also for establishing guidelines and skills development programmes throughout the company. It does take away some of the flexibility for the sales force, as they have to adhere to guidelines established by the experts. However, the trade off is that they will have new skills to help them sell on value and understand the impact of the pricing offers they make. This brings more consistency and predictability to the business.

Similar to centre-supported pricing, centre-led design improves pricing processes and takes functional ownership of pricing systems. In addition, the experts will establish new processes that aid in the goal of profit improvement. By collaborating with all levels of the organization, it will also institute a pricing intelligence community. This brings information from many areas to a central point where trends, opportunities and threats can be identified, evaluated and considered for strategic direction. It also helps the company better assess and respond to any competitor moves in the market such as whether a price change is a local phenomenon or a concerted action.

Centralized pricing brings the maximum level of control to pricing. A central team of experts and analysts are responsible for all pricing in the organization. This is usually focused on controlling and is autocratic in nature. Key measurements are profit and compliance to the standards. In a large organization, a strongly centralized pricing can ensure that price erosion is kept under control and that clients are treated consistently. The pricing function is responsible for all processes, systems, analysis and ultimately for the content of all offers made to clients. Due to the nature of the analysis and approval process, it is seen as being restrictive to the sales force and discourages initiative taking. The response time to clients is increased and can result in loss of sales from the lack of flexibility. Companies will sometimes deploy this model in times of a crisis and then move to a centre-led design once control is established and they understand better the amount of flexibility that might be needed.

The practical exposé on the four types of organizational design for pricing does not give any clear answer on which design works best for an organization. Each design offers advantages and disadvantages that practitioners and leaders in the firm need to consider in detail. As discussed, depending on the situation the firm faces in the market and the level of pricing maturity, a firm might start with one design and transition to another once the pricing skills and processes are in place. There is no silver bullet solution to organizing for pricing. Leaders need to establish their pricing goals and strategies and then design the best architecture to increase their pricing power. In the process they will have to consider trade-offs between various variables related to pricing: delegation, speed of response to customers and the sales force, approach to price decisions, etc.

Research design and methods

Following our in-depth literature search and practical exploration on the centralization construct, we conducted qualitative and quantitative research projects to investigate the elements impacting the organization of the pricing function in firms and the impact of these elements on relative firm performance. In both studies, the organization of the pricing function emerged as an important theme. More details on our empirical studies and their findings follow in the next sections of the paper.

Qualitative survey
Methodological approach

We conducted a qualitative study using semi-structured interviews to develop a grounded theory (Corbin and Strauss 2008) about how organizational factors affect the adoption of a pricing approach in industrial firms. We aimed to get a better understanding of how managers in these firms make pricing decisions and what roles they play in the firm's pricing process.

Sample

Our sample consisted of 44 managers in 15 small and medium US industrial firms. Relying on the principal researcher's professional network and advice by the Professional Pricing Society, over 36 small and medium US firms were identified in three industries: building materials, transportation products and plastics products. Seven firms were small as defined by the Small Business Administration 2007 size standards by industry (www.sba.com/size) as having between 50 and 380 employees; and eight were medium-sized with between 900 and 2,200 employees. More information of sample characteristics is available in the Appendix.

Data collection

The primary method of data collection was semi-structured interviews conducted over a three-month period from April to June 2010. Thirty-seven interviews were conducted in person at the respondents' place of employment and seven were conducted by telephone. The interviews, averaging 60+ minutes, were digitally recorded and subsequently transcribed by a professional service.

Data analysis

Consistent with a grounded theory approach, data analysis commenced simultaneously with data collection. The audio recordings of each interview were listened to several times and the transcripts of each interview read repeatedly. Three stages of rigorous coding then ensued (open, axial and selective coding). The process resulted in a reduction in the number of categories from 92 to 40 yielding seven major themes and capturing 781 of the total 'codable moments' out of the 2,554 ones originally identified.

Quantitative survey

Methodological approach

To test our hypotheses, we designed a cross-sectional, self-administered survey to measure the latent variables associated with our conceptual model. Marketing, pricing, commercial and management professionals and leaders involved in managing pricing activities for their firms constituted our population. The Professional Pricing Society (PPS), a professional organization dedicated to the education and networking of pricing professionals around the world, supported our research. The survey was emailed to 18,300 PPS members in April 2011. Responses were returned over an eight-week period. About 300 'bounced back' and were assumed not to have reached the intended recipients. Of the remaining 18,000, 1,148 surveys were returned partially or fully completed for a response rate of 6.4 per cent. We determined 748 were usable for further analysis. Our response rate is consistent with surveys targeted at large professional organizations not typically asked to participate in academic research. Sample characteristics are provided in the Appendix.

Measure development and assessment

Since there was little empirical precedent to measure the degree to which a centre-led pricing team supports an organization with specific pricing activities, a multiple-item scale was also developed by the team in accordance with an operational definition as suggested by Kerlinger and Lee (2000: Chapter 3) and by relying on our fieldwork and on extant research. We used seven items ranging from 1 – 'rarely done' to 7 – 'frequently done' to operationalize this scale as shown in Table 2.1 below.

TABLE 2.1 Centre-led survey items

Items	Centre-led pricing management (CLED)
CLED1	Conducts pricing training with divisional decision makers and top executives
CLED2	Manages specific pricing projects or programmes to support divisional marketing programmes
CLED3	Assists in the design and/or implementation of pricing tools
CLED4	Conducts pricing research activities to support pricing decision making process
CLED5	Assists decision makers with price setting process as part of the formal product development process
CLED6	Provides top management with pricing reports and trends
CLED7	Provides knowledge with overall pricing process (for example, pricing increases, pricing reviews)

This scale was refined through pretests and pilot testing using established item development procedures and guidelines (Churchill 1979). Content validity was determined through comprehensive review of the literature, pilot tests and assessment by a panel of practitioners and academics to ensure that measurement items covered the domain of the constructs (Nunnally 1978; Churchill 1979). To assess the survey's quality, face-to-face interviews with pricing practitioners were conducted using Bolton's pretesting methodology (Bolton 1993). We pretested our scale items with a small panel of academics and pricing and business practitioners. Next, a pilot test involving 150 professionals representing pricing, business and general manager functions from companies in both manufacturing and service industries provided 70 complete and usable responses.

Findings

Qualitative study

We discovered stark differences in the locus of the pricing function, the nature of the pricing process, the organizational structure, the diffusion of pricing capabilities and in leaders' behaviours in firms with a value-based pricing orientation versus those with cost- or competition-based orientations.

Finding 1: Firms using value-based pricing (VBP) support pricing decisions by reliance on formal market research, scientific pricing methods and 'expert' recommendations while those using other orientations (cost or competition) rely on experience, prior knowledge, gut and intuition.

Three out of four firms in our sample that had adopted VBP conducted formal quantitative market research to calculate customers' value and to derive final pricing points. These firms used scientific methods, such as conjoint analysis, KANO and customer acceptance testing, to define a range for the price point. Respondents claimed these methods reduced the level of uncertainty when managers made the final price point definition thus increasing the level of rationality in the decision

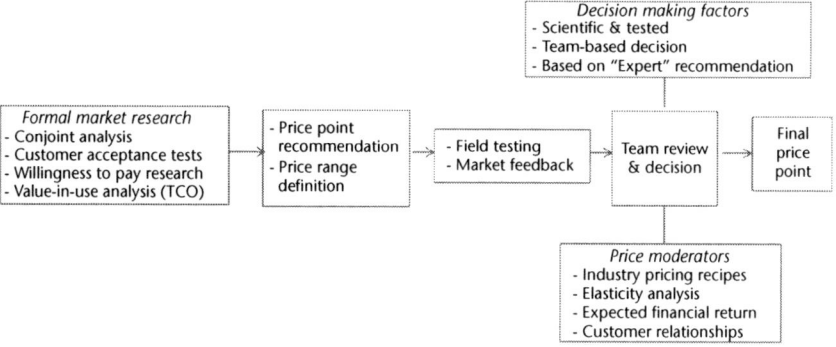

FIGURE 2.2 Price point definition process for value-based pricing (VBP)

making process. Figure 2.2 illustrates the VBP price point definition process highlighting the role of internal experts and consultants from 'central' or centre-led pricing teams as critical to support, test and validate pricing decisions.

As illustrated in Figure 2.4, of the six firms which used cost-based pricing (CBP), most developed advanced cost models – and all used margin targets – to inform pricing decisions. When faced with uncertainty, managers of all firms reported using prior knowledge and experience and half admitted to relying on intuition and guessing to define the final price point (see Figure 2.5). Most of these managers (five out of six firms) characterized their pricing process as 'unscientific' despite

	Scientific decision making process
VB1 – SM	'Basically, we give one recommendation ... and we try to make this recommendation with a proof, with an evidence that this is right. And this is done in this Phase 4 (of Stage Gate), for example, within the second customer contact phase, which can be a conjoint analysis because then you have facts and data that support your recommendation.'
VB1 – EL	'The large decision-making is up to the product manager, of course. He will follow the recommendation of the (functional) guy based on the controlled research.'
VB4 – SM	'We try and get feedback from our testing. So whenever you have tests done and you can quantify the performance of the new product versus the other alternatives that customers have access to (and) then we try and see if we can quantify the benefit that this product will deliver based on all the benefits we think it brings. We will survey as many customers as we have access to, or as much test data as we have generated and have access to .... We ask them to test it, test the hypothesis. Instead of saying every analysis you come up with is wrong and therefore cannot be implemented, you create an implementation plan that allows you to test.'
VB2 – FA	'We do an analysis of the investment, definitely .... For something like that, because it would be like a new product and we would be investing, we have a process internally where, before we finalize anything, it goes before the executive team, and we review the pricing. We review our returns on the project.'
	Unscientific decision making process
CB5 – EL	'I would love to say it's scientific, but it ain't, I mean, it ain't ... it's a gut check that's made that.'
CB3 – EL	'Yeah, it's not a highly scientific, there's not an algorithm I could give you.'
COB1 – SM	'Now what that premium is, is highly, in my mind, unscientific. That's almost (as much) art as it is science .... A quantification of the value of the system is the Holy Grail for me.'
COB3 – EL	'We had information coming in from Japan. We had information coming in from China. So we knew we were in a favourable position, which I think gave us the confidence to go a little bit higher, but I can't say at the end of the day I did a spreadsheet and put in all the factors and came out with a number and said, "That's the number we're going to".'
COB2 – EL	'As far as having some working formula that enables us to say that this marketplace enables us to mark up 50 per cent of what we would normally do, it's probably not as sophisticated as that. It is more a sense of understanding the marketplace and the pricing associated with the applications, and then the value add that we bring to the table to ensure that we achieve maximum pricing.'

FIGURE 2.3 Differences in the decision making process between firms using value-based pricing and those that did not

Organizational design of pricing function   37

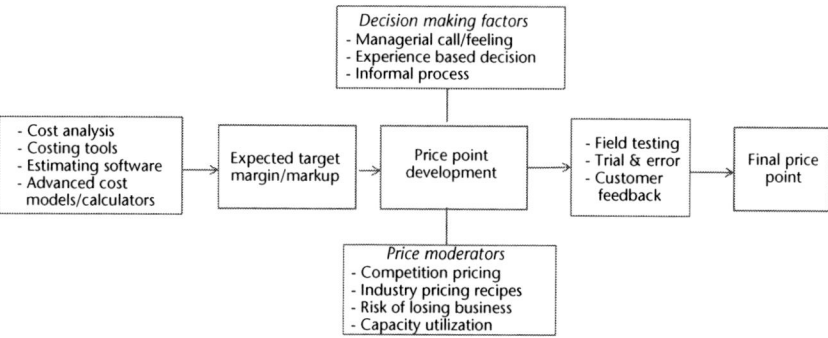

FIGURE 2.4 Price point definition process for cost-based pricing (CBP)

VB1 – EL	'We have dedicated (functional) managers. They don't do anything else, and then just (customer research), and this is observation of the customer. It's videotaping of the customer. It's understanding what is the unarticulated needs of the customer, and of course, also the articulated needs.'
VB3 – EL	'The way (company) works is we have the business units in (country) which are in charge of development. So they bring the products and then they bring overall pricing guidelines worldwide.'
VB3 – SM	'You've got the senior manager of pricing, which is responsible for the pricing processes; continuous improvement for (Corporation) overall ... and then within that group you have a few analysts who help manage the pricing within the system: one technical person, one person who helps on the reporting .... one individual who helps out with projects like agreement review process (and) strategic business pricing. And we also have a group that focuses in on day-to-day maintenance of making sure price points in the system don't go below a certain threshold.'
VB4 – EL	'In a development group ... there's three people like (name) who are development managers. We've got hundreds of development people in the world .... That's all they do. They don't sell a thing .... So they're doing the advanced design, advanced development.'
VB2 – SM	'We have engineering services, our project managers ... (who) can put together is a cost justification analysis .... The department is called Engineering Services ... they'll bring in all the formulas/cost justifications from our customer's end.'
VB2 – EL	'We have a pricing department. It's four people that are split by market segment, and they're responsible for doing quotes for new business or large – anything that's not under contract should come to them for pricing, to do a quote.'

FIGURE 2.5 Evidence of role specialization in firms that use value-based pricing

the fact that it was based on financial data and was formulaic in nature. Figure 2.3 provides evidence of the scientific versus unscientific nature of decision making processes in these firms.

Finding 2: Pricing is an orphan in industrial firms using cost or competition pricing orientation.

No dedicated pricing function existed in the 11 firms in our sample using cost or competition pricing orientation. In these firms, pricing activities were highly fragmented, followed informal pricing review processes, and focused only on margins versus prices (7 out of 11 firms). By contrast, all firms using VBP had dedicated pricing functions (involving 3 to 15 members), tracked specific pricing key performance indicators (KPIs) and led specific monthly pricing reviews.

Finding 3: The locus of pricing responsibility varies based on pricing orientation.

In the 11 firms using CBP and competition-based pricing (COBP), the locus of both tactical and strategic pricing responsibility was situated in the sales function. In all firms using VBP, the pricing function reported into the marketing organization. In these industrial firms, marketing was responsible for strategic pricing resulting in greater integration of pricing programmes in the overall marketing planning process.

Finding 4: Firms using VBP designed formalized processes and established centralized or centre-led pricing expertise.

All firms using VBP created specialized units composed of highly skilled professionals whose mission was to support the pricing decision making process. These units included, as illustrated in Figure 2.5, a packaging engineering group, a dedicated pricing team acting as internal consultants or a specialized market research team dedicated to voice of the customer projects. The role of these units was to provide project-related support to managers who made business unit-specific pricing decisions.

In these firms, pricing responsibility was centre-led and the department provided pricing support to the entire organization. Our findings (see Figure 2.6) suggest a definition of centralization in which knowledge and capabilities were concentrated to create the concept of a centre of excellence for pricing. Five out of six sales and marketing respondents in firms using VBP indicated that this central

VB1 – EL	'… we have three full-time equivalents for voice of the customer studies. We have that centrally. So whenever we develop a product for this market, we get them here and they set the whole system because it's a very formal thing.'
VB3 – SM	'The overall team supports all of the (Company) North America … the profit desk underneath the pricing team can look to see whether or not the price points are too low.'
VB3 – FA	'Pricing is actually at the corporate level here, it's marketing that has that pricing team underneath. So marketing is responsible for defining the price points.'
VB4 – SM	'I am a corporate function; I go from business to business.'
VB4 – EL	'When we wanna do something different and new, we hooked up with them (Central Team) (and) when we said, "You know, on our mature business, we got too many price points. We need to simplify this thing. How do you help us simplify?" … there's this group out there that knows (and) consults on this all the time. Why don't we tap into them, and let's start a project. (That) group is kinda looking for the best of the best in (Company) and in cross-training.'
VB4 – SM	'We tap into our corporate sales and marketing (team) (and) say, "Hey, they've got professionals that know the terminology, the theory, and the strategy associated with pricing in general." And you do a little bit of negotiation role-playing and that sort of thing. So that's probably once a year or once every year and a half.'

FIGURE 2.6 Evidence of expertise centralization in firms that use value-based pricing

pricing function acted as a strong resource to improve managerial pricing management. None of the firms using CBP (0 out of 6 firms) reported the existence of a centralized pricing function.

Quantitative study

An exploratory factor analysis (EFA) was conducted on the dataset of 748 pricing and business professionals using principal axis factoring with Promax rotation. The EFA resulted in six factors, consistent with our conceptual model. The summary statistics for the centre-led pricing management construct are shown in Table 2.2 and construct correlations are shown in Table 2.3. Each item loaded on its respective factor with a value greater than .40 and no cross-loadings of more than .20 (Hair et al. 2010; Igbaria et al. 1995). Two items did not load properly and were removed from the model.

We conducted a confirmatory factor analysis (CFA) to validate the factor structure. The measurement model was constructed incorporating each construct and associated items. The model was further trimmed and appropriate covariance relationships were added when theoretically justified (Byrne 2009). The composite reliability (CR) for the centre-led management construct is provided in Table 2.4. The CR value exceeds the acceptable threshold level (>0.70) and the average variance extracted (AVE) value confirming the reliability of the indicators and demonstrating convergent validity. For discriminate validity we show that for this construct the maximum shared variance (MSV) and average shared variance (ASV) are less than the AVE (Fornell and Larcker 1981).

Supported by our theoretical review and the results of our qualitative inquiry, we hypothesized that centre-led pricing management was one critical organizational

TABLE 2.2 EFA summary statistics

Construct	No. of Items	Loadings	Cronbach alpha
Centre-led pricing management	5	0.667; 0.589; 0.613; 0.669; 0.688	0.784

TABLE 2.3 Construct correlation scores

Constructs	Mean	Standard deviation	Cronbach alpha	Centre-led pricing management
Centre-led pricing management	5.20	1.48	0.784	**0.43**
Pricing capabilities	4.31	1.50	0.906	0.445
Relative performance	4.82	1.31	0.915	0.328
Organizational confidence	5.07	1.41	0.851	0.317
Championing behaviours	4.94	1.59	0.959	0.449
Organizational change capacity	4.93	1.46	0.919	0.363

TABLE 2.4 Results of the measurement model

Constructs and corresponding items	Cronbach alpha	Mean	Standard deviation	Standardized regression weights	Standard error	Critical ratio	Composites reliability	Average variance extracted	Maximum shared variance	Average shared variance
Centre-led pricing management (CLED)	**0.784**						**0.79**	**0.43**	**0.26**	**0.20**
CLED2		5.01	1.598	0.617	0.078	14.436				
CLED3		5.56	1.389	0.584	0.069	13.504				
CLED4		4.70	1.603	0.645	0.078	15.252				
CLED5		5.15	1.509	0.692	0.072	16.67				
CLED7		5.58	1.292	0.729	0.06	17.792				

TABLE 2.5 Results of the structural model

Hypothesis	Beta	Supported
H2a: Centre-led pricing management has a positive effect on pricing capabilities	0.354***	Yes
H2b: Centre-led pricing management has a positive effect on organizational confidence	0.013	No

TABLE 2.6 Pricing capabilities R square decomposition

Independent variables	Dependent variables	Correlations	Standardized estimates	Portion of variance explained by IV
Championing behaviours	Pricing capabilities	0.551	0.351	36%
Centre-led pricing management	Pricing capabilities	0.445	0.359	29%
Organizational change capacity	Pricing capabilities	0.477	0.135	12%
Controls	Pricing capabilities			23%
Total				100%
Pricing capabilities R square decomposition		0.543		

element associated with pricing that influenced pricing capabilities and organizational confidence in pricing as shown below:

HYPOTHESIS 2a *Centre-led pricing management has a positive effect on pricing capabilities.*

HYPOTHESIS 2b *Centre-led pricing management has a positive effect on organizational confidence.*

Our results indicate that centre-led pricing management has a positive effect on pricing capabilities but not on organizational confidence as shown in Table 2.5.

Furthermore, the decomposition of the R square for pricing capabilities as shown in Table 2.6 revealed the strong contribution of championing behaviours (36 per cent) and centre-led pricing management (29 per cent) in explaining its total variance. Finally, organizational change capacity was the stronger contributor to the R square of organizational confidence with 38 per cent of explained variance.

Implication for innovation in pricing

The goal of this paper was to propose a thorough review of the potential organizational designs for pricing management as well as to summarize the findings of our empirical research projects. We believe that the content of this paper makes strong contributions to the fields of pricing management and organizational design.

First, we have reviewed literature related to the centralization construct as well as proposed the four types of potential design of the pricing function in firms from a practical perspective. Leaders in firms wishing to design for pricing can review these options and consider the implications for their pricing function. Then, we have proposed that firms comprised in our sample using value-based pricing all adopted a centre-led management design leading to the successful adoption of this modern and advanced pricing orientation.

Finally, we have designed a unique quantitative scale to measure the activities of centre-led pricing teams. This scale can be used in future research projects related to pricing. Our findings suggest that centre-led pricing management is one of the five organizational factors related to pricing leading to firm performance. We therefore show that organizing for pricing using the centre-led model can benefit firms and can increase the level of capabilities and confidence related to pricing. Pricing teams play a strong role in boosting expertise, skills and confidence. As a result, they receive a high level of credibility and acceptance from commercial teams located in business units and divisions. Centre-led management of pricing is therefore a unique design where compliance is obtained because the central team of experts are dedicated to the pricing success of their counterparts in business units. Centre-led pricing teams act as internal consultants dedicated to the pricing success of their divisions as well as their entire corporations.

Much more needs to be studied and written on the topic of organizational design for pricing. The debate about centralized versus decentralized pricing is still ongoing. We contribute to this discussion by adding an innovative design for the pricing function called the centre-led management of pricing. We also propose that this design leads to superior performance in firms. Many firms (DSM, DuPont, ITT, Parker Hannifin, 3M, Philips Health Care, etc.) have adopted this design and have created central marketing or commercial excellence teams in charge of pricing management. These companies have pioneered the centre-led design for pricing excellence. We conjecture that it is the best organizational design for superior pricing and that it needs to be largely adopted.

Appendix: Sample characteristics from qualitative and quantitative studies

TABLE 2.7 Qualitative survey sample characteristics

Criteria	Characteristics	Firms
Firm size	Small	8
	Medium	7
Industry	Building products	4
	Transportation products	5
	Resins and plastics products	6

TABLE 2.7 Continued

Criteria	Characteristics	Firms
Pricing orientation	Cost-based pricing	6
	Competition-based pricing	5
	Value-based pricing	4
	Total firms	15

Criteria	Characteristics	Respondents
Functions	Executive leadership	15
	Sales and marketing	18
	Finance and accounting	11
Nature	Face-to-face interviews	37
	Phone interviews	7
	Total interviews	44
States	Pennsylvania, North Carolina, South Carolina, Oklahoma, Michigan, Massachusetts, Georgia, Wisconsin, Delaware and Kentucky	

TABLE 2.8 Quantitative survey sample characteristics

	Count	%		Count	%
Main activity			*Function of respondents*		
Manufacturing firm	415	55	General management	65	9
Service organization	206	28	Marketing and sales	177	24
Distribution/retail company	107	14	Finance and accounting	29	4
			Pricing and revenue management	427	57
Missing data	20	3			
Nature of firm			Administrative and operations	27	4
Publicly traded	437	58	Missing	23	3
Privately owned	257	34	*Geography of firm HQ*		
Both	25	3	North America	508	68
Do not know	9	1	Latin America	10	1
Missing	20	3	Europe	180	24
Firm size – employee numbers			Asia Pacific	21	3
Less than 250	78	10	Middle East/Africa	2	0
251 to 500	43	6	Missing	27	4
501 to 1,000	45	6	*Geography of respondents' location*		
1,001 to 10,000	233	31	North America	532	71
More than 10,000	329	44	Latin America	22	3
Missing	20	3	Europe	140	19
Total respondents	**748**		Asia Pacific	25	3
			Middle East/Africa	2	0
			Missing	27	4

References

Aiken, M., Bacharach, S. and French, J. L. (1980) Organizational structure, work process, and proposal making in administrative bureaucracies. *Academy of Management Journal*, 23 (4), pp. 631–52.

Argyres, N. S. and Silverman, B. S. (2004) R&D, organization structure, and the development of corporate technological knowledge. *Strategic Management Journal*, 25 (8–9), pp. 929–58.

Bolton, R. N. (1993) Pretesting questionnaires: content analyses of respondents' concurrent verbal protocols. *Marketing Science*, 12 (3), pp. 280–303.

Byrne, B. M. (2009) *Structural equation modeling with AMOS: Basic concepts, applications, and programming*. New York: Psychology Press.

Campbell, A., Kunisch, S. and Müller-Stewens, G. (2011) To centralize or not to centralize. *McKinsey Quarterly*, June, pp. 97–102. McKinsey & Company, Inc.

Churchill Jr, G. A. (1979) A paradigm for developing better measures of marketing constructs. *Journal of Marketing Research*, 16 (1), pp. 64–73.

Corbin, J. and Strauss, A. (2008) *Basics of qualitative research*. Thousand Oaks, CA: Sage Publications, Inc.

Cummings, S. (1995) Centralization and decentralization: The never ending story of separation and betrayal. *Scandinavian Journal of Management*, 11 (2), pp. 103–17.

Deaker, J. and Zang, X. (2006) How to organize the pricing discipline. *The Pricing Advisor*, November, pp. 1–4.

Dutta, S., Bergen, M. E., Levy, D., Ritson, M. and Zbaracki, M. (2002) Pricing as a strategic capability. *MIT Sloan Management Review*, 43 (3), p. 61.

Ecker, K. (2010) *Choosing the right type of pricing organisation for your company*. European and Global Pricing Conference, Brussels, Belgium.

Evaristo, J. R., Desouza, K. C. and Hollister, K. (2005) Centralization momentum: The pendulum swings back again. *Communications of the ACM*, 48 (2), pp. 66–71.

Fayol, H. (1949) *General and industrial administration*. London: Sir Isaac Pitman & Sons, Ltd.

Fornell, C. and Larcker, D. F. (1981) Evaluating structural equation models with unobservable variables and measurement error. *Journal of Marketing Research*, 18 (1), pp. 39–50.

Grant, R. (1996) Toward a knowledge-based theory of the firm. *Strategic Management Journal*, 17, pp. 109–22.

Hage, J. and Aiken, M. (1967) Relationship of centralization to other structural properties. *Administrative Science Quarterly*, 12 (1), pp. 72–92.

Hage, J. and Aiken, M. (1970) *Social change in complex organizations*. New York: Random House.

Hair, J. F., Black, W. C., Babin, B. J. and Anderson, R. E. (2010) *Multivariate data analysis*, 7th edition. Englewood Cliffs, NJ: Pearson-Prentice Hall.

Hall, R. (1977) *Organization, structure, and process*, Volume 2. London: Prentice-Hall.

Hall, R., Johnson, N. and Haas, J. E. (1967) Organizational size, complexity, and formalization. *American Sociological Review*, 32 (6), pp. 903–12.

Hinterhuber, A. (2004) Towards value-based pricing – An integrative framework for decision making. *Industrial Marketing Management*, 33 (8), pp. 765–78.

Hinterhuber, A. (2008) Customer value-based pricing strategies: why companies resist. *Journal of Business Strategy*, 29 (4), pp. 41–50.

Igbaria, M., Iivari, J. and Maragahh, H. (1995) Why do individuals use computer technology? A Finnish case study. *Information & Management*, 29 (5), pp. 227–38.

Ingenbleek, P. (2007) Value-informed pricing in its organizational context: literature review, conceptual framework, and directions for future research. *Journal of Product & Brand Management*, 16 (7), pp. 441–58.

John, G. and Martin, J. (1984) Effects of organizational structure of marketing planning on credibility and utilization of plan output. *Journal of Marketing Research*, 21 (2), pp. 170–83.

Kerlinger, F. and Lee, H. (2000) *Foundations of behavioral research*. Fort Worth, TX: Harcourt College Publishers.

Kruisinga, H. J. (1954) *The balance between centralization and decentralization in managerial control*. Leiden: HE Stenfert Kroese.

Lawrence, P. and Lorsh, J. (1967) *Organization and enviroment*. Boston: Division of Research, Harvard Business School.

Malhotra, N. K. (1996) The impact of the Academy of Marketing Science on marketing scholarship: An analysis of the research published in JAMS. *Journal of the Academy of Marketing Science*, 24 (4), pp. 291–8.

March, J. (1994) *A primer on decision making: How decisions happen*. New York: Free Press.

March, J. (1999) *The pursuit of organizational intelligence*. Oxford: Wiley-Blackwell.

March, J. and Simon, H. (1958) *Organizations*. New York: Wiley.

Miller, D., Droge, C. and Toulouse, J.-M. (1988) Strategic process and content as mediators between organizational context and structure. *Academy of Management Journal*, 31 (3), pp. 544–69.

Mitchell, K. (2011) *The current state of pricing practice in U.S. firms* (opening speech). Professional Pricing Society Annual Spring Conference, Chicago, USA.

Noble, P. and Gruca, T. (1999) Response to the comments on industrial pricing: Theory and managerial practice. *Marketing Science*, 18 (3), pp. 458–9.

Nunnally, J. (1978) Fundamentals of factor analysis. In: Nunnally, J. C. (ed.) *Psychometric theory*. 2nd ed. New York, NY: McGraw-Hill Book Company, pp. 327–404.

Pfeffer, J. (1978) The micropolitics of organizations. In: Meyer, M. W. (ed.) *Environments and organizations*. San Francisco: Jossey-Bass, pp. 29–50.

Simon, H. A. (1961) *Administrative behavior*. NewYork: Macmillan.

Simon, H. A. (1965) *The shape of automation for men and management*. New York: Harper & Row.

Simon, H. A., Guetzkow, H., Kozmetsky, G. and Tyndall, G. (1954) *Centralization vs. decentralization in organizing the controller's department*. New York: Controllership Foundation, Inc.

Van de Ven, A. and Ferry, D. (1980) *Measuring and assessing organizations*. New York: Wiley.

3
ORGANIZATIONAL BARRIERS AND THE IMPLEMENTATION OF CUSTOMER VALUE MAP ANALYSIS

A case study of a global manufacturing firm in the polymer technology industry

Niklas L. Hallberg

Linn Andersson

Introduction

Customer value map analysis (CVMA) is often recommended as a technique for implementing value-based pricing (e.g. Dolan and Simon 1996; Marn *et al.* 2004; Monroe 2003). CVMA is a technique for the competitive positioning of products based on their customer value and the prices of competing products. While there are detailed recommendations on how to identify customer value and competitor prices in the literature (Forbis and Mehta 1981; Kortge and Okonkwo 1993; Marn *et al.* 2004; Monroe 2003; Shapiro and Jackson 1978; Smith and Nagle 2005), the internal coordination and control mechanisms that determine firms' ability to *implement* value-based pricing are often vaguely described. For example, coordination and cooperation between different business departments (Dolan 1995; Dutta *et al.* 2002; Lancioni 2005b; Lancioni *et al.* 2005; Monroe 2003; Nagle and Holden 2002; Vogel *et al.* 2002) is identified as a key success factor for a more effective pricing but seldom elaborated. This is troubling since prior studies have found that firms often find it difficult to replace less effective pricing strategies, such as cost-based pricing and competition-based pricing, with value-based pricing (Hinterhuber 2008). One reason for this is that firms lack clearly specified authority levels for granting list price discounts to customers and systems for monitoring the sales force (Hinterhuber 2008; Stephenson *et al.* 1979).

One important element of sales force management is the development of guidelines on how sales representatives should handle customer discounts (Hinterhuber 2008; Marn *et al.* 2004; Monroe 2003; Simon *et al.* 2003). However, the accumulated empirical evidence on whether pricing authority should be delegated to sales representatives is inconclusive. Some studies recommend that pricing authority should be delegated to the sales representatives because of their superior information about the demands and willingness-to-pay of individual customers (e.g. Frenzen *et al.* 2010; Lal 1986; Weinberg 1975). Other studies are more critical of delegating pricing authority to sales representatives and highlight the tradeoff firms face between utilizing sales representatives' better information and the control-related problems that delegation can cause (Mishra and Prasad 2004; Stephenson *et al.* 1979), such as managing differences between the firm's objectives and the goals of the sales representatives (Joseph 2001; Mishra and Prasad 2005).

Since the purpose of CVMA is to set prices that match customer value and to position products relative to competing products, it requires that the firm accurately estimates the value of its products to each of its customer segments and is able to coordinate its prices across different customer segments. Hence, even if a decentralized pricing authority is suitable for estimating customers' willingness-to-pay (e.g. Frenzen *et al.* 2010; Lal 1986; Weinberg 1975), it might also prevent the firm from setting coordinated and competitively well-positioned prices. Thus, sales force price delegation might create an organizational barrier to the implementation of CVMA, which could limit firms' ability to reap the benefits from this technique. Organizational barriers may take the form of structural impediments, strategy obstacles, and systems barriers (Harris 2000). In this longitudinal case study of a firm implementing value-based pricing through the means of CVMA, we examine the nature of these organizational barriers by studying the mechanisms by which different levels of sales force price delegation affects the effectiveness with which CVMA can be used to implement value-based pricing strategy. In other words, we address the question of *how sales force price delegation affects the effectiveness with which firms use CVMA to implement value-based pricing strategy?* Our basic research model is outlined in Figure 3.1.

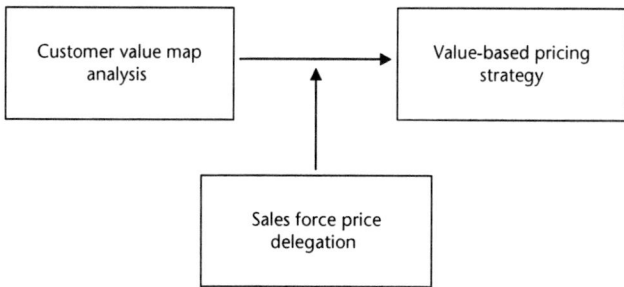

FIGURE 3.1 The moderating effect of sales force price delegation on the relationship between customer value map analysis and value-based pricing strategy

Theoretical foundation

Publications on price management include a variety of recommendations on how firms should price their products. For example, firms are recommended to base their pricing on customer value (Anderson and Narus 1998; Forbis and Mehta 1981; Kortge and Okonkwo 1993; Marn *et al.* 2004; Monroe 2003; Shapiro and Jackson 1978; Smith and Nagle 2005), competitor prices (Akintoye and Skitmore 1992; Duke 1994), customer price sensitivity (Dolan and Jeuland 1981; Monroe 2003; Nagle 1984; Vogel *et al.* 2002), and opportunities for price discrimination across customer segments (Cannon and Morgan 1990; Monroe and Lee 1999; Tellis 1986). However, despite the large body of research on different pricing strategies and analytical pricing techniques (such as how to estimate the customer value), empirical research on organizational barriers and control-related problems associated with the implementation of value-based pricing is sparse. To the extent that these issues are examined, it is mainly in terms of the different monetary incentives that can be provided to decision-makers at different levels in the organization to increase the likelihood of decisions with a positive effect on profit margin (Hinterhuber 2004, 2008; Marn *et al.* 2004; Nagle and Hogan 2006; Vogel *et al.* 2002). Hence, differential internal control mechanisms and organizational forms have traditionally been given little attention. Naturally, there are exceptions, for example, research stressing top-management involvement (Richards *et al.* 2005; Simon *et al.* 2003; Urbany 2001; Vogel *et al.* 2002), coordination and cooperation between departments (Dolan 1995; Dutta *et al.* 2002, 2003; Lancioni 2005b; Lancioni *et al.* 2005; Nagle and Holden 2002; Vogel *et al.* 2002) and organizational conflicts (Dutta *et al.* 2003; Zbaracki and Bergen 2010).

Value-based pricing strategy

Value-based pricing strategy, which is claimed to be the most profitable pricing strategy (Anderson and Narus 1998; Cannon and Morgan 1990; Hinterhuber 2008; Ingenbleek *et al.* 2003), is defined by Hinterhuber (2008: 42) as using "the value a product or service delivers to a predefined segment of customers as the main factor for setting prices" (see also Dolan 1995; Monroe 2003; Morris and Calantone 1990; Thompson and Coe 1997). We define customer value as "a customer's perceived preference for and evaluation of those product attributes, attribute performance, and consequences arising from use that facilitate (or block) achieving the customer's goals and purposes in use situations" (Woodruff 1997: 142).

Contrary to our definition, customer value is sometimes defined as the difference between the benefits received and the sacrifices made by the customer (see Lapierre 2000; Marn *et al.* 2004; Menon *et al.* 2005; Shapiro and Jackson 1978; Teas and Agarwal 2000). In these definitions, sacrifices refer to what the customer gives up when acquiring the product, such as price and time, whereas customer benefits are linked to the customer's perception of the received value of acquiring and using the product. As will be made clear in the next section, defining customer value in terms of the benefits received by the customer net of the price paid is highly problematic in the context of CVMA since this technique builds on plotting the relationship between customer value and price for a focal product and its substitutes.

Customer value map analysis

The estimation of customer value plays an important role in the implementation of value-based pricing that firms often experience as difficult (Anderson and Narus 1998). CVMA is in this context often recommended as a useful technique (see Dolan and Simon 1996; Marn et al. 2004; Monroe 2003). Hence, CVMA is a technique for plotting a firm's products against competing products based on the products' differential customer value and price. The benefit of this technique is that it allows the analyst to visualize the attractiveness of different competitive positions from the perspective of a potential customer.

The first step in applying CVMA is thus to quantify the *customer value* of the product in question. Forbis and Mehta (1981) suggest a method for accomplishing this. According to this method, the maximum price the customer is willing to pay is equivalent to the price of a reference product plus or minus the aggregated difference in value provided by the differentiating features of the focal product (e.g. difference in productivity, cost for maintenance, product life-time, payback time, or return on investment) (see Marn et al. 2004; Monroe 2003).

Once the customer value of the focal product is quantified, the same analysis is performed for competing products. As exemplified in Figure 3.2, the result is plotted in a two-dimensional chart with the product's customer value on the y-axis and the product's price on the x-axis. Products plotted on the dotted line are consequently those products for which price equals customer value. Product P illustrates the focal product whereas Product C1 and C2 represent competitive products.

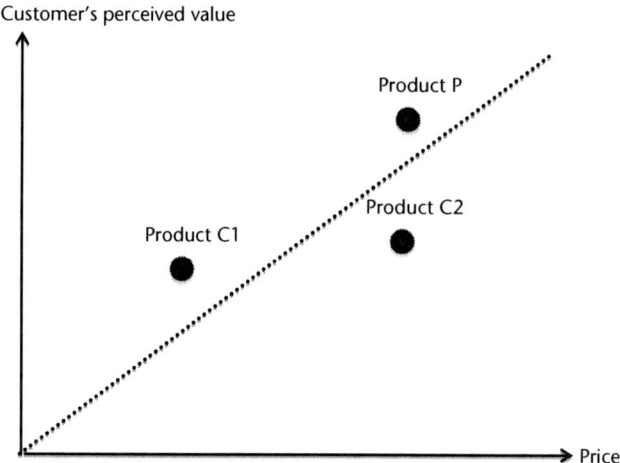

FIGURE 3.2 Graphical illustration of CVMA

As will be discussed in the next section, while CVMA might be a useful technique for analyzing the competitive consequences of different prices, firms often encounter difficulties when implementing the result from this analysis. These difficulties might ultimately lead firms to implement more traditional cost-based or competition-based strategies (Hinterhuber 2008). This indicates that there are important organizational barriers that might prevent firms from successfully using techniques, such as CVMA, and that these organizational barriers should be taken into account when implementing a value-based pricing strategy. For example, prior studies have shown that sales force control is an important factor to consider when implementing new pricing strategies (Hinterhuber 2008; Marn *et al.* 2004; Monroe 2003; Simon *et al.* 2003).

Sales force price delegation

Coordination and cooperation between business departments is often stressed as an important factor for managing price since pricing requires information held by different departments (Dolan 1995; Dutta *et al.* 2002; Lancioni 2005b; Lancioni *et al.* 2005; Monroe 2003; Nagle and Holden 2002; Vogel *et al.* 2002). For example, the sales department might hold important information about customers; the marketing department might be responsible for developing the pricing strategy, while the finance department is responsible for financial control (Dolan 1995). However, even though there is a consensus that firms often encounter internal coordination problems when implementing new pricing strategies (Lancioni 2005a), it is not yet fully understood what the sources of these problems are (Lancioni *et al.* 2005). It has been suggested that organizational barriers are created due to a lack of support from management (Richards *et al.* 2005; Simon *et al.* 2003; Urbany 2001; Vogel *et al.* 2002), internal conflicts (Dutta *et al.* 2003; Lancioni *et al.* 2005), and an unclear delegation of the pricing authority (Hinterhuber 2008).

Among other questions, there is an ongoing debate over whether pricing authority should be delegated to the individual sales representatives or not. Studies pointing to the benefits of delegation emphasize the impact of information asymmetries between the sales force and higher-level managers that puts the individual sales representative in a better position to set prices that match the individual customer's willingness-to-pay (Frenzen *et al.* 2010; Lal 1986; Weinberg 1975). Those in favor of price delegation also argue that the sales representative is motivated by the responsibility that follows with a full authority to set prices (Dolan and Simon 1996). A centralized pricing authority is, on the other hand, advocated in cases where there is no information asymmetry between the sales representatives and managers (Lal 1986; Mishra and Prasad 2004). This indicates that an important determinant of whether firms should delegate pricing authority is the level of information asymmetry between sales representatives and managers.

Empirical studies on the subject show that full delegation of pricing authority has a negative impact on profit margins because sales representatives tend to seek to increase volume rather than profit margin (Stephenson *et al.* 1979), a tendency that, for example, might cause sales representatives to give too large discounts

(Joseph 2001; Mishra and Prasad 2005). The main recommendation that can be derived from this literature is thus that firms should delegate pricing authority to the individual sales representative and provide incentives that secure that the sales representatives' goals are aligned with business goals. In the following, we examine this implication in detail based on an empirical case study.

Methods

We studied a global manufacturing company (ManComp) in the polymer technology industry. ManComp sells standardized product for the agriculture industry. ManComp was selected because between 2006 and 2010 it significantly changed its pricing organization and successfully implemented a value-based pricing strategy. ManComp's main markets are Western Europe and North America.

Data collection

The data was collected through interviews and internal documents (e.g. reports related to the pricing project, presentation material for internal use, annual reports, internal training material, and pricing self-assessments). Eight respondents were interviewed at the head office of ManComp. Each interview lasted up to three hours. The respondents held positions such as marketing manager, pricing manager, sales manager, sales representative, finance manager, and CEO. The respondents were selected based on a request to interview employees involved in the pricing process. The interview questions covered the project aimed at changing the pricing practice, the past and current practice for setting prices, as well as pricing techniques, pricing authority, customer relationship management, and the competitive market situation (see Appendix). Each interview was recorded and transcribed. In order to control the validity of our findings, a report was sent to the pricing project manager who was given the opportunity to comment on the results in a phone interview.

Data analysis

The transcribed interviews and relevant data from internal documents were first structured chronologically to give a full account of the events that had transpired from the initiation of the pricing project at ManComp to its completion. This allowed us to sort and describe events at ManComp according to the sequence in which the new pricing project had developed. The case description was then structured according to *a priori* specified constructs such as *pricing strategy* (i.e. cost-based and value-based pricing), *pricing techniques* (e.g. CVMA is a pricing technique when performing value-based pricing), and *sales force price delegation* (e.g. the sales representatives authority to grant discounts) (Eisenhardt 1989: 536). This allowed us to empirically examine the effects of different levels of sales force price delegation and pricing techniques on ManComp's ability to effectively implement a value-based pricing strategy. The empirical pattern that emerged from this analysis was then matched against the recommendations that had been identified in the literature review (Yin 2009).

ManComp's implementation of customer value map analysis

In 2001, a large corporate group in the polymer technology industry acquired ManComp from a competitor. ManComp was, as a part of the agreement, given the permission to license the competitor's brand until the end of 2010. In 2006, ManComp launched a project with the purpose of rebranding its products. Since the competitor from which ManComp was acquired was recognized as a premium brand, whereas the acquiring group was more or less unknown within this particular industry, management at ManComp feared that the customers would request lower prices and change to competing products. Thus, the purpose of the rebranding project was to protect market share and to maintain price levels. Hence, in order to maintain profit margin and sales volume, management initiated a pricing project with the purpose of changing the pricing practice at ManComp. The following four sections present the project of changing the pricing practice at ManComp. This includes pricing practices prior to the change, the actions that were taken in order to accomplish a change of the pricing practices, the pricing practice after the change, and the perceived performance outcomes of the project. Table 3.1 summarizes the changed pricing practice at ManComp in terms of the pricing strategy, sales force price delegation, and pricing techniques.

Pricing at ManComp prior to the pricing project

At the time when the pricing project was initiated, ManComp was using two different sales channels, original equipment manufacturers (OEMs) and dealers. Roughly 55 percent of the products were sold to OEMs, whereas the remaining 45 percent were spare parts sold to dealers. The OEMs are generally larger, global players that are handled centrally at the head office. The prices to the OEMs are negotiated for each customer and agreement. Due to the limited number of OEMs, their large turnover, and the long-term customer relationships, specific sales representatives were assigned for each OEM and pricing authority was delegated to these sales representatives.

The sales representatives responsible for the OEMs used his or her experience and gut feeling when setting prices. As a result, the prices were largely based on customer history. The dealers, on the other hand, which are generally smaller, local firms, that sell within a limited geographical area, were given price lists (with standardized rebates). The price lists were issued by the regional market offices, which autonomously set prices and handled customer negotiations. The pricing strategy used at this stage was, for both OEMs and dealers, cost-plus profit pricing. The pricing techniques that were used were profitability analysis for the different product categories (for the dealers) and individual OEM profitability. All these activities were performed on a monthly basis by a pricing manager at the head

TABLE 3.1 ManComp's pricing prior to the pricing project, actions taken, and pricing after the project

	Prior to the pricing project	Actions taken	After the pricing project
Pricing strategy	• Cost-plus pricing		• Value-based pricing
Sales force price delegation	• Pricing authority regarding the dealers delegated to the regional market offices • Pricing authority regarding the OEMs delegated to the individual sales representatives at the head office • A pricing manager working dedicated with pricing	• A project team consisting of managers and internal pricing experts was given the task of analyzing the pricing organization and providing recommendations for improvement • A communication campaign addressing both employees and customers was conducted • Approximately 10% of the sales force was laid off • Top management had a high focus on pricing • A new IT tool was constructed and implemented in order to allow for better information management	• A centralized pricing authority for all customers • Strict guidelines regarding the sales representatives' authority to give discounts • Sales representatives rewarded on gross profit margin • Pricing lists issued by head office instead of the regional market offices • A pricing manager working dedicated with pricing

Continued

TABLE 3.1 Continued

	Prior to the pricing project	Actions taken	After the pricing project

Pricing techniques	• Prices were set based on the individual sales representatives' experience/gut-feeling and customer history
	• Customer-profitability was analyzed for the OEMs
	• Product profitability was analyzed on an aggregated level for the different product categories
		• Sales representatives were provided with training in value-based pricing techniques
		• Employees were hired based on their pricing skills
			• CVMA with the support of:
			  ○ Price elasticity of demand analysis
			  ○ Inter-country price coherent reports
			  ○ Quantification of customer's buying criteria
			  ○ Identification and analysis of competitors' prices and products
			  ○ Customer-profitability analysis
			  ○ Product-profitability analysis
			  ○ Customer segmentation
			  ○ Revenue leakage analysis

office. Prices across different regional markets were not monitored, neither was the sales representatives' performance in terms of gross profit margin achievement.

Actions taken

When initiated in 2006, the project team, consisting of the pricing manager, marketing manager, sales managers, and the CEO, started by analyzing the pricing organization and formalizing an action plan in order to prevent possible negative consequences from the acquisition and the change in brand. The project team identified two main problems with the current pricing practice: inconsistent price level throughout sales regions which hindered the company from practicing competitive price positioning, and that the sales representatives were lacking the ability to set prices that match customer value. According to the marketing director at ManComp, the problem was that the individual sales representatives placed too much focus on revenue and competitors' prices rather than profit margin and customer value. He explained:

> The sales people always think of a market price, but the problem is that they cannot define the market price and they cannot determine the willingness of the customer to pay for that. They are not capable of doing that. It is not easy and probably they are much more short term driven. They want the product to be sold right now.

In order to address the two identified problems, a decision was made by management to implement value-based pricing and increase the consistency of prices across different sales regions. CVMA was decided to be a central feature of the new pricing practice. According to the project members, the pricing project was highly prioritized by management from the very beginning. The marketing director, one of the project team members, explained the high level of management support:

> There was a focus from the top, no doubt about that. That was the only way because pricing need time and resource so if it is not coming, the commitment from top-management, you cannot have resources. The time that you dedicate to prices means that you cannot dedicate to something else. So if it is not in the priority of the company it cannot be in the priority of the employee. I think it is quite easy to understand.

Before any changes were implemented, an information campaign addressed to both employees and customers was launched. The part of the campaign that was directed toward employees was initiated one year before any actual changes were implemented. Its purpose was to convince the employees of the benefits of the new pricing practice. Approximately 10 percent of the employees within sales did not accept the new pricing practice. These employees were laid-off as a result of their refusal to accept the new pricing practice. The part of the campaign that was directed toward the customers was designed to convince them that ManComp's products, and the quality of products, would remain the same after the change in brand.

Implementing competitive price positioning

According to the CEO, the competitive positioning of ManComp's products were perceived as essential both in order to signal the value of the product to the customer and to prevent internal predatory pricing which, in the long run, might lower the average price level. Hence, the next step in the pricing project was to centralize pricing authority for all customers in order to secure that the products were sold at a premium price. Thus, the decision was made to issue the price lists to the dealers from the head office, rather than from the regional market offices. Further, the sales representatives' authority to grant discounts was restricted. According to the marketing manager, the decision to centralize the pricing authority and restrict the sales representatives' authority to grant customer discounts allowed management to limit the sales representatives' tendency to prioritize revenue over profit margin. The CEO explained:

> Pricing is about positioning. I consider pricing to be the most important thing to influence the customer's perception of the value. So that is why we have decided since the beginning to position ourselves on the top and be a price leader in the market. This is mandatory in this company. Then of course you need to be consistent. You cannot have countries where your position is low because this is a global market. Your premium price position needs to be coherent with the rest of the world.

Matching prices according to customer value

Next, the sales representatives were provided with training on how to identify and quantify the customer value of products and to communicate how ManComp's product created value for different customer segments. Further, the sales representatives were trained in how to analyze price elasticity and perform competitive price positioning. This new employee skill-set was particularly premiered when hiring new sales representatives. The training material was published on the intranet for easy access.

Additionally, in order to facilitate the implementation of value-based pricing and the handling of required data (e.g. competitors' prices and customer history), a new IT system allowing better information management and price analysis were constructed. This includes a toolbox of pricing techniques that enable the pricing manager to perform price elasticity of demand analysis, revenue leakage analysis, CVMA, and inter-country price coherency reports.

Pricing at ManComp after the pricing project

The pricing project at ManComp was completed in 2010. The results of the project exceeded targets. Major changes had been made in several key areas as a result of ManComp's implementation of CVMA. As listed in Table 3.1, changes were made regarding the level of sales force price delegation and the use of different pricing techniques. These changes regarding sales force price delegation and the implemented pricing techniques are presented in the following sections.

Sales force price delegation

As a result of the new centralized pricing authority, the sales representatives' authority to allow discounts was restricted to 2 percent per year. In other words, the individual sales representatives could give the full 2 percent discount to one single customer or freely distribute it across several customers. Hence, discounting decisions were almost fully centralized, leaving only a small range for the sales representatives to negotiate. The limited possibility of sales representatives to offer discounts led to a decreased pressure to reduce the prices in customer negotiations. One of the sales representatives explained:

> In the discussion with the customer, it is always about the price, that's always what the customer wants to talk about. The challenge is to convince the customer that the added value that [ManComp] sells is worth paying extra for. The restricted discounts makes it easier because we simply cannot go lower in price, even if the customer asks us to.

Thus, the restricted pricing authority resulted in a decreased focus on price in customer negotiations: when asked by the customer to lower the prices, the sales representatives either referred to the customer value provided by the product, or offered a product with a lower quality and price. As indicated above, in some cases, if the sales representative judged that the customer had great future potential, the sales representative was able to offer a discount within their limited discount authority. Generally, the sales representatives did not experience that they were losing customers because of the new restricted discount policy. This was due to the greater precision in the competitive price positioning analysis. In other words, the customers were usually not able to buy similar products from a competitor at a lower price.

Training the employees in CVMA

As a substitute for using discounts as a tool in customer negotiations, the sales representatives were instead each year provided with training sessions on value-based pricing, for example, on how to perform CVMA, or how to communicate product value to the customers. The sales representatives responsible for the OEMs were obligated to perform CVMA for their respective customers, whereas the pricing manager, responsible for producing the price lists for the spare parts sold through the dealers, performed CVMA for a selection of these products. Performing CVMA on all of the spare parts would be too time consuming. Thus, rather than quantifying the customer value according to the logic used for the OEMs, the pricing manager relied on price elasticity of demand analysis when adjusting the price levels for the standardized products.

Price elasticity of demand analysis

As a result of the centralized pricing authority, the pricing manager at the head office now issued the price lists to the dealers. The pricing manager monitored the prices charged to each customer and conducted revenue leakage analysis for each product category. By dividing the change in the average price level with the change in sales volume, the pricing manager was able to perform price elasticity analysis for each product category within the different sales regions. Based on these analyses, the pricing manager quickly detected changes in volume due to price changes and responded accordingly. The CEO explained the importance of price elasticity of demand analysis:

> We do a lot of studies in price-volume-elasticity in order to understand exactly what impact we can expect on volume from a price increase. We are actually at the moment doing a study because we need to raise the price and we might lose some volume, we might lose a lot. But again, the gross contribution that we are going to get from the price increase is much higher than the additional volume we may get if we don't increase the prices at the level we would like to increase it.

Pricing new products according to CVMA

ManComp conducted CVMA each time they launched a new product. This involved testing customers' buying criteria and benchmarking competing products according to these parameters. For new product launches, an external organization, a university for example, was often hired to perform certified tests. These tests in combination with the cost for maintenance and product life time were benchmarked with competing products and analyzed according to CVMA.

Competitive price positioning

In order to perform competitive price positioning, new procedures for monitoring price levels between different sales regions were introduced. When conducting the monthly inter-country price comparison analysis, the pricing manager compared the average price level for each product category within each sales region with the average price of the competitors' products sold in the same region. The competitors' prices were obtained from product catalogues and the information the sales representatives received from customers. The sales representatives were responsible for reporting this information to the regional marketing office, which in turn reported it to the pricing manager.

The monthly inter-country prices comparison analyses enabled the pricing manager to both detect price differences between sales regions and provide him with the actual price position of each product category relative to competing products. According to the pricing manager, his analysis revealed that the competitor's prices differed between different sales segments, implying that many competitors lacked the capability to effectively perform price positioning. According to the sales representatives, knowing the prices of the competitors gave them better self-esteem when going into the customer meeting because they were confident that the prices were correct.

The CEO explained the advantages with the competitive price positioning:

> I can see our prices compared to our competitors' and break it down in detail country by country. In order to position yourself, you need to know exactly where you are, market by market, so that is why we have people in all the markets that are doing this job daily, just collecting information on prices. They produce a lot of information that tells me exactly in any segment and product category where we stand. We are quite centralized when you talk about pricing because we know that inconsistent prices will reduce the average price level instantly. We give freedom in any thinking to the subsidiary but when we talk about pricing, we would like to keep everything under control because we need to coordinate, because we need to make sure that we are coherent in our image all over the world and that is the basis of our pricing strategy today.

Pricing culture

The internal awareness of the strategic importance of pricing was facilitated by the marketing meetings being held two or three times each year, during which there was always a session dedicated to pricing. Additionally, during the monthly meetings with the highest management level, where all of the departments, such as sales, marketing, manufacturing and finance were represented, the first hour of the meeting was always dedicated to pricing. The pricing review for the last month was discussed, including raw material trends, competitive scenario, performance on the key performance indicators for pricing, such as inter-country price consistency, profitability, and gross profit margin. In order to facilitate a focus among the sales representatives on profit margin, they were measured and rewarded on the gross profit margin that they achieved.

Perceived performance outcomes from the pricing project according to self-assessment

Once the pricing project was completed in 2010, the result exceeded targets. The market share in Europe had more than doubled and the average price level had increased to the same level as the leading competitor. This made ManComp one of two actors in the highest European price segment. But perhaps most importantly, the profit margin (earnings before interest, taxes, depreciation, and amortization, EBITDA) had doubled.

The marketing director explained the outcome as resulting from the decision to centralize the pricing authority. He believed that the sales representatives would have been unable to maintain a premium price level if they had maintained authority to grant customer discounts. Hence, the results from the pricing projects showed that the sales representatives, once they were provided with training in value-based pricing, were able to better explain the value of the products to the customers and thus get the customers to accept premium prices.

When commenting on the results from the pricing project, the marketing director said that maintaining a competitive positioning in the highest price segment was the key success factor in order to ensure that the customers would understand the value of the products:

> I wouldn't believe it and I also think that they [top-management] didn't even consider the possibility to increase the market share and to reduce the price gap [between ManComp and the competitor in the highest price segment]. Probably they just wanted to keep the gap and keep the position but the results were exceeding the expectations. There is a lot of reasons why, we have been analyzing why it was good. For sure, one of the reasons, one part of the success is because of the price, because of what we've been doing. So I think it's been really a pillar in the brand switch project and I will take that with me in the future in the sense that when one wants to run a brand switch it is really risky not prioritizing pricing first. It is extremely important because pricing has an enormous effect on the perception of the value, enormous.

Conclusion

The results of our study indicate that innovation in sales force management, or more specifically, sales force price delegation (such as ManComp's radical centralization of pricing authority), is a key success factor for the implementation of value-based pricing. While some prior studies recommend that pricing authority is delegated to the individual sales representatives, because they supposedly hold better information about the customers' willingness-to-pay, our study indicates that there are important benefits of centralized pricing authority. Hence, we argue that the sales representatives should, instead of being given guidelines for how to deduct discounts and incentives that reward profit margin achievement, be provided with training on how to explain the centrally decided prices to the customers in terms of the value provided by the firm's products.

The decision of whether to delegate pricing authority to the individual sales representative should not primarily be seen as a question of information asymmetry (cf. Frenzen et al. 2010; Lal 1986; Mishra and Prasad 2004; Weinberg 1975) and the alignment of sales representatives' and management's goals (cf. Joseph 2001; Marn et al. 2004; Mishra and Prasad 2005; Vogel et al. 2002). Rather, the key question is whether the firm has adequate knowledge and skills at the organizational level where pricing decisions are made, and enough control over decision-makers at this level to guarantee that prices are consistent and coordinated.

Prior studies have found that firms often find it difficult to implement innovative pricing strategies, such as value-based pricing, due to the organizational barriers they face in the implementation process (Hinterhuber 2008). We identify three organizational barriers related to sales force price delegation that prevent an effective use of CVMA and the implementation of value-based pricing strategy.

First, allowing individual sales representatives, or even regional sales offices, to independently issue prices causes inconsistency. This is highly problematic when using CVMA since it undermines the competitive price positioning of products, a central aspect of CVMA that requires consistent prices within and across sales regions. In other words, an effective use of CVMA requires that pricing authority is centralized and not spread across different decision-makers. Naturally, there are benefits of a decentralized pricing authority in terms of local and fast responsiveness to customer demand. However, our study indicates that, despite these benefits, decentralization is a deceitful path to customer satisfaction. Ultimately, value-based pricing builds on knowing what the products are really worth to the customer, and consistently communicating this value to the customer. Local responsiveness in terms of asking individual customers to estimate their perceived value of the product is not the solution, but part of the problem.

Second, sales representatives operating in cost-based business environments do not normally have the training or techniques for identifying and quantifying customer value. Naturally, this presents a challenge to firms attempting to change from cost- to value-based pricing. Managers are thus left with the choice of either centralizing pricing authority to a level where sufficient knowledge and control can be achieved (e.g. a pricing manager) or spending substantial resources on retraining its sales force. Given the cost of retraining the sales force and the limited benefits of having a sales force that is itself capable of delivering value-based prices (due to the coordination problems discussed above), this speaks in favor of centralizing pricing decisions. The managerial implications of this is that the implementation of pricing innovations in traditional organizations (such as ManComp) should be accomplished with a strict top-down, rather than bottom-up, focus in order to avoid organizational coordination problems that might otherwise offset the benefits of these innovations.

Third, our study shows that granting sales representatives authority to give discounts makes the sales representatives more inclined to offer substantial discounts to customers, and less inclined to spend time and effort on communicating the rationale behind the price in terms of customer value. In other words, granting sales representatives authority to give discounts leads to prices that correspond to what the customers claim to be their willingness-to-pay, rather than the actual customer value provided by the firm. Presumably, this is simply the effect of sales representatives' willingness to please their customers: If both the sales representative and the customer know the amount of money that is on the table (i.e. the size of the discount that the sales representative is allowed to give), both parties' attention will be directed toward how this amount of money can be divided in a way that is perceived to be equitable to both parties (e.g. splitting it in half).

Implications for innovation in pricing

We offer the following three recommendations to managers that, like the managers at ManComp, are dedicated to innovation in pricing and are about to begin the process of replacing their traditional cost-based pricing strategy with a value-based pricing strategy:

- Local responsiveness in terms of asking individual customers to estimate their perceived value of the product is not a solution to the challenges faced by firms in the implementation of value-based pricing; it is part of the problem. The solution is to identify the organizational level within your firm where decision-makers possess the right mix of product- and market-specific knowledge that may enable them to make pricing decisions that are both consistent (i.e. meet the requirement of competitive price positioning) and accurately reflect the value provided to customers.
- The implementation of pricing innovations, such as value-based pricing strategy, in more traditional industries (where firms normally rely on cost-based pricing) should be accomplished with a strict top-down, rather than bottom-up, focus in order to avoid organizational coordination problems that might otherwise offset the benefits of these pricing innovations.
- Granting sales representatives authority to give significant discounts leads to prices that correspond to what the customers claim to be their willingness-to-pay, rather than the actual customer value provided by the firm. All negotiation games are structured by the parties' prior commitments. Make sure that the negotiation games your sales representatives play are structured so that they stand a chance of capturing a fair share of the money that is on the table.

Appendix: Interview guide

Customer relationship management
- character of customer relations
- customers' buying criteria and determinants of purchasing decision
- delivered customer value
- customer feedback
- different pricing practices depending on different customers and/or sales regions
- the role of the customer's customer.

Competitors
- competitive situation
- information about competitors.

The project of changing the pricing practice
- Which pricing strategy was used at ManComp prior to the pricing project?
    - discount policy
    - pricing authority
    - intensive programs for sales representatives
    - pricing techniques
    - customer relationship management.

- Why was the decision made to launch the pricing project?
  - Why was it initiated and by whom?
  - Were there any other alternatives and, if so, how were they evaluated?
  - What was the expected outcome from implementing the new pricing strategy?

- How was the pricing project carried out?
  - Who was responsible?
  - How was it carried out?

- What was the outcome from the pricing project?
  - Which changes have been made?
  - Have there been any changes regarding prices?
  - Have there been any reactions from the customers, competitors and/or suppliers?
  - discount policy
  - pricing authority
  - intensive programs for sales representatives
  - pricing techniques.

Pricing strategies and techniques
- pricing skills among employees in general and sales representatives in particular
- procedure for setting prices
- discount policy
- procedures for changing prices
- pricing techniques
- information management
- pricing of new products
- hiring of pricing talent.

Coordination and management involvement
- management involvement on pricing decisions
- pricing authority
- management involvement when price changes are imposed and when new products are priced
- communication between management and lower-level
- communication between different departments/functions/divisions regarding pricing
- key performance indicators (KPIs) tied to pricing objectives
- sales force management.

References

Akintoye, A. and Skitmore, M. (1992) Pricing approaches in the construction industry. *Industrial Marketing Management*, 21 (4), pp. 311–18.

Anderson, J. C. and Narus, J. A. (1998) Business marketing: Understand what customers value. *Harvard Business Review*, 76 (6), pp. 53–65.

Cannon, H. M. and Morgan, F. W. (1990) A strategic pricing framework. *The Journal of Service Marketing*, 4 (2), pp. 19–30.

Dolan, R. J. (1995) How do you know when the price is right? *Harvard Business Review*, 73, pp. 174–83.

Dolan, R. J. and Jeuland, A. P. (1981) Experience curves and dynamic demand models: Implications for optimal pricing strategies. *Journal of Marketing*, 45 (1), pp. 52–63.

Dolan, R. J. and Simon, H. (1996) *Power pricing: How managing price transforms the bottom line.* New York: The Free Press.

Duke, C. R. (1994) Matching appropriate pricing strategies with markets and objectives. *Journal of Product and Brand Management*, 3 (2), pp. 15–27.

Dutta, S., Bergen, M., Levy, D., Ritson, M. and Zbaracki, M. (2002) Pricing as a strategic capability. *MIT Sloan Management Review*, 43 (3), pp. 61–7.

Dutta, S., Zbaracki, M. J. and Bergen, M. (2003) Pricing process as a capability: A resource-based perspective. *Strategic Management Journal*, 24 (7), pp. 615–30.

Eisenhardt, K. M. (1989) Building theories from case study research. *The Academy of Management Review*, 14 (4), pp. 532–50.

Forbis, J. L. and Mehta, N. T. (1981) Value-based strategies for industrial products. *Business Horizons*, 24 (3), pp. 32–43.

Frenzen, H., Hansen, A. K., Krafft, M., Mantrala, M. K. and Schmidt, S. (2010) Delegation of pricing authority to the sales force: An agency-theoretic perspective of its determinants and impact on performance. *International Journal of Research in Marketing*, 27 (1), pp. 58–68.

Harris, L. C. (2000) The organizational barriers to developing market orientation. *European Journal of Marketing*, 34 (5), pp. 598–624.

Hinterhuber, A. (2004) Towards value-based pricing – An integrative framework for decision making. *Industrial Marketing Management*, 33 (8), pp. 765–78.

Hinterhuber, A. (2008) Customer value-based pricing strategies: Why companies resist. *Journal of Business Strategy*, 29 (4), pp. 41–50.

Ingenbleek, P., Debruyne, M., Frambach, R. and Verhallen, T. M. (2003) Successful new product pricing practice: A contingency approach. *Marketing Letters*, 14 (4), pp. 289–305.

Joseph, K. (2001) On the optimality of delegating pricing authority to the sales force. *The Journal of Marketing*, 65 (1), pp. 62–70.

Kortge, G. D. and Okonkwo, P. A. (1993) Perceived value approach to pricing. *Industrial Marketing Management*, 22 (2), pp. 133–40.

Lal, R. (1986) Delegating pricing responsibility to the salesforce. *Marketing Science*, 5 (2), pp. 159–68.

Lancioni, R. (2005a) Pricing issues in industrial marketing. *Industrial Marketing Management*, 34 (2), pp. 111–14.

Lancioni, R. A. (2005b) A strategic approach to industrial product pricing: The pricing plan. *Industrial Marketing Management*, 34 (2), pp. 177–83.

Lancioni, R., Schau, H. J. and Smith, M. F. (2005) Intraorganizational influences on business-to-business pricing strategies: A political economy perspective. *Industrial Marketing Management*, 34 (2), pp. 123–31.

Lapierre, J. (2000) Customer-perceived value in industrial contexts. *The Journal of Business and Industrial Marketing*, 15 (2), pp. 122–45.

Marn, M. V., Roegner, E. V. and Zawada, C. C. (2004) *The price advantage*. Hoboken, NJ: John Wiley & Sons, Inc.

Menon, A., Homburg, C. and Beutin, N. (2005) Understanding customer value in business-to-business relationships. *Journal of Business to Business Marketing*, 12 (2), pp. 1–38.

Mishra, B. K. and Prasad, A. (2004) Centralized pricing versus delegating pricing to the salesforce under information asymmetry. *Marketing Science*, 23 (1), pp. 21–7.

Mishra, B. K. and Prasad, A. (2005) Delegating pricing decisions in competitive markets with symmetric and asymmetric information. *Marketing Science*, 24 (3), pp. 490–7.

Monroe, K. B. (2003) *Pricing: Making profitable decisions*, 3rd edition. New York: McGraw-Hill Higher Education.

Monroe, K. B. and Lee, A. Y. (1999) Remembering versus knowing: issues in buyers' processing of price information. *Journal of the Academy of Marketing Science*, 27 (2), pp. 207–25.

Morris, M. H. and Calantone, R. J. (1990) Four components of effective pricing. *Industrial Marketing Management*, 19 (4), pp. 321–30.

Nagle, T. (1984) Economic foundations for pricing. *The Journal of Business*, 57 (1, Part 2: Pricing Strategy), pp. S3–S26.

Nagle, T. T. and Hogan, J. E. (2006) *The strategy and tactics of pricing: A guide to growing more profitably*, 4th edition. Upper Saddle River, NJ: Pearson Education, Inc.

Nagle, T. T. and Holden, R. K. (2002) *The strategy and tactics of pricing: A guide to profitable decision making*, 3rd edition. Upper Saddle River, NJ: Pearson Education, Inc.

Richards, J. D., Reynolds, J. and Hammerstein, M. (2005) The neglected art of strategic pricing. *Financial Executive*, 21 (5), pp. 26–9.

Shapiro, B. P. and Jackson, B. B. (1978) Industrial pricing to meet customer needs. *Harvard Business Review*, 56 (6), pp. 119–27.

Simon, H., Butscher, S. A. and Sebastian, K.-H. (2003) Better pricing processes for higher profits. *Business Strategy Review*, 14 (2), pp. 63–7.

Smith, G. E. and Nagle, T. T. (2005) A question of value. *Marketing Management*, 14 (4), pp. 38–43.

Stephenson, P. R., Cron, W. L. and Frazier, G. L. (1979) Delegating pricing authority to the sales force: The effects on sales and profit performance. *The Journal of Marketing*, 43 (2), pp. 21–8.

Teas, R. K. and Agarwal, S. (2000) The effects of extrinsic product cues on consumers' perceptions of quality, sacrifice, and value. *Journal of the Academy of Marketing Science*, 28 (2), pp. 278–90.

Tellis, G. J. (1986) Beyond the many faces of price: An integration of pricing strategies. *Journal of Marketing*, 50 (4), pp. 146–61.

Thompson, K. N. T. and Coe, B. J. (1997) Gaining sustainable competitive advantage through strategic pricing: selecting a perceived value price. *Pricing Strategy & Practice*, 5 (2), pp. 70–9.

Urbany, J. E. (2001) Justifying profitable pricing. *Journal of Product & Brand Management*, 10 (3), pp. 141–59.

Vogel, H. M., Bright, J. K. and Stalk Jr, G. (2002) *Organizing for pricing*. BCG Perspectives, Boston Consulting Group Report.

Weinberg, C. B. (1975) An optimal commission plan for salesmen's control over price. *Management Science*, 21 (8), pp. 937–43.

Woodruff, R. B. (1997) Customer value: The next source for competitive advantage. *Journal of the Academy of Marketing Science*, 25 (2), pp. 139–53.

Yin, R. (2009) *Case study research: Design and methods*, 4th edition. Thousand Oaks, CA: Sage Publications, Inc.

Zbaracki, M. J. and Bergen, M. (2010) When truces collapse: A longitudinal study of price-adjustment routines. *Organization Science*, 21 (5), pp. 955–72.

4
CEO CHAMPIONING OF PRICING AND THE IMPACT ON FIRM PERFORMANCE

Stephan M. Liozu

Andreas Hinterhuber

Sheri Perelli

Toni M. Somers

Introduction

Compared to other management responsibilities, pricing receives relatively little attention from practitioners and scholars (Malhotra 1996; Carricano et al. 2010). The Professional Pricing Society, the world's largest organization dedicated to pricing, estimates that fewer than 5 per cent of Fortune 500 companies have a full-time function exclusively dedicated to pricing (Mitchell 2011) and, similarly, among AACSB (The Association to Advance Collegiate Schools of Business) accredited business schools, only 9 per cent offer courses that put a significant emphasis on pricing (McCaskey and Brady 2007). Yet several studies suggest pricing has substantial and immediate effects on company profitability: small variations in price influence the bottom line by as much as 20 per cent to 50 per cent in both directions.

Several studies have examined how firms make pricing decisions and how pricing decisions influence profitability (Ingenbleek et al. 2003; Smith 1995). Others have demonstrated that CEOs, as architects of corporate strategy (Andrews 1971), impact firm performance (Mackey 2008) by committing organizations to specific courses of action (Harrison and Pelletier 1997).

Curiously, however, the question of how CEOs influence organizational performance via pricing has not been studied. From a practical perspective this question is relevant. Warren Buffet, a prominent CEO and investor, observes:

> The single most important decision in evaluating a business is pricing power. If you've got the power to raise prices without losing business to a competitor, you've got a very good business. And if you have to have a prayer session before raising the price by 10 per cent, then you've got a terrible business.
> (Frye and Campbell 2011)

Understanding the link between CEO commitment to and involvement in pricing and the design and performance of an organization allows us to further shed light on a specific type of strategic actions – pricing activities – through which CEOs can influence firm performance. To address this phenomenological gap, we surveyed 557 business owners, presidents and CEOs in firms from around the world to measure the effect of championing of pricing on firms' organizational design and relative performance. Our inquiry contributes to the fields of pricing and organizational behaviour by linking championing behaviours on pricing to three organizational factors – pricing capabilities, collective mindfulness and decision making rationality – and subsequently to relative firm performance. Most importantly, our data highlight the role of organizational champions in support of the pricing function and imply that purposeful championing of pricing influences organizational design for pricing and may impact perceived firm performance.

Theoretical background and hypotheses

The development of our theoretical research model (show in Figure 4.1) draws from related streams on pricing literature and firm capabilities and resource-based view of the firm as well as from critical dimensions of organization theory from a decision making perspective such as bounded rationality, organizational champions and collective mindfulness.

Pricing literature from an organizational perspective

Several studies have examined pricing practices from the perspective of organizational decision processes but, among them, only a handful have linked the bodies of knowledge on pricing and organizational behaviours. Cyert and March (1992), who studied pricing behaviours in a retail environment, suggest that, over time, simplifying 'rules of thumb' emerge within the firm. They argue that prices are 'negotiated' between various departments of the firm as a way to reach consensus and achieve negotiated objectives. Finally, they propose that cost-based pricing practices are included among these rules of thumb or routines. Lancioni

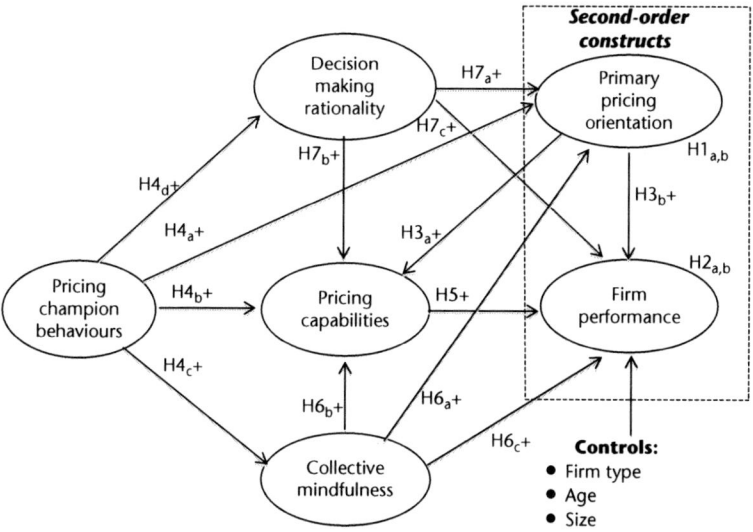

FIGURE 4.1 Research model and proposed hypotheses

et al. (2005) researched the intraorganizational influence on business-to-business pricing strategies and more specifically the importance of interdepartmental rivalry and conflicting interests on the pricing process. The findings show that resistance to progressive pricing strategies emanate from many groups in firms each of them 'having parochial interests and agendas'. The most dominant resistance and roadblocks were created by the finance department which was ranked as the most difficult to work with in developing a comprehensive pricing policy. Senior management was also ranked high because of its desire to control the pricing process. Finally, Ingenbleek (2007) conducted a meta-analysis of 53 pricing studies drawn from cost-principle theory, decision making theory and marketing strategy. Although no empirical research was conducted, Ingenbleek proposed a conceptual framework and several directions for future research in the field of value-informed pricing. His review of the literature suggests that information sources represent a key resource to be acquired, developed and deployed within the firm. However, the availability of information does not guarantee success in value-informed pricing – the degree to which information is processed, interpreted, communicated and used can influence the implementation of it. Thus the pricing process within the firm can influence the management of information related to customer value perceptions. Ingenbleek (2007) made the following critical conclusions with regard to pricing literature: (1) it is highly descriptive and lacks statistical significance; (2) research insights on pricing practices are often not cumulative; and (3) theory about how price decisions are made in firms is limited. We hope to build on the scholarly work of Cyert and March, Lancioni, and Ingenbleek by bridging the fields of pricing and organizational behaviour.

Pricing literature on orientation and firm performance

The notion of pricing orientation in firms has not been appropriately defined and explored. A handful of academic papers reviewed pricing approaches in business markets (Hinterhuber 2008b) while others discussed pricing practices and their relationship to new product market performance (Ingenbleek et al. 2003, 2010). Managerial pricing orientation 'deals with decisions relating to setting or changing prices. It also includes price positioning and product decisions introducing new pricing points to the business unit's product or service mix' (Smith 1995). Smith defined it as consisting of four dimensions (information getting and processing, pricing objectives, policies and beliefs, organizational decision processing, and organizational responsiveness) and proposed four distinct managerial pricing orientations – cost, sales, competition and strategy. We, however, define pricing orientation with three dimensions: cost, competition and customer value (Hinterhuber 2008b). We consider pricing orientation from a firm's strategic perspective and define it as all pricing practices, methods, behaviours and processes leading to pricing decisions with the goal of maintaining and sustaining firm competitive advantage. Moreover, methodological emphasis is placed on conceptualizing pricing orientation as a second-order factor and defining the three dimensions as first-order factors.

HYPOTHESIS 1a *There are three distinct dimensions of a firm's pricing orientation.*

HYPOTHESIS 1b *Each dimension contributes to a second-order construct of a firm's pricing orientation.*

Most pricing practitioners agree that pricing orientation and the lack of scientific and systematic return on investment (ROI) calculations for pricing strategies constrain visibility of pricing in the C-suite and restrain firm adoption of modern pricing approaches. In addition, marketing and pricing literature is silent about both the consequences of pricing orientations on overall company performance (Cressman Jr 1999; Ingenbleek 2007; Hinterhuber 2008b) and, more specifically, on how value-based pricing might lead to superior firm performance. Ingenbleek et al. (2003) tested the relationship between pricing approach and new product success and found value-informed pricing had the overall strongest positive effect on product performance. A subsequent study (Ingenbleek et al. 2010), showed value-informed pricing positively influenced new product market (but not new product financial) performance (noting the latter link may require a more complex model including data on sales, costs and other information) (Ingenbleek et al. 2010).

We believe firm performance may be better represented as a higher-order construct. Consequently, firms' relative performance is operationalized as a second-order factor measured by sales, profit and pricing. Conceptualizing firm performance in this manner recognizes that the construct's interpretation is derived from the content of the items used in its operationalization. Thus we posit:

HYPOTHESIS 2a *There are three distinct dimensions of a firm's relative performance.*

HYPOTHESIS 2b *Each dimension contributes to a second-order construct of a firm's relative performance.*

HYPOTHESIS 3a *The firm's pricing orientation will be related positively to its pricing capabilities.*

HYPOTHESIS 3b *The firm's pricing orientation will be related positively to its relative performance.*

Organizational champions

Leaders can influence both functional management commitment and the adoption of innovative technology and practices in firms (March and Simon 1958: 219). Top management support strongly impacts functional management commitment. This type of top management support needed for initiatives such as total cost of ownership (TCO) (Wouters *et al.* 2005) or value-based pricing (Hinterhuber 2008a), which require inter-functional cooperation. Hinterhuber (2008a), for example, reported lack of support from senior management was an obstacle for 50 per cent of respondents involved in value-based pricing implementation. Senior management support for customer-value management processes is a requirement when firms try to implement a 'philosophy' of doing business based on demonstrated value to customers (Anderson *et al.* 2007: 13). Senior management must 'take a broader view of persuasively conveying this value merchant mind-set and culture to everyone working in the business and to the customers' (Anderson *et al.* 2007: 123). Hinterhuber (2008a: 49) argued that 'senior management (support) can be obtained through various means, including lobbying, networking, and bargaining. If such support is gained, middle-ranking executives can then implement value-based pricing strategies'.

Top management plays a key role in defining and promoting corporate-wide priorities and new strategic programmes but also in identifying, allocating and deploying strategic resources to support these programmes (Chandler 1973: 4). Executive experience, overall personality and risk aversion behaviours help determine the course and rate of structural adaptation and innovation (Chandler 1973: 283; Jaworski and Kohli 1993). The influence, skills and drive of upper management are a resource leading to better strategy and greater economic rents by firms (Barney and Clark 2007). Leadership styles (authoritative versus participative) and backgrounds (legal, finance or marketing) also impact the organization (Chandler 1973: 317; Simon 1961: 159).

Scholars and practitioners have focused on the role of champions from a leadership perspective. Organizational champions have been defined as charismatic leaders (Nadler and Tushman 1990), transformational leaders (Bass 1985: 22; Wang and Huang 2009) and champions of change (Nadler and Nadler 1997: 98). Champions may exhibit a 'constellation of behaviours' (Howell *et al.* 2005) that can be nurtured and learned – including 'communicating a clear vision of what innovation could be or do, displaying enthusiasm and demonstrating commitment to it, and involving others in supporting it' (Howell and Higgins 1990). They may increase 'effort-accomplishment expectancies' by reinforcing collective efficacy and increase self-efficacy and collective efficacy by expressing positive evaluations (Tasa et al. 2007) and showing confidence in people to perform effectively and to meet challenges (Nadler and Tushman 1990).

HYPOTHESIS 4a, b, c, d *The more the involvement of the 'champion on pricing' the stronger the firm's pricing orientation, (b) pricing capabilities, (c) collective mindfulness, (d) decision making rationality.*

Capabilities and resource-based view of the firm

The resource-based view of the firm (Wernerfelt 1984), which seeks to explain and predict why some firms are able to establish positions of sustainable competitive advantage leading to superior returns or economic rent, perceives the firm as a 'unique bundle of resources and capabilities where the primary task of management is to maximize value' (Grant 1996). These resources include 'all assets (physical and nonphysical), capabilities, organizational processes, firm attributes, information, knowledge etc. controlled by the firm that enable a firm to conceive and implement strategies that improve its efficiency and effectiveness' (Barney 1991: 101). A specific combination of these tangible and intangibles resources and capabilities is valuable, rare and difficult to imitate or acquire by competitors (Barney and Clark 2007; Dierickx and Cool 1989; Hall 1993) and cannot be captured on a piece of paper (Nadler and Tushman 1990: 18).

Dutta et al. (2003) highlight the role of pricing capabilities for increasing company performance. In contrast to the marketing capability literature, these authors define pricing capabilities as a set of complex routines, skills, systems, know-how, coordination mechanisms and complementary resources. Pricing capability refers to, on the one hand, the price setting capability within the firm (identification of competitor prices, setting pricing strategy, and translation from pricing strategy to price) and, conversely, to the price setting capability vis-à-vis customers (convincing customers on the price change logic, negotiating price changes with major customers). In this and subsequent research settings, pricing capabilities are found to be positively related to company performance (Berggren and Eek 2007; Dutta et al. 2002, 2003; Hallberg 2008). In these studies, pricing capabilities are complex, difficult-to-imitate processes which span organizational boundaries. These studies investigate exclusively the link between pricing capabilities and firm performance. All of these studies use qualitative research. In other words, the link between a somewhat more complex view of pricing capabilities and organizational performance has not yet been explored empirically. Thus we posit:

HYPOTHESIS 5 *The firm's pricing capabilities will be related positively to its relative performance.*

Organizational mindfulness

Mindfulness, originally characterized by Langer (1989) as a state of alertness that is manifest in active information processing, includes: creating new categories rather than relying on categories present in our memory; welcoming new information by being open and attending to changed signals; and welcoming more than one view and being aware of multiple interpretations. Fiol and O'Connor (2003: 60) observed that 'the greater the level of mindfulness of decision makers, the more likely it is they will use decision making mechanisms to expand their search for information'. Weick et al. (1999) extended the concept of individual mindfulness (Langer 1989, 1997) to the collective, describing it as the widespread adoption and diffusion of mindfulness by the organization's members. Mindfulness helps organizations to notice more issues, process them with care, and detect and respond to early signs of trouble (Weick and Sutcliffe 2007). Weick and Sutcliffe (2007); Weick et al. (1999) describe five cognitive processes that constitute organizational mindfulness: (1) preoccupation with failure; (2) reluctance to simplify interpretations; (3) sensitivity to operations; (4) commitment to resilience; and (5) deference to expertise. We contend that these characteristics of high reliability organizations can also be applied to the adoption and implementation of pricing strategies in firms.

Firms engaged in the development of modern pricing practices invest in developing pricing capabilities of their front line personnel through pricing training for sales employees in order to equip them with the tools and capabilities to achieve the firm's pricing goals. Sensitivity to operations also entails adjusting pricing programmes by taking into account the knowledge of people who actually do the work (Weick and Sutcliffe 2007). Commitment to resilience is strongly influenced by executive champions' internal development of shared beliefs, courage and resilience when implementing pricing strategies. Finally, firms defer pricing decision expertise and influence to centre-led pricing teams. Decision makers in business units rely on the expertise of these specialized centres of excellence to optimize pricing decisions and the firm's performance.

HYPOTHESIS 6a, b, c *The firm's collective mindfulness will be related positively to: (a) pricing orientation, (b) pricing capabilities and (c) relative performance.*

Decision making rationality

Simon (1961: 93) posits that actual behaviour of managers in firms when making decisions or making choices falls short of objective rationality in three ways: (1) the incompleteness of knowledge; (2) the difficulties in anticipation of the consequences that will follow choice; and (3) the choice among all possible alternative behaviours. Managers also suffer from a possible 'bottleneck of attention' that impacts their ability to deal with more than a few things at a time (Simon 1961: 90). Bounded rationality refers to the notion that rational actors are significantly constrained by limitations of information and calculations (Cyert and March 1992: 214). Behavioural theorists conjecture that managers in organizations simplify the decision making process by using various behaviours (Cyert and March 1992: 264): satisficing (March 1978); following rules of thumb (Schwenk 1988); and defining standard operating procedures and organizational routines (Feldman 2000; Pentland and Reuter 1994). Others will define frames of reference (March and Simon 1958: 159) which will be determined 'by the limitations of the rational man's knowledge'. Experienced managers will draw from their memory, training and experience (Simon 1961: 134). They construct and use 'cognitive heuristics' (Brownlie and Spender 1995) or mental models (Porac et al. 1989) to simplify complex strategic issues and engage in intuitive and judgemental responses to decision demanding situations (Barnard and Andrews 1968; Oxenfeldt 1973). The resolution of uncertainty is 'to create a rationality, a recipe or an interpretative scheme' (Brownlie and Spender 1995) leading to a choice or a decision.

HYPOTHESIS 7a, b, c *The firm's decision making rationality will be related positively to: (a) pricing orientation, (b) pricing capabilities and (c) relative performance.*

Methodology

Data collection and sampling

Following the total design method (Dillman et al. 2009), a cross-sectional self-administered electronic survey was sent in April 2011 to 7,897 active members of the Young President Organization International (YPO). YPO is a for-profit organization with 18,000 business owner/executive members in 110 countries. Members of YPO must meet eligibility criteria, such as age (under 45 years old), title (President, Chief Executive Officer, Chairman of the Board, Managing Director, and/or Managing Partner), enterprise value (minimum $10 million), number of employees (minimum 50) and annual sales revenues (minimum $8 million for sales, service and manufacturing corporations, $160 million for financial institutions and $6 million for agency-type businesses). To our knowledge, no other empirical studies have used the YPO database.

Consequently, the survey was emailed to 7,897 targeted respondents of which 376 were returned for reasons of email discrepancies. Of the remaining 7,521, 902 surveys were returned partially or completed for a response rate of 12 per cent. We deemed 557 usable for analysis. Our response rate is consistent with the surveys of other top executives (Hambrick et al. 1993; Simsek et al. 2010).

Eighty per cent of the firms in our study identified themselves as manufacturing or service firms with the remaining classified as retail/distribution firms. Over half (61 per cent) were business-to-business (B2B) firms vs. business-to-consumer (B2C). About 11 per cent were publicly traded while 87 per cent reported being privately owned. Seventy-three per cent indicated they owned the firm. Half (50 per cent) had fewer than 250 employees, 22 per cent had 251–500, 13 per cent had 501 to 1000 employees and 15 per cent had more than 1,000 employees (of that, 3 per cent had over 10,000 employees). Fifty-three per cent reported the age of their firm as older than 10 years but less than 50 years old. Thirty-four per cent indicated their firm had been in business for longer than 50 years. Business management was reported as the educational background of 48 per cent of the respondents, 20 per cent had technical, industrial or engineering backgrounds, 17 per cent finance and accounting and 14 per cent sales and marketing. Most

(60 per cent) of the firms were headquartered in North America, 13 per cent in Europe, 11 per cent in Asia/Pacific, 8 per cent in the Middle East and 7 per cent in Latin America.

Measure development and assessment

Although most scale items were adapted from those in the existing literature, with slight modifications to reflect our focus, a new scale was developed to measure a firm's pricing capabilities. The scale was refined through pretests and pilot testing using established item development procedures and guidelines (Churchill 1979).

Content and face validity were determined through a comprehensive review of the literature, pre- and pilot tests, and assessment by a panel of practitioners and academics to ensure that measurement items covered the domain of the constructs (Churchill 1979; Nunnally 1978). To assess the quality of the survey items, in-depth, face-to-face interviews with pricing practitioners were conducted using Bolton's 'talk aloud' methodology (Bolton 1993). We pretested all scale items with a small panel of academics and pricing and business practitioners. A pilot test involving 150 professionals representing pricing, business and general manager functions from companies in both manufacturing and service industries provided 70 complete responses. The survey was iteratively modified to incorporate all relevant test results. None of the pretest or pilot test participants was included in the final sample. The survey instrument is presented in the Appendix.

Behaviour of champion on pricing

A six-item scale adapted from Howell *et al.* (2005) was used to assess pricing champion behaviours (CBE). Each item was measured using a seven-point Likert scale anchored at the extremes by 'strongly disagree' to 'strongly agree'.

Pricing capabilities

Since there was little empirical precedent to measure pricing capabilities (PC), a multiple-item scale was developed by the academic team in accord with an operational definition (Kerlinger and Lee 1999), by relying on our fieldwork, and on extant literature. We used 12 items ranging from 1 – 'much worse than competitors' to 7 – 'much better than competitors' to operationalize this scale.

Pricing orientation

We adapted the scales developed by Ingenbleek *et al.* (2001) to measure value based pricing (VBP) (5 items), competition based pricing (COB) (6 items), and cost-based pricing (CB) (5 items). Items were measured using a seven-point Likert scale anchored at the extremes by 1 – 'not at all taken into account in price setting' to 7 – 'very much taken into account in price setting.'

Collective mindfulness

The 12-item scale used to measure collective mindfulness (CM) was based on adapting existing measures (Knight 2004) and conceptual definitions in the literature (Weick and Sutcliffe 2007). Reluctance to simplify (4 items), sensitivity to operations (4 items) and commitment to resilience (4 items) were assessed using seven-point, Likert-type scales anchored with 'strongly agree' at the extreme positive end and 'strongly disagree' at the opposite end of the scale.

Decision making rationality

Four items measured the level of analysis involved in decision making. The four-item scale was developed and validated by Miller (1987). The seven-point scale was anchored with 'does frequently' at the extreme positive end and 'does rarely' at the opposite end of the scale.

Firm performance

Similar to Morgan et al. (2009), firm performance was operationalized as a second-order construct consisting of three first-order reflective constructs – sales, pricing and profit performance. The measures for sales and profit were adapted from Morgan et al. (2009) and include six items, while the other two measures were from the work of Ingenbleek (2007).

The use of subjective performance measures was required for a number of reasons. First, because our sample contained many privately owned firms for which objective accounting data on their performance would not be accessible, we followed the convention (Simsek et al. 2005; Simsek 2007) of asking CEOs to compare their *firm's relative performance* to that of their competitors on eight different dimensions for the past year (e.g. growth in sales, return on investment, return on sales and so forth) using a scale ranging from 1 ('much worse') to 7 ('much better') than competitors. Second, since firms in our sample were of various types and from various geographical zones, a multidimensional measure based on perceptual firm performance facilitates comparisons across firms and contexts, such as across industries, time horizons and economic conditions (Song et al. 2005). Finally, earlier studies have shown that perceptual performance measures tend to be highly correlated with objective indicators (Dess and Robinson Jr 1984) and are used in strategy research (Anderson and Paine 1975). Taken in the aggregate, subjective or perceptual measures of firm performance can provide a broad indication of a company's health (Quinn and Baily 1994).

Firm-level control variables

We controlled for a number of likely determinants of performance by including demographic characteristics of the firm, such as firm type, age and firm size (Amburgey and Rao 1996).

Non-response bias

A commonly used method for estimating the bias in strategy research (for examples see Armstrong and Overton 1977; Simsek et al. 2010) is to compare early – those who responded within the first week (74 per cent) – and late (26 per cent) responses among the study variables; a late respondent is considered a proxy for a non-respondent. First, chi-square tests comparing demographic characteristics across the two groups revealed no significant biases when number of employees ($\chi^2_{(4)} = 1.45$; $p = 0.835$), type of firm ($\chi^2_{(2)} = 2.39$; $p = 0.303$) and age ($\chi^2_{(4)} = 4.72$; $p = 0.317$) were examined. Next, one-way ANOVA tests, performed at the item level, indicated no significant differences in data derived from early vs. late responders, except on 1 of the 58 (1.73 per cent) study variables. Consequently, it appears that bias present from the time of response is due to chance.

Common method bias

Surveys from a single set of respondents can introduce common method bias (CMB) in the data. Consequently, we took several steps to mitigate, detect and control for a common method bias. We carefully constructed all survey items, and wherever possible, used pretested, valid, multidimensional constructs (Huber and Power 1985). We varied the scale anchors and format in the questionnaire, performed a series of scale-validation processes before distributions, and randomized questions.

Several *post hoc* tests determined the extent to which common method bias was present in our data. First, using Harman's single-factor test, all 58 items were entered into an unrotated principal components factor analysis to determine the number of factors necessary to account for the variance in the variables. Accordingly, if a single factor emerged or a single general factor explained most of the variance between the independent and dependent variables, common method variance may be present (Podsakoff *et al.* 2003). Our results indicated the presence of ten potential factors (all with eigenvalues greater than one); each factor explained roughly equal variance, and explained over 65 per cent of the total variance. These results provide initial evidence that response bias does not appear to be a problem in the data (Podsakoff and Organ 1986).

Second, we used the confirmatory factor analysis (CFA)-based Harman's single-factor test in which we hypothesized a single CMB factor as causing all the indicators. The CMB factor extracted 17 per cent of the variance. A χ^2 difference ($\chi^2 = 17.021$, $p = .000$) test between the baseline with all the CMB paths free floating, and the CMB with all paths equal to zero, indicated items loaded significantly on the single factor, suggesting that CMV might be a source of variance in the observed items.

Third, an unrelated construct, a *marker* variable, determined *ex post* to have no signification correlation with other items in the constructs was added to the measurement model (Lindell and Whitney 2001). Since we did not measure an unrelated construct *a priori*, we used a modified test in which a weakly related construct – CEO perceptions of pricing – a four-item scale was used (Pavlou and Gefen 2005). High correlations among any of the items of the study's constructs and pricing perception would indicate common method bias. Since the highest correlation of pricing perceptions and the constructs was $r = 0.15$, there appeared to be minimal evidence of common method bias.

Fourth, we examined multicollinearity and CMB with linear regression analysis on the study constructs and found low variance inflation factors. Further, multicollinearity can be ruled out because no two predictor variables correlated more strongly than

0.70 (Hair et al. 2010). Finally, we examined the correlation matrix, as shown in Table 4.1, and found no highly correlated factors (highest correlation is $r = 0.61$), whereas evidence of common method bias should have resulted in extremely high correlations ($r > 0.90$). Based on these tests, multicollinearity is not present and common method bias does not appear to pose a problem with our analysis.

Confirmatory factor analysis
First-order factors

Four of the six constructs (champion of pricing, pricing capabilities, collective mindfulness and decision making rationality) were measured as first-order constructs, while the other two (pricing orientation and performance) were operationalized as second-order factors in our CFA models. The measurement models were estimated using AMOS (Analysis of Moment Structures) software, a covariance-based structural equation modelling technique. In this model, no unidirectional path was specified between any latent variables.

The psychometric properties of the four latent constructs involving 25 items were evaluated simultaneously in one CFA.[1] The sample size of 557 was deemed sufficient, given acceptable values on the Hoelter's Critical N test,[2] and the model was expected to converge using maximum likelihood estimation.

As seen in Table 4.1, almost all correlations were significant. Discriminant validity was assessed by comparing the square root of the AVE associated with each construct to the correlations among constructs (Fornell and Larcker 1981). To provide evidence of discriminant validity, the square root of the AVE associated with a particular construct must be greater than its correlations with other constructs (Fornell and Larcker 1981). Accordingly, this is confirmed by the estimates provided in Table 4.1. Internal consistency reliability was assessed in two ways – using Cronbach's alpha (CA) coefficient and composite reliability (CR). Table 4.1 indicates each type of reliability exceeded the recommended 0.70 threshold (Fornell and Larcker 1981; Nunnally 1978), with one exception on the margin (CA = 0.69 price performance).

Convergent validity can be assessed by examining individual item loadings on their theorized latent variables (Hair et al. 2010). All individual items loaded on their intended constructs and no undesirable cross-loadings emerged. An item is significant if its factor loading is greater than 0.50 (Hair et al. 2010). As shown in Table 4.2, the standardized factor loadings of all the items were significant ($p < 0.01$) and ranged from 0.53 to 0.86, meeting the threshold and demonstrating convergent validity at the item level.

It is recommended that multiple indices be considered simultaneously when overall model fit is evaluated.[3] We paid less attention to the sample size sensitive model chi-square ($\chi^2_{(256)} = 466.77$; $p = 0.000$). As an alternative to chi-square, we examined the Browne-Cudeck test of close fit (BCC) and compared the BCC value across the hypothesized, saturated and independence model (Browne and Cudeck 1993). The BCC was lower than the saturated model, suggesting a good

TABLE 4.1 Descriptive statistics, reliability, correlations and discriminant validity

Construct	No. of items	M	SD	CA	CR	1.	2.	3.	4.	5.	6.	7.	8.	9.	10.
1. **Champion on pricing**	6	5.54	.99	.846	.84	**0.71**	0.170	0.153	0.131	0.086	0.022	0.075	0.035	0.069	0.061
2. **Pricing capabilities**	8	3.35	1.53	.855	.92	0.412	**0.67**	0.091	0.173	0.081	0.029	0.108	0.125	0.182	0.178
3. **Collective mindfulness**	7	5.96	.72	.863	.92	0.391	0.302	**0.69**	0.036	0.100	0.034	0.058	0.059	0.033	0.061
4. **Decision making rationality**	4	4.58	.97	.768	.88	0.362	0.416	0.190	**0.70**	0.053	0.023	0.136	0.010	0.024	0.028
5. **Value based**	4	5.52	1.12	.852	.85	0.293	0.285	0.316	0.231	**0.77**	0.066	0.071	0.036	0.051	0.052
6. **Competition based**	4	5.48	1.19	.870	.85	0.149	0.171	0.184	0.150	0.257	**0.77**	0.091	0.013	0.001	0.003
7. **Cost based**	3	5.16	1.24	.700	.76	0.273	0.328	0.240	0.369	0.267	0.301	**0.71**	0.037	0.016	0.032
8. **Sales performance**	3	5.38	1.05	.830	.84	0.187	0.354	0.243	0.098**	0.190	0.112**	0.192	**0.80**	0.185	0.235
9. **Price performance**	2	4.80	1.08	.690	.70	0.262	0.427	0.181	0.156	0.225	0.016$_{n.s.}$	0.125**	0.430	**0.73**	0.370
10. **Profit performance**	3	5.21	1.21	.930	.93	0.246	0.422	0.246	0.166	0.228	0.059$_{n.s.}$	0.178	0.485	0.608	**0.89**

Notes: All coefficients significant at $p < 0.001$ (one-sided test) except where noted.
M = mean; SD = standard deviation; CA = Cronbach's alpha; CR = composite reliability.
Square root of Average Variance Extracted (AVE) are bolded values along diagonal; values above diagonal are squared correlations.
* $p < 0.05$; ** $p < 0.01$; *** $p < 0.001$.

TABLE 4.2 Measurement model results for first-order constructs

Constructs & items	Regression weight	Standardized regression	Critical ratio
Champion of pricing (CBE)			
CBE1	1.208	0.858	23.400
CBE2	1.000	0.806	21.991
CBE3	0.878	0.763	19.402
CBE4	0.782	0.559	13.732
CBE5	0.600	0.533	12.978
CBE6	1.003	0.650	16.504
Pricing capabilities (PC)			
PC1	0.918	0.691	16.993
PC2	0.860	0.660	15.816
PC3	0.912	0.770	19.889
PC6	0.894	0.590	14.122
PC7	0.833	0.617	14.708
PC8	0.775	0.575	13.483
PC9	0.814	0.556	12.875
PC12	0.851	0.585	14.039
Collective mindfulness (CM)			
CM5	0.797	0.763	18.864
CM6	0.708	0.645	15.649
CM7	0.569	0.617	14.721
CM8	0.600	0.642	15.345
CM9	0.610	0.680	14.978
CM10	0.602	0.659	15.837
CM11	0.660	0.713	16.473
Decision making rationality (DMR)			
DMR1	1.069	0.595	12.582
DMR2	1.430	0.713	13.596
DMR3	1.666	0.809	15.735
DMR4	1.296	0.616	13.020

fit (Floyd and Widaman 1995). Steiger and Lind's (1980) root-mean-square error of approximation (RMSEA), with 90 per cent confidence interval, was used to reflect both the fit and parsimony of the model at hand. The RMSEA, known as the most sensitive index to models with misspecified factor loadings (Hu and Bentler 1998) was 0.038 and the 90 per cent confidence interval was small (0.033 to 0.044) suggesting a close fit (Browne and Cudeck 1993). The Normed χ^2 (1.823) at a ratio of less than 2:1 indicated a good 'rule of thumb' model fit (Tabachnick and Fidell 2007). We also used the Non-Normed Fit Index, NNFI (Tucker and Lewis 1973), the Comparative Fit Index (CFI) (Bentler 1990), and Incremental Fit Index (IFI) as other goodness-of-fit measures that are independent of sample size and reflect the proportionate improvement in fit of the measurement model over a more restricted baseline model. Hu and Bentler (1999) suggested values 'close to .95' (p. 27) as indicating satisfactory fit. The NNFI, CFI and IFI all exceeded 0.95. Consequently, the measurement model was deemed acceptable to proceed to structural modelling.

Second-order factors

We conducted a second-order CFA of pricing orientation and relative performance to provide empirical support for their measurement at the second-order level. We modelled the items for the first-order factors as reflective items because they are moderately correlated among themselves (Bassellier and Benbasat 2004). For pricing orientation and relative performance, all first-order factors had a significant ($p < 0.001$) relationship with their respective second-order constructs. The path coefficients indicate the factors' relative importance in reflecting the second-order constructs. Further, we assessed convergent and discriminant validity of the items and the contributions of the factors to the second-order constructs.

Figure 4.2a shows pricing orientation is operationalized as a second-order factor with the facets as its indicators (Gerbing et al. 1994). The facets define specific domains related to a firm's pricing orientation – value based, competition based, cost based. Each facet is defined by a unidimensional set of items adapted from the literature (Ingenbleek et al. 2003). The items load 0.66 and higher on their respective factors and the first-order factors are strongly related (0.50 to 0.59) to the pricing orientation dimension. Composite reliability ranged from 0.76 to 0.85, all AVEs exceeded the 0.50 threshold, and squared multiple correlations ranged from 0.25 to 0.35, thus supporting H_{1a}. Validation of this model and support for H_{1b} is demonstrated by several fit statistics (Normed $\chi^2 = 1.735$, CFI $= 0.99$, IFI $= 0.99$; NNFI $= 0.98$ and RMSEA $= 0.036$; CI$_{RMSEA} = 0.02$–0.05).

As seen in Figure 4.2b, first-order factors for firm performance had high loadings (0.64 for sales, 0.88 for pricing and 0.84 for profit dimensions; $p < 0.001$). Items loaded at 0.70 or higher on their respective factors and all were significant ($p < 0.001$). Composite reliability ranged from 0.70 to 0.93 and all AVEs exceeded 0.50, thereby providing support for H_{2a} squared multiple correlations ranged from 0.40 to 0.78 suggesting the correlations are below the 0.90 threshold considered acceptable (Bagozzi et al. 1991). Further, support for H_{2b} was found by acceptable goodness-of-fit statistics ($\chi^2/df = 1.806$, CFI $= 0.983$, IFI $= 0.98$; NNFI $= 0.98$ and RMSEA $= 0.05$). These results suggest that it is appropriate to model pricing orientation and relative performance as multidimensional second-order factors (Anderson and Gerbing 1988).

Power analysis

We relied on the MacCallum et al. (1996) framework to estimate the power of RMSEA fit measure. Consequently, since our objective was to test relationships between the constructs of interest, we used a 'test of not close fit' for RMSEA in order to assess the adequacy of the sample size. Using a desired alpha of 0.05 with 256 degrees of freedom, a hypothesized population RMSEA of 0.05, and a sample size of 557, we calculated the statistical power to be .99 (Preacher and Coffman

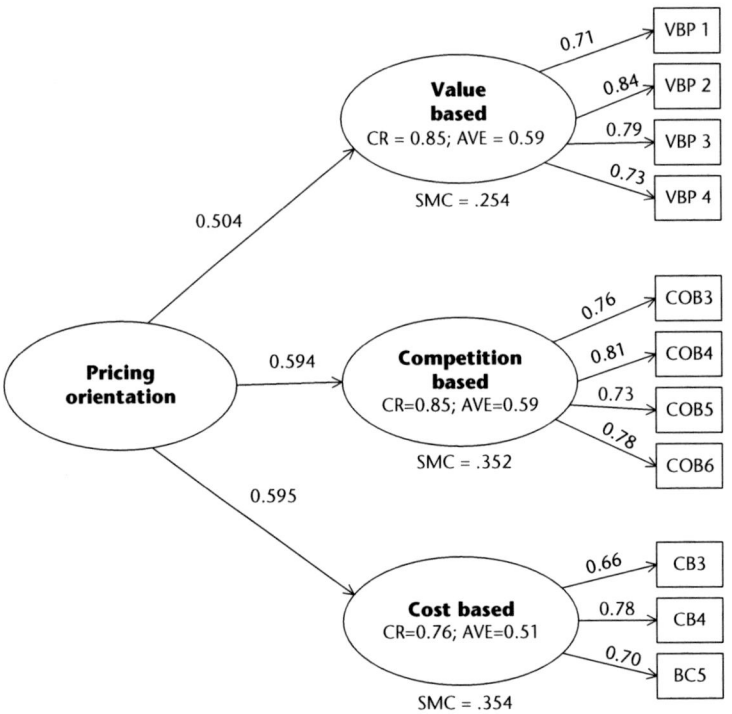

FIGURE 4.2a Second-order measurement model results for pricing orientation

Notes: Standardized estimates shown; Significant at $p < 0.001$.
Composite Reliability (CR); Average Variance Extracted (AVE); Squared Multiple Correlation (SMC).

2006) which exceeds the commonly accepted criterion of 0.80.[4] Accordingly, we can be relatively confident that the sample is large enough to support the statistical inferences made regarding the relationships between the constructs.

Results

We tested our hypotheses using structural equation modelling (SEM). SEM was particularly appropriate because it allows estimation of multiple associations, simultaneously incorporates observed and latent constructs in these associations, and accounts for the biasing effects of random measurement error in the latent constructs (Medsker et al. 1994).

The results are presented in Table 4.3. All hypothesized relationships are significant, except for two of the six ($H3_b$ and $H7_c$), explaining 26 per cent of the variance for relative performance, 28 per cent for capabilities, 20 per cent for pricing orientation, 15 per cent for collective mindfulness and 13 per cent for decision making rationality. The fit indices for the model indicated this model reached an

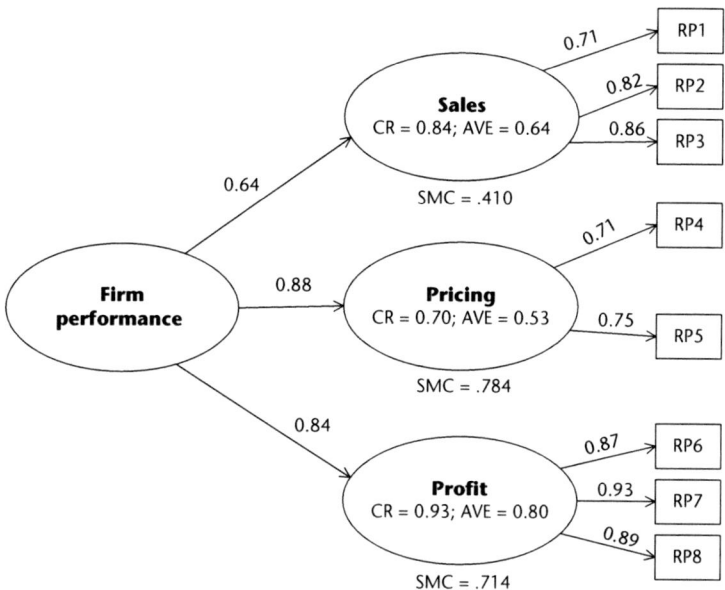

FIGURE 4.2b Second-order measurement model results for relative performance

Notes: Standardized estimates shown; All loadings significant at $p < 0.001$.
Composite Reliability (CR); Average Variance Extracted (AVE); Squared Multiple Correlation (SMC).

acceptable level for goodness of fit ($\chi^2_{(17)} = 27.79$; $p = 0.047$, $\chi^2/\text{df} = 1.635$, CFI = 0.984, IFI = 0.985; NNFI = 0.96 and RMSEA = 0.034; CI$_{\text{RMSEA}}$ = 0.01–0.05).

First, the hypothesized impact of pricing orientation on pricing capabilities (0.175, $p < .001$), H3$_a$, was supported. However, pricing orientation (0.064) was not significantly related to performance (H3$_b$ not supported). Second, the champion of pricing had a positive and significant impact on pricing orientation (0.13, $p < 0.001$), pricing capabilities (0.22, $p < 0.001$), collective mindfulness (0.28, $p < 0.01$), and a strong impact on decision making rationality (0.56, $p < 0.001$). These findings support H4$_{abcd}$. Third, pricing capabilities (0.166, $p < 0.001$) impact on firm performance provided support for H5. Fourth, collective mindfulness is both positive and significantly related to the firm's pricing orientation (0.287, $p < 0.001$) and firm performance (0.173, $p < 0.001$), thereby validating H6$_a$ and H6$_b$. Also, collective mindfulness had a significant impact on pricing capabilities (0.152, $p < 0.01$) providing support for H6$_c$. Finally, decision making rationality (0.132, $p < 0.001$) relationship to orientation and pricing capabilities (0.166, $p < 0.001$) provided support for H7$_a$ and H7$_b$. Decision making rationality (0.042) had no effect on firm performance, thus H7$_c$ was not supported.

We controlled for type of company, age and size. Since the firms participating in this study came from a variety of industries, it was necessary to control for the different industries under which the firms operated (manufacturing, service and retail/distribution). We controlled for firm size, which has frequently been used in

TABLE 4.3 Structural model results

Hypothesized paths	Regression estimate	Standardized estimate	Critical ratio	Hypothesis supported
$H3_a$: pricing orientation → pricing capabilities	0.175	0.156***	3.882	Yes
$H3_b$: pricing orientation → firm performance	0.064	0.060	1.453	No
$H4_a$: champion behaviour → pricing orientation	0.127	0.147***	3.355	Yes
$H4_b$: champion behaviour → pricing capabilities	0.217	0.223***	5.336	Yes
$H4_c$: champion behaviour → collective mindfulness	0.282	0.391***	10.026	Yes
$H4_d$: champion behaviour → rationality	0.560	0.362***	9.164	Yes
H5: pricing capabilities → firm performance	0.432	0.452***	10.750	Yes
$H6_a$: collective mindfulness → pricing orientation	0.287	0.239***	5.802	Yes
$H6_b$: collective mindfulness → performance	0.173	0.134***	3.396	Yes
$H6_c$: collective mindfulness → pricing capabilities	0.152	0.112**	2.797	Yes
$H7_a$: rationality → pricing orientation	0.132	0.235***	5.781	Yes
$H7_b$: rationality → pricing capabilities	0.166	0.263***	6.637	Yes
$H7_c$: rationality → firm performance	−0.042	−0.070	−1.724	No
Controls:				
Age → firm performance	−0.035	−0.044	−1.044	
Type of firm → firm performance	−0.057	−0.046	−1.125	
Number of employees → firm performance	0.044	0.056	1.344	

Goodness-of-fit statistics:
$\chi^2 = 27.795$; df = 17; $p = 0.047$
Normed $\chi^2 (\chi^2/df = 1.635)$
CFI = 0.984; IFI = 0.985; TLI = 0.958
RMSEA = 0.034

R^2 rationality = 0.131
R^2 collective mindfulness = 0.153
R^2 pricing orientation = 0.202
R^2 pricing capabilities = 0.286
R^2 firm performance = 0.264

*$p < 0.05$; **$p < 0.01$; ***$p < 0.001$.

previous studies involving firm performance (Morgan *et al*. 2009) and firm age. All three variables had no significant effect on performance.

Implications for the pricing field

Our objective was to improve our understanding of how CEO and top executive championing of the pricing within their firms might influence relative firm performance. Our intention was to construct a strong bridge between the fields of pricing and organizational behaviour to contribute to the development of the pricing literature from an organizational perspective. Our findings shine a new light on the findings of previous studies and offer four substantive contributions.

First, our results support the proposition that a purposeful championing of pricing activities by top executives strongly influences the firm's organizational design to support the pricing process in critical areas (decision making rationality, collective mindfulness, capabilities and pricing orientation). All relationships between championing behaviours and other organizational characteristics were positive and significant. Our study found strong links between championing in pricing, organizational design and relative firm performance. By providing evidence of these relationships, we uniquely begin the exploration of organizational drivers of the pricing function. Most scholars and practitioners agree that pricing receives scant attention from the C-suite (Cressman Jr 2009; Hinterhuber 2008a). Our conclusions suggest that once top executives realize the importance of pricing and purposefully decide to champion it, the impact on the organization and its performance is significant.

Second, our results support resource-based theory that pricing capabilities positively and significantly influence firm performance vis-à-vis competition. Previous studies on marketing capabilities suggest a positive link between pricing capabilities – a subset of marketing capabilities – and firm performance (Morgan *et al*. 2009; Vorhies and Morgan 2005). However, these studies measured pricing capabilities as part of a much wider subset of marketing capabilities. Our findings show that pricing capabilities are significantly influenced by championing behaviours, decision making rationality, mindfulness and overall pricing orientation. In turn, these capabilities in pricing positively influence firm performance vis-à-vis competition.

Third, our findings suggest that the role of executives in the corporate suite is essential for the design and sustainable implementation of pricing strategies in firms. A unique organizational architecture for pricing and the promotion of a culture of change and pricing knowledge diffusion should become a top priority for CEOs and other senior executives. By investing to build pricing capabilities that generate a sustainable and inimitable competitive advantage (Dierickx and Cool 1989; Dutta *et al*. 2003), champions of pricing forge shared vision, a collective 'can do' mentality and a sense of resilience in the firm that lead to superior levels of organizational efficacy (Bohn 2001) and superior outcome. Dutta *et al*. (2002: 66) posit that 'most CEOs will never set a single price. They can, however, give their managers the ability to win price wars, maintain price leadership and hold a competitive edge in pricing.'

Finally, although we did not establish a significant relationship between decision making rationality and relative firm performance, our results highlight the criticality of creating an environment where pricing decisions are made on a more scientific and rational basis and not solely on intuition or gut feeling. Our findings indicate that greater levels of decision making rationality influence the pricing orientation that firms adopt as well as their levels of capabilities in pricing. In recent years, there has been a resurgence of interest in intuition and gut feeling in decision making theory in part due to the general dissatisfaction with the concepts of rationality and its limitations (Sadler-Smith and Shefy 2004). Making decisions by intuition is increasingly viewed as a viable and acceptable approach in today's business context (Burke and Miller 1999). Intuition may be an appropriate decision making process in certain situations and business scenarios, especially in situations of uncertainty or turbulence (Khatri and Ng 2000), novelty or in situations related to human resources. Scholars relate the intuitive skills of managers to the intuitive skills of chess masters or physicians (Simon 1987). Experienced managers have in memory a large amount of experience, schemas and patterns gained through experience and organized 'in terms of recognizable chunks and associated information' (Simon 1987). Managers need to be able to combine both approaches to reach a greater level of decision effectiveness (Dane and Pratt 2007; Simon 1987). Intuition can then become a complement to an appropriate pricing decision after a thorough analytical and scientific process. This process conducted by pricing experts can help decision makers narrow the decision range and remove as much uncertainty and ambiguity out of the price setting process as possible.

Limitations

Despite its significant contributions, the present study is not without limitations. First, the sample was derived from the entire worldwide listing of CEO and business owners belonging to a professional society. Consequently, the relatively small sample size is a limitation in this study. Second, the performance measures utilized in this research are perceptual, although using perceptual or subjective data has been advocated in the strategic management literature (Dess and Robinson Jr 1984). We cannot rule out that the observed performance differences could be a function of different firm goals rather than of differences in objective firm performance. As a consequence, caution should be taken when interpreting the performance results. Third, we used the key respondent approach to our survey study and directed our questionnaire to the CEO or business owner because they were best positioned to answer the questions; however, their responses may not be without some bias. Fourth, our research model is tested using cross-sectional data; we can report associations but are not able to determine causality, because we implemented a passive observation design (i.e. survey). Fifth, even though the relationships between the constructs in our research model are argued based on theory, longitudinal studies should be done to offer stronger empirical evidence for the observed relationships. Finally, multiple measurement methods and data sources should be used to control potential common method bias in future studies (Burton-Jones 2009).

Appendix: constructs, definitions, coded items and source

Construct/Dimensions	Definition	Items	Source
PRIMARY PRICING ORIENTATION	The primary orientation used by firm respondents based on customer value, cost and competition information. Because the use of customer value, competition and cost information are a matter of degree rather than mutually exclusive categories, the result of the measure will report a primary firm orientation.	**To what extent does your organization take into account the following factors when setting prices for its products and services?** (1 = *Not at all taken into account in price setting* to 7 = *Very much taken into account in price setting*) *Value-based pricing* VBP1: Advantages of the product compared to competitors' products/services VBP2: Customer perceived value of the products/services VBP3: Customer willingness to pay for the unique benefits of the product/services VBP4: Balance between advantages of products/services and price *VBP5: Differentiated value drivers of our products/services compared to substitutes *Competition-based pricing* *COB1: Price of competitors' products/services *COB2: Competitors' current price strategy COB3: Likelihood of competitors' strength to react COB4: Market structure (number and strength of competitors) COB5: Degree of competition on the market COB6: Competitive advantage of competitors in the market	Adapted from Ingenbleek *et al.* (2003) Value-based pricing; 5 items (AC: 0.81) Competition-based pricing; 6 items (AC: 0.91) Cost-based pricing; 5 items (AC: 0.75)

Continued

Construct/Dimensions	Definition	Items	Source
	Cost-based pricing *CB1: Variable costs of products/services *CB2: Price necessary to break-even CB3: Investments in products/services CB4: Target margin guidelines CB5: Target return on sales levels		
DECISION MAKING RATIONALITY	Rationality relates to the concepts of analysis, future orientation and planning, explicitness of the strategy, and systematic scanning of the environment. These concepts all relate to the 'synoptic and planning modes' and represent systematic, analytical decision making. This contrasts with the purely spontaneous, intuitive modes found with severely bounded rationality.	**Indicate the extent to which your organization does the following activities to support pricing decisions.** *(1 = Does rarely to 7 = Does frequently)* **DMR1:** Applies pricing research techniques such as conjoint analysis and pricing/value simulations to make major product/service pricing decisions **DMR2:** Conducts brainstorming with senior management groups for novel solutions to pricing problems **DMR3:** Conducts formalized, systematic pricing review process as part of the product/service development process (like Stage Gate) **DMR4:** Uses staff specialists to investigate and provide recommendation on major pricing decisions	Adapted from Miller (1987). Level of analysis: 4 items (AC: 0.74)

Construct/Dimensions	Definition	Items	Source
PRICING CAPABILITIES	Pricing capabilities are part of marketing capabilities which concern the firm's adequate management of individual 'marketing mix' processes such as product development and management, pricing, selling, etc. as well as marketing strategy development and execution. These capabilities may be rare, valuable, non-substitutable and inimitable source of advantage that can lead to superior firm performance.	**Rate your organization relative to your major competitors in terms of its capabilities in the following areas:** *(1 = Much worse than competitors to 7 = Much better than competitors)* **PC1:** Using pricing skills and systems to respond quickly to market changes **PC2:** Knowledge of competitors' pricing tactics **PC3:** Doing an effective job of pricing products/services ***PC4:** Monitoring competitors' prices and price changes ***PC5:** Sticking to price list and minimizing discounts **PC6:** Quantifying customers' willingness to pay **PC7:** Measuring and quantifying differential economic value versus competition **PC8:** Measuring and estimating price elasticity for products/services **PC9:** Designing proprietary tools to support pricing decisions ***PC10:** Conducting value-in-use analysis or total cost of ownership ***PC11:** Designing and conducting specific pricing training programmes **PC12:** Developing proprietary internal price management process	Construct definition included Morgan et al. (2009) and the researcher qualitative research (Liozu et al. 2011). Result of the pilot survey with 70 responses yielded an AC of 0.885 with these 12 items.

Continued

Construct/Dimensions	Definition	Items	Source
CHAMPIONING BEHAVIOURS	Transformational leaders motivate followers to achieve performance beyond expectations by transforming followers' attitudes, beliefs and values. They take on the role of organizational champions by demonstrating specific behaviours to lead and support organizational implementations.	**To what extent do you agree or disagree with the following statements about your involvement with pricing** *(1 = Strongly disagree to 7 = Strongly agree)*. **CBE1:** I enthusiastically promote the pricing function **CBE2:** I express confidence in what pricing can do **CBE3:** I show tenacity in overcoming obstacles when changes in pricing are needed **CBE4:** I get pricing problems into the hands of those who can solve them **CBE5:** I get key decision makers involved in the pricing process **CBE6:** I act as a champion of pricing	Adapted from Howell *et al.* (2005):

Construct/Dimensions	Definition	Items	Source
COLLECTIVE MINDFULNESS	Weick et al. (1999) extended the concept of individual mindfulness (Langer 1989) to the collective entities, describing it as the widespread adoption and diffusion of mindfulness by the organization's members. Mindfulness helps organizations to notice more issues, process them with care, and detect and respond to early signs of trouble (Weick and Sutcliffe 2007). They describe five cognitive processes that constitute organizational mindfulness: (1) preoccupation with failure; (2) reluctance to simplify interpretations; (3) sensitivity to operations; (4) commitment to resilience; and (5) deference to expertise.	**To what extent do you agree or disagree with the following statements about your organization.** *(1 = Strongly disagree to 7 = Strongly agree)* *CM1: Seeks input from diverse sources to solve problems *CM2: Approaches unexpected events with novel solutions *CM3: Expects employees are familiar with tasks beyond their immediate jobs *CM4: Supports divergent viewpoints CM5: Fosters a climate that encourages open, ongoing communication CM6: Pays attention to real-time information CM7: Believes that regular updating, and refreshing of our employees' skills are essential CM8: Strives to make ongoing assessments and continual updates in our operations CM9: Does not give up on solving problems CM10: Encourages employees to 'bounce back' from mistakes CM11: Takes steps to correct errors before they worsen *CM12: Treats failures as indicators of reliability of operations	Adapted from Knight (2004) based on the work of Weick and Sutcliffe (2007) Reluctance to simplify interpretations: 4 items (AC: 0.80) Sensitivity to operations: 4 items (AC: 0.84) Commitment to resilience: 4 items (0.87)

Continued

Construct/Dimensions	Definition	Items	Source
PERCEIVED RELATIVE PERFORMANCE	Respondents' perceived evaluation of their organization's performance relative to their competition.	**Please evaluate the performance of your major line of business over the past year relative to your major competitors.** *(1 = Much worse/lower than competitors to 7 = Much better/higher than competitors)* **RP1:** Acquisition of new customers **RP2:** Increase of sales to current customers **RP3:** Growth in total sales revenues **RP4:** Absolute price levels **RP5:** Pricing power in the market **RP6:** Business unit profitability **RP7:** Return on sales (ROS) **RP8:** Return on investment (ROI)	Two items adapted from Ingenbleek (2007). Six items adapted from Morgan *et al.* (2009). Market effectiveness: 3 items (AC: 0.90) and profitability: 3 items (AC: 0.95) Our pilot survey with 70 respondents yielded an AC of 0.929.

Notes: *Item eliminated due to insufficient reliability and validity; AC = Alpha Coefficient.

Notes

1 Nine items were trimmed from the model because of insufficient reliability and/or validity.
2 This is the largest sample size at which we would accept the model at the .05 (sample size = 276) or .01 (sample size = 286) levels. Since our sample is 557 we can expect decreasing significance of the χ^2 statistic leading to possible rejection of the model based only on that statistic.
3 We selected normed chi-square (χ^2/df), the comparative-fit index (CFI), the incremental fit index (IFI), and the root mean squared error of approximation (RMSEA) based on their relative stability, robustness, uniqueness of information provided, and independence of sample size. Recommended thresholds indicating good fit are $\chi^2/\mathrm{df} < 3$; IFI, CFI and NNFI > 0.90, and RMSEA < 0.05.
4 This is the power level at which an RMSEA of 0.08 is excluded from the RMSEA confidence interval. If the hypothesized RMSEA were the same as observed (0.038), then statistical power would still be .99.

References

Amburgey, T. L. and Rao, H. (1996) Organizational ecology: Past, present, and future directions. *The Academy of Management Journal*, 39 (5), pp. 1265–86.
Anderson, C. R. and Paine, F. T. (1975) Managerial perceptions and strategic behavior. *The Academy of Management Journal*, 18 (4), pp. 811–23.
Anderson, J., Kumar, N. and Narus, J. A. (2007). *Value merchants: demonstrating and documenting superior value in business markets*. Boston, MA: Harvard Business School Press.
Anderson, J. C. and Gerbing, D. W. (1988) Structural equation modeling in practice: A review and recommended two-step approach. *Psychological Bulletin*, 103 (3), pp. 411–23.
Andrews, K. R. (1971) *The concept of corporate strategy*. Homewood, IL: Richard D. Irwin.
Armstrong, J. S. and Overton, T. S. (1977) Estimating nonresponse bias in mail surveys. *Journal of Marketing Research*, 14 (3), pp. 396–402.
Bagozzi, R. P., Yi, Y. and Phillips, L. W. (1991) Assessing construct validity in organizational research. *Administrative Science Quarterly*, 36 (3), pp. 421–58.
Barney, J. (1991) Firm resources and sustained competitive advantage. *Journal of Management*, 17 (1), pp. 99–120.
Barnard, C. and Andrews, K. (1968). *The functions of the executive*. Cambridge, MA: Harvard University Press.
Barney, J. and Clark, D. (2007) *Resource-based theory: creating and sustaining competitive advantage*. New York: Oxford University Press, USA.
Bass, B. (1985) *Leadership and performance beyond expectations*. New York: Free Press.
Bassellier, G. and Benbasat, I. (2004) Business competence of information technology professionals: conceptual development and influence on IT-business partnerships. *MIS Quarterly*, 28 (4): pp. 673–94.
Bentler, P. M. (1990) Comparative fit indexes in structural models. *Psychological Bulletin*, 107 (2), pp. 238–46.
Berggren, K. and Eek, M. (2007) *The emerging pricing capability*. Master thesis, School of Economics and Management, Lund University.
Bohn, J. (2001) *The design and validation of an instrument to assess organizational efficacy*. Unpublished Dissertation, University of Wisconsin, Milwaukee.
Bolton, R. N. (1993) Pretesting questionnaires: content analyses of respondents' concurrent verbal protocols. *Marketing Science*, 12 (3), pp. 280–303.

Browne, M. W. and Cudeck, R. (1993) Alternative ways of assessing model fit. In: Bollen, K. A. and Long, J. S. (eds) *Testing structural equation models*. Thousand Oaks, CA: Sage Publications, pp. 136–62.

Brownlie, D. and Spender, J. (1995) Managerial judgement in strategic marketing. *Management Decision*, 33 (6), pp. 39–50.

Burke, L. A. and Miller, M. K. (1999) Taking the mystery out of intuitive decision making. *The Academy of Management Executive (1993–2005)*, 13 (4), pp. 91–9.

Burton-Jones, A. (2009) Minimizing method bias through programmatic research. *MIS Quarterly*, 33 (3), pp. 445–71.

Carricano, M., Trinquecoste, J. F. and Mondejar, J.-A. (2010) The rise of the pricing function: origins and perspectives. *Journal of Product & Brand Management*, 19 (7), pp. 468–76.

Chandler, A. (1973) *Strategy and structure*. Cambridge, MA: MIT Press.

Churchill, G. A., Jr. (1979) A paradigm for developing better measures of marketing constructs. *Journal of Marketing Research*, 16 (1), pp. 64–73.

Cressman Jr, G. (1999) Commentary on industrial pricing: Theory and managerial practice. *Marketing Science*, 18 (3), pp. 455–7.

Cressman Jr, G. (2009) Why pricing strategies fail. *The Journal of Professional Pricing*, (Second Quarter 2009).

Cyert, R. and March, J. (1992) *A behavioral theory of the firm*. Oxford: Wiley-Blackwell.

Dane, E. and Pratt, M. G. (2007) Exploring intuition and its role in managerial decision making. *Academy of Management Review*, 32 (1): pp. 33–54.

Dess, G. G. and Robinson Jr, R. B. (1984) Measuring organizational performance in the absence of objective measures: The case of the privately held firm and conglomerate business unit. *Strategic Management Journal*, 5 (3): pp. 265–73.

Dierickx, I. and Cool, K. (1989) Asset stock accumulation and sustainability of competitive advantage. *Management Science*, 35 (12), pp. 1504–11.

Dillman, D. A., Smyth, J. D. and Christian, L. M. (2009) *Internet, mail, and mixed-mode surveys: The tailored design method*, 3rd edition. Hoboken, NJ: John Wiley & Sons.

Dutta, S., Bergen, M., Levy, D., Ritson, M. and Zbaracki, M. (2002) Pricing as a strategic capability. *MIT Sloan Management Review*, 43 (3): pp. 61–6.

Dutta, S., Zbaracki, M. J. and Bergen, M. (2003) Pricing process as a capability: a resource based perspective. *Strategic Management Journal*, 24 (7): pp. 615–30.

Feldman, M. (2000) Organizational routines as a source of continuous change. *Organization Science*, 11 (6), pp. 611–29.

Fiol, C. and O'Connor, E. (2003) Waking up! Mindfulness in the face of bandwagons. *The Academy of Management Review*, 28 (1), pp. 54–70.

Floyd, F. J. and Widaman, K. F. (1995) Factor analysis in the development and refinement of clinical assessment instruments. *Psychological Assessment*, 7 (3), pp. 286–99.

Fornell, C. and Larcker, D. F. (1981) Evaluating structural equation models with unobservable variables and measurement error. *Journal of Marketing Research*, 18 (1), pp. 39–50.

Frye, A. and Campbell, D. (2011) Buffet says pricing power more important than good management. *Bloomberg*, 18 February 2011.

Gerbing, D. W., Hamilton, J. G. and Freeman, E. B. (1994) A large-scale second-order structural equation model of the influence of management participation on organizational planning benefits. *Journal of Management*, 20 (4), pp. 859–85.

Grant, R. (1996) Toward a knowledge-based theory of the firm. *Strategic Management Journal*, 17, pp. 109–22.

Hair, J. F., Jr., Black, W. C., Babin, B. J. and Anderson, R. E. (2010) *Multivariate data analysis*, 7th edition. Upper Saddle River, NJ: Prentice Hall.

Hall, R. (1993) A framework linking intangible resources and capabiliites to sustainable competitive advantage. *Strategic Management Journal*, 14 (8), pp. 607–18.

Hallberg, N. (2008) *Pricing capabilities and its strategic dimensions*. PhD thesis, School of Economics and Management, Lund University.

Hambrick, D. C., Geletkanycz, M. A. and Fredrickson, J. W. (1993) Top executive commitment to the status quo: Some tests of its determinants. *Strategic Management Journal*, 14 (6), pp. 401–18.

Harrison, E. F. and Pelletier, M. A. (1997) CEO perceptions of strategic leadership. *Journal of Managerial Issues*, 9 (3), pp. 299–317.

Hinterhuber, A. (2008a) Customer value-based pricing strategies: why companies resist. *Journal of Business Strategy*, 29 (4), pp. 41–50.

Hinterhuber, A. (2008b) Value delivery and value-based pricing in industrial markets. *Advances in Business Marketing and Purchasing*, 14, pp. 381–448.

Howell, J. and Higgins, C. (1990) Champions of technological innovation. *Administrative Science Quarterly*, 35 (2), pp. 317–41.

Howell, J., Shea, C. and Higgins, C. A. (2005) Champions of product innovations: Defining, developing, and validating a measure of champion behavior. *Journal of Business Venturing*, 20 (5), pp. 641–61.

Hu, L. and Bentler, P. M. (1998) Fit indices in covariance structure modeling: Sensitivity to underparameterized model misspecification. *Psychological Methods*, 3 (4), pp. 424–53.

Hu, L. and Bentler, P. (1999) Cutoff criteria for fit indexes in covariance structure analysis: Indexes in covariance structure analysis: Conventional criteria versus new alternatives. *Structural Equation Modeling*, 6, pp. 1–55.

Huber, G. P. and Power, D. J. (1985) Retrospective reports of strategic level managers: Guidelines for increasing their accuracy. *Strategic Management Journal*, 6 (2), pp. 171–80.

Ingenbleek, P. (2007) Value-informed pricing in its organizational context: literature review, conceptual framework, and directions for future research. *Journal of Product & Brand Management*, 16 (7), pp. 441–58.

Ingenbleek, P., Debruyne, M., Frambach, R. and Verhallen, T. (2001) *On cost-informed pricing and customer value: A resource-advantage perspective on industrial innovation pricing practices*. University Park, PA: The Pennsylvania State University, Institute for the Study of Business Markets, pp. 1–33.

Ingenbleek, P., Debruyne, M., Frambach, R. T. and Verhallen, T. M. (2003) Successful new product pricing practices: a contingency approach. *Marketing Letters*, 14 (4), pp. 289–305.

Ingenbleek, P., Frambach, R. T. and Verhallen, T. M. (2010) The role of value informed pricing in market oriented product innovation management. *Journal of Product Innovation Management*, 27 (7), pp. 1032–46.

Jaworski, B. and Kohli, A. (1993) Market orientation: antecedents and consequences. *The Journal of Marketing*, 57 (3), pp. 53–70.

Kerlinger, F. N. and Lee, H. B. (1999) *Foundations of behavioral research*. Belmont, CA: Wadsworth.

Khatri, N. and Ng, H. A. (2000) The role of intuition in strategic decision making. *Human Relations*, 53 (1), pp. 57–86.

Knight, A. (2004) *Measuring collective mindfulness and exploring its nomological network*. Thesis, Master of Arts, University of Maryland, College Park.

Lancioni, R., Schau, H. J. and Smith, M. F. (2005) Intraorganizational influences on business-to-business pricing strategies: A political economy perspective. *Industrial Marketing Management*, 34 (2), pp. 123–31.

Langer, E. (1989) *Mindfulness*. Reading, MA: Addison-Wesley.

Langer, E. (1997) *The power of mindful learning*. Reading, MA: Addison-Wesley.

Lindell, M. K. and Whitney, D. J. (2001) Accounting for common method variance in cross-sectional research designs. *Journal of Applied Psychology*, 86 (1): pp. 114–21.

Liozu, S., Boland, R., Hinterhuber, A. and Perelli, S. (2011) *Industrial pricing orientation: The organizational transformation to value-based pricing*. Paper presented at First International Conference on Engaged Management Scholarship, 2 June 2011.

MacCallum, R. C., Browne, M. W. and Sugawara, H. M. (1996) Power analysis and determination of sample size for covariance structure modeling. *Psychological Methods*, 1 (2), pp. 130–49.

McCaskey, P. H. and Brady, D. L. (2007) The current status of course offerings in pricing in the business curriculum. *Journal of Product & Brand Management*, 16 (5), pp. 358–61.

Mackey, A. (2008) The effect of CEOs on firm performance. *Strategic Management Journal*, 29 (12), pp. 1357–67.

Malhotra, N. K. (1996) The impact of the Academy of Marketing Science on marketing scholarship: an analysis of the research published in JAMS. *Journal of the Academy of Marketing Science*, 24 (4), p. 291.

March, J. (1978) Bounded rationality, ambiguity, and the engineering of choice. *The Bell Journal of Economics*, 9 (2), pp. 587–608.

March, J. and Simon, H. (1958) *Organizations*. New York: Wiley.

Medsker, G. J., Williams, L. J. and Holahan, P. J. (1994) A review of current practices for evaluating causal models in organizational behavior and human resources management research. *Journal of Management*, 20 (2), pp. 439–64.

Miller, D. (1987) Strategy making and structure: analysis and implications for performance. *The Academy of Management Journal*, 30 (1): pp. 7–32.

Mitchell, K. (2011) *The current state of pricing practice in U.S. firms (opening speech)*. Professional Pricing Society Annual Spring Conference, Chicago, USA.

Morgan, N. A., Vorhies, D. W. and Mason, C. H. (2009) Market orientation, marketing capabilities, and firm performance. *Strategic Management Journal*, 30 (8), pp. 909–20.

Nadler, D. and Nadler, M. (1997) *Champions of change: How CEOs and their companies are mastering the skills of radical change*. San Francisco, CA: Jossey-Bass.

Nadler, D. and Tushman, M. (1990) Beyond the charismatic leader and organizational change. *California Management Review*, 32 (2), pp. 77–97.

Nunnally, J. (1978) *Fundamentals of factor analysis. Psychometric theory*, 2nd edition. New York: McGraw-Hill Book Company, pp. 327–404.

Oxenfeldt, A. (1973) A decision-making structure for price decisions. *The Journal of Marketing*, 37 (1), pp. 48–53.

Pavlou, P. A. and Gefen, D. (2005) Psychological contract violation in online marketplaces: Antecedents, consequences, and moderating role. *Information Systems Research*, 16 (4), pp. 372–99.

Pentland, B. and Reuter, H. (1994) Organizational routines as grammars of action. *Administrative Science Quarterly*, 39 (3), pp. 484–510.

Podsakoff, P. M., MacKenzie, S. B., Lee, J.-Y. and Podsakoff, N. P. (2003) Common method biases in behavioral research: A critical review of the literature and recommended remedies. *Journal of Applied Psychology*, 88 (5), pp. 879–903.

Podsakoff, P. M. and Organ, D. W. (1986) Self-reports in organizational research: Problems and prospects. *Journal of Management*, 12 (4): pp. 531–44.

Porac, J. F., Thomas, H. and Baden-Fuller, C. (1989) Competitive groups as cognitive communities: The case of scottish knitwear manufacturers. *Journal of Management Studies*, 26 (4), pp. 397–416.

Preacher, K. J. and Coffman, D. L. (2006, May) Computing power and minimum sample size for RMSEA [Computer software]. Available from http://quantpsy.org.

Quinn, J. B. and Baily, M. N. (1994) Information technology: Increasing productivity in services [and executive commentary]. *The Academy of Management Executive (1993–2005)*, 8 (3), pp. 28–51.

Sadler-Smith, E. and Shefy, E. (2004) The intuitive executive: Understanding and applying 'gut feel' in decision-making. *The Academy of Management Executive (1993–2005)*, 18 (4), pp. 76–91.

Schwenk, C. R. (1988) The cognitive perspective on strategic decision making. *Journal of Management Studies*, 25 (1), pp. 41–55.

Simon H. A. (1961) *Administrative behavior*. New York: Macmillan.

Simon, H. A. (1987) Making management decisions: The role of intuition and emotion. *The Academy of Management Executive (1987–1989)*, 1 (1), pp. 57–64.

Simsek, Z. (2007) CEO tenure and organizational performance: an intervening model. *Strategic Management Journal*, 28 (6), pp. 653–62.

Simsek, Z., Heavey, C. and Veiga, J. F. (2010) The impact of CEO core self evaluation on the firm's entrepreneurial orientation. *Strategic Management Journal*, 31 (1), pp. 110–19.

Simsek, Z., Veiga, J. F., Lubatkin, M. H. and Dino, R. N. (2005) Modeling the multilevel determinants of top management team behavioral integration. *The Academy of Management Journal*, 48 (1), pp. 69–84.

Smith, G. (1995) Managerial pricing orientation: the process of making pricing decisions. *Pricing Strategy & Practice*, 3 (3), pp. 28–39.

Song, M., Droge, C., Hanvanich, S. and Calantone, R. (2005) Marketing and technology resource complementarity: an analysis of their interaction effect in two environmental contexts. *Strategic Management Journal*, 26 (3), pp. 259–76.

Steiger, J. H. (1998) A note on multiple sample extensions of the RMSEA fit index. *Structural Equation Modeling: A Multidisciplinary Journal*, 5 (4), pp. 411–19.

Steiger, J. H. and Lind, J. (1980) *Statistically-based tests for the number of common factors*. Annual Spring Meeting of the Psychometric Society, Iowa City.

Tabachnick, B. G. and Fidell, L. S. (2007) *Using multivariate statistics*. Boston, MA: Pearson Education.

Tasa, K., Taggar, S. and Seijts, G. H. (2007) The development of collective efficacy in teams: A multilevel and longitudinal perspective. *Journal of Applied Psychology*, 92 (1), pp. 17–27.

Tucker, L. and Lewis, C. (1973) A reliability coefficient for maximum likelihood factor analysis. *Psychometrika*, 38 (1), pp. 1–10.

Vorhies, D. W. and Morgan, N. A. (2005) Benchmarking marketing capabilities for sustainable competitive advantage. *Journal of Marketing*, 69 (1), pp. 80–94.

Wang, Y. and Huang, T. (2009) The relationship of transformational leadership with group cohesiveness and emotional intelligence. *Social Behavior and Personality: An International Journal*, 37 (3), pp. 379–92.

Weick, K. and Sutcliffe, K. (2007) *Managing the unexpected: Resilient performance in an age of uncertainty*. San Francisco, CA: Jossey-Bass.

Weick, K. E., Sutcliffe, K. and Obstfeld, D. (1999) Organizing for high reliability: Processes of collective mindfulness. In: Sutton, R. S. and Staw, B. M. (eds) *Research in organizational behavior*, Volume 1. Greenwich, CT: JAI Press, pp. 81–123.

Wernerfelt, B. (1984) A resource-based view of the firm. *Strategic Management Journal*, 5 (2), pp. 171–80.

Wouters, M., Anderson, J. and Wynstra, F. (2005) The adoption of total cost of ownership for sourcing decisions – a structural equations analysis. *Accounting, Organizations and Society*, 30 (2), pp. 167–91.

5

WHO IS IN CHARGE OF VALUE?

The emerging role of Chief Value Officer

Ronald J. Baker

Stephan M. Liozu

Introduction

THE WORLD of business and economics changes fast and is becoming more complex every decade. Firms are faced with the choice to adapt, reinvent and differentiate themselves or die. Over the past few years, the nature and intensity of these changes in the business landscape have created organizational disruption and a realistic need to redesign organizational structure and leadership approaches. As a result, the nature and structure of the C-suite has also been changing to respond to these exogenous trends. Whereas traditionally C-level positions were focused on operations (Chief Operations Officer), on finance (Chief Financial Officer), on information systems (Chief Information Officer) and on innovation (Chief Innovation Officer), we have witnessed the emergence of a flurry of new C-level titles emanating from new management theory (Chief Learning Officer, Chief Knowledge Officer), from increased business regulations (Chief Compliance Officer, Chief Ethics Officer, Chief Sustainability Officer, Chief Risk Officer) and from increased focused on markets and customers (Chief Customer Office, Customer Experience Officer, Chief Growth Office, Chief Commercial Officer and Chief Marketing Officer).

Today more and more firms realize that they cannot cut their way to prosperity and that their growth potential has been severely reduced due to the continued recessionary trends. Businesses are looking at their business models and reinventing their value propositions in order to generate customer excitement, boost value-creation programmes and capture value through value-based pricing. This trend towards value begs the question of who is in charge of value-management processes and programmes in firms and how they design and implement comprehensive, systematic long-term value initiatives. For the past decade, the authors have promoted the role of Chief Value Officer in professional firms to lead such programmes and initiatives (Baker 2006). In this paper, we explore the need for the creation of a Chief Value Officer role for both service and manufacturing firms. We offer a practical comparison of the customer- and market-related CXO positions and propose two potential job descriptions for the role of Chief Value Officer (CVO). Our goal is to recommend the creation and adoption of the CVO role and to elevate the value discussion to the C-suite. There has never been a better time to focus on the topic of business and customer value. Who is in charge of value in your organization?

What does value mean?

> Price is what you pay. Value is what you get.
>
> Warren Buffett

Adam Smith (1723–90) was confounded. One of the greatest economic and social thinkers in the history of ideas struggled with the so-called diamond–water paradox, which Smith explained in Chapter 4 of Book I of *Wealth of Nations*: 'Nothing is more useful than water: but it will purchase scarce anything .... A diamond, on the contrary, has scarce any value in use; but a very great quantity of other goods may frequently be had in exchange for it' (Skousen and Taylor 1997: 27).

Most people confronted with this paradox – including Smith – would resolve it by replying that the supply of diamonds is sparse compared with water, and hence they command a higher price. This is an intuitive, and very reasonable, solution. After all, water is approximately 71 per cent of the earth's surface, while diamonds are found in only a limited number of places in the world.

Yet the scarcity theory lacks explanatory power. Just because something is scarce does not mean it is valuable. There must be a better theory that solves this puzzle, so let us explore the antecedents of the theory of value.

Throughout history, man has always correlated labour with value, inputs with outputs. In medieval English, the word 'acre' meant the amount of land a team of eight oxen could plough in a morning. Even Adam Smith identified two separate forms of value – 'value in use' and a 'value in exchange', which gave rise to the famous diamond–water paradox, since certain items for one's own use were highly valuable (e.g. water) but commanded little in exchange for other goods, such as diamonds. In essence, Smith decided to ignore a commodity's value in use and just focus on value in exchange. Indeed, to this day, one sees various pricing books distinguishing value in use from value in exchange.

Yet, Smith understood that there were factors other than labour that went into the cost of producing commodities, such as the cost of capital, equipment, rent and the risk the entrepreneur was assuming. All these factors also had to be compensated for in the price of the final commodity, so Smith posited a 'cost of production' theory of value, in effect 'adding up' labour, profit, rent and cost of capital to determine price. Of course, this still begs the question of how a company could ever lose money by following this theory, since even the most inept businessperson would be able to add up all these factors to derive a price that generates a profit.

Here we have an eminent economist – although called a moral philosopher in his day – who struggled to develop a unifying and credible theory of value. It would take another influential economist to popularize a theory of value that appeared to advance his utopian objectives.

Karl Marx is far from dead. His labour theory of value still wields enormous influence over our present-day concept of value and price. Here is how Marx explained his theory in *Value, Price and Profit*, originally published in 1865:

> A commodity has *a value*, because it is a *crystallization of social labour*. The *greatness* of its value, or its *relative* value, depends upon the greater or less amount of that social substance contained in it; that is to say, on the relative mass of labour necessary for its production. The *relative values of commodities* are, therefore, determined by the *respective quantities or amounts of labour, worked up, realized, fixed in them*. The *correlative* quantities of commodities which can be produced in the *same time of labour* are *equal*. [italics in original]
>
> (Marx 1995: 31)

This, too, sounds quite reasonable, until you test this theory to see whether it can explain how people spend their money in the marketplace. Marx's theory cannot explain how land and natural resources have value, since there is no labour contained in them. Taken to its extreme, the labour theory of value would predict those countries with the most labour hours – such as China or India – would have the highest standards of living. But this is demonstrably false, and what we witness instead in countries with *less* labour inputs and more entrepreneurship – as well as secure private property and other institutions conducive to economic growth – are vastly higher standards of living, including shorter hours for workers.

If Marx's theory was correct, a rock found next to a diamond in a mine would be of equal value, since each took the same amount of labour hours to locate and extract. Yet we do not see many rocks in the local mall's jewellery store. If one were to have pizza for lunch, under Marx's theory, the tenth slice would be just as valuable as the first, since each took the same amount of labour hours to produce. One glaring flaw in Marx's theory was that it did not take into account the law of diminishing marginal utility, which states that the value to the customer declines with additional consumption of the good in question.

Another Marxian flaw is that the very nature of a transaction between a willing buyer and seller is based not on an equality of labour but rather on the *inequality* in the subjective value of the good bought and sold. This takes us back to one of Adam Smith's central insights: that both buyer and seller must gain from an exchange, or it will not take place. Were this not so, a contractor could build any type of house *he* wanted, hire incompetent and lazy workers, tally up his costs, add a desired profit and still receive his full price.

In the middle of the nineteenth century, economic theory was at a dead end. Serendipitously, three economists, from three different countries, originated the marginalist revolution: William Stanley Jevons (1835–82), from Great Britain; Leon Walras (1834–1910), from France; and Carl Menger (1840–1921), from Austria. Swedish economist Knut Wicksell, who lived through the marginalist revolution, described it as a 'bolt from the blue' (Skousen 2008: 169). What made this new theory so revolutionary? As Menger explains in his book *Principles of Economics*, written in 1873 when he was 33 years old:

> Value is ... nothing inherent in goods, no property of them. Value is a judgement economizing men make about the importance of the goods at their disposal for the maintenance of their lives and well-being. Hence value does not exist outside the consciousness of men .... [T]he value of goods ... is entirely subjective in nature.
> (Ebenstein 2003: 23)

> The value of goods arises from their relationship to our needs, and is not inherent in the goods themselves .... Objectification of the value of goods, which is entirely subjective in nature, has nevertheless contributed very greatly to confusion about the basic principles of our science .... The importance that goods have for us and which we call value is merely imputed.
> (Menger 1873: 120–1, 139)

Value is like beauty – it is in the eye of the beholder. This theory has enormous explanatory and predictive capabilities, because it explains, for instance, why people dive for pearls. Karl Marx would say that pearls have value because people dive for them (thus supplying labour, commensurate with his labour theory of value). The marginalists would retort that people dive for pearls because other people value them.

Philip Wicksteed, a British clergyman, wrote a scientific critique of the Marxian labour theory of value in 1884, in which he explained that:

> A coat is not worth eight times as much as a hat to the community because it takes eight times as long to make it .... The community is willing to devote eight times as long to the making of a coat because it will be worth eight times as much to it.
> (Howey 1989: 157)

So why are diamonds more expensive than water? Water tends to be priced based on the marginal satisfaction of the last gallon consumed. The German economist Hermann Heinrich Gossen (1810–58) developed what is known as Gossen's Law: The market price is always determined by what the last unit of a product is worth to people.

While the first several gallons of water may be vital for your survival, the water used to shower, flush the toilet and wash the dishes is less valuable. Less valuable still is the water used to wash your dog, your car and hose down your driveway. The market price of water reflects the last uses of the good for the aggregate of all consumers of water. On the other hand, the marginal satisfaction of one more diamond tends to be very high.

If water companies knew you were dehydrated in the desert, they would be able to charge a higher price for those first vital gallons consumed, and then gradually adjust the price downwards to reflect the less-valuable marginal gallons. Since they do not possess this information – the cost of doing so would be prohibitive – the aggregate market price for water tends to be based on its *marginal* value.

As a consumer, if one is dehydrated in the desert, near death, a bottle of Evian water is *priceless*, compared with the same quantity of water used to wash the dishes or dog. If one's basement is flooded with water, it now has a *negative* value, since one will have to pay someone to remove it. Value is not only subjective, it is contextual.

Economic historian Thomas Sowell explains how the economics profession finally overcame the absurd notion of the labour theory of value:

> By the late nineteenth century, however, economists had given up on the notion that it is primarily labour which determines the value of goods . . . . This new understanding marked a revolution in the development of economics. It is also a sobering reminder of how long it can take for even highly intelligent people to get rid of a misconception whose fallacy then seems obvious in retrospect. It is not costs which create value; it is value which causes purchasers to be willing to repay the costs incurred in the production of what they want.
> (Sowell 2004: 177)

To argue that you can measure value by labour is to argue that the value of Jonas Salk's polio vaccine is based on how long it took him to develop. One might as well plunge a ruler into the oven to determine its temperature. Labour is the wrong measurement of value.

None of this discussion is meant to imply that businesses cannot *create* the demand for a product. No one 'demanded' – or subjectively valued – a Sony Walkman or the Apple iPad before they were produced and offered in the market. Quite often, supply does indeed create demand, especially as it relates to innovations and new technologies. But there is no guarantee of consumer acceptance just because costs were incurred; the high rate of product failures is a testament to this fact. Nonetheless, in the long run, a product or service will only *continue* to be produced if people value it, and if its price can cover its full costs of production, including profit.

Value at the organizational level

'Value' is probably one of the most frequently used words in business. Yet it is extremely difficult to define, to assess its drivers and fully capture it with customers.

Given that most companies create their own social construction of value, we propose to explore what it might mean and introduce some practical steps to increase your understanding of it.

Why is it that few suppliers in business markets are able to define and measure value? In a 2008 survey of business executives, 79 per cent attributed this difficulty to a lack of capabilities and skills needed to assess value, apply the appropriate methods, and extract the exact value differential between two products (Hinterhuber 2008a). Second to the value-assessment issue, communicating value to the market was associated by 65 per cent of the executives with difficulty in elevating the value message above the advertising noise in the market. Bottom line: there is a need for more research related not only to theory on value (Ulaga 2001) but also to marketing tools for understanding, assessing and delivering value in business markets (Cressman Jr 2010). Scholars agree that there are six characteristics of business value that make value difficult to measure: value is (1) a subjective concept, (2) a trade-off between benefits and sacrifices, (3) multidimensional, (4) defined relative to competitors, (5) segment-specific and (6) future-oriented (Hinterhuber 2008b).

We conjecture that value must be elevated to the organizational level. Firms must put business value at the centre of their existence (Forbis and Mehta 1981; Slater 1997), make it part of their DNA (Liozu *et al.* 2011), and focus on creating sustainable value for stakeholders. Figure 5.1 depicts a framework for the creation and capture of business value. This framework highlights the fact that business value exists at various stages of the commercial cycle and resides in multiple functions of the firm: innovation, strategy, marketing, pricing and financial management.

By continuously creating, assessing and capturing value, firms can reap the fruits of their holistic value-management programmes and can reinvest significant portions of their incremental profitability into innovation. Simply put, enterprises need to innovate for growth and price for profit. Profit is the price an enterprise pays to create the future; both innovation and profit depend on value creation.

Who is in charge of value?

> The final question needed in order to come to grips with business purpose and business mission is: 'What is value to the customer?' It may be the most important question. Yet it is the one least often asked. One reason is that managers are quite sure that they know the answer. Value is what they, in their business, define as quality. But this is almost always the wrong definition. The customer never buys a product. By definition the customer buys the satisfaction of a want. He buys value.
>
> Peter Drucker, *Management: Tasks, Responsibilities, Practices*, 1973

Whenever this question is posed to a group of businesspeople – 'Who's in charge of value in your company?' – someone will inevitably shout out, 'Everyone!' Really? If everyone owns something, no one does. Adam Smith demonstrated that the *division and specialization of labour* were a central cause of the wealth of nations; they

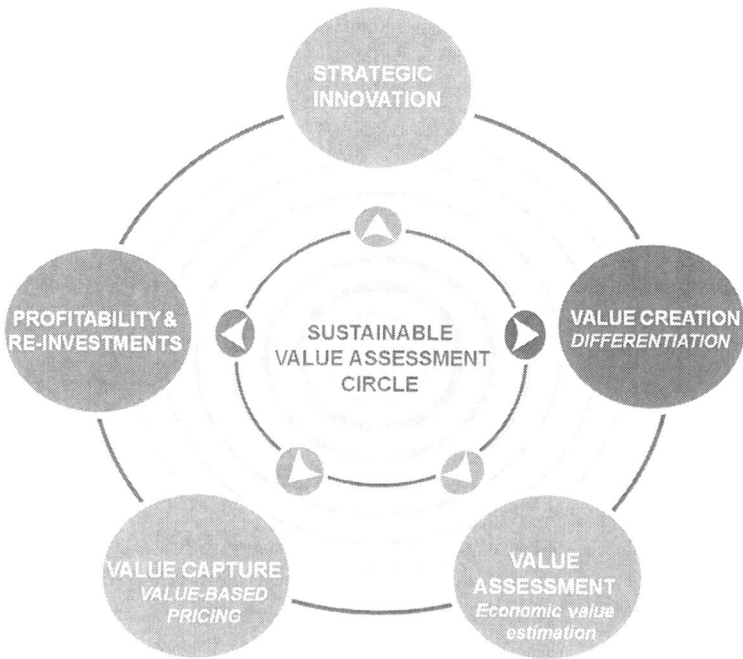

FIGURE 5.1 Sustainable value-assessment circle

are also the central cause of the success of a business. Not everyone can be good at everything.

In a company, someone needs to own the value and pricing functions, someone who can be held accountable for creating and capturing value across the entire range of customers. When you consider how much executive attention the purchasing function receives in most organizations – with the elevation of a new title, Chief Purchasing Officer (CPO) – shouldn't the pricing function receive the same level of executive commitment, attention and resources as a function designed to control costs? A report by the London Business School and Ariba, a software company, claims that the new CPOs at 70 per cent of European firms report directly to the board of directors, an increase of 20 per cent over the prior year (*The Economist*, 'A Rise in the C-Level,' 26 February 2005: 60). Many Fortune 500 companies have a Chief Revenue Officer, or Chief Pricing Officer; and while these appointments are a step in the right direction towards making pricing a core competency within a company, we posit that there still exists a lacuna in most companies: understanding and measuring value.

Since price, ultimately, is determined by value – and now that we have explored in detail the subjective theory of value, we have a better understanding of this concept – shouldn't someone within the company be in charge of comprehending, communicating and capturing value? All businesses talk about value, and all agree it is essential to create, and constantly add to, but who is in charge of it? Until it is elevated to the executive suite, it is not going to receive the attention, resources and alignment with overall corporate strategy that it merits. After all, a business exists to create wealth – value – outside of itself, and until someone is held responsible and accountable for understanding the impact on customers, companies will continue to operate below potential in the value-creating function. Let us appoint a CVO in order to take a stand for customer value within the organization.

Unlike a biological organism, the true test of a company's success lies outside of its four walls. As Peter Drucker wrote, 'All results are external, there is no such thing as a profit centre'; there are only cost, activity and effort centres. The only profit centre in your company is a customer's cheque that doesn't bounce.

Yet in many companies, according to McKinsey & Company, marketing is poorly linked to corporate strategy. According to a McKinsey survey of 30 large US companies, more than a third reported that their boards spent less than 10 per cent of their time on marketing- and customer-related issues. How can a company continually create value, let alone capture it with more effective pricing strategies, if it does not have someone overseeing this responsibility?

Any company that does not understand the value of its own offerings will, by default, perform a suboptimal job communicating it to its customers. Yet your customers purchase relatively infrequently, while your company sells many more times. Is it not worth gaining a deeper understanding of value so you can leverage that knowledge across your entire customer base, rather than just a few sales? This is precisely why the role of CVO was created. The CVO role grew out an experiment conducted with professional knowledge firms around the world. Initially, a pricing council was established, composed of a group of people who would have ultimate responsibility for pricing across the entire firm.

In any company, pricing exists at the crossroads of almost every other discipline, such as marketing, sales, finance, project management and even research and development. Yet these various functions sometimes have conflicting objectives and priorities. Marketing tends to focus on brand awareness and market share, while finance may insist on maintaining certain margins, and sales is interested in making the next sale. Pricing tends to become an afterthought, taking a backseat to these other functions that normally secure executive attention and clout.

What was learned with the pricing council experiment was enlightening. While every firm that implemented the idea became a better pricer, and focused on the customer more effectively, some of the councils degenerated into what Paul Kennedy, partner at O'Byrne & Kennedy, chartered accountants in the United Kingdom, described as 'an auction house'. He said:

> We'd sit around and discuss a particular contract for a client and when we finished with scope and an obligatory nod to value, we started throwing out prices. One member would say £10,000, the next £12,500, on up to £20,000. It dawned on me after this scenario was repeated several times we were becoming as inward focused as cost accountants. Yes, we had moved up from costing the job to placing a more strategic price upon it, but we were

still not giving proper attention to the outward value we were creating, or should have been creating, for the customer. This was an epiphany for us. Soon thereafter, we created a value council, whereby the focus is, first and foremost on value, then price. This has been much more effective, and has resulted in happier customers and greater profits for the firm.

In this particular firm, the value council has become the eyes, ears and voice for the customer. Rather than merely setting prices, they have begun to think strategically about value – we have become 'obsessed with value', as Paul now says – which should be the basis for how prices are set.

Brendon Harrex, at age 31, was the world's first CVO, appointed in March 2005 by his former chartered accounting firm in New Zealand. In May 2007, he launched his own firm, The Harrex Group. Brendon describes what he learned as CVO in his prior firm, in Case Study 1.

BOX 5.1 CASE STUDY 1: WHAT BRENDON LEARNED AS CVO

- I am learning so much in the CVO role. It is like climbing a mountain – just when you think you are nearing the top, you find it merely another ridgeline and the horizon still is a distant vision.
- I am coming to realize what a wimpy pricer I really am. I think sometimes we price for the 80 per cent of the job that everyone else can do and forget to capture the real value that being focused and fanatical brings to a customer.
- I am learning very quickly that as an individual and a business you can not be all things to all people and you have to say no quite a lot more than I am used to.
- I am learning how scared many of us are of change, even if there is no logical or illogical argument supporting the status quo.
- I am learning that business value is maximized when we realize that the customer owns the shop.
- I am learning that fun is maximized when we realize the customer owns the shop and start acting like it.
- I am learning that, as in life, control in business is just an illusion. Yet we allocate valuable resources into sustaining the illusion.
- I am learning that vision drives the structure and sometimes the structure needs changing to assist fulfilment of the vision.
- I am learning the value of a decision and the high cost of indecision.
- I am learning that the less we focus on our own importance, the more important we become.
- I am learning that one wrong doesn't overcome another.
- I am learning the importance of laying the foundation before beginning to build.

Brendon Harrex, Founder, The Harrex Group, Invercargill, New Zealand

No customer buys costs, efforts or activities, yet many businesses continue to price on a cost-plus basis. The customer wants to see the baby, not hear about the labour pains. However, consider how most companies have traditionally been taught to think of the pricing function:

Cost-plus pricing

Product → Cost → Price → Value → Customer

Notice that you start with the product (or service), determine its cost, mark up that cost with a desired profit to set the price, and then pray that the customer values the output at a level higher than the price they are being asked to pay. Notice where the customer is in this chain of events – at the end! Value-based pricing inverts this chain to correspond with the economic realities of the marketplace.

Value-based pricing

Customers → Value → Price → Cost → Product

This value chain recognizes that value is like beauty; it is in the eye of the beholder. It is in total alignment with the *subjective* theory of value. Customers do not care about your internal costs, or your profit desires. They demand value higher than the price they are paying.

This inversion reveals a further fact of economic life: your costs do not determine your price; rather, your price determines your costs. This is anathema to a cost accountant, but self-evident to a pricer. A firm needs to determine, before producing a product or service, whether the price charged – based on value – will allow it to invest in the costs required to develop the product or service at a profit the company can tolerate – *price-led costing*. If not, it should not undertake production. The important point about this process is *when* costs are considered – *before* the product is produced, not after. This is the problem with historical standard cost accounting – it can only allocate past costs, once they have been spent.

CVOs understand that the hardest part of this new value chain is determining value. After all, cost is relatively easy to determine, since most companies employ cost accountants capable of allocating fixed and variable costs to each widget. Setting price above cost is also not difficult – even the most inept businessperson should be able to accomplish this. In determining value, cost accounting provides little help, since customers purchase value, not a bundle of allocated costs.

Since the CVO position is relatively new, more is being learned every day about this responsibility within firms. It is an unusual position, to say the least. The firms that have implemented it so far have reported favourable results, so much so that the idea warrants further testing. One question that continually arises is, what are the traits of a successful CVO?

The framework for the Chief Value Officer
CVO versus other commercial-oriented C-level positions

Our intention in this paper is not to propose a detailed and final description of various C-level positions. We intend to launch a conversation about the role of the CVO compared with other C-level positions that are related to market and customer activities. The Chief Marketing Officer (CMO) and Chief Commercial Officer (CCO) positions have been more widely accepted over the past decade. While the role of CCO is relatively new, about 200 CCOs have been appointed worldwide since the role emerged (Abele and Stevenson 2009). Similarly, the number and presence of CVOs is accelerating around the world. In 2006, Spencer Stuart identified more than 30 CMOs in FTSE top 50 companies. In the USA, among Fortune 100 firms, 23 had a CMO as the head of marketing in 2008 (Grewal and Wang 2009). The acceptance of the role of Chief Pricing Officer (CPO) and Chief Value Officer (CVO) has a long way to go. First of all, in most companies, the pricing and value-management function receives limited attention. Data from the Professional Pricing Society, the world's largest organization dedicated to pricing, reveal that fewer than 5 per cent of Fortune 500 companies have a full-time function exclusively dedicated to pricing (Mitchell 2011). After an in-depth review in Google, only two or three firms have a clearly identified CVO function.

Reviews of the published roles of CVO, CPO, CMO and CCO allowed us to prepare the summary data shown in Table 5.1. We propose that all four roles are different but present some overlapping characteristics or critical functions. While job descriptions might differ from firm to firm, we find that the CVO function best captures the systematic and holistic creation, assessment and capture of value.

The LACEY framework

The acronym LACEY is a useful framework for identifying what characteristics are essential for a successful CVO:

Leadership
Attitude
Commitment
Experimentation
Youth

Let us examine each of these attributes, and discuss the functions required for each one.

Leadership

A company will never rise above its leadership. CVOs implicitly and explicitly understand that the company's prices are the language in which they strategically communicate value to customers. Even though companies are becoming more sophisticated with respect to the pricing function, value too often has been put aside. Now that we have a theory for value – the subjective theory of value – it should be promoted to the executive suite as the basis for all pricing decisions.

CVOs understand that there is nobility in being paid what the company is worth. Nothing is more satisfying than customers who believe – and act on the

TABLE 5.1 Critical function of commercially related C-level positions

Chief Marketing Officer	*Chief Pricing Officer*
Product management	Firm pricing orientation
Market management	Pricing strategies and tactics
Strategic marketing excellence	Pricing realization excellence
Strategic pricing management	Value management process
Marketing communications	Systems, tools and infrastructure
Chief Commercial Officer	*Chief Value Officer*
Commercial strategies and tactics	Value management process
Commercial excellence	Strategic pricing management
Product management	Innovation management
Market and customer insights	Market and customer insights
Customer experience management	Learning and knowledge management

premise – that they get what they pay for. Perhaps the first important characteristic of a successful CVO is high self-esteem; they believe that their company's products and services are worth every penny they charge. They are more concerned with developing a value proposition based on value, not price or cost.

In today's competitive business environment, low self-esteem is a competitive disadvantage, whereas high self-esteem confers a competitive advantage. Yet, how can people feel good about themselves, their work and their service to the customer and the greater community if they believe they are commodities and are constantly being beaten up over their price? *You will never get paid more than you think you are worth*. And if a company's leaders do not think they are worth more than cost-plus pricing, why would its customers?

In addition to high self-esteem, a CVO must have demonstrable leadership skills, while commanding respect and creditability across multiple functions within the company. He or she will be responsible for communicating the importance of pricing and value to the media, thereby negating price wars within the industry. Since competitors tend to judge a company's pricing behaviour based on its most ruthless actions, think of the message that appointing a CVO would send to others in the industry about how committed a firm is to price for value and not engaging in self-destructive price wars.

The CVO is also responsible for establishing the value council, a group of motivated team members who look upon pricing as an enormous opportunity, not a limitation. The size of the council will vary by company size, industry and customer segment, but experience suggests that smaller is better. It should not consist of executives only, but should comprise a cross-selection of disciplines, from finance, marketing, sales and so forth. Some companies have made one-half of the positions rotate, perhaps on a two- or three-year basis, in order to bring in fresh perspectives, while spreading the value message throughout the organization.

The final determination of the value council's membership should be made by the CVO, possibly in conjunction with the CEO. But it is important to emphasize that the council is not a jury; it does not require unanimous consent to make decisions. The CVO always holds the tie-breaking vote, in order for there to be true leadership and accountability. Margaret Thatcher, former Prime Minister of Britain, was fond of pointing out, 'Consensus is the negation of leadership.'

Examples of mission statements for the value council are:

- To ensure [company name] prices on purpose, according to the value received by the customer, not the costs incurred.
- To make pricing for value a core competency within [company name].
- To change the marketing culture within [company name] to one that comprehends, creates, communicates, convinces and captures the value of the products we provide to our customers.

Attitude

The CVO and members of the value council must view pricing as an enormous opportunity for the company to create and capture value, rather than a limitation imposed on them over which they have no control, like the weather. Pricing is far too important to assign to narrow minds. Pricers must be intellectually curious, constantly learning and studying why humans behave the way they do.

Look for a CVO who is constantly learning, and who is moving through the five levels of learning: awareness, awkwardness, application, assimilation and art. Pricing is an iterative process of the mind. Although it may require substantial investment – to purchase sophisticated pricing software, for example – it will always require human judgement; otherwise, it will be the embodiment of garbage in, garbage out. Pricing strategy, ultimately, is a human endeavour.

Commitment

A CVO who does not have the support of the CEO is destined to be feckless. Effective centralized pricing must have total authority, which we believe needs to be vested in one individual so that there is one throat to choke. Taking it a step further, if value creation is truly the purpose of a company, the CVO should report directly to the CEO. This will send a powerful message throughout the organization that the leaders are serious about value and pricing, as well as to competitors, thereby possibly reducing the threat of price wars.

The commitment to a CVO also provides a competitive advantage, since competitors can monitor only historical pricing, not value. Value creation and pricing competence create a sense of self-worth among team members, and although nearly impossible to measure quantitatively, can certainly be observed in morale.

Experimentation

CVOs must take a stand on behalf of the customer, constantly asking how the organization can provide more value. They must be willing to experiment and cannot be prisoners of the past. 'That is the way we have always done it' draws nothing but contempt from CVOs, since they have little respect for the status quo.

They seek change not simply for change's sake but to fulfil the purpose of the organization.

If you have ever been bribed off an oversold airplane – with a free flight voucher, upgrade or airline money equivalent – you have the late economist Julian Simon to thank. Until 1978, travellers were bumped off overbooked planes rather capriciously – the airlines preferred to bump old people and military personnel on the theory they would be least likely to complain – and this caused enormous amounts of customer complaints and ill will. Sometimes an entire flight would be cancelled and rebooked at proper capacity, causing even greater outrage. Worse yet, the problem fed upon itself, because passengers began to expect being bumped and so would book several flights under various names to ensure a seat on at least one; this caused the airlines to increase bookings even more in order to ensure decent load factors. A flight attendant friend who worked for United Airlines told Simon of this problem:

> The next day when shaving it occurred to me that there must be a better way; indeed, an auction market could solve the problem by finding those people who least mind waiting for the next flight. The practical details fell into place before the shave was complete.
>
> In 1966 and 1967 I wrote to all the airlines suggesting the scheme. The responses ranged from polite brush-offs, to denials that they overbooked, to assertions that the scheme could not work, to derision.
>
> [...] I was unable to persuade any airline (or the Civil Aeronautics Board) to conduct an experiment for even one day on a single airline at a single airport at a single boarding gate – an experiment that I believed would be sufficient, even with the inevitable breakdowns in any new activity.
>
> (Simon 2003: 289–94)

Had the airlines employed a CVO, Simon's idea would have been tested much sooner, to the benefit of both the airlines and their customers.

Soren Kierkegaard wrote, 'Purity of soul is to will one thing.' What is more important than to champion the cause of value creation within today's companies? A CVO is never satisfied with the status quo because he or she will constantly be searching for new ways of doing things, all the while eliminating procedures and processes that do not add value to the customer. This is the CVO mandate.

Youth

> *Age is, of course, a fever chill*
> *that every physicist must fear.*
> *He's better dead than living still*
> *when once he's past his thirtieth year.*
>
> Paul Dirac, 1933 Nobel Laureate in Physics

Of all the characteristics in LACEY, there is a certain amount of uncertainty about the implications of this last one. Facts are indeed stubborn things; we are all entitled to our *opinions*, but we are not entitled to our *facts*. Consider these facts:

- The average age of the signers of the Declaration of Independence was 45, Benjamin Franklin being the oldest at 70 and Thomas Lynch, Jr (South Carolina) the youngest at 27.
- The average age of the delegates to the Constitutional Convention was 43, the oldest being Benjamin Franklin at 81 and the youngest Jonathan Dayton at 26.
- The average age of the Marginalist Revolution economists was 35.
- Adam Smith was 36 when he wrote his first book, *The Theory of Moral Sentiments*, containing the genesis of his later masterpiece *Wealth of Nations*.
- Blaise Pascal, who proved Euclid's 32nd theorem, was 28 by the time he completed most of the scientific work for which he is famous.
- Albert Einstein developed his theory of relativity at age 26.
- The average age of the Manhattan Project scientists was 25.
- Steve Jobs was 21 and Steve Wozniak 26 when Apple Computer was founded; they were 29 and 34, respectively, when the Macintosh was launched.
- Walt Disney was 27 when Mickey Mouse was introduced to the world.

Charles Murray, Bradley Fellow at the American Enterprise Institute, wrote an absolutely fascinating book, *Human Accomplishment*, wherein he identified 4,002 individuals who basically invented, developed or proved the most consequential ideas in the history of the world, from 800 BC to 1950:

> It is a fact that takes some getting used to, but the evidence for it is overwhelming: When you assemble the human résumé, only a few thousand people stand apart from the rest. Among them, the people who are indispensable to the story of human accomplishment number in the hundreds. Among those hundreds, a handful stand conspicuously above everyone else.
>
> (Murray 2003: 87)

We truly do stand on the shoulders of these giants. The mean age of these individuals was 40. What does all of this mean? We will admit to not being entirely sure. One thing is certain: if organizations want innovation and dynamism, they will have to confer greater authority and responsibility onto their youthful team members. Organizations, like people, tend to calcify with age, and youth can keep the blood pumping at a more vigorous pace. No doubt they will make more mistakes and incur more failure, yet risk is where profits come from. What is the alternative? Ossification is not an option.

Chief Value Officer job description

CVOs are focused on systematically creating, assessing and capturing value across all processes and functions of the firm. SAP's CVO supports our view:

Value is created in three stages – value discovery, value realization, and value optimization. We believe partners can look at these three areas and offer services around them, such as change and programme management to help customers unleash the potential of what is being offered.

CVOs make sure that all programmes, actions, initiatives, new products, services and investments create and capture customer value. They challenge the decision-making process to bring forward customer needs, value propositions and value models as well as how value is captured in the process. CVOs live and breathe value management, as the eyes, ears and voices within the organization advocating value creation for the customer.

There are two options for designing the role of the CVO, as shown in Figure 5.2. A first way is to establish a project management office (PMO) dedicated to the management of value and driving all programmes, processes and systems associated with value management. We call this approach a process-focused CVO.

The second approach proposes to design this role by grouping all functions associated with value management (marketing, innovation, pricing, value, strategy) and to fold them under one function reporting to the CEO. This approach resembles a more traditional one, closer to the role of Chief Marketing Officer with innovation and strategic responsibilities. We call this approach a functionally focused CVO with more direct responsibility. The selection of one versus the other approach depends on the firm's process orientation and its capacity to change at the organizational level. Our opinion is that both approaches offer great potential to put value management where it belongs, that is, in the C-suite.

In this paper, we also propose to go further and to offer readers a potential job description for a process-focused CVO. For this we build on the work of Deloitte (Dalton and Wortman 2004) and add additional dimensions to the position, as shown in Figure 5.3.

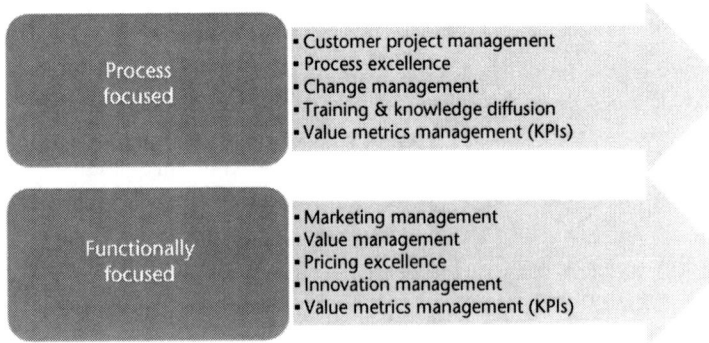

FIGURE 5.2 Two options for CVO role design

Note: KPI, key price indicator.

Job title:
Chief Value Officer (CVO)

Reports to:
ECO and Board of Directors

Objective of the role:
To lead the development and execution of an integrated performance management process focused on the creation and capturing of long term business value.

Scope:
This role encompasses all elements of performance management, including development and update of strategic plans, management of the project portfolio, determination and approval of capital investments and new product introductions, establishment of performance measures and targets, and the evaluation and reward of performance. Organizational scope includes an overall corporate perspective, with responsibility for providing direction to all business units, aligning their strategies within the contex of enterprise value, and optimizing the enterprise portfolio.

Main responsibilities:

- Lead the continuous assessment of the business environment, customer trends and value models, and assessment of possible scenarios, as well as the changes in direction implied by potential changes.
- Review and approval of all plans, projects, investments, measurements, targets, and performance assessments for completeness and consistency with overall corporate value-creation and value-creation and value-capturing goals and objectives.
- Establishment, review, and maintenance of a consistent, integrated performance management process across all parts of the organization – including timelines, outputs, and systems to be used.
- Review and approval of all compensation and reward programs for consistency and alignment with corporate goals.
- Develop training and intellectual capital management programs to promote the value management.

Experience & skills required
A demonstrated knowledge of marketing, value assessment, pricing and finance.
Excellent business acumen including a passion for delivering superior outcome.
The ability to lead and direct diverse cross-functional teams to a common goal.
Strong experience leading value-creating and capturing processes.
A passion for holistic thinking and continuous improvement.
An ability to manage and direct the corporate and multi-functional project portfolio.
Strong change management experience and passion for communication.

FIGURE 5.3 Proposed process-oriented CVO job description

While the initial job description was well designed and captured more important elements of the role, we added the dimensions of learning and knowledge management as well as added required skills in change management. Putting value at the centre of the firm's DNA requires an organizational transformation (Liozu et al. 2011). The CVO will be required to drive this difficult transformation with passion. He or she will act as a champion of value in the firm and will reinforce collective efficacy by expressing positive evaluations (Tasa et al. 2007), showing confidence in people to perform effectively and to meet value challenges (Nadler and Tushman 1990), awakening spirits to rally the troops (Hacker and Roberts 2003), and energizing members across the organization (Nadler and Tushman 1990; Thompson 2009: 100).

Conclusions

In this paper we have attempted to bring forth arguments for why firms should comprehensively and systematically manage business value at the organizational level. We have also highlighted the need to have business value managed centrally through the creation of the position of Chief Value Officer.

Implications for innovation in pricing

In this essay, we make several contributions to the field of marketing, value and pricing management. First, we propose a different definition of business value and also support the need to elevate the value discussion to the C-suite. Many CEOs believe that it is their role to manage value day in and day out. We take a different position and argue that CEOs cannot improvise and focus fully on comprehensive value management. They need a full-time pool of resources that will make value leadership a priority project with the intent to create, assess and capture value. CEOs need to put business at the centre of the firm's existence and delegate that mission to value experts. CMOs, CPOs and CCOs may be able to assist in the management of value but they will also suffer from the same issues of multitasking, attention misallocation and lack of dedicated expertise that CEOs contend with.

Second, we propose a couple of different design options for CVOs as well as a potential job description based on Deloitte's 2004 work (Dalton and Wortman 2004: 31). We hope that further research will be conducted on the role and function of the CVO and that practitioners will draw from our work to advance the cause of value management in the C-suite.

Third, we clearly establish a separation between pricing management and value management in the firm. While they are not separated in the overall process, they must be managed differently and cannot be integrated with each other. Pricing strategies and tactics are used to capture value in the marketplace with customers. Prior to being captured, however, value must be created and assessed. Reciprocally, value cannot be captured without sound pricing strategies. Therefore, we posit that pricing belongs in the value-management process led by a CVO, and not simply a CPO reporting to the CEO or working in the C-suite.

If you are competing against a company with a CVO – either for customers or talent – you may be at a severe competitive disadvantage. The Roman God Janus had two sets of eyes, one set to see what lay behind and the other to see what lay ahead. A CVO is an outward-looking position, with duties carried out in a world of risk, uncertainty, innovation and faith in the future, where value is solely determined by the customers your company is privileged to serve. If the only set of eyes you possess look behind you – at historical costs and efforts – you are destined for a perilous future.

So, who is in charge of value in your company?

References

Abele, J. M. and Stevenson, J. M. (2009) *The rise of the chief commercial officer*. Heidrick & Struggles White Paper, pp. 1–4.
Baker, R. (2006) *Pricing on purpose: Creating and capturing value*. Hoboken, NJ: John Wiley & Sons.
Cressman Jr, G. E. (2010) Selling value-based pricing strategies: Making pricing strategy work. *Journal of Professional Pricing*, (First Quarter 2010), pp. 16–19.
Dalton, B. and Wortman, B. (2004) The value habit: A practical guide to creating value. *Straight Talk*, 6, pp. 1–34.
Drucker, P. (1973) *Management: Tasks, responsibilities practices*. New York: Harper & Row.
Ebenstein, A. O. (2003) *Hayek's journey: The mind of Friedrich Hayek*. New York: Palgrave Macmillan.
Forbis, J. and Mehta, N. (1981) Value-based strategies for industrial products. *Business Horizons*, 24 (3), pp. 32–42.
Grewal, R. and Wang, R. (2009) The chief marketing officer: New vintage, or just old wine in a new bottle. *The Chief Marketing Officer Journal*, 1, pp. 29–33.
Hacker, S. and Roberts, T. (2003) *Transformational leadership: Creating organizations of meaning*. Milwaukee, WI: ASQ Quality Press.
Hinterhuber, A. (2008a) Customer value-based pricing strategies: Why companies resist. *Journal of Business Strategy*, 29 (4), pp. 41–50.
Hinterhuber, A. (2008b) Value delivery and value-based pricing in industrial markets. *Advances in Business Marketing and Purchasing*, 14, pp. 381–448.
Howey, R. S. (1989) *The rise of the Marginal Utility School, 1870–1889*. New York: Columbia University Press.
Liozu, S., Boland, R., Hinterhuber, A. and Perelli, S. (2011) *Industrial pricing orientation: The organizational transformation to value-based pricing*. (June 2, 2011). First International Conference on Engaged Management Scholarship, 2011.
Marx, K. (1995) *Value, price and profit*. International Publisher (paperback edition, originally published in 1865).
Menger, C. (1873) *Principles of economics*. New York: New York University Press.
Mitchell, K. (2011) *The current state of pricing practice in U.S. firms (opening speech)*. Paper presented at the Professional Pricing Society Annual Spring Conference, Chicago, USA.
Murray, C. (2003) *Human accomplishment: The pursuit of excellence in the arts and sciences, 800 BC to 1950*. New York: HarperCollins.
Nadler, D. A. and Tushman, M. L. (1990) Beyond the charismatic leader and organizational change. *California Management Review*, Winter, pp. 77–97.
Simon, J. (2003) *A life against the grain: The autobiography of an unconventional economist*. New Brunswick, NJ: Transaction Publishers.
Skousen, M. (2008) *The making of modern economics: The lives and ideas of the great thinkers*. Armonk, NY: M. E. Sharpe, Inc.
Skousen, M. and Taylor, K. C. (1997) *Puzzles and paradoxes in economics*. Cheltenham, UK: Edward Elgar Publishing.
Slater, S. (1997) Developing a customer value-based theory of the firm. *Journal of the Academy of Marketing Science*, 25 (2), pp. 162–67.

Sowell, T. (2004) *Basic economics: A citizen's guide to the economy*. New York: Basic Books.

Tasa, K., Taggar, S. and Seijts, G. (2007) The development of collective efficacy in teams: A multilevel and longitudinal perspective. *Journal of Applied Psychology*, 92 (1), pp. 17–27.

Thompson, M. (2009) *The organizational champion: How to develop passionate change agents at every level*. New York; London: McGraw-Hill Professional.

Ulaga, W. (2001) Customer value in business markets an agenda for inquiry. *Industrial Marketing Management*, 30 (4), pp. 315–19.

6

B2B PRICING SYSTEMS

Proving ROI

Mark Stiving

Introduction

Data, data, data. Virtually every transaction today is conducted electronically. Consumer purchases are rung up on scanners. Most business-to-business (B2B) transactions involve electronic data interchange (EDI). Sales call information is stored on customer relationship management (CRM) systems. Businesses have computerized every aspect of their operations including quotes, invoices, shipments, inventory, reports and more. The quantity of this data is growing rapidly. The trouble is that the *quality* of useful information derived from it is not. That's where pricing systems offer a competitive advantage. Pricing systems turn that data into information that feeds best practices for pricing products and creating day-to-day quotes.

Although pricing systems have been around for a long time (PROS, a leading pricing system company, was founded in 1985, for example), few potential users have adopted one (Gartner 2011). This low rate of adoption is especially surprising considering the huge potential payback. Pricing system vendors provide case studies of customers increasing profitability by 5 per cent or more of revenue annually. This is $50 million per year for a $1 million company. Yet companies have been reluctant to adopt them for two basic reasons:

1. Implementing a pricing system is like any other major strategic pricing decision – it requires a massive change management effort. Pricing touches or is touched by many different departments: sales, sales operations, marketing, finance and every P&L centre. That means executive commitment is required for both resources and active support, which in turn means executives must first be convinced the investment is worth the effort.
2. Pricing systems are confusing. It is difficult to understand what a pricing system is, what it does, and how it is different from current processes. It comes down to, 'Prove it!'

In order for a pricing organization to convince management that a multi-million dollar investment in a pricing system is warranted, they must clearly articulate the return. They must explain the problem, provide examples of the increase in profitability, and then demonstrate through number crunching that the return is real. Many pricing organizations, guided by system vendors, make broad claims regarding pricing system return on investment (ROI). Although such claims are likely true, they rarely convince executives. Data and facts move executives much more quickly than vendor-backed claims of ROI.

Observations related to pricing systems

What exactly is a pricing system? Several vendors offer these software applications (see Appendix), and many firms create their own custom pricing systems using their Information Technology (IT) resources, their Enterprise Resource Planning (ERP) system and their CRM system.

Pricing systems support one or more of the following three major pricing functions: execution, analytics and/or science.

Execution

Pricing execution is the process of getting a price delivered to an end customer. Start-up companies and small enterprises have it easy. Someone asks for a price and the CEO or vice president of marketing sets the price that is then delivered by the salesperson.

As the company grows in size, in scope and in depth, so does the complexity of delivering prices. Then the trouble starts. Early on, the business is quoting enough customers that management creates guidelines and processes so that the executives don't have to be involved. As the company continues to grow, quotes come in from international locations, from multiple channel partners, from customers of all sizes and for many new products. The rules become more confusing. They conflict with each other. The people quoting prices to the customers are overwhelmed with the number of products, customers, channels and rules – mistakes appear more frequently.

Not surprisingly, this scenario is filled with profit leakages:

- Customers and channels aren't represented in a single intuitive system, and the rules don't always get followed.
- Accounting is often unable to properly invoice the customers since the systems don't easily collect all of the pertinent data points.
- The person at the quote desk doesn't have easy access to all of the quote history so will make mistakes.

Each of these leakages and many more cost the company revenue and profit. The company's typical solution? Throw some IT resources at the problem, one issue at a time. This band-aid approach grows with the company until someone makes a decision to install a proper system to replace it. This is the execution portion of a pricing system. Execution minimizes leakage by enforcing the pricing rules and making it easy for both the quote desk and accounting to successfully complete their jobs.

Besides the potential large financial return (discussed later) that comes from implementing the execution advantage of systems, this function also helps companies collect more and cleaner data that are vital to analytics.

Analytics

Imagine a product manager looking at a scatter plot, with price on the Y-axis and volume on the X-axis. The green dots are won quotes, the red ones are lost. Something looks funny in the plot between 1,000 and 10,000 volume so they zoom into that section. She or he clicks on a green dot that was below market pricing and discovers it was an unknown customer. Why would a small customer get such a great price? She or he pulls up that customer history to see what else they purchased. At the same time they look at the customer's overall pocket margin and finds it is very low. All of which means new action should be taken. Analytics makes this possible.

Analytics in pricing systems offer two significant advantages over traditional business intelligence tools like Business Objects and Cognos. First, analytics in pricing systems come with expertise. Each pricing system company calls on their industry and pricing expertise to provide ready-made charts and graphs. In addition, the systems often come with hands-on consulting and/or playbooks outlining what to look for and even what actions to take once discovered. The second major advantage is that pricing systems are much faster at analytics than business intelligence tools. This speed makes them easier to use and therefore more people are inclined to use them. They provide simpler user interfaces intended for pricing that both examine the big picture and allow drill downs to greater details. This is especially valuable when trying to determine why something happened. For example, if revenue in Singapore fell last month, what was the cause? One customer? Average sales price (ASP) decrease? Product mix?

Although analytics are useful to many actors in the firm, the quote desk and the product managers responsible for pricing will benefit most. The quote desk can quickly determine appropriate pricing for situations slightly outside of normal yet still within their authority levels. And product managers can use these tools to set more appropriate pricing guidance for the quote desk to follow.

Science

Pricing system vendors offer 'science'. They call it science to identify the process used to create hundreds or thousands of segments. 'Science' in this context really means micro-segmentation. Science is especially valuable for companies with tens of thousands of customers. The pricing system vendors gather a year or two of historical transaction/quote data and use statistical techniques like cluster analysis to group similar customers together into segments. Each segment is then broken down into quartiles based on how much each customer actually paid. For any given micro-segment it is soon apparent which customers got away with paying too little. When future customers that fit in that segment request a quote, their price will be closer to, if not above, the median price for that segment.

This simple act of knowing which micro-segment each customer belongs to more closely identifies that customer's willingness to pay. This, in turn, allows companies to win more business at the highest margins possible. Note, however, that science is not possible without reasonably clean data and an execution mechanism designed to deliver the best price to each customer.

The data elements

Pricing systems turn data into information, but that data has to be clean. The old phrase 'garbage in, garbage out' is extremely appropriate here and always represents a huge risk. Therefore, companies may focus on four types of data to achieve the cleanest results possible: Master Data Management (MDM), transaction, waterfall and competitor pricing.

For pricing systems, MDM typically refers to a clean customer master; a list of customer names and locations so every customer location is represented exactly once. Such a customer master offers three important capabilities:

- aggregate duplicate customer names
- the ability to link customers between disparate systems
- the ability to provide one or more hierarchies.

This is the foundation of a pricing system. Without knowing the customers, a pricing or quoting tool cannot correctly interpret historical data. As a quick example, a salesperson could enter a quote for I.B.M. Then the quote desk gets a quote request from a distributor from IBM. Another distributor then asks for a quote for IBM Corp. All three may be the same piece of business, but a computer thinks they are all different customers. An MDM system links these three customer interactions under a single customer name, even if sales and the quote desk are using different systems.

Once the customer master is in order, transaction data is the next most important to capture and clean. Transaction data includes quotes, purchases, point of sales reports from channel partners and even leads. There is immense information available when an opportunity can be completely tracked from lead to quote to end-customer purchase to repeat purchase. Pricing execution systems excel at managing the data from these customer interactions and making the resulting information available to product managers and quote desks.

Waterfall charts are common in pricing systems, but they require specific data that is not always captured – the cost to serve any given customer. Customers are treated differently depending on their size, their location, their industry and even the capabilities of their purchasing departments. One common example is payment terms. Different customers may negotiate different payment terms. Each different payment term has a different cost associated with it. In order for a company to truly understand its customers, know which ones are more profitable and which ones may even be unprofitable, the costs to serve each customer must be tracked. Pricing systems can provide invaluable information on customer type and profitability if this type of data is collected.

Competitor pricing data in the world of B2B is hard to come by. However, companies that truly believe in value-based pricing know that value is measured relative to their competitors' prices. Efficient and effective price maintenance means some mechanism to monitor competitor prices must be in place. Many business-to-consumer (B2C) companies use web scraping to monitor competitors' websites. Third party companies have also sprung up to collect and sell industry pricing data. Unfortunately, it is not always that simple. Some companies collect competitor pricing during the quote process, but the accuracy of the data is certainly suspect. A more reliable gauge (though not perfect) is pricing data collected from distribution channels, either directly through channel partners or by web scraping partners' websites. Yet this dataset is traditionally ignored.

Understanding, collecting and managing the appropriate data types ensures realistic ROI is achieved as well as increased profitability.

Where to find ROI

There are five ways to impact profitability (ROI): higher margin, higher win rates, increased number of opportunities, reduced costs and reduced liabilities.

Higher margin

Higher margin is where every pricing system rightfully claims to help. By providing the tools and the proof to raise prices (even a little) without affecting demand, margins can increase and profits rapidly improve. Improved margin likely drives the largest portion of ROI, but understanding where else to look can add significantly to the overall ROI case.

Increased margin due to a pricing system comes from many places. In execution, simply eliminating quoting and invoicing errors improves margin. Analytics and science enables the marketers to set better prices and possibly just as important, provide confidence to the sales force that they can win at those prices.

Higher win rates

High win rates come from winning sales opportunities that are typically lost. These are driven by price segmentation and faster quote times. Typically, lost deals can be won with lower pricing, but the company must be careful not to lower pricing on deals they would otherwise win (at higher prices). The key is knowing which opportunities should be priced lower. This is where pricing science helps. Getting this balance correct increases win rates, and that translates to increased profits (but not necessarily margins).

A second key way to increase win rates is faster response time when quoting, typically provided by the execution portion of a pricing system. Many companies focus on how long it takes to get a quote to a customer believing they want to get the business 'off the street', sometimes before their competitors can even quote.

Increased number of opportunities

Pricing systems can help companies realize more opportunities through better customer relationships. When companies price quickly, consistently and fairly with their customers and channel partners it is very likely that these customers and partners will rely on them more often. This increases the number of opportunities the company sees.

As pricing becomes more automated and the data analysis becomes easier it will require fewer resources to accurately quote. Similarly, pricing systems often simplify the process of accurately invoicing customers the correct price, eliminating the need for manual reconciliation.

Cost reductions

Not only can the company reduce costs through reallocating resources, pricing systems typically make the remaining employees more satisfied since they are contributing more with the proper tools. The increased profitability from these reduced costs is typically small compared to the profit growth when growing margin or revenue with a pricing system. However, some companies overvalue cost savings and undervalue revenue growth when making large investment decisions. The cost element shouldn't be ignored.

Reduction of liability

Finally, pricing systems can reduce liability. Companies enter into contracts with customers and channel partners, sometimes with clauses on pricing. These clauses are frequently yet unintentionally violated, creating potentially huge liabilities. One common example is a Most Favoured Nation (MFN) clause, which guarantees a specific customer a price for a specific part that is less than or equal to the price to any other customer. Without a systematic method of tracking, these clauses are challenging to comply with.

Proving ROI

Companies that offer pricing systems commonly claim a return of 1–5 per cent of revenue in additional profit. They base their claims on results from previous installations. Unfortunately, few executives are willing to commit millions of dollars based solely on vendor claimed case histories.

Thus the first step of successfully proving ROI is to find specific examples where the pricing system can anecdotally and numerically demonstrate one of the five areas of return cited above. These examples typically come from interviewing the people involved in pricing, quoting and sales. Questions revolve around what is wrong with current pricing processes and how it affects the company. These interviews will bring many examples and areas for improvement to light.

The next step is to select several areas for improvement where a pricing system can both address the problems at hand and offer a very high potential return. In each of these areas a few anecdotal stories will help explain the issue, but quantitative analysis determining realistic ROI must also be performed. This often requires manual work, looking at transactions for specific behaviours.

As an example, here is one way to quantify the liability of a MFN clause. Start by collecting all contracts that have MFN clauses. List all of the products covered by that clause. Then find the price at which each customer purchases. The lowest of these prices can be called the MFN price. Then search all sales and quote history for transactions and/or quotes with prices lower than the MFN price. Finally, add up the financial impact of lowering the prices to the companies with the MFN clause to meet the lowest prices for the parts. This is a solid estimate of the liability for one specific area that can be reduced through a pricing system.

A detailed and quantitative estimate of return should be done in every area where a pricing system could potentially yield a substantial return. The total return from all of these areas is the numerator in the ROI analysis. Most of these areas are annual returns, making the results even more significant.

Although this process seems daunting, it is critical to acquiring executive commitment to such a large and all-encompassing system. Yet, the pricing system vendors are able and usually willing to help. They have the experience to help. They all have case studies that can be used as examples or guidance. Many will analyse potential customers' transactional data, look for areas of return, and provide estimates of the value of fixing the profit leaks. There is still a lot of work for the customer, collecting and cleaning data, but the expertise of the system vendors can prove valuable.

Conclusions

Implementing a pricing system requires executive level buy-in and commitment, which does not come easily. Before committing, the executive must understand what a pricing system is and then believe it is the best place to invest the available resources. Pricing professionals need to be well prepared in three areas:

1. A clear explanation of what it is. Pricing systems can be confusing. It is imperative that the pricing professional understand and be able to explain the functional areas of execution, analytics and science. Each function solves a different set of pricing problems. Also, pricing systems are always driven by data. The pricing team must clearly articulate the issues with the data both before and after the implementation of a pricing system.
2. Anecdotes of problems that will be fixed. Before and after stories are effective at describing the value that can be achieved through a pricing system. Anecdotes are required for each area where a hard ROI estimate will be presented, but

this is also the best opportunity to present important areas that are harder to put numbers to. For example, a critical element and advantage of a pricing system is the management of complexity in pricing and the overall business. Hard to capture in numbers, but an example or two could prove useful.
3. A hard estimate of ROI based on historical data. This is the challenging work of listing all of the problems solved, prioritizing them based on a rough estimate of a return, and then gathering and analysing a sample of the necessary data. Although the focus will mostly be on increased margin, there are several other potential ways for a pricing system to put additional profit on the bottom line: higher win rates, more opportunities, lower costs and reduced liabilities.

Implications for the pricing field

Pricing is one of the most fascinating topics because it requires knowledge of almost every aspect of business. Every customer touch point either creates or destroys value; pricing captures it. Product development, done well, creates more value for pricing to capture. Well-executed marketing creates perceived value, which pricing can capture. Pricing touches all of the business, so effective pricing professionals must be conversant and trusted in every one of these areas.

Convincing corporate executives to invest in a pricing system adds even more complexity to the pricing team's role. Without knowledge of how executives think, or experience proposing huge projects, pricing professionals frequently struggle.

Our experience shows that convincing companies and their top executive to invest in pricing systems is not an easy task. Many attempts to convince them succeeded while others failed despite strong relationships and experience with pricing system vendors. Here are a summary of relevant observations:

- Most business people do not understand what a pricing system is and what it can do. Many pricing professionals are in the same boat as well.
- Many pricing professionals think 'getting a pricing system' solves their problems, but they have not taken the time to figure out what those problems are or how a pricing system actually solves them.
- Pricing professionals often submit ROI numbers that are too small thinking it's easy to justify them. A return of 5 to 10 times the investment is needed to get attention.

Our contribution to the field of pricing is to demonstrate that pricing systems do solve real problems. They can have phenomenal ROI and give companies the abilities to execute leading edge pricing strategies. But pricing professionals must realize they have to sell this concept. Executives do not invest millions of dollars to solve a few problems. They invest millions of dollars on things they understand and that they believe will earn many more millions of dollars than they invest.

Appendix

Pricing vendors covered in the Gartner (July 2011) report:

Model N
Navetti
Oracle
PROS
Servigistics
SignalDemand
Vendavo
Vistaar Technologies
Zilliant

References

Gartner (2011) *MarketScope for price optimization and management software for B2B.* July 29, 2011.

PART III
Innovation in pricing strategy

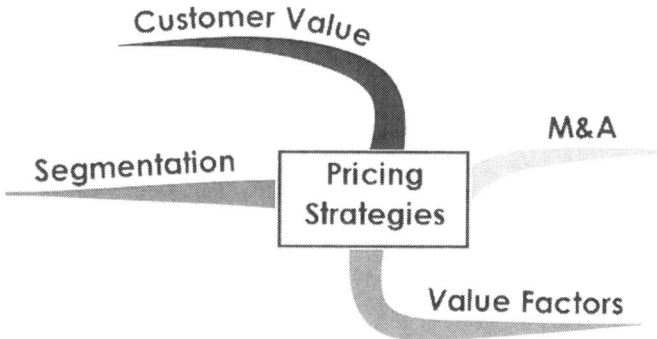

7
INNOVATION IN B2B PRICING

Rafael Farrés

Alternative pricing methods in business-to-business (B2B)

Pricing has gained much importance in recent years. Now that companies have exploited all other possible ways to improve the bottom line, pricing is widely seen as the biggest lever for profitability.

Companies must build up not only knowledge and experience in pricing but also an infrastructure around it. A common pricing language, effective pricing metrics and supportive IT systems are key elements in this infrastructure. What is not measured cannot be controlled. Managing pricing requires a gradual replacement of subjective interpretations with analyses of hard data. Pricing requires a dedicated approach. Many pricing initiatives start with the first available information without questioning whether it is appropriate for pricing. I analyse this in the next sections.

Pricing segmentation

Market segments are often defined to suit the purposes of marketing. Customers can be segmented by business profile, product or technological requirements, or other criteria. This helps to define what products are appropriate for the segment and the appropriate go-to-market strategy. But these segmentation criteria do not always coincide with the pricing requirements. Customers may be interested in the same products but be prepared to pay for them in different ways. A pricing segment can be defined around a group of customers that will be sensitive to a full bundled price offer, while others prefer to buy individual components. Some will prefer on-time delivery, expecting the supplier to hold the inventory, while others will prefer to place orders in advance with a scheduled delivery. Price segmentation needs to identify these differences. This means that irrespective of the already existing marketing segmentation, a dedicated price segmentation may be needed.

Capturing the full value from a price segment is not easy. Specific customer offerings must be designed. These differentiated offers need to consider the cost of these additional services versus the price the customer is prepared to pay.

Strategy around pricing

Companies tend to be simplistic in their pricing strategies, or to have no strategy at all. Often the question is limited to 'Should we go for volume or price?' But the answer to this simple question cannot in itself define the strategy. Companies today tend to be more complex, and are confronted with rapidly changing business environments as well as multiple product offerings. Customers perceive value in different ways, and products can be at different stages of their life cycle. A pricing strategy should include all these different dimensions in order to capture all the value potential.

There has been recently much hype around so-called value pricing, to the point that one may think that, if value pricing seeks to capture the maximum value from a product, this strategy should be applied in all circumstances. But is this advisable, and is it even possible? Let's analyse this in more detail.

In normal business situations, companies are confronted with existing product portfolios (some may not be ideal), existing investments that must be amortized, ongoing R&D projects to which much effort has already been deployed, and often a limited budget. These define the business constraints. The challenge is to obtain the maximum value from the situation in which the company exists. This means that it will be necessary to extract the maximum value from products that are not necessarily better than the competitors', or from the existing investments, because those required to bring the product offer to the desired level are not affordable. In some cases, it may be necessary to maximize sales of a product to achieve a critical volume in order to maintain a certain investment. In general, companies are confronted with business restrictions related to budget availability or business-intrinsic limitations which render following the desired roadmap impossible.

In my view, it is better to take a realistic approach to pricing, considering the real situation of the different products and markets to define an appropriate strategy. A realistic approach will always lead to a more effective strategy.

Let's look in some detail at the three different pricing strategies that can be applied.

Value-based pricing

If a product, in a given market, has the potential to provide a specific value to its customers, in comparison to the other available products, then the price can be defined around this value instead of the product cost. This is what we call value pricing. In a value-pricing approach, the price of something is based not on a markup on its cost, or on a competitor's price, but on the value it provides.

In this situation, a good evaluation of the product's value is critical to defining its price. Applying value pricing may imply identifying advantages for the product's customers, which are not visible at first glance. Conjoint analysis and total cost of ownership (TCO) are techniques that can help us determine the value that the product provides to its customers. Then, with this information, we can set the price around this value.

But let's not forget the obvious. It may be that the perceived value of a product is close to its cost or even lower. What to do then? Value pricing is interesting when the perceived value of something is greater that the market price of its cost. Where this is not the case, value pricing cannot be applied.

Value pricing must take many things into consideration. Are there features that can be added to a product to provide specific advantages versus the competitors'? Can the product be bundled with others to offer an advantage? The costs of constructing this advantage should be considered as well.

If the analysis shows that the product offers a significant advantage above the market price, the sales price can be set around this value. This will give the company an additional margin, and the customer will remain satisfied because they will benefit from these advantages. We will elaborate further on the value-pricing implementation with a special focus on B2B companies.

If after the analysis a differential advantage cannot be built at an affordable cost, it is better to follow a different pricing strategy.

Market-based pricing

There are many situations in which market pricing cannot be ignored. Following a value-based price strategy when there are no differential values can be very ineffective. Trying to set the price around a nonexistent product value will shift focus from the important parameter in this case, which is the market price.

In market-based pricing it is important to differentiate between the perceived market price and the real market price. This perceived market price, especially in B2B, where prices are less transparent, tends to be lower than the real market price. The reason for this is the following.

In B2B, pricing is defined between two companies, where a price is agreed on between the supplier and the customer against certain conditions. These may include specific delivery, service and payment conditions. In B2B, prices are not visible like they are in retail shops. The price agreement between these two companies may include a multiplicity of terms. It will often start from a list price, going down to a net, net–net, and often triple-net price after all discounts and conditions are applied. Therefore, comparing competitors' prices implies a good understanding of these trading conditions, which are normally not visible.

Smart purchasing managers will try to make suppliers think that they have a very good competitor's price in order to force them to come back with more attractive prices. In addition, sales executives receive biased information on competitor price levels: They receive immediate feedback when their own prices are lower than competitor prices, but far less feedback on instances where competitive price levels are higher. All these combinations imply that the perceived market price is lower than the real market price. If B2B companies could sell at the real rather than the perceived market price, they could enjoy a nice price differential.

Thus, a market-price intelligence process to identify this real market price is a key element in a market-based pricing strategy. But measuring market price is not easy and requires, among other things, a systematic analysis of contracts gained and lost. The conditions in which companies gain or lose contracts and in which competitors' conditions are confronted can provide a good overview of the true market price. Many companies forget this and leave a lot of value on the table by following the perceived market price.

But market-based pricing also has its limitations. When a market price is not high enough to cover the costs, companies must find another limit to define how far to go without destroying value. This brings us to the next pricing strategy.

Cost-plus pricing

This is also not a simple topic. Pricing based on cost may look simple, but it is not, and if there is no other option than to pursue a cost-plus model, it is important to do it effectively.

Pricing based on cost instead of on value or market price may be required in certain circumstances, such as when there is a lot of excess capacity in the market and competitors have difficulty removing this capacity or transforming it to produce other products. Competitors may fight to be the last one standing in a given technology, trying to force others to close available capacity. In these situations companies may be competing with prices that are close to cost, or even below it.

To manage cost-plus pricing requires strong price controlling to ensure that price agreements strictly follow the price policy defined, and that all additional costs to serve are effectively monitored so that any deviations from the strict agreement can be charged for separately.

But the main difficulty with the cost-plus model is the measuring of the cost itself. The cost of a product is not a fixed number and is influenced by many factors, ranging from achievable volume to sales conditions.

The volume achieved has an important effect on a product's costs. The amount of fixed costs that can be absorbed in manufacturing depends on the volume produced. If a production line works at full capacity, fixed costs per unit produced will be much lower than when the line works at only 50 per cent. This means that a straight cost line cannot be defined. The cost-plus model requires a sound cost analysis that takes into consideration all these elements. A good overview of the full costs per different volumes and the incremental costs can truly define the price limits.

This notion of incremental costs is important. By incremental costs, we mean the sum of all variable costs, excluding fixed costs. This corresponds to the costs of incremental production. To understand this better, consider a given product line with excess capacity of 70 per cent and calculate the cost to produce something more, but always below full capacity, for example, at 10 per cent, because exceeding that capacity will require new investments, adding a new element to the costs. In the case we were describing, fixed costs and amortization are already covered at the current production level, and only extra variable costs such as raw materials, incremental energy, and, eventually, increased labour will be needed. Whatever can be gained on top of this cost will contribute to covering part of the fixed costs. This defines the minimum price. If prices are set below this level, value is effectively being destroyed, because the price does not cover the incremental cost of this extra production. These incremental costs define a true price floor. It is important to know this floor thoroughly before applying a cost-plus strategy.

Another element to consider is that cost-plus models require strict debundling. If prices are defined at the cost limits, the additional services that are provided need to be charged for as well. Shipping conditions, payment conditions and built-in services, need to be either added to the incremental cost as cost to serve and included in the selling price, or given to the customer as an option and charged for separately if the customer demands them. In cost-plus pricing this extra cost does not create a perceived value that allows for the setting of a high price. Pricing is defined at the limits of profitability, and these variables should be known and controlled in full detail.

In practice, companies must set prices in a variety of products and markets. The solution is not to apply value pricing wherever possible but to have a well-formulated pricing strategy that considers the situation of each product in its market and to apply that strategy effectively. This means that there will be areas (product–market combinations) where value pricing can be applied, and others in which the strategy will be market-based or cost-plus pricing.

Whether pricing is based on value, the market or cost plus, it is much more effective to choose the most appropriate method and to apply it strictly. It will be highly ineffective to apply cost plus in a situation where value pricing applies, because much value will be left on the table. But it is also inefficient to look for value pricing in a situation where it is not applicable rather than to formulate and follow up with a cost-plus model where it applies.

The real nature of B2B business

B2B companies do business between themselves. We must see these companies as part of a complex value chain. A B2B product is not a finished product in itself but the means to make one that reaches the consumer. For example, a company producing and selling perfume will buy from many B2B companies the different components needed, such as chemicals, bottles, packaging, advertising material, marketing services, legal services and so on. The company buying the bottles will also buy products and raw materials from others. This means that in B2B, a product or service provided to another company is an element in a value chain. As part of this value chain, a product or service will be part of the product cost of this company, either as an operating or capital expense. This is, in my view, the essential difference between B2B and business-to-consumer (B2C) companies.

When a consumer buys a product, the motives influencing this decision are mainly his or her own preference, and the way that the individual consumer views the price–value relationship. The appearance of the product and the reputation of the brand, for example, play an important role in the value perception. We can see this in many areas. In the food industry, for example, products should not only taste good but also look tasty. Clothing or perfume purchases are driven by the consumer's feelings about them. Consumers' buying motives may be very different, but, with some exceptions, will not be driven by complex seller–buyer negotiations involving return on investment (ROI) calculations and the like.

In the case of B2B companies, since purchasing a product will affect the P&L of the buying company, the selling price will be influenced by this effect. Therefore, the proposed price will be challenged by different people in the buyer organization. These people, normally from different departments, will have differing views about the product. Not only will the purchasing department have to be convinced by the seller, but also the departments using it will be consulted and involved in this decision. This introduces a different element into B2B: the price negotiation.

How B2B companies perceive value

In this environment, perceived value cannot be measured by the customer in the same way it is measured in B2C. As indicated above, in B2B, the value is perceived not by an individual but by a company. This means that the perceived value will be a combination of the values perceived by a group of people. In addition, B2B companies will try to translate this perceived value into monetary terms. Since the product represents a cost to the company, customers will try to evaluate it in terms of savings potential, the extra margin generated, or the ROI. In B2B, this needs to be considered when defining product values. The ROI and/or the TCO that the product provides to the buyer's P&L is an important and highly tangible measure of the product's value that cannot be ignored. The risk is that if the supplier does not consider these calculations, the customer will perform them.

This does not mean that subjective value perception does not count in B2B. Brand value, as an example, is important. Brand value and previous experience with the company will result in a lower risk perception and higher security. How much value can be attributed to this is difficult to calculate, and must be considered, but the former objective elements such as ROI or TCO also cannot be ignored.

On the other hand, measuring the impact of a product in the full value chain can unveil unexpected value, which can allow the product price to be set at a premium. This price could be even higher than the initial perceived value of the product. In this case, this value cannot be missed. If the analysis shows that a product adds value to the customer's value chain, one can establish a price differential around it.

The ROI and TCO that a product provides can also be different from one customer to the next. This introduces another element: market segmentation. How value chains vary within different customer segments is an element that a company needs to take into account in order to set prices effectively.

BOX 7.1 IDENTIFYING VALUE IN B2B: CASE STUDY

Let's take the example of a company that launched a new product free of chemicals. This is a product that customers can use without any type of chemicals. At first glance, the perceived advantage was the reduction in chemical costs for the company using the product. The product could be sold easily at a premium price by increasing the price just below these costs.

Continued

Extensive testing and customer focus-group meetings revealed that this was not the only advantage. By not using chemicals in the process, customers saved additional money associated with the recycling and disposal costs of the chemicals. These costs involved the amortization of the recycling units, the labour involved, and fees to external companies to take care of the disposal of the residual chemicals. But this was not the only saving. By not using chemicals, the production process was more stable because one of the production variables was eliminated. Customers could reduce start-up times, as well as the cost of the materials used in the start-up process. Service maintenance costs could also be reduced.

The result was that the value that the new process provided was much greater than just the cost of the chemicals. A strict analysis of these elements made it possible to quantify each one. They included chemicals consumption, recycling cost, recycling units amortization, disposal fees, reduced start-up costs, reduced maintenance and increased productivity.

Each of these elements had an impact on company performance, whether product costs, capital expenditures or increased output. This gave this company a very good basis for defining a premium price, and a solid sales argument to support the sales actions to increase the market penetration with this product.

This example also illustrates excellently the pricing segmentation mentioned above. Not all customers used the same process, meaning that the value of the different elements varied from one customer to the next. These different processes were linked to a special application. Therefore, the customers could be segmented based on this concept, which made it possible to differentiate pricing between these segments. In addition, recycling costs are linked to environmental regulations, which vary from country to country. This introduced another element to consider in the value that the product offers.

The fact that the product value measured in this way will vary by segment or application or country does not mean that the price should be differentiated in the same way. It is not possible to introduce certain price differentials if customers find out that the same product can be bought somewhere else on more favourable terms. But segmentation provides a good basis for defining a price premium, introducing a level of differentiation per segment or country, and being able to exploit all the value potential.

Pricing analysis, metrics and key performance indicators (KPIs)

The pricing building requires a solid foundation. This is the only way any of the pricing strategies can work and deliver results. Let's look at the different elements of this foundation in more detail.

The language

One of the first elements in this foundation is the pricing language. This should include the pricing terms used, and clear definitions of all of them. Companies involving multiple departments and countries will find different price terms in use. These different terms may have the same meanings; conversely, different meanings may be associated with the same term. This may result from local terms wrongly translated from other languages, or from misinterpretation of terms used by different departments. It is important to identify these pricing terms and to redefine them in order to create a harmonized language in the company. The new pricing language needs to be defined and the terms well described and communicated internally to avoid confusion. This new language will be fundamental to internal communication and to understanding the new pricing metrics required.

Pricing metrics

Price must be measured. To do so, several KPIs must be defined as part of the pricing language. These pricing metrics are another key element in the pricing foundation. Once the language is in place, one must formulate how to measure pricing. In reality there are many ways to measure pricing, and each will have its own interpretation, so it is also important to define one's internal price-metrics conventions and pricing KPIs.

Many companies do not measure price effectively because they take the first available pricing data rather than the data that the organization, especially sales, has the capacity to understand and influence. Specifically, most IT systems have been designed around stock keeping units (SKUs), to support logistics and accounting purposes. So it is very easy for most IT systems to provide a price per SKU. This provides easy and immediate price information that companies can use from day one. But they must also consider whether this is the best information with which to measure price – in other words whether this pricing corresponds to what is used in price negotiations, and whether this is the way that sales departments and customers understand pricing.

As indicated above, SKUs are normally defined based on logistics criteria, as they must serve this purpose. But this may not necessarily coincide with pricing requirements. Customers may or may not recognize a price per SKU, but may instead use litres, kilograms, metres squared or some other unit of measure. If this is the case, the systems must be redesigned to reflect this market metric. In other cases, customers are offered bundles of SKUs. Again, if this is the case, the IT systems should capture this element, and measure the price of these bundles rather than individual SKUs. The conclusion is that price needs to be measured as it is going to be used in the market rather than as it is used in internal processes.

But this is not the only complexity to address. Price is the result of product turnover divided by volume. So far, this is a simple definition, but the issue in measuring price is how these two denominators are defined.

Turnover is the result of the value we invoice, taking into consideration credit notes, rebate provisions and the like. In addition to the price conditions agreed upon with the customer, *ad hoc* discounts or further given conditions that may reduce the agreed-upon price must be analysed. Here we are confronted with different turnover values: the turnover from the invoice, the turnover that we see after all other non-invoice conditions are applied, and the final turnover we obtain. What is the turnover that we want to analyse in order to calculate the price? In our view it is interesting to be able to analyse all of them and to be able to differentiate the turnover resulting from the agreed-upon terms versus the final turnover after the one-off effects are eliminated. These two values are important because the difference indicates how much our final price deviates from the one that was agreed upon.

The *turnover per product* corresponds to the previous definition applied to a given product, but the issue now is how a product is defined, either as SKU, product or product category. If a group of SKUs are priced based on the same criterion, such as a unit of measurement, then this is the price we need rather than the price per SKU. In the same way, SKUs may be grouped to form a package or a bundle, and in this case the price we are interested in is the price of this selling unit. The conclusion is that we cannot always take the first price we get but must take the price around the sales units that are recognized in the negotiations with customers.

Volume is another of the key denominators in the price calculation. Similar to what we have defined above, we need to consider the unit we use to measure volume, whether it is number of units, kilograms or any other unit of measurement. Whatever measurement we take, it should be aligned with the language used in sales, because the objective is to obtain price information that can be understood by those in the organization who can act on it, and these are mainly the sales departments.

Once all these variables are defined, we will obtain a pricing that the organization can recognize. With this we can establish the pricing KPIs and analyse price variations.

The price waterfall

The price waterfall is a good way to make visible the different price levels, from the list price to the final net price.

If we combine the different price points obtained by dividing the different turnovers by the volume, we can obtain a price waterfall that clearly illustrates our pricing structure (see Figure 7.1). A price waterfall shows how pricing goes from the initial list price to the final net price after all discounts and special terms given to customers are applied.

Visualizing the different discounts that contribute to the final price can help us understand when these are given in excess, and define policies that can reduce them to improve pricing.

The price waterfall is also a good way to illustrate the price language. Pricing tends to use a terminology based on common knowledge, but often these are not

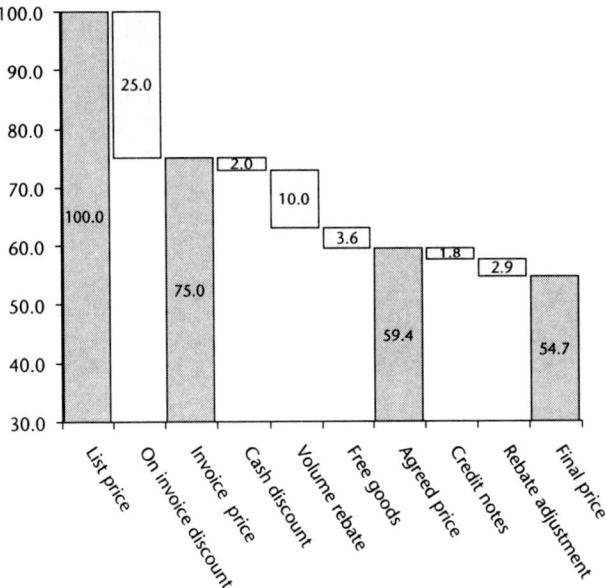

FIGURE 7.1 The price waterfall

understood in the same way by everyone, as we have already shown. The pricing department needs to obtain consensus and define a price terminology with clear definitions of the terms used.

Different price levels

Everybody understands the concept of *list price*, but the term *net price* can be unclear. One could argue that a cash discount triggers a lower financial cost, and therefore should not be included in the net price. Others will argue that this discount often exceeds in value the financial gain, and therefore it should be included. In addition, financial costs change over time. In our view, the net price should be calculated after all discounts, regardless of the reason of these discounts. This makes things easy and more transparent. The cost decreases related to price agreements can be measured and compared with the price as well. But whatever position one takes, the key message is that this needs to be defined and agreed on upfront. However, there are many other debatable elements in the net price, such as special credit notes, complaint-related concessions and so on. All of these render the meaning of *net price* unclear, and this is precisely the term that must be well defined. For this reason, we introduce the concept of three net-price levels.

Net1 price or invoice price

This is the price after all discounts have been applied, and that is visible on the invoice.

Net2 price or agreed-upon price

This is the price after applying all agreed-upon customer terms, including non-invoice concessions such as volume rebates or promised free goods to be delivered at the end of a given period or any other agreed-upon condition, such as advertising, training support or any other agreed-upon concession. The key is that this price reflects all agreed-upon conditions of any nature.

Net3 price or the final net price

This is the price after applying all agreed-upon conditions plus any *ad hoc* concessions that may be given such as credit notes or those similar to the ones mentioned above but that were not part of the initial price agreement. This is the final price from which the net turnover is built.

These definitions help to introduce different measurements, such as the deviation between the net price and the agreed-upon price. The formula (Net2 − Net3) × Vol gives us an idea of the value differential between the final price and the price agreed upon with a customer. This is a good calculation for determining whether the pricing problem arises from poor price agreements or from a lack of enforcement of negotiated prices. We elaborate on this further in the next section.

Pricing targets and KPIs

As in any other areas of the business, pricing, too, requires targets. Therefore, it is important to introduce, as part of the pricing language, the terms *target price* and *price floor*. These are both important terms. The use of the term TMP (target market price) can be very effective. This term refers to a price estimate made by a marketing department, and should reflect the marketing view of the price that is achievable in the market. This price can be different by region or country, depending on the market conditions. A TMP should be also a dynamic price, in the same way that market conditions change. It is important that marketing departments define a methodology for calculating and updating TMPs using measurements that are as objective as possible. We indicated above the need to determine the pricing strategy, whether value-based, market-based, or cost-plus pricing. A TMP defined by marketing can result from a conjoint analysis or a TCO calculation, if a value-pricing strategy has been chosen for this product. A TMP can be an estimate of the competitors' price following a price-intelligence process, or a cost-plus calculation if one of these is to be the strategy. The deviation of our final pricing from TMP can be analysed and discussed to define the corrective measures.

Price floors are also important. Price floors are typically a level below the TMP. A price floor is defined as the level at which management wants to be informed so that the prices are formally approved. This helps the VP of sales in particular to focus on the large negotiations with critical pricing issues. Like TMPs, pricing floors need to be dynamic as the market conditions change, so as not to overload management with requests for price exceptions. Management can use this to set an example of how to analyse and decide on critical price negotiations and to establish a model for price decisions through the whole organization. Price floors can be defined at different management levels if needed.

Integrating price into the organization

Once price foundations are in place, the different departments in a company can be involved in pricing actions. This is very important, because price improvement is the result not of the actions of a single department, such as sales, but of a collective action. Sales are at the front end of pricing, but they require support and guidance to achieve optimal prices.

Many companies have started pricing actions by appointing a pricing manager and creating a price department, but the first question that comes to a manager's mind is the following: Where should we put the pricing department? Or, in other words, to whom should the pricing manager report?

The role of the pricing manager

A pricing manager should have the capacity to involve all the different departments, often breaking company silos, and make them work together. The personality of the manager and the level of support he or she receives will be the key success factors. Strong hierarchical companies typically will have more trouble working this way, unless the pricing manager has a high hierarchical status. Companies that are more used to working on projects, and that have lower hierarchical barriers, will have less trouble implementing more sophisticated pricing actions, even if the pricing manager is not at VP level. Starting a pricing action as a project, with a project team guided by the different VPs involved, can help break down these barriers, because the pricing person will have sufficient authority and support to be accepted at all the levels required. In the end, when all initial measures have been taken and the entire infrastructure is in place, marketing is the ideal department for pricing because it is already at an intermediate point between sales and the other departments of the company.

The link to new product development is also important. Pricing has to do with the way a product is presented to the customer, and this involves all areas of the organization. Reaching pricing excellence requires combining the way the product is designed, its features and how they should be presented, delivered and invoiced for. Understanding the complexity of all the different business processes and being able to create new products or new ways of presenting them will be key to the pricing manager's success. This is not easy and will require not only support but also a good learning process. The pricing manager should be able to understand the additional cost of his or her requirements and balance them with the estimated price advantage. It is for this reason that we emphasize the need for a good translation of price to value in the way it has been explained above. This is very important, because it will help in these discussions where, inevitably, every department will consider the additional costs of changing a product or process.

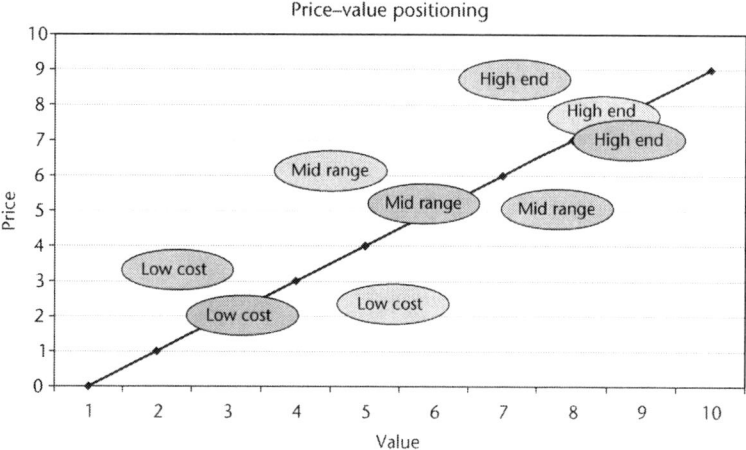

FIGURE 7.2 The price–value map

Price decision support: selecting appropriate pricing tools

A number of pricing tools are available, and companies can be overwhelmed by the number of software offerings, losing track of the critical question: What information does one need to make effective pricing decisions? Let us look at some of them and try to select the most important tools and how they can be used.

Defining pricing at launch: price–value graphs

When a product is launched, it should be positioned on a price–value graph that illustrates its intrinsic values and a clear comparison with its competitors' equivalents (Figure 7.2).

Price–value graphs position the prices of a company's products against its competitors' equivalents. The above example depicts three competitors as ovals with three different product types. The lowest group of ovals cover the low-cost area; the middle group, the middle-cost area; and the highest, the high-performance segments. Price is indicated along the y-axis, and the x-axis represents the value of the product. A product may have a different value for different segments of customers; in this case it is advisable to select the value delivered to the most important customer segment. If a product is above the solid black line, its price is too high compared with its competitors' equivalents. Additional values not considered in the graph can be subject to discussion. If the products fall below the line, the immediate conclusion is that their price is too low and may need to be reviewed.

Deciding on price–volume trade: turnover build-up

The first KPI to get a quick overview of pricing is the turnover build-up (Figure 7.3). Using the price value as described above can provide an overview of how turnover has changed from a given reference, such as the previous year or a defined target, to the actual results.

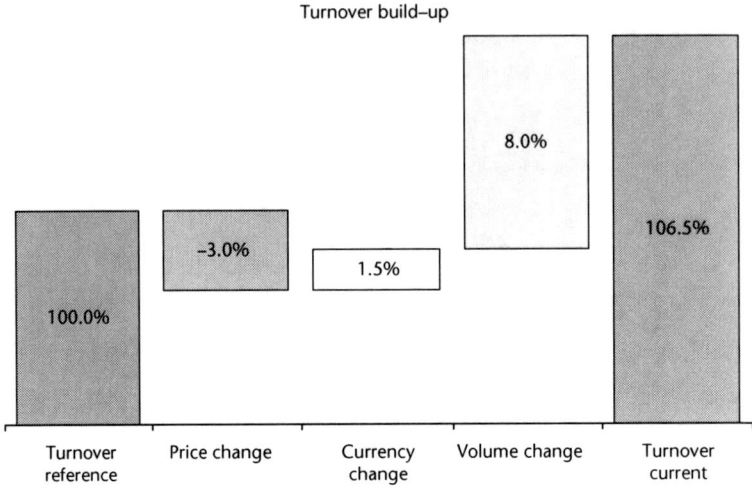

FIGURE 7.3 Turnover build–up

In the above example, a turnover increase of 6.5 per cent is the result of a price decrease of 3 per cent in value, a 1.5 per cent currency gain, and an 8 per cent gain in volume. Depending on the average margin, one can easily determine whether the volume increase has been high enough to compensate for the decrease in price. In the example, if the average gross margin is below 37.5 per cent, the price decrease is not compensated for by the margin generated by the new sales.

The percentages indicated in the graph can also be shown in terms of absolute value. This KPI is very visible, and it provides a quick overview of price-change impact.

Enforce price discipline

Figure 7.4 below shows with every dot a product's price position with respect to the volume purchased during the period. If we add to it the pricing targets and cost of goods sold (COGS) lines, the outliers can be easily identified. This provides an immediate overview of the customers that deviate from the pricing policy, so that a company can decide to correct these prices or modify the policy.

Customers with prices below cost, the COGS line in the example, should be the first to look at. But customers below the price floor, the Floor line in the example, require attention as well.

Correct leaks in the pocket price: price waterfall

Once the target customers have been identified, the price waterfall is a good way to understand the details of the price agreements, how a new price proposal can be defined, which conditions can be challenged, and how a new price proposal to correct the situation can be defined.

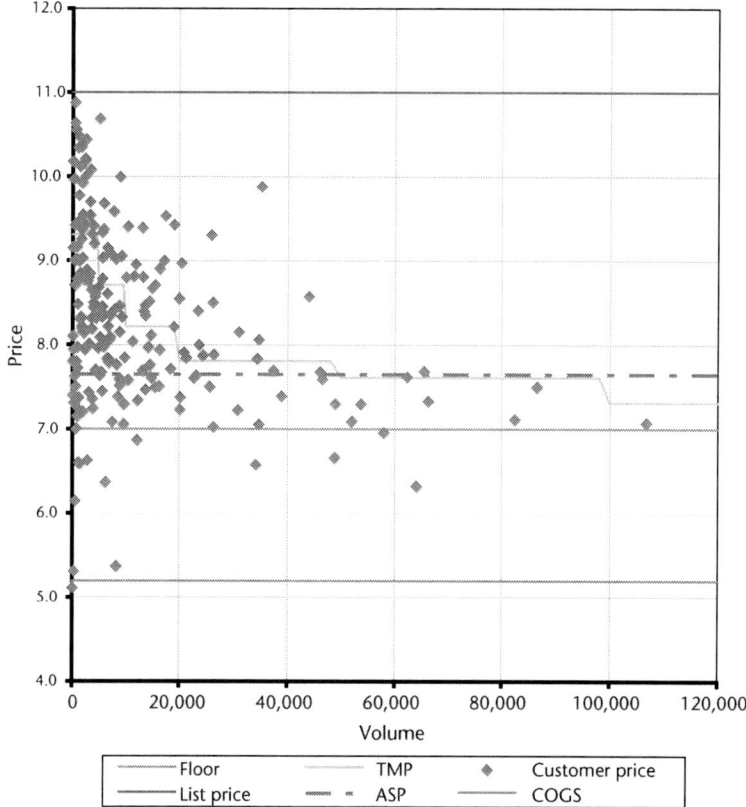

FIGURE 7.4 Price floors, list prices and target prices

The first element to understand through the waterfall is whether the pricing problem is related to the price agreement for the final price. If the low price is driven not by the price agreements but by offline concessions, these may need to be reviewed, and programmes established to enforce the agreement. If the agreement already delivers a low price, it will be necessary to review the agreement itself. The waterfall is a good way to identify these elements and correct them.

Document the price agreements: the terms and conditions (T&C) tool

Documenting price agreements in a structured way is good practice. The T&C tool provides a template for documenting the complete price agreement for a given customer (Figure 7.5). It should include all possible discounts and rebates for each product. Pricing thresholds should be included in the tool to show whether the price proposal is above or below the target price and the floor. Different colour scales can be used to indicate (a) that the price is above the target price, (b) that the price is below the target price but above the floor price and (c) that the price is below the floor price. This facilitates following up on the price-approval process.

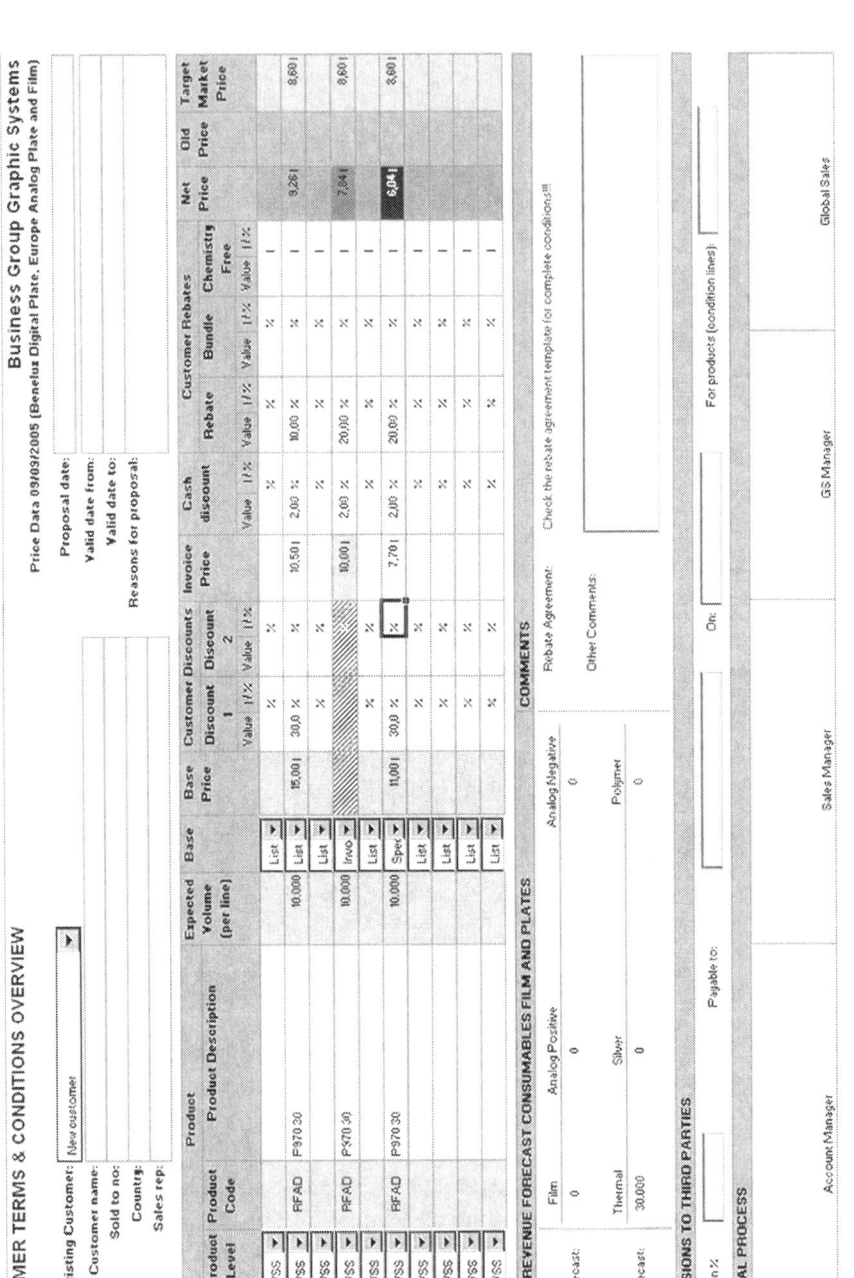

FIGURE 7.5 The terms and conditions (T&C) tool

Adding the volume estimates to the T&C tool permits one to quantify the price change versus the target prices or the previously agreed-upon prices, using the price–value formulas indicated above. This provides very valuable information for making pricing decisions. A section for comments allows further explanation for any elements not covered by the numbers.

Keeping track of these templates also makes it easy to review issues related to price deviations. It also permits good documentation of lost deals, when the proposed prices are not accepted by the customer.

Pricing explorer

All these tools can be combined in a master tool to analyse customer profitability from the price agreement to the price finally realized, volumes purchased, price and volume evolutions per period, and the price waterfall (Figure 7.6).

Pricing clouds can also be included for every sales region so that the price distribution per region can be analysed in detail.

The main objective of these tools is to provide the information necessary to make effective pricing decisions. Because there can be a lot of information available it is important to select and visualize critical data that will facilitate the decision-making process.

There are many other KPIs and variables that could not be considered in this chapter. However, we have provided a number of elements that must be considered and that should provide a good basis on which to start looking at pricing in a professional way. Price improvement is a long journey, and companies need to build up experience and know-how around it. This can only be accomplished by building up knowledge and experience inside the company. Companies are very different and face many different situations in the market. In the same way, pricing actions will have to be company-specific.

Implications for innovation in pricing

In the first section, I analysed three different pricing strategies: cost-plus pricing, market-based price and value-based pricing. It would be wrong to link innovation to value-based pricing only: there is much innovation potential in cost-plus and market-based pricing as well. In a cost-plus model, for example, by analysing in detail the product cost structure and its dependencies, suppliers can see which of these costs are influenced by customer behaviour. This can help companies define specific price models in order to obtain a reasonable price level while reducing unnecessary costs. It is by looking at supplier–customer processes as an integrated whole that one can identify inefficiencies and propose creative pricing solutions.

A company tends to look at its own universe, understanding it in terms of itself and its customers, but this is not enough. Its vision must reach beyond this. A B2B company is part of a complex value chain in which several companies cooperate to produce a product.

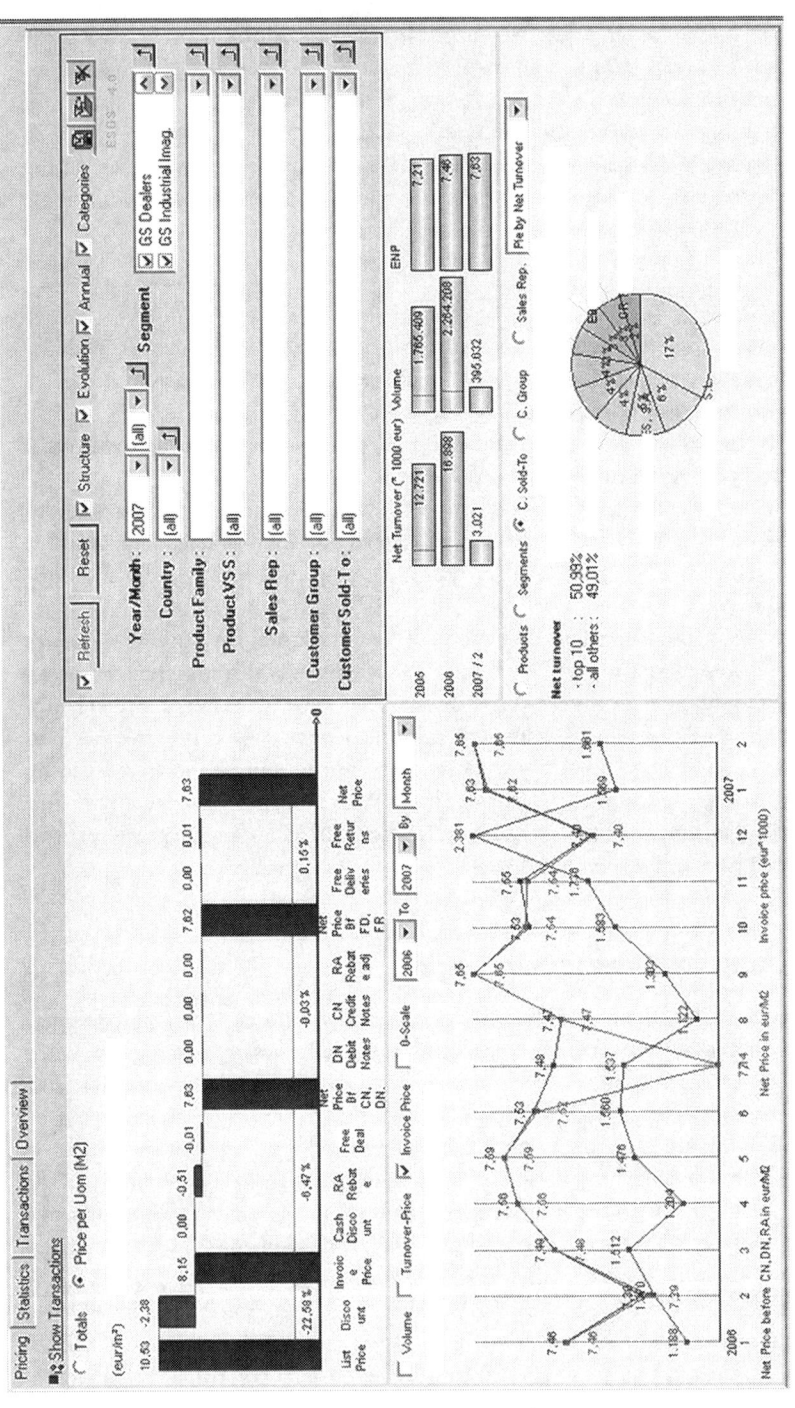

FIGURE 7.6 The pricing explorer

Innovation in B2B pricing **149**

The value chain involves our suppliers, our customers and even their customers. It is the understanding of this value chain that can help us to identify which new products can be more attractive, and which pricing methods can maximize value. This is well illustrated in the VAT concept, according to which companies are taxed not for the product they produce but for the value they add to it. In the same way, we need to look not at the product we make, but at the value we add to produce the final one.

In B2B, more interesting than customer satisfaction interviews are focus group discussions in which the different participants of a given value chain can be involved. This can be a very effective way to identify opportunities for profit improvement via pricing. Some companies have done it very successfully, taking the initiative to involve representatives of the industries they serve, as suppliers of other products, their customers and representatives of the industries these customers serve. This provides an integral view of the industry and the opportunities to optimize the processes in an integral way, and helps to find the right balance between the product they are providing and the conditions in which it will be used in the full value chain.

Let's illustrate this with a practical example: the production of most printed material, whether a book, magazine or newspaper. As illustrated in Figure 7.7, the main steps in the value chain are the creation of the content, the print preparation in which the content will be put into the appropriate format, the printing itself and the distribution. This process can take place within a single company that executes it from beginning to end, or in multiple companies, each of which performs one step in the process.

If it is not integrated, this process can become slow and inflexible, with a lot of intermediate inventories that become easily obsolete. The increase in connectivity between different companies around a given publication has made the process much more efficient. Making content work available online means that print preparation can be initiated before all content is available. Printers can also source all the necessary elements to begin the printing as soon as the preparation is finished. In the same way, distribution can be initiated just in time. The result is a true print-on-demand model that is much faster and that does not require intermediate inventories.

With this connectivity, missing elements can be identified very easily and corrected in less time to avoid publication delays and extra costs. In this environment, pricing can be defined in different ways. When companies work more in isolation, the process can only begin when the other company has finished it. In addition, the price of a product or service must contain provisions for process inefficiencies,

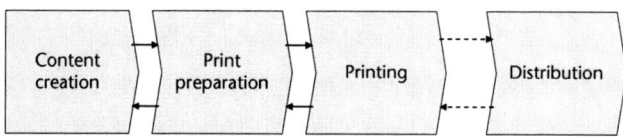

FIGURE 7.7 Sample value chain

to average out what in practice is happening. In an integrated process, these inefficiencies can be easily identified and corrected, and a price can be set for the process itself without any extra provision for inefficiency risks.

In B2B, a good understanding of complete value chains in which various companies are participating is key to pricing innovation. These complex value chains often involve many different companies, which at the same time may participate in different value chains in other industry segments. The best solution is to try to see how the process would work if the full value chain were to work within a single company. This defines a new way to operate that can be easily translated to the different companies that are now in the chain by creative pricing models.

8
WHY SEGMENTATION MATTERS

Linda Trevenen

Introduction

Segmentation matters – especially when firms face the challenge of intense competition and eroding profitability brought on by declining prices. Consider the case of Dow Corning (Gary 2004). As a perennial leader in the silicone market, they admittedly had become complacent in the face of aggressive competitors who were offering lower prices. They also faced increasing costs for innovation and service. To cope with these challenges they employed market segmentation to better understand the structure of their market. In their segmentation of the market, they learned that not all customers had the same set of needs. Some required more service than others, some valued innovation more than others, while others were trying to improve the profitability of their own businesses. They also learned that one segment no longer needed the added value of service, innovation, or a broad product assortment of the silicone products they purchased; instead they just wanted the best price.

Dow had been treating all these customers the same, yet each of four identified segments required a different bundle of benefits. It became painfully evident to their managers that they were providing expensive services to some customers who did not even need them. Therein lies the most critical reason why segmentation matters in business – *profits can be lost by treating all customers the same in terms of their pricing*. This is not just a practical matter, but one grounded in traditional economic theory.

As Thomas (2012) notes, the theory that supports segmentation is based primarily on the economics literature of price discrimination developed during the 1920s and 1930s (Chamberlin 1965; Pigou 1920; Robinson 1954), and is widely accepted in the marketing literature (Smith 1956; Frank *et al.* 1972). The theory suggests that customer heterogeneity supports the existence of demand-based segments from which firms can generate greater profit by shaping different offerings and prices for segments than by providing the same offering and price to the whole market. This is exactly what Dow Corning did to overcome their predicament.

The segmentation approach by Dow Corning actually redefined their entire business strategy. Instead of offering their products and services at the same prices to all customers, they created different offerings for the needs of the different segments. They allowed each customer to choose the types of products and services they needed and these were priced accordingly. However, the segment of customers who wanted only low prices with little or no service posed a special problem. Dow Corning could not just offer them low prices because other customers would want those low prices as well. To create a barrier between this segment and the others, Dow Corning chose to launch a new brand called Xiameter. Through this brand they offered a limited number of their most popular products at competitive prices with no services. They used an Internet-based business model to maintain a low cost approach to manage the business while meeting this segment's needs. Their entire needs-based segmentation approach was so successful that it was reported to have paid for itself in three months (Gary 2004).

What we learn from this example is that segmentation is a promising management process that can lead to opportunities for improved profitability. However, these opportunities are not the same for all firms. Segmentation is highly situational and each firm must take the challenge to use it to achieve a business strategy, or alternatively, as in the case of Dow Corning, to completely revise its strategy.

This chapter will introduce some of the challenges pricing professionals face related to conducting customer needs-based segmentation and how to overcome them. In addition, pricing professionals will learn best practices for implementing segmentation so that their price plan takes advantage of the value in their offering and maximizes the profit relative to their customer segments. Three important objectives addressed in this chapter help to understand why segmentation should matter a lot for pricing professionals:

1. To recognize the importance of segmentation and how to offer value through optimized solution offerings for customer segments
2. To learn the strategic and practical activities and implications for needs-based segmentation
3. To understand how to implement segmentation best practices into the organization so that a segmentation strategy realizes greater profitability.

Segmentation, value, and pricing

Many companies view segmentation as expensive and requiring more effort than the expected return. This raises one of the more important first steps in segmentation: Is it right for your firm in your business situation?

Lesson 1: Know exactly why you want to use segmentation and what its expected benefits might be for you.

At the outset, write down the outcome you expect from using a segmentation approach to improve your pricing decisions. In general, I recommend using segmentation when you must make one or more market-based decisions that are important to your firm's performance and when you face a high degree of uncertainty around the outcome of these decisions. For example, you may have some high costs-to-serve programs that you offer to your customer base as part of your offering. If your sales representatives are providing these high cost services to *all* customers without regard for return on sales, then you are losing money. To that end, segmentation could benefit by determining which customers value the programs and are willing to pay for your services and which ones believe these programs are less useful. Or, you may decide that your sales force is spread too thin given the base of customers who require field support and you are looking for a way to improve their efficiency and productivity per visit. If the customer base is not well understood, then your sales representatives are inefficient and calling on customers who may not deliver revenue given the resources spent on visiting them. For less important decisions in which you are fairly certain about the outcome, you may gain little from segmentation.

Among the more important decisions facing firms is pricing. Pricing is the gateway to customer purchases as well as the firm's profitability. Pricing professionals instinctively know many of their decisions are important, but often do not have the necessary marketing competency in segmentation to effectively complete their pricing plan. Also, some pricing decisions will vary in the amount of uncertainty faced in the market place. Without a proper understanding of the segmented structure of the market, a pricing decision that is important and facing uncertainty may miss its mark. Understanding what makes your customers different from one another based on what they value is the required ingredient for a successful needs-based segmentation that leads to more profitable pricing. Only then, can pricing professionals establish the appropriate fences that their customers find meaningful and distinct. Surprisingly, very few companies have successfully implemented segmentation on a regular basis as part of their pricing plans, let alone their entire marketing plans (Thomas 2012). This is why I advocate a rather systematic approach to this process.

The second important step in performing segmentation for pricing is recognizing the variables you will use to divide your market into meaningful groups that are similar within each group and different between each group.

Lesson 2: When it comes to pricing, segments based on value will be most productive.

Value is the relationship between what customers perceive as benefits in an offering and the price they pay for those benefits. Customer benefits are driven by their needs, and hence are helpful in implementing needs-based segmentations. By identifying customer needs and formulating benefits to meet them, a basis for weighting them against willingness to pay for those benefits can be established through marketing research (in the next section I will address in more detail the important aspects of qualitative and quantitative market research to measure customer value).

Pricing professionals will recognize market research as a key element in their pricing plan – understanding the customer's willingness to pay for different offerings.

Once your organization conducts the market research, and collects the data at the individual customer level, it is possible to categorize customers into clusters according to their willingness to pay for the different benefits. Cluster analysis (and its variants) provides the primary tool for identifying similarities within groups and differences between groups. The purpose of this chapter is not to describe the details of cluster analysis or other statistical tools, but rather to make sure that managers involved in pricing recognize there are analytical tools and techniques available that can help realize the promise of segmentation.

The next step in the segmentation process is to identify potential market segments and describe them.

Lesson 3: Accept the fact that most value-based segments will not be precisely different, yet they will be sufficiently different to guide pricing decisions.

One of the challenges in a segmentation project is determining the segments that make sense for your business. The database generally contains many variables, such as how your customer receives information, how they obtain referrals, what types of brands they prefer, how they perceive educational programs, whether they value sophisticated methods of managing their business information, size of firm, formalized business plans, and/or attitudes toward vendors to name a few examples. Many firms utilize research companies who have experience in segmentation and are familiar with the different techniques for segmenting databases. These firms first look at how many clusters the data presents to determine the number of possible segments. The minimum or appropriate size of a segment depends on the markets being analyzed. Statisticians look for natural clusters, specifically the number of customers who answered similarly for a particular variable. When there are several variables that are similar across groups, then they may become a cluster. It may also help to describe your segments as personality types because there may be many characteristics that make up a segment and understanding the drivers in each of these makes it easier to understand the customer's motivation in that particular segment. Segment names, for example, might include: "The Efficiency Expert"; "Referrals Rule"; and "The Risk Taker."

Keeping the end in mind

When you first embark on a segmentation project, you need to ask yourself:

- What does success look like for your firm?
- How do you plan to use the segmentation information once you have it?
- What results do you expect segmentation to provide once implemented?

Write down your hypothesis and share them with key stakeholders at your firm. These people could be leaders in sales, marketing, customer service, field support, technical support, and/or R&D. It is important to identify your stakeholders and their perceptions of success if segmentation were implemented. Objectives need to be agreed upon by key executives in your firm so you have endorsement and support. Many firms want to drive more profitable growth without reducing their revenue base; however, they may not be willing to execute a specific "target" strategy with specific customer groups identified from the segmentation project. If a company decides to conduct a segmentation study, and then identifies targets but does not alter the way they call on these targets so they can realize greater productivity from their sales force, then perhaps they should not start the project at all.

Lesson 4: Uncover how much the firm is willing to change their behavior if the research findings suggest that they make changes to messaging, field force allocation, resource allocation, and solution offering.

Establishing your starting point in a segmentation project is critical to determining its eventual success. Executive commitment, clear expectations, and the ability to view its implementation are necessary before committing to conducting a segmentation project. Too often firms want to start with price setting but miss the point that price is simply the outcome of perceived value. Therefore, start with a segmentation plan first so you can identify how value differs among your customers and then link price later. Without understanding what your customers value, you will have a hard time assigning price, setting fences between offerings, and managing your customer targets. Segmentation enables you to understand the key elements that matter most to your customers so you can develop the appropriate offerings and price.

Lesson 5: Start with a good segmentation plan to identify customer value before thinking about setting price.

It may be helpful to create your own Segmentation Preparation Plan (Figure 8.1) to ensure you are setting yourself up for success. The plan is broken out into three parts to ensure that you have a successful result.

1. Diagnosing your firm's readiness (Q1, Q2)
2. Aligning business objectives across your firm (Q3, Q4)
3. Establishing metrics for your project (Q5, Q6)

	High influence in firm	
Challengers		Advocates
Keep in close communication		Involve and communicate frequently
Close-minded		*Open-minded*
Inform only		Inform and involve – create positive word of mouth
	Low influence in firm	

FIGURE 8.1 Segmentation preparation plan

1. List names of executives who are have a high degree of influence and are open-minded to the idea of creating customer segments.
2. Uncover any prior experience with segmentation that these stakeholders have had in their careers. What type of segmentation experience have they had? How successful was it? (Understanding your internal stakeholders well will assist you with mitigating and managing expectations.)
3. List out the business objectives by stakeholder focusing on those in the "Advocates" box.
4. List challenges for your project using the closed-minded high influence group of stakeholders or "Challengers."
5. List success factors based on the high influence stakeholders listed above.
6. Determine metrics for the top three business objectives that you listed in Question 3.

Developing your segmentation plan

Now that you have established the outline for success, you will need to formalize your plan so it can be broadly distributed in the firm. Be sure to familiarize your plan with many stakeholders – the more who understand what you are trying to accomplish, the better. It is also important to establish up front that you plan to conduct a pilot to test your offering and the messaging on your target segments. Most folks agree that understanding your customers at a deeper level is worthwhile. You will need to remind folks throughout the project that your main goal is to uncover the elements that your customers truly value in your offering set so your firm can differentiate itself relative to competition with their offering set.

Your action plan should include the following elements:

1. Purpose
    a. This section describes your business problem and why you are undertaking a segmentation initiative.
    b. It lists the key strategic questions that you expect to answer as a result of this initiative.
    c. It lists the business objectives (obtained by your pre-work).
2. Stakeholders/team members
    a. Core team members
    b. Executive sponsors
3. Tasks/deliverables for achieving field pilot (suggests a pilot before full approval)
    a. Measure of team's success (this section includes metrics for a field pilot)
        i. inputs (Was the typing tool used to identify our target segments effective?);

ii. outcomes (Was the activity time spent with a key target more valuable than time spent with a non-target customer? Was pre-call planning more efficient as a result of the segmentation data?);
iii. process (Were you able to close your target customers more effectively given the targeted messaging tools created for these targets?).

Now that your plan is in place, assign teams who will be responsible for actively engaging in this project as it progresses. These teams are best if you have a few cross-functional members involved besides marketing, e.g. sales management, sales operations. The duties of this team include:

- DEFINE – Evaluating Request for Proposals (RFP) from the market research firms.
- DATA COLLECTION – Performing qualitative interviews to determine the key areas of further research for the quantitative phase of the research: this step requires that your teams are trained in the proper techniques for collecting voice of customer data. If not, then you may want to have your market research firm conduct these preliminary interviews to determine the areas that will be surveyed in greater depth in the quantitative phase.
- ANALYSIS – Ensuring quantitative immersion of the data once collected to associate the data groups with the clusters identified.
- NAME – Naming of the segments.
- DEVELOP RECOMMENDATION – Formulating the strategy for developing offerings to these segments.
- PILOT – Deploying your segmentation offerings in the sales field to your pre-determined clusters to test your hypothesis.
- MEASURE – Measure the outcomes of the pilot.
- CONFIRM – Determining price bands for specific target segments.

Documenting your plan, distributing it to a wide audience, holding update meetings, and ensuring there is high involvement among marketing and sales will ensure you have a successful outcome. The reason for your pilot is to ensure you have a plan that can be executed by the average and below average sales person. By testing in the field, you will learn whether you met your stated objectives of the project, i.e. increased sales force effectiveness, improved pre-call planning, achieved willingness to pay, and/or improved differentiation.

Lesson 6: Conduct a field pilot involving sales management that measures the effectiveness of your segmentation data before rolling-out to the larger sales organization.

If successful, then proceeding with a larger scale plan makes sense.

Identifying what matters

The goal of segmentation is to identify what matters most to your target segments. One of the first steps is identifying your target segments based on the segment clusters that the database presents. Your clusters may have been presented to you but deciding on which cluster is right for you depends on what is important to your firm. Many choose targets using a grid based on segment attractiveness and competency factors among the firm. Segment attractiveness criteria are generally chosen by your cross-functional team of sales and marketing personnel and may include:

- growth of a market segment
- price sensitivity of customers
- number of competitors/entrants
- customer loyalty to competition
- number of customers in that segment.

Competency factors may include:

- sales force effort required to meet segment needs
- ability of product to meet needs of potential buyers
- fit with corporate strategy
- sales force competency to sell "solutions"
- uniqueness/differentiation.

Managers wishing to choose a target segment may use a combination of judgment and data to rate each segment on the above criteria and use this as a basis for selecting one or more target segments. It should be noted that more than one segment can be targeted, although if doing so, pay careful attention to defining a different offering for each segment. An offering is defined not solely as a technology but rather all the elements of the total solution including services, financing, programs, etc. This becomes especially important for pricing decisions when it may be necessary to establish boundaries or price fences between segments to better manage profitability. It should also be noted that a targeting decision is preliminary in the sense that as you learn more from designing a marketing strategy for the segment, you may need to revise your target.

By deploying value based segmentation, whether targeting a single segment or multiple segments, you are focused on the "value elements" that matter most to your customers. Your clusters may reveal that educational programs are important to one segment and not important to another; or managing one's database to drive new revenue is important for one group but to another driving new customer volume matters more. Recall that the key characteristics of your segments are identified during the clustering process.

The next step is determining the value that each of these characteristics have relative to your offering and whether your target is willing to pay for them. Your offerings can be created using a menu with the basic elements already valued by your audience. Start with creating a base offering and then layer on the elements that your target values. The core elements may be technology, financing, and marketing programs and the variable offerings may include other options from the base along with educational programs, and frequency of field visits. You can test your theory in the field pilot. Before going into the field, your segments will be predetermined using a typing tool (a tool that filters your customers into segments based on the key criterion that separates the segments) so you can test your theory of different offerings with different segments. Each offering will have a different price and it is at this point you can establish price "fences" (Nagle and Holden 2002).

Lesson 7: Establishing your segment offerings first before determining your price provides the sales force with the knowledge they need for a flexible and profitable negotiation.

Price fences represent the minimum and maximum pricing parameters for each of your offering elements so that there is no room for interpretation. Knowing what matters to your customers determines how you will price elements in your offering. Your offering set will be determined by who you want to attract in a particular market. Price fences help to avoid "gray areas" of value overlap illustrated when a sales person throws in an extra service for a customer who is not meant to receive it and now inequities are created within a segment. For example, if you have three target segments who value your offering elements as in Table 8.1, you can establish fences that enable your sales force to effectively negotiate with each of these customer groups. For Segment 1, your sales force will not talk about educational programs but will emphasize the multiple delivery options and field programs that can be estimated as part of their proposal. For Segment 3, your sales force will focus on the value of the educational programs and the breadth and value of their technology offering. All elements will have prices assigned so your sales force can understand what is included in the offering and what is not.

Depending on the structure of your offering and internal company policies, it is often best for some segments to be given à la carte pricing so that you can

TABLE 8.1 Segment and value offering

Scale 1–5: 1 – Low value, 5 – High value	Segment 1	Segment 2	Segment 3
Educational programs	1 – Low value, has trainer in house	3 – Moderate	5 – High value, has no trainer
Field service programs	5 – High value	2 – Low value	1 – Low value
Technology	2 – Low value	3 – Moderate	5 – High value
Delivery	5 – High value, has small warehouse	3 – Moderate	2 – Low value, has warehouse

subtract or add an element into their contract based on the pricing approach you have established. If you don't have price fences established up front, it is too easy for sales reps to offer what they think is "fair." By doing the work up front and identifying what matters to customers, you are creating price integrity for your established offerings. Fences provide rules for the sales force ensuring that you are getting an adequate return on the resources applied to each customer.

Lesson 8: Emphasize the importance of adhering to your price fences to avoid adding free extras that increase the cost to serve and dilute the integrity of your price fences.

Set price fences and offering elements in accordance with your strategy. If you wish to penetrate a particular segment, then you may choose to be more aggressive with that particular group. "True" perceived value is tested in your field pilot where you can approach your targets with these offerings to test their receptivity. Without good discipline and adherence to price fences, your sales force may simply try to "match" a lower price from competition and erode profitability.

Sales strategy, maximizing profitability

A segmentation project is only successful if the sales force can execute it effectively in the field. Therefore, when you introduce your segmentation data to your sales organization, be sure to share it in three parts: (1) explain segmentation so they are aware of how it can help them make resource and offering decisions; (2) describe what your customer data shows and how targets were determined; and (3) assist in developing strategic options for specific customers so their field time is optimized with customers expected to grow.

Target segments and sales goals should be chosen by your core team and executive leaders. It is critical to show how your sales leaders can use the segmentation information for developing their sales strategy. To be consistent with a strategic pricing effort, sales leaders decide which current and potential customers to invest, maintain, or divest in their area (Table 8.2). Customers within the chosen target group are seen as growth opportunities and should be developed or defended given that the target group is aligned with segment attractiveness and competencies of the organization. These customers become the ones that deserve your sales force's attention.

In addition to assigning a sales strategy to targets and non-targets, sales can overlay other criteria such as profitability (low, medium, high), breadth of purchase,

TABLE 8.2 Sales strategy

HIGH *Profit*	Develop selectively	Defend	Develop or Defend
	Use few resources	Defend or Maintain	Develop
	Fewest resources deployed	Use few resources	Develop selectively
LOW		*Future Growth*	HIGH

Why segmentation matters 161

and/or loyalty to the brand before setting an exact price within the price band for the targets. If a typing tool exists and your sales organization can discern between your target and other segments, then consider looking at existing data within your firm to assist your sales team in making more informed resource decisions relative to cost-to-serve, thus driving profitability in a positive direction.

Lesson 9: To execute a value-based segmentation plan, tie it to a tangible sales strategy that distinguishes between profitable and unprofitable customers.

It should be emphasized with your sales force that they regularly make many daily decisions that affect profitability. When you consider the possible combinations available to a sales representative as shown in Table 8.2, you understand just how important it is to understand what your customers really care about so that your sales representative is not giving too much away in the transaction. In Figure 8.2, there are over 1,080 possible decisions that a sales rep can make at any time with any customer. Thus, the creation of a price policy that sets price by segment for the standard offering will assist your sales organization with the boundaries. A price policy is a more comprehensive document that clearly articulates rules around pricing practices and discounts for specific segments. Rules should be created and followed when it comes to decisions about if and when the sales force can or cannot extend services or price discounts to particular customers. Price fences are different in that they establish differences between the solution offering elements and what can and cannot be included in a negotiation with an assigned value.

Now that your sales representative knows who to target, why to target them, and understands to follow a prescribed price policy, it is also important that an escalation policy or "exception" policy be available as part of your pricing program. For consistent behavior, sales managers should provide a clear escalation policy describing the process that defines what a sales person should do if they want to

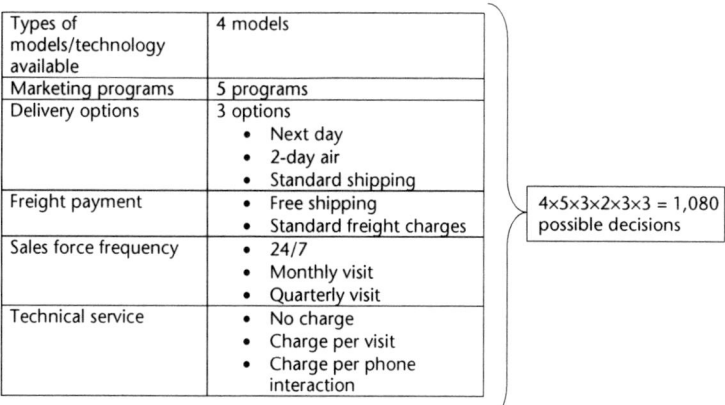

FIGURE 8.2 Example of a medical device firm

go outside of the assigned fences or price bands for their customer. As a rule, there should be few exceptions made and escalations should be backed up with a form describing why this customer falls outside of the fence limits. Escalations are usually viewed by an established "price desk" in an organization who has authority to decide "no."

Lesson 10: An escalation policy is an essential part of the pricing program because it provides flexibility for possible exceptions.

Conclusions

In summary, needs-based (value-based) segmentation is the heart of a pricing plan because you need to identify customer needs first before setting price. The strategic choice to segment your customers before setting price is essential for maximizing profit potential within your firm. Effective price setting is achieved when you have created offerings that are tailored to your customer segments with clearly established and communicated price fences that inform your sales team about what is included or not included in the offering – all of which can avoid the undisciplined free giveaway. Lastly, segmentation plans are only effective if they can be executed to have impact on sales behavior related to price setting and adherence. Profitability is dependent on the quality of segmentation, sales strategy, and how well your sales force adheres to the policies given to them. Clarity of offerings, price fences, and escalation will ensure a more profitable future.

Implications for the pricing field

Segmentation may not be new, however, when done with careful thought and planning to match a firm's pricing challenge, it can transform the way the firm sells its solutions to its customers. It also forces new behavior from your sales team and establishes integrity of your prices thereby improving profitability. The ten lessons from this chapter are:

Lesson 1:	*Know exactly why you want to use segmentation and what its expected benefits might be for you.*
Lesson 2:	*When it comes to pricing, segments based on value will be most productive.*
Lesson 3:	*Accept the fact that most value-based segments will not be precisely different, yet they will be sufficiently different to guide pricing decisions.*
Lesson 4:	*Uncover how much the firm is willing to change their behavior if the research findings suggest that they make changes to messaging, field force allocation, resource allocation, and solution offering.*
Lesson 5:	*Start with a good segmentation plan to identify customer value before thinking about setting price.*
Lesson 6:	*Conduct a field pilot involving sales management that measures the effectiveness of your segmentation data before rolling-out to the larger sales organization.*

Lesson 7:	*Establishing your segment offerings first before determining your price provides the sales force with the knowledge they need for a flexible and profitable negotiation.*
Lesson 8:	*Emphasize the importance of adhering to your price fences to avoid adding in free extras that increase the cost to serve and dilute the integrity of your price fences.*
Lesson 9:	*To execute a value-based segmentation plan, tie it to a tangible sales strategy that distinguishes between profitable and unprofitable customers.*
Lesson 10:	*An escalation policy is an essential part of the pricing program because it provides flexibility if certain exceptions exist.*

References

Chamberlin, E. H. (1965) *The theory of monopolistic competition*. Cambridge, MA: Harvard University Press.

Frank, R. E., Massy, W. F. and Wind, Y. (1972) *Market segmentation*. Englewood Cliffs, NJ: Prentice Hall.

Gary, L. (2004) Dow Corning's push for organic growth. *Strategy and Innovation*, 2, pp. 3–5.

Nagle, T. T. and Holden, R. K. (2002) *The strategy and tactics of pricing: A guide to profitable decision making*, 3rd edition. Upper Saddle River, NJ: Prentice Hall.

Pigou, A. C. (1920) *The economics of welfare*. London: Macmillan.

Robinson, J. (1954) *The economics of imperfect competition*. London: Macmillan.

Smith, W. (1956) Product differentiation and market segmentation as alternative marketing strategies. *Journal of Marketing*, 21, pp. 3–8.

Thomas, R. J. (2012) Business-to-business market segmentation. In: Lilien, G. L. and Grewal, R. (eds) Handbook on business-to-business marketing. Cheltenham, UK: Edward Elgar Publishing Ltd, pp. 182–207.

9
THE FIVE FUNDAMENTAL VALUE FACTORS

Ralf Drews

Introduction

Just 17 percent of companies apply the value-based pricing model (Liozu *et al.* 2011), and many of them do so only very late in the stage-gate process of developing a product. An even smaller percentage understand that value is defined by the customer, who not only considers the value of the offering itself but also is consciously or unconsciously driven by other values such as service, product delivery, and company brand. Knowing that there exists a wide variety of buying preferences across different customer segments and global cultures makes it even more challenging for companies to set the right price point. A strong company strategy considers all of these variables and defines them well before a voice of the customer (VOC) study is run and a product concept is created that is later to be embedded in the overall go-to-market approach.

In everyday business life, executives often view pricing not strategically but tactically: a value-based price accounts for the value of the product in the context of its use but disregards other value drivers outside the offering as well as the value perception of different customer characteristics. Unless all important value factors are considered, the negative impact can be a hit on the bottom line: if the price is too high, sales stay below expectations; if the price is too low, margin is wasted. In addition, the disconnect between price and strategy can lead to wrong conclusions if corrective actions must be taken to improve a product's financial performance.

This chapter provides a comprehensive overview of all five fundamental value factors in their logical order. Anyone seeking to define the right price for an offering can easily apply this approach to their business.

The five fundamental value factors

Value Factor 1: Pick the right focus industries
Value Factor 2: Understand the buying influence structure

Value Factor 3: Prioritize other important buying-decision factors outside the offering
Value Factor 4: Define the buying characteristics and the ideal customer profile
Value Factor 5: Apply a voice of the customer (VOC) study at the beginning of the stage-gate process

The following example illustrates the application of the five value factors.

The fictitious company High Pressure Technology (HPT) develops, manufactures, and sells high-pressure cleaners. It is headquartered in Switzerland and has a strong brand in Europe. The next-generation product is to be created, and the company's goal is to gain significant market share in North America, where HPT has traditionally been weak. The products are of premium quality and are made for industrial applications. Even though this market has become very competitive, HPT can still differentiate based on three strong value propositions, which set the company apart from other manufacturers:

- outstanding cleaning results without degradation of surfaces due to patented technology
- low cost of ownership due to premium-quality design
- productivity enhancements due to reduced cleaning time.

The company's executive team seeks to leverage those strengths in their go-to-market strategy.

Value Factor 1: Pick the right focus industries

The most common decision criteria for market selection are market volume, market growth, market profitability, and market barriers. Other less-common but very important criteria are related to the strength of the enterprise in the vertical market: market share, brand value, fit with global focus markets, and, most important, power of the value proposition. A strong *company* value proposition (not *product* value proposition!) is unique, provides true value to customers, and is sustainable.

Tables 9.1 and 9.2 show how companies in three different industries select their focus vertical markets; Figure 9.1 depicts the final result.

Table 9.2 indicates the most critical enterprise strengths related to the vertical markets. It is critically important for profitable pricing that the company's value proposition fits with the buying preferences of the vertical market. Misalignment between company strengths and what the customers appreciate will result in poor product margins.

Figure 9.1 illustrates the positioning of the different vertical markets. Based on these results, HPT picks the chemical industry as their focus market because of the strong position shown on the x-axis and the high overall attractiveness (y-axis) in combination with a considerable market volume (bubble size).

Although Figure 9.1 shows that waste water treatment is almost as attractive as the chemical industry, HPT decides to target the latter because it is a much better

TABLE 9.1 Industry attractiveness independent of the company's strengths

	Weight (1–10)	Chemical industry	Waste water treatment	Ship building
Market size	7	8	7	3
Portfolio fit	9	8	8	5
Profit margin	7	7	7	4
Market growth	9	6	5	5
Competitive intensity	5	3	5	6
RESULT		**246**	**240**	**169**

TABLE 9.2 Strength of enterprise

	Weight (1–10)	Chemical industry	Waste water treatment	Ship building
Market share	5	2	1	1
Brand value	3	3	2	2
Fit with global focus markets	7	7	7	3
Power of value proposition	10	8	4	5
RESULT		**148**	**100**	**82**

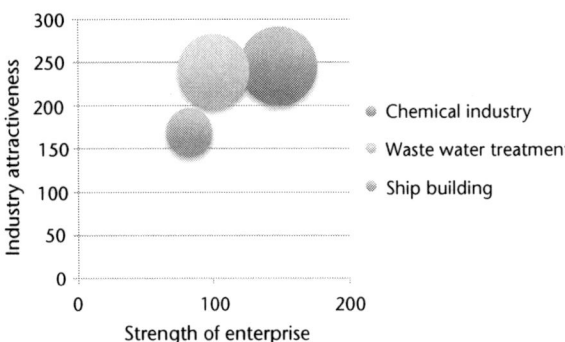

FIGURE 9.1 Market prioritization

fit in terms of HPT's value proposition (8 versus 4): this is because the chemical industry has a higher degree of cleaner use, and this is where reduced downtime as a result of greater robustness and higher cleaning efficiency make a big difference.

> When exploring new marketplaces, the power of the company's value proposition is a major market-selection criterion!

The next step is to better understand the buying decision-making process associated with this specific industry.

Value Factor 2: Understand the buying influence structure

Once the focus industry has been defined, the main buying influences and their say in the decision-making process need to be understood. Of course, the distribution of decision power varies slightly from company to company. However, since roles and responsibilities within the target industries are similar, the information in Table 9.3 is sufficiently accurate for a clear product and pricing definition.

Identifying the buying influences and their decision-making power can be performed by the marketing department. In real life, however, sales departments typically understand very well who has the greatest and second-greatest influence when it comes to buying decisions. This information is critical for an effective VOC study since it means prioritizing the requirements of the buying influences in the order of their decision-making power. Meeting the needs of the most-influential decision maker most likely means achieving the best price for one's offering. In this example, HPT determined the operations manager to have the greatest influence. This means that he will drive the decision based on the value he sees in HPT's offering. His focus is clearly the process efficiency improvement of 20 percent compared with the next-best competitor:

$$\text{Cost savings} = \text{increased cleaning efficiency} \times \text{cleaning hours per year} \times \text{hour} = \text{value}$$

This equation translates into the following value for the operations manager:

$$20\% \times 600 \text{ hours} \times \$15/\text{hr} = \$1{,}800 \text{ savings per year per cleaner.}$$

Assuming the average life of a cleaner is 5 years, the customer benefit translates into $5 \times \$1{,}800 = \$9{,}000$. Based on that analysis, a pricing approach might look like this: HPT charges \$4,500 more than their next-best competitor; in addition,

TABLE 9.3 Distribution of decision-making influence

Buying influence	Role in the chemical industry	Decision-making influence	Values
Economic buyer	Purchaser	20%	Low costs of purchase
Technical buyer	Operations manager	50%	Low downtime
			Decreased cleaning time
			(20% better than competition)
			Excellent cleaning results
User buyer	Industry worker	30%	Ease of use
			Excellent cleaning results

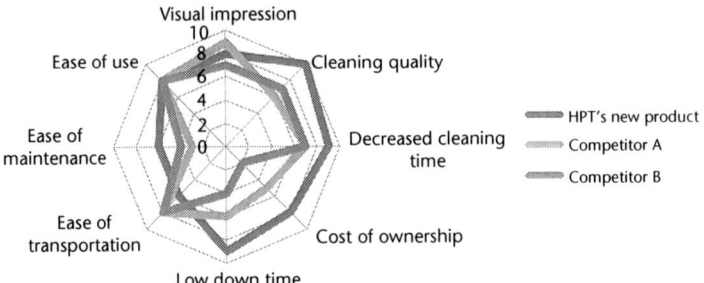

FIGURE 9.2 Target product value profile reflecting the needs of the most powerful buying influence

they still offer a $4,500 value advantage, which results in a very attractive ratio of price to performance.

This example shows how important it is to align the decision-making structure in the key vertical market with the company's value proposition.

Once a company thoroughly understands the decision-making process, they can determine the main value drivers of their offering: Figure 9.2 shows that the focus of the product value propositions matches the needs of the most powerful buying influence.

A common tool for identifying the value of product features based on the preferences of buying influences is conjoint analysis, which is explained in more detail later.

Value Factor 3: Prioritize other important buying-decision factors outside the offering

Once the company's value proposition has been defined, the key market selected, and the buying-influence structure understood, the next questions are: "What are the six to eight most important buying criteria from the perspective of all buying influences?" and "Which of those buying influences are outside the offering itself, and how does the company's performance in those areas impact the pricing of the offering?"

> Companies have to wake up to the fact that they are more than just a product on a shelf. They're behaviour as well.
>
> Robert Hass, Levi Strauss

The key message of Hass's statement is that a buying decision is driven not only by the offering's ratio of price to performance itself but also by other factors like brand (= trust), delivery performance, and service. An offering's outstanding price-to-performance ratio can compensate for performance disadvantages of other value factors. Thus it is important to define the company's strategy canvas (Figure 9.3).

The five fundamental value factors **169**

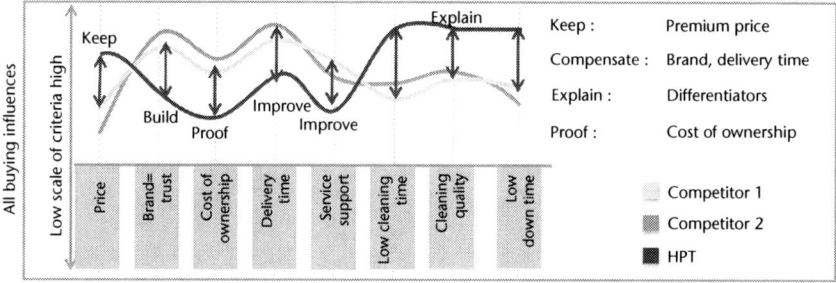

FIGURE 9.3 HPT's eight most important buying criteria and its positioning against the competition

This canvas shows how HPT (represented by the black line) is positioned in the marketplace. Although there may be up to 30 buying-decision criteria, the x-axis shows the eight most important criteria (Pareto). Those criteria predominantly drive the buying decision of the three buying influences as described in Value Factor 2. HPT will differentiate itself from its competitors based on its higher cleaning performance at lower costs of ownership. Its challenges are its weak brand, poor delivery, and service performance.

Generally, a buying decision considers more than eight buying-decision criteria. So, how are the eight most important buying criteria being defined?

First, as described earlier, it is important that customers in HPT's target market appreciate the company's value proposition. For example, if HPT had decided to enter the lower-end performance market in the US, the company DNA – producing quality products – could not have been leveraged. Thus the "power of the value proposition" is a key market-selection criterion. Following this logic, four of the eight buying criteria are already defined: little downtime, high cleaning quality, low cost of ownership, and high productivity.

Second, in order to understand the importance of value factors outside the offering, one can also apply conjoint analysis since the purpose is very similar: down-selection of buying criteria. Conjoint analysis is mostly used for market segmentation, pricing, and product development. The following simple example explains how conjoint analysis generally works.

It would be important for an automotive manufacturer to determine how significant the factors "brand," "motor power," and "colour" are with regard to buying decisions. In a conjoint analysis, several options are created (e.g. a red Audi with 170 HP, a gray Mercedes with 170 HP, or a blue BMW with 190 HP) and presented to test persons who rank or rate these different options. By analyzing how they assign preference to these options, the manufacturer can determine the implicit valuation of the individual elements making up the product or service. One possible result in this example is that the persons being surveyed are strongly oriented toward a certain manufacturer (most important feature), for example toward BMW (most important characteristics) when it comes to purchasing a new car.

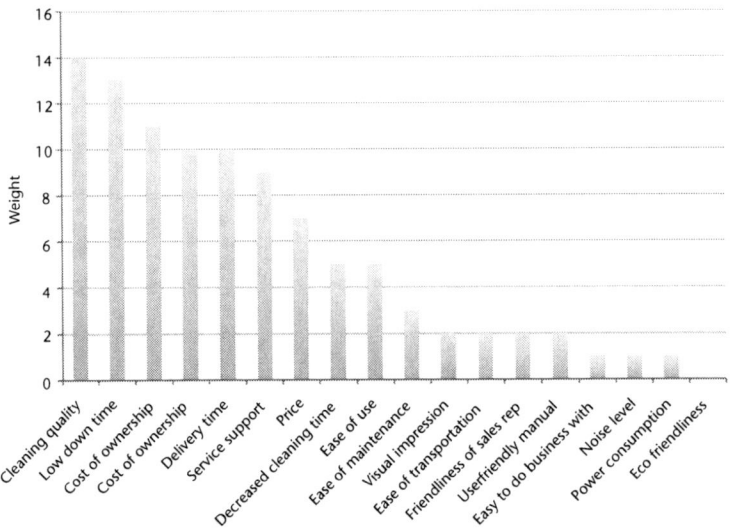

FIGURE 9.4 Analysis of the eight most important buying criteria by means of conjoint analysis

The strategic marketing department should survey the initial definition of all buying criteria. Figure 9.4 shows the result of HPT's conjoint analysis. The key takeaway is that 80 percent of the weight is distributed over the first eight buying criteria; these criteria are reflected in the company's strategy canvas.

As mentioned above, HPT's challenges are its lack of brand value and brand awareness. Since brand equals trust, a well-known brand is sold more easily just because the buyer has a higher degree of confidence that he or she is buying the right product.

The company's delivery time lags behind that of its competitors, as does its service support. The lack of a good service network means that buyers might hesitate to accept the risk of a long downtime in case of a product issue.

These three value issues must be either eliminated or compensated for in the **overall value equation** (Figure 9.5). Since HPT's brand, delivery, and service provide negative value compared with the competition, HPT must decide how they want to create the competitive advantage needed to penetrate the US market. It might be viable to lower the price of their offering, assuming this would not affect the company's brand position.

Value Factor 4: Define the buying characteristics and the ideal customer profile

Having worked on Value Factors 1 through 3, the focus market is now defined, the influence of the different buyers is revealed, and the price position of the offering is determined in the context of the most relevant buying-decision criteria by means of the strategy canvas and the overall value equation (Figure 9.5).

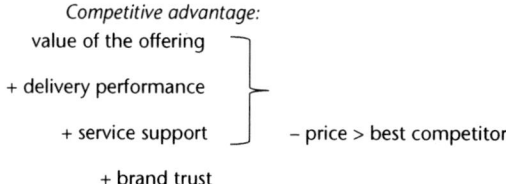

FIGURE 9.5 The overall value equation

At this point, the strategic homework is nearly done. There is just one step left to ensure that the strategy is effective and the margins are optimized in the selling process: the definition of the ideal customer profile. What is an ideal customer? Mercedes Benz's ideal customer is most likely someone who is wealthy, and who likes luxury, has a solid financial background, prefers comfortable driving over sporty driving, and is willing to pay for a brand. In this example it seems obvious that Mercedes sales representatives would not spend much time on teenagers since this customer category does not (most likely) comply with the ideal customer's profile. Many companies forget to make this distinction. As a result, their sales force spends time with customers who are unwilling to pay for an offering's extra value. Returning to HPT, if their sales representatives talked to those chemical industry customers who might prioritize initial purchase costs over shorter cleaning time and shorter downtime, the discounts offered would increase, and such a deal would typically result in lower margins. Over time, the brand could be damaged as well. Practical experience shows that management struggles with defining the ideal customer because doing so shrinks the accessible market significantly. However, the Mercedes example shows how ridiculous it would be if Mercedes did not clearly define the ideal customer in the automotive market but sold their product to anyone.

So, what is the ideal customer profile? What are the relevant factors, and how does one describe this customer? Answering that question requires revisiting the strategy canvas (see Figure 9.3).

What could be the **personal win** and the **personal risk** for a buyer choosing an HPT product?

The strategy canvas identifies the following risks: First, there is HPT's weak brand (if something were to go wrong with the HPT cleaner, the buyer might be blamed by his or her superior for having bought a no-name product, and his or her career might suffer). Another risk is the lack of service support. This could lead to long downtimes and loss of productivity. Therefore, HPT's ideal customer is someone who takes risks, who is a global thinker (considers buying a Swiss product), and is open-minded and willing to be different. This person constantly seeks changes to improve his or her business. All these traits describe the customer's emotional side.

What about personal wins? Lower costs of ownership and better cleaning results with less labor could make this buyer a successful change agent in the eyes of his or her superior.

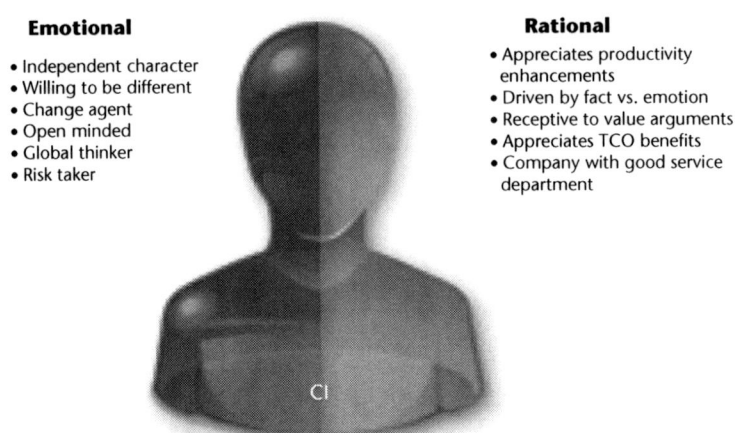

FIGURE 9.6 The ideal customer profile of HPT

In addition, our ideal customer is someone who truly appreciates the benefits of quality products and is willing to pay for them. All these traits describe the customer's rational side (Figure 9.6).

Summing up, in this case the rational part of the ideal customer is aligned with the differentiators (strengths) presented in the strategy canvas. The emotional part is aligned with the challenges presented in the strategy canvas.

> The ideal customer profile helps to keep discounts low through a good alignment of product-value propositions and customer-value appreciation in relation to the emotional burdens that the customer must bear.

Value Factor 5: Apply a voice of the customer (VOC) study at the beginning of the stage-gate process

Now that all important value factors are defined, HPT is ready to run a VOC for the new product development, which is focused on the US market. One of the most efficient and effective ways to do this is to have dedicated in-house resources that specialize in this process. HPT's VOC team, for example, would most likely be composed of human-interface experts, industrial psychologists, and strategic marketing people. The benefit of having an in-house team is that every VOC project significantly increases the company's market intelligence to an extent and a level of detail that a regular product manager would not reach. One main reason for this is the intense involvement in the customer's processes by means of customer observations that is required. Another reason is that the skill set and passion of VOC people are different from what a good product manager will most likely bring to the table. The following step-by-step procedure illustrates what a VOC process can

TABLE 9.4 Workflow for the installation of a cable duct

Activity	Time spent	Type of work
Measurement	28%	Manual
Drilling	17%	Machine
Insert wall plug	10%	Manual
Fit holders	24%	Manual
Fit cable ducts	21%	Manual

look like, how new valuable (high-margin) features can be discovered, and how the main features of the new product are selected.

Step 1: Customer interviews and observations to identify articulated and unarticulated customer needs in the target industry. This is the most challenging and most critical part, because at this point the customer's unsolved problems can be discovered. If HPT were the first company to solve a newly discovered problem, they could charge the dollar equivalent of the problem's value without facing any competitive pressure.

Table 9.4 illustrates an example in which a detailed workflow analysis of a drilling machine manufacturer leads to exactly this result. The conclusion of the workflow analysis is that the time required for taking the measurement represents 28 percent of the overall time needed to install a cable duct. The drilling itself takes just 17 percent of the time. So instead of squeezing another 1 or 2 percent out of the drilling time, it makes much more sense to find a way to reduce the measurement time by 50 percent.

This is a good example to illustrate that the customer himself probably would not have discovered this efficiency-improvement potential because he was unaware of this problem. The result of this discovery was the development of a laser gauge that helped to reduce the measurement time by 50 percent.

Another helpful approach to discovering and identifying important product functions is the "day in a life" approach. Unlike in the cable ducts example, this approach observes all interactions between human and machine throughout the day. In the case of HPT, a VOC would analyze storage, sign-out, transportation to the workplace, installation and setup, cleaning, soap refill, and cleaner maintenance. This process would be written down and documented in great detail (Figure 9.7).

All interactions, especially those at the interface stages, potentially create additional value for the customer as soon as a problem is discovered.

In Step 1, the most important functions that a product must perform in this specific industry application are identified (Figure 9.8).

Step 2: Competitive benchmarking to identify the strength and weaknesses of the company's target competitors. In this stage the performance of the competitor's products are evaluated in terms of the identified functions (Figure 9.9). Independent people using the products in the context of the application perform the evaluation.

FIGURE 9.7 Result of the "day in a life" approach

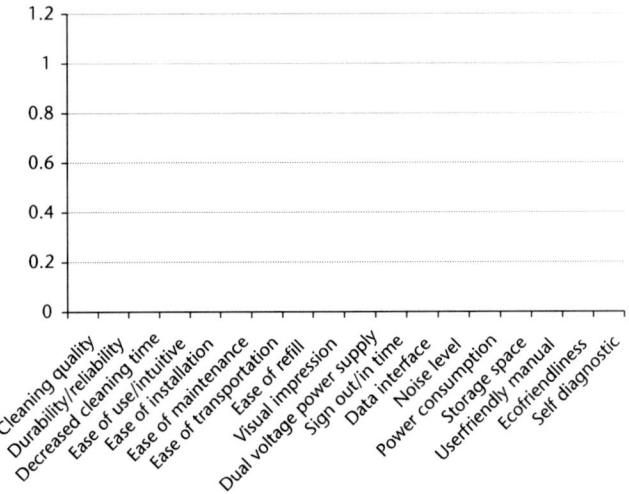

FIGURE 9.8 Unweighted relevant functions of the HPT cleaner

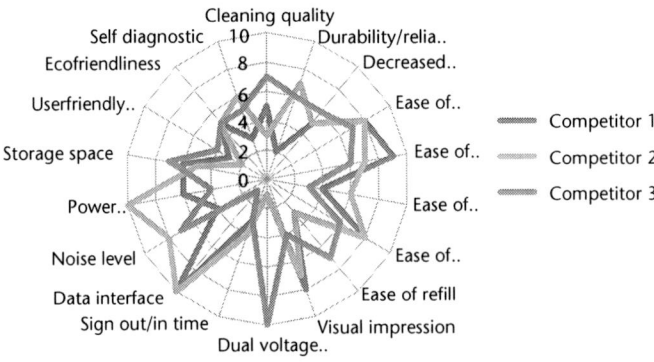

FIGURE 9.9 Performance of the competitors' products in all relevant functions

Step 3: Prioritization of functions by HPT's ideal customer. In this step, the VOC team creates the target performance profile of the new product development. Before the target profile is created, it is important to understand which functions the ideal customer appreciates the most. Conjoint analysis, as described earlier, is once again applied. The result is shown in Figure 9.10.

The process involves identifying the most important product functions, then assessing the target competitor's product performance, and, last but not least, prioritizing product functions by considering the buying preferences of the ideal customer.

With this result, HPT obtained good verification that their ideal customers truly value the properties as outlined in the strategy canvas (durability = low downtime and low cost of ownership). The final step is to define the target profile of the new product. The relevant factors are the weights of the functions as shown in Figure 9.11 and the costs of realizing those functions. The ideal product would

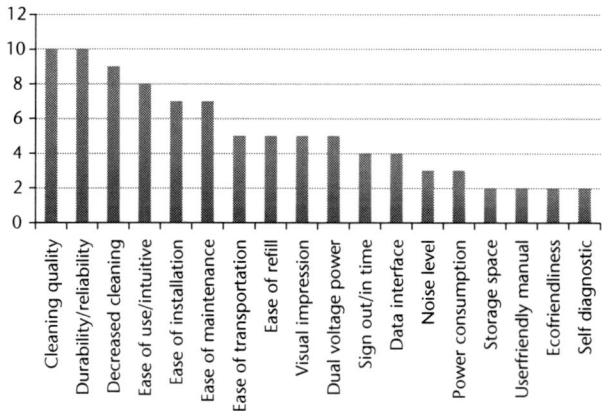

FIGURE 9.10 Importance of the functions from the ideal customer's point of view

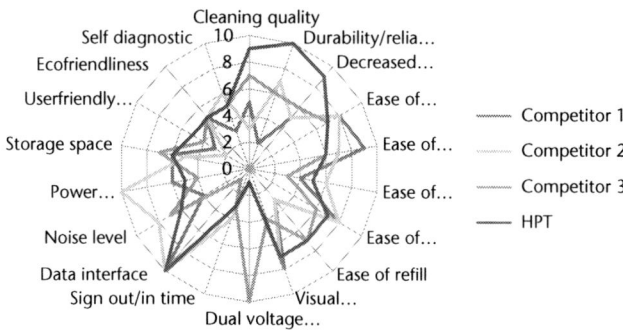

FIGURE 9.11 Target profile of HPT's new cleaner

show maximum performance in every function; however, such a product would most likely not be competitive because it would be too expensive.

Once this target profile has been defined, the marketing team will fit the new product into HPT's strategy canvas and derive the price point from it. This price combined with the target margin defines the target production costs for R&D. From a product concept and pricing perspective, the R&D project is ready to be launched.

Conclusions

In a growing number of publications about pricing, one can read that pricing should become a priority of the CEO and CFO in companies. However, most companies continue to leave pricing to their marketing departments alone.

This chapter explains why product pricing must be embedded in the overall company strategy and why this should be a priority of companies' senior executives. Strategic elements like company value proposition, focus markets, buying-influence structure, ideal customer, go-to-market strategies, and VOC studies should not be looked at separately but can be nicely integrated into a powerful overall strategic approach. If this happens all company functions are aligned to support a strong and consistent offering, which optimizes margins and sales.

The five fundamental value factors integrate all the above-mentioned strategic elements and deliver a simple approach for the practitioner.

Implications for the pricing field

Market segmentation has long played an important role in the pricing process. In addition, VOC studies and conjoint analysis have been very useful tools for pricing. The truly innovative thought of the five fundamental value factors is the integration of all important strategic factors, innovation approaches, and pricing tools. If this approach is used for pricing, companies will

- discover inconsistencies or gaps in their company and marketing strategy and, more importantly, will now know how to correct them
- understand better how emotional and unconscious buying criteria influence the go-to-market strategy
- align the value propositions of products better with non-product-related value factors.

The application of the five value factors leads to stronger strategies, to profitable growth, or to deliberate discontinuation in certain marketplaces. In addition, the reader of this chapter will understand why it is critical to link pricing to the VOC process: no R&D dollar should be spent before all relevant value drivers are identified and prices are evaluated.

References

Liozu, S., Boland, R., Hinterhuber, A. and Perelli, S. (2011) *Industrial pricing orientation: The organizational transformation to value-based pricing.* Paper presented at the International Conference on Engaged Management Scholarship, Case Western Reserve University, Cleveland, OH.

10

THE JOURNEY TO PRICING EXCELLENCE

The case of a mid-sized manufacturing firm

W. Michael Crouch

Greg Hunsicker

The challenge

Companies that have enjoyed a long history of success and profitability, even those that occupy the premium space in their category, have seen significant challenges during the last few years of economic crisis. The recent collapse in demand in many industries, combined with a reduction in available capital, has caused customers to rethink the products they need and how much they are willing to spend. "Good enough" has become a more common refrain and customers are now more willing to make trade-offs between performance and price. This shift in thinking has forced companies who sell in the premium segments to prove and dollarize the value of their products and services like never before. It has pressed many historically cost-plus organizations to consider a move to a more value-based way of thinking. A purely "cost-plus" or margin driven mentality can leave a company vulnerable to under- or overpricing, margin deterioration, or volume loss.

The following are symptomatic of these types of companies:

- A long history of high product margins and cost pass-through without regard for competitors.
- Cost-plus price setting, with margin minimums by product.
- Lack of a formal pricing process.
- Lack of formalized organizational design for pricing.
- Little to no customer segmentation (same price for all customers).
- Some level of "selling arrogance" – little true quantification of value.

Many times, companies have the products, technology, and services to command a premium position, but lack the organizational culture, common language, methodology, and tools to develop and defend this position in front of customers. The economic collapse has pushed many organizations to reach out for new solutions.

The challenge then is to transform a company's culture to embrace a value-based philosophy, to build on a strong brand and premium orientation, and to be able to demonstrate and quantify value in products and services. While the journey to value-based pricing is significant for all companies, it is absolutely vital for those companies that sell innovation and premium products.

The strategy

Companies have employed many methods and strategies for building pricing excellence and value-based pricing in their organizations. We have found that changing a culture, including norms, beliefs, language, meanings, etc., takes time, can be tenuous, and is a journey rather than a destination. The most sustainable way of changing culture starts with a firm foundation and then a building process through distinct stages. The journey is then measured through a series of steps rather than as one complete event. Here are the steps:

Step 1: Senior management commitment

The first and most important step is to build consensus in the organization that value-based pricing and pricing excellence are a benefit to growth and profitability. Top management, and preferably CEO, support and involvement is critical. However, involvement might not be enough to break the obstacles and barriers to change. Top management needs to champion the transformational journey and provide energy, passion, and conviction to the organization. The most important statement for the organization coming from the "C-suite" is to make pricing excellence a key strategic pillar and a well-resourced one in that strategic program. Actions speak louder than words!

Step 2: Resource dedication

A dedicated resource (or resources) is essential. Someone has to champion, be the leader, and be the constant driver for cultural change and training. With many organizations the individual selected will come from a finance background, but needs to have the ability to communicate well with internal and external customers. As the culture moves to a more value-based organization, the pricing function should move to marketing. This is the logical home for pricing since value-based pricing excellence is targeted on the customer needs, preferences, and perceived value. Sustainable change is driven internally, not from consultants or outside in. While consultants are appropriate for training and support, developing in-house expertise is necessary. The decision to develop in-house capabilities creates a number of positive impacts. In addition to the obvious expense savings, developing internal capabilities improves employees' commitment to the program, builds competitive advantage for the long term and aligns the vocabulary and methods used by all involved in the project. Additionally, the change message comes from an internal voice versus someone from the outside telling your organization what to do and how to do it.

Step 3: Building a knowledge base and a common language

After gaining commitment and resources, then comes the educational process. A strong start is to make the Professional Pricing Society's (PPS) Certified Pricing Professional (CPP) program a requirement for key individuals in the organization who participate in pricing decisions. This should include members of marketing, sales, and finance. Be prepared for a long road here, and a lot of patience. This education process will take one to two years to build a knowledge base and common vocabulary among all actors. In addition to the CPP process, the pricing leader can start internal training on the concepts of value-based pricing and the importance of price relative to profitability.

Step 4: Establish a "pricing council"

The creation of a pricing council is a vital step to help ensure early success and monitor progress. This guarantees that, on a regular basis (monthly in our case), a group of key individuals from sales, marketing, operations, and finance meet to spend time dedicated to the management of pricing. The pricing council creates a forum for discussion of major pricing topics, such as key performance indicators, competitive data, dollarization models and new product pricing.

Step 5: Build the right tools and deploy the right systems

Last but not least, when all previous steps are implemented, it is time to focus on decision making support models, tools, and systems. Pricing cannot be forever managed in Excel and home-made tools. At some point, and to increase the systematic adoption of value-based pricing, the adequate professional tools have to be designed and deployed to support the pricing decision making process.

The results

Over two years into the process a substantial change has occurred; however, the transformation is still very much in progress. It is a journey! Notable improvement areas are:

Pricing process implementation

Systematic analysis is now done in all areas concerning pricing. During a pricing event, whether a new product, special price or promotion of existing, there is now a process in place to review, quantify, and understand product value and competition. As a result, the pricing and value messages are more cohesive than ever before.

Communication of quantifiable benefits

Customer benefits are becoming points of emphasis, with increasing quantification as opposed to just listing all the product features. Information flow and dialog is also on-going with all proper parties to make sure that value drivers quantification is dynamic and reliable.

An increased awareness of customer needs

A shared language is created and shared across the organization. Topics such as dollarization, customer value and customer needs are commonly discussed across all functions. People adhere to the concept of capturing value and the worth of products and services in the eyes of the customers.

The new product introduction process

The NPI process has been revised to include more pricing and value quantification, and involves more individuals in the organization. In addition, pricing discussions are taking place much sooner in the process, providing insights into the future viability of the product. Post-launch discussions are also encouraged to evaluate the effectiveness of our pricing strategy.

The unexpected findings

The "journey"

Even if anticipated, the "journey" part of the journey to pricing excellence may be the most surprising finding. Bumps in the road on a major culture shift such as this should be seen as the expected rather than the unexpected. PPS case studies often stated transition time of five to seven years to achieve a full internalization of value-based pricing. This is not an exaggeration but rather a reality. This is a very long slow process that takes continuous reinforcement and training.

There are many ways and directions for this journey. The ARDEX journey has first focused on building a strong pricing process and strong internal capabilities before discussing the transition to value-based pricing (Figure 10.1). We have therefore focused on pricing realization first and then changing the pricing orientation. Bringing the knowledge base up and creating a common language among pricing actors were top priorities for us. With over 20 CPPs in the business now, we are able to move faster toward value-based pricing.

Value quantification

The investment in time and attention on the topic of value driver quantification is tremendous. Quantifying product-related value drivers will eventually get done. Quantifying services and gaining consensus on their value has proven to be more difficult. More investment and time than anticipated may be necessary to capture real customer value-based data. Companies cannot improvise and rely on internal data only. At some point, properly conducted market research projects are needed to support value maps and dollarization exercises.

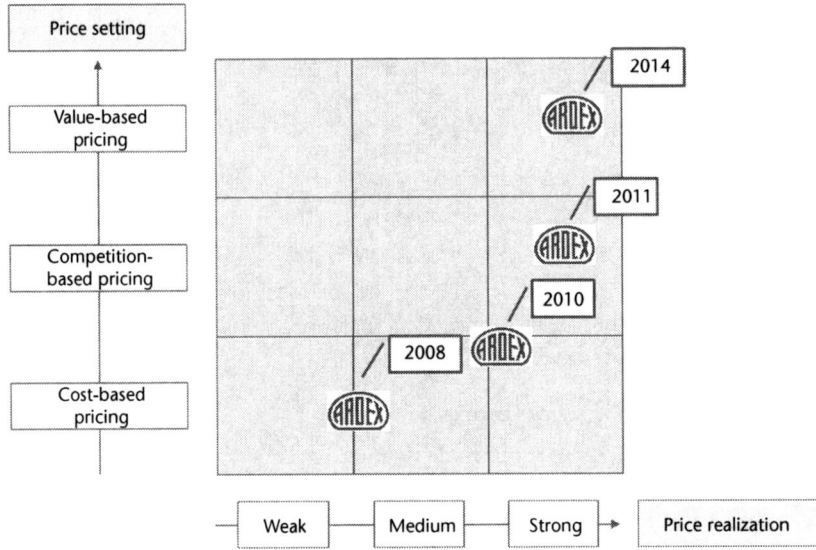

FIGURE 10.1 The ARDEX journey

Key lessons

- Stay the course – this is a long hard process so be prepared and patient.
- Education is essential – the knowledge base is the foundation for everything.
- A champion of the process is required – a knowledge and training "Sherpa."
- Top management support – without it, the process will deteriorate over time.
- Pricing may start in finance, but will inevitably end up in marketing.
- Pricing excellence leads to increased understanding of customer value.
- Pricing transformation is a journey and you might never reach the destination.

11
PRICING PROCESSES IN FAST PACED BUSINESS-TO-BUSINESS SETTINGS

Magnus Johansson

Introduction

The concept of pricing capability (Dutta *et al.* 2002, 2003; Vogel *et al.* 2002) applies a resource based perspective on the topic of pricing in order to capture the organizational aspects of pricing. Pricing capability is thus a highly important contribution as it turns the attention towards the organizational processes, routines and resources required to perform pricing activities and thus capture value through pricing. The concept of pricing capability originates from the recognition that (1) pricing activities are not costless (Bergen *et al.* 2003) and (2) pricing activities are associated with internal and external uncertainties (Dutta *et al.* 2003; Hinterhuber 2008b). Pricing capabilities capture the processes, routines and resources that the organization can strive to build in order to improve cost efficiency and manage uncertainty.

However, the process oriented capability definition applied in Dutta *et al.* (2003) is based on a single case study where the value creation processes are rather well known in advance of pricing activities. In other settings, the distinction between value creation and pricing is not necessarily as clear. For instance, high levels of customization of products involve iterative, intertwined sales and development activities with customers. Pricing processes are therefore less distinctly divided between internal and vis-à-vis customer processes, as defined by Dutta *et al.* (2003). This is due to the fact that in such settings the internal pricing processes do not start by a pre-defined value level as value creation is an ongoing iterative process. Furthermore, fast paced innovative settings involve a continuous interaction between product development activities and value assessment of future deliveries. Thus, competitive as well as value based pricing approaches will draw on resources for value assessment which will also be essential for decisions in association with ongoing value creation activities. The processes involved for future value assessment thus also challenge the implicit assumptions in Dutta *et al.* (2003) that value is defined in advance of the pricing process.

Through theoretical studies and examples from a unit within the semiconductor industry, this chapter shows that for markets involving fast paced innovation and high levels of customization of products to customer needs it may be difficult to explicitly isolate pricing processes and thus pricing capabilities from value creation processes. Thus, for certain settings, the chapter illustrates the difficulties of applying the pricing capabilities concept based on pricing processes without taking into consideration the value creation processes involved. It also suggests that pricing processes should enable proactive pricing activities.

Theoretical foundation

Pricing process as capability and price changes

Pricing capability evolved as a response to the focus on value creation in association with capabilities. Dutta et al. (2002) illustrate how price setting is a strategic capability which the organization must develop and maintain. Through case studies and empirical examples they argue that pricing, and the ability to price, has a key role in the strategy of the firm. They identify three capitals of pricing: human, systems and social capital that contribute to the firm's pricing capability. One of the prime reasons to invest in pricing capabilities is for the firm to be able to handle uncertainty in association with pricing. Dutta et al. (2003) provide a few examples of uncertainties related to customers, competitors and the internal organization. Hinterhuber (2008b) describes the uncertainties inherent in value assessment, a key aspect of value based approaches to pricing.

Of particular importance in association with pricing capability is the ability of the firm to handle price changes and the costs that they incur (Dutta et al. 2002). Bergen et al. (2003) explore this area further by focusing on the internal and external costs of price changes and how to manage price changes. The internal costs may refer to administrative costs but perhaps more importantly to managerial costs involved in pricing, i.e. how much time do managers spend on price changing activities and at what cost. The external costs are related to interaction with customers in order to communicate and gain acceptance for price changes. Dutta et al. (2003) also adhere to the internal and external perspective in association with pricing when they discuss pricing capability from a process perspective. They state that 'In setting prices, firms face two issues: appropriating rents and balancing competing internal interests. A pricing capability consists of the systems and processes that a firm develops to address these two issues' (Dutta et al. 2003: 616). Vogel et al. (2002) also view pricing capabilities in relation to price changes and external and internal aspects when they propose that policies and processes are key parts of building a pricing capability.

Based on a study within a business-to-business setting, Dutta et al. (2003) outline two pricing processes: internal and vis-à-vis customers. They state that the firm normally moves between these two processes in iterative cycles or loops, but they also state that a price changing sequence is typically initiated by the internal price setting process. The internal price setting process encompasses the identification of competitor prices, setting of pricing strategy and transferring pricing strategy to prices. The vis-à-vis customers process revolves around the bargaining process and thus focuses on the convincing of customers of changes in prices and in pricing logic and the negotiation of prices with customers. Thus, a price changing sequence is typically initiated by a stage in which strategy is transferred into generic price levels, in the form of, for instance, list prices. The next stage takes these price levels to the customer level for adaptation and bargaining. Phillips (2005) makes a slightly different distinction as he is primarily concerned with the tactical level of pricing: between list pricing and customized pricing. Whereas Dutta et al. (2003) focused their study on a business-to-business setting, Phillips discusses list and customized pricing across consumer as well as business-to-business markets. Among the examples of customized pricing the business-to-business cases are in the majority. Customized pricing is characterized, according to Phillips, by the one-to-one quoting of price to each customer. Thus, the seller can quote a different price for each request.

Common for the above descriptions of pricing situations and processes is the assumption of value as created ahead of the pricing process. This is at its clearest in the case of mass-products or services, which are most clearly associated with list prices. But also in association with what Phillips refers to as customized pricing, the pricing sequence largely assumes that the value level of the product or service can be pre-defined. In the following sections, this chapter will illustrate two settings where the pricing process, and thus the value capture process, and the value creation process cannot be as easily distinguished from each other.

It is vital to note that although Dutta et al. (2003) is a highly important study as it provides in-depth insights into the character of pricing processes, it is a single case study. As such, it is limited to the character of the empirical pricing setting. This chapter tries to expand our knowledge of pricing processes, and capabilities, by deliberately studying partly different pricing settings where the pricing processes are likely to have slightly different characteristics. Furthermore, although Dutta et al. (2003) captures several aspects of different pricing approaches, or strategies, it does not explicitly deal with that dimension of the field of pricing. This chapter explicitly tries to take into consideration cost, competition and value based pricing approaches, with a particular focus on the latter. The next section provides an overview of the main pricing strategies and the main value based approaches to pricing.

Value based pricing

Even though the literature suggests numerous different pricing strategies, there are three main categories that researchers in general are able to agree on: (1) cost-based pricing, (2) competition-based pricing and (3) customer value based pricing (Hinterhuber 2008a). The approach of customer value based pricing can be defined as: 'Customer value based pricing approaches use the value a product or service delivers to a predefined segment of customers as the main factor for setting prices' (Hinterhuber 2008a: 42).

Within the value based pricing approach two main value definitions can be identified: customer perceived value (e.g. Cannon and Morgan 1990; Thompson and Coe 1997) and differentiation value (Forbis and Mehta 1981). Smith and Nagle (2005) elaborate on the differences between these two main categories and provide an overview of four types of value. They distinguish between: (1) value in use, i.e. the actual value to the customer of the product or delivery in use (cf. the concept of acquisition utility in Thaler 1985); (2) value in exchange, i.e. economic value, similar to the prior one, with a focus on differentiation and a referenced commodity value; (3) perceived value, here with a focus on the perceived market value, i.e. it captures how customers perceive value, and more specifically the economic value and (4) willingness to pay.

Of particular interest in association with a value based approach is the assessment of value. For instance in Hinterhuber (2008a) value assessment is ranked as the main obstacle towards implementing value based pricing. In the review by Hinterhuber (2008b) the above two value definitions, customer perceived value and differentiation value, reappear. But Hinterhuber also stresses the aspect of uncertainty in association with value in business markets due to the future orientation of values. The origin of uncertainty is the interaction between buyer and seller and the process where 'two parties exchange resources (e.g. money, goods, services, rights, or intellectual property) in the expectation of certain future benefits resulting from consuming these resources' (Hinterhuber 2008b: 390). This chapter will address the issue of uncertainty of value assessment in two particular settings and further elaborate on its relation to the value creation process in each case.

Assessing customer value and applying it in association with pricing activities is closely associated with the pricing literature; see, for instance, the discussion on value based pricing in Smith and Nagle (2005), Nagle and Hogan (2006) and Bernstein and Macias (2002). However, this explicit part of the pricing process is not dealt with extensively in Dutta *et al.* (2003). Dutta *et al.* provide one example that shows the importance of the pricing function in leading the assessment of product and reference value, i.e. the value of the competitor product alternative (Nagle and Hogan 2006). The example also illustrates that the process transfers beyond the traditional pricing or marketing function boundaries. But, limited attention is given to the uncertainty and future orientation inherent in a business-to-business setting.

When viewing value assessment in relation to processes, one issue is whether to associate value assessment with the pricing capability or other capability definitions. It would for instance be possible to attribute reference value assessment processes to other capability distinctions, such as outside-in processes (Day 1996). However a complete value assessment process is, as the pricing process and capability in Day (1996), a spanning process which links internal and external perspectives. Thus, a value assessment process (if such a process can be isolated and defined) will also be a spanning process. This is apparent in association with value based pricing where external information of customer perceived value and competitor reference value must be considered together with internal data on the actual value set of the product or service of the firm in order to set the price. Therefore, from the perspective of capability as process, when working with value based pricing, the pricing process must include activities that incorporate internal and external perspectives. This is contrasted by a pure cost-based pricing approach where a firm may rely on internal data only.

Methods

In the following sections, two pricing settings will be studied. It will be done mainly from a value based perspective, and by considering the pricing processes involved. The settings studied differ from the one studied by Dutta et al. (2003) by their nature of value creation. The two settings are studied through a definition of the pricing setting based on the value creation character. Each section reviews theoretical descriptions of pricing practices in the particular setting but also utilizes examples from a case firm.

The studied firm, headquartered in Europe, is one of the major players among a number of semiconductor firms supplying combined hardware and software solutions for consumer electronics original equipment manufacturers (OEMs). Most of the firms in this section of the industry have a focus on the design and development of products and are mostly fabless, although they still depend on the characteristics of the industry inherent from semiconductor manufacturing. The studied firm has several development sites and serves customers from all over the world.

The case firm combines two different types of value creation to generate its customer offerings and thus works with two different pricing settings. The first type of value creation is related to generic products in a business-to-business setting. In that sense it does not differ significantly from the settings studied by Dutta et al. (2003). However, the firm acts in a fast paced industry with substantial, but quickly eroding, innovation premiums. The first price setting therefore considers pricing processes related to the pricing of technologically innovative products with a temporary monopoly character.

The second price setting is characterized by value created by adapting, or customizing, the generic products to customer specific needs and demands. This is thus another, but very different, monopoly pricing setting with barriers of entry which are often created over longer periods of time through long-term customer relationships. Some of these aspects are captured by Dutta et al. (2003) in their study. However, by applying a value creation framework in order to identify different settings in which pricing processes appear this chapter provides additional detail to the perspective of pricing capability as a process. Although a single firm is studied, the two settings as described above are substantially different in their value creation character which, as will be shown, also influences the pricing processes. Therefore, although it is a single firm, the empirical part of this study consists of two cases depicting two different pricing settings due to the value creation character.

The differences between the two pricing settings will be outlined through a theoretical review of value creation types and pricing approaches in association with these. Examples and descriptions from the case firm will help to clarify the character of pricing in the settings and the particularities of the processes. This paper is empirically based on a case study. Studies of the firm were done as an observing participant (Alvesson 1999) over a period of more than two years, which has enabled closeness to the firm (cf. Brundin 2007). Observing as a participant was made possible through working with a corporate group that provided support to the majority of the firm's business areas in fields such as business planning, pricing and strategic analysis.

Findings

Fast paced innovation and pricing

The first pricing setting of this chapter deals with innovative contexts where value perishes rapidly over time. The setting is largely similar to what is described by Dean (1950); a monopoly pricing setting where innovation price premiums can be applied for innovative products. However, here the prime focus is on the changes in the products and not whether the products are radically new or not. For instance, the case example in this section comes from an industry where products fulfil the same type of market needs over time but where the main features due to the fast technological pace evolve very rapidly from one product generation to the next.

When applying pricing with value based features in association with innovation we can distinguish two (non-exclusive) approaches, in accordance with value definitions. The first adheres to the concept of value in use (Smith and Nagle 2005; and see also acquisition value in Thaler 1985). The process of new product pricing in association with value in use is described for instance in Bernstein and Macias (2002) who through a case study outline the customer value research involved in such activities. Customer value (value in use) studies are particularly important for new features or new use cases where the price sensitivity of the customer is hard to determine (cf. Nagle and Hogan 2006).

The second approach is closely intertwined with environments with fast paced new product introduction (cf. Nagle and Hogan 2006) and relates to market value and more specifically the reference value which forms a basis for distinguishing economic value. Fast paced innovative environments are characterized by players who adopt a semi-structured, rhythmic, time-paced transition process (Brown and Eisenhardt 1997, 1998). This rhythmic behaviour is proposed to be related to three types of internal or external adaptations. The first has to do with the interaction between staff with a focus on future orientation and those focused on current development. Rhythmically paced transitions enable these to interact in an efficient manner and balance changes with established ways of working. The second is that the rhythm enables work to be paced and thus creates a smooth flow in activities. The third reason is that the rhythm arises in association with external factors. This may for instance correspond with market cycles and timing of market windows, or the overall pace of the industry. Thus, pacing related to external factors may depend on adaptation to an external technological rhythm but it might also be related to the rate at which the market can absorb innovation.

One of the prime examples in Brown and Eisenhardt (1998) is how Intel works with time pacing. They discuss how Intel have enabled and adjusted their pace to stay ahead of competition and in line with market demand and absorption of innovation. Intel did this through time paced innovation of products, time-paced investments in production facilities and alignment of complementor pacing. Time pacing (Brown and Eisenhardt 1998) requires a proactive approach rather than the reactive alternative of event pacing.

The most recent example of Intel product development time pacing is the Tick-Tock model (Intel Tick-Tock Model 2011) where every other year sees a change in process architecture and process node reduction respectively. An industry coloured by such 'pacing' of innovation follows a path which can be predicted with some accuracy. It is important to note that the innovative pace in this example also encompasses continuous (or rather incremental, stepwise) change in existing product lines. Thus, the innovative pace does not necessarily generate new types of products or expand the industry or user targets. Rather the fast innovative pace is a necessity in order to keep up with continuously increased feature demands from customers or increased feature or technology competition in existing product areas.

Rutherford and Wilhelm (1999) describe how future market prices can be forecasted on fast paced markets by studying key feature development and price erosion on the notebook market. They propose a three stage process. The first phase relates computer price to main features during a time period. Phase two quantifies how feature evolution affects market value and phase three applies these findings in order to forecast a competitive selling price with a specific set of features. Applying such a forecast for decision making is of course only valid when the industry is not subject to disruptive innovative changes (Christensen 1997) which may alter the importance of the specific features but follows a pace such as described above. However, the approach shows how on a market with a fast but predictable price and feature development the market reference value can be forecasted.

The approach as described by Rutherford and Wilhelm (1999) is associated with new product development or continuous refinement of existing product lines whereas Bernstein and Macias (2002) include market innovation aspects which require deeper understanding of customer adoption and expected customer value in use. Depending on the situation, key input to pricing decisions rely on these value assessment processes. But, the value creation process also depends on these value assessment processes as they can provide key input to investment decisions. Furthermore, pricing decisions are most often not just taken the moment before introduction but are the result of a long iterative process in which they also must be considered in the light of other products in a portfolio and their timing (cf. the decision problems in Moorthy and Png 1992). Thus, the value creation and value capture process must execute in parallel. The distinction between them is also difficult as they rely on the same key input and the establishment of future market value.

Therefore, in highly innovative markets the distinction between value creation and value capture processes is much less obvious.

The role of pricing and future value assessment as a key influencer on value creation could also be seen in the case study of this chapter. The studied firm is one of the key players within a segment of the semiconductor industry. It incorporates hardware and software design but primarily outsources its production. Customers are typically electronics manufacturers who design and produce high technology consumer goods. Firms in the segment, in which the case firm acts, has a high ratio of R&D expense over net sales, typically close to one third of net sales. Partly, the segment follows similar industry pacing as the Intel Tick-Tock example above due to similar semiconductor manufacturing dependence.

During the period which I studied the firm, an attempt was made at estimating future market value based on feature development and price erosion. This provided a very different picture compared to the cost-based models used previously in the firm. It revealed significant price premiums at the early stages of upgraded feature levels in the market, which then eroded quickly. But it also revealed that products needed to be balanced with regard to feature innovation and cost efficiency. This balance had to be pursued in order to capture the initial premiums but also to survive long enough in the market to reach pay-back levels. This showed a market which required a different approach to research and development than currently employed. The value studies, as a key part of the pricing planning, was central to revealing this.

This setting also involves a certain level of uncertainty due to future orientation. The uncertainty comes from the fact that the market is changing at a rapid pace. If it were sufficient to assess value at the time of launch this would not be a problem, but in these settings value assessment, as well as strategic pricing, must provide guidance long in advance, from an external price changing perspective as well as in the form of guidelines towards value creation processes.

From a pricing capability perspective this case illustrates the importance of routines related to tracking competitor prices (cf. Dutta et al. 2003), and not least, how competitor products change over time. But as discussed above, in the specific setting these routines also involve forecasting of future market prices in order to estimate future product pricing (cf. Rutherford and Wilhelm 1999) and revenue levels.

High levels of customization and pricing

Pricing literature and discussions on value most often relate to products or services that are of a generic and repeatable character. In particular, the product perspective on value dominates the discussion. And for many firms, in relation to pricing, it is highly important that they are able to move towards value based pricing (as promoted in Hinterhuber 2004, 2008a, b).

However, for firms with a high level of customization in their deliveries a substantial share of customer value will be generated by adaptation or design to customer unique demands and requirements. To some extent this area of pricing has been covered by Phillips (2005). But his discussion primarily revolves around limited customization of products which includes a bidding process between competing suppliers, not higher levels of customization depending on longer-term relationships.

Therefore, the second pricing setting that will be considered is the one where value is created in close interaction with customers through iterative customization processes. Such value creation settings can be found in association with professional services such as consulting services, but also in industrial business-to-business contexts. Descriptions of the character of such a value creation setting can be found for instance in Stabell and Fjeldstad (1998) where shop logic value creation deals with customization to customer unique problems. In such settings, problem solving activities drive the allocation of resources. The interaction of the firm with the customer for which to solve a problem is cyclical and spiraling (Stabell and Fjeldstad 1998), which affects how the capabilities of the organization will evolve.

Whereas industrial organizations most often are associated with the value chain (Stabell and Fjeldstad 1998), professional service firms are associated with the value shop (Stabell and Fjeldstad 1998). The value chain is a configuration of activities in a chain-like fashion whereas the value shop consists of an iterative sequence of diagnosis and solving of a customer's problem, and thus the customization of a delivery to a customer's specific needs. A high level of customization is consequently a key characteristic of professional services (Løwendahl 1997). Industrial organizations, on the other hand, are traditionally associated with their ability to standardize in order to enable economies of scale through repetition. But customization can be an important feature of an industrial organization. And in fact, this is not a new phenomenon. Customization has always been significant on industrial markets (Spring and Dalrymple 2000).

The character of value creation in this setting and especially the close customer interaction affects pricing activities. Dawson (2005) emphasizes the importance of customer relationships in relation to value based pricing as value based pricing strategies often require a certain level of mutual trust in order to gain insights into the value effects for the customer. In turn, client relation based strategies often rely on individually based long-term interactions (Løwendahl 1997). The project orientation, which can be associated with professional service firms, can also be found in industries with a similarly high level of customization. Thus other firms, such as construction firms (Akintoye and Skitmore 1992), have similar pricing situations.

For further insights into the contrast of pricing depending on a shop value creation model I will initially turn to professional service firms such as consulting firms. In consulting industries it is not unusual that pricing utilizes cost-plus models based on hourly rates. This enables certain flexibility in problem solving situations where the exact time required to solve the customer problem may be hard to estimate. Time and cost pricing is a common pricing method for professional services (cf. Dawson 2005). It is thus a cost based approach directly related to the prime resources applied in professional service delivery – human resources. Time based charging is also often the underlying principle of setting price levels for fixed fees or they may appear in combined models together with fixed fees (Dawson 2005). Dawson (2005) also mentions commission models and retainers and membership fees as common models. Retainers and membership fees are typically applied in order to access information and knowledge services.

What are then the consequences of applying value based pricing on consulting or other shop logic value creation settings? When viewing the price setting situation from a value based perspective it is important to separate between different parts of the value creation process and the value delivered. Interaction between customer and supplier typically starts off by identifying a problem to be solved through a pre-study. After that a first agreement is made which includes a compensation target for the supplier for solving the problem. This first phase, which in itself creates customer value (compare consultative services for product selection in Hinterhuber 2008a), is the one which has the strongest iterative character. The value of this initial process is partly overlooked by, for instance, Weiss (2002). For consultative services associated with product choices (DeVincentis and Rackham 1998; Hinterhuber 2008b with references to Corey 1989), this phase may very well be prominent. The next stage is the execution phase (see approaches to value based pricing for these processes in, for instance, Weiss 2002). This stage also requires close interaction (cf. Løwendahl 1997) as it revolves around problem solving together with the customer. The iterative character of both of the phases increases the intertwinement between the internal price setting process and the price setting process towards the customer. This tendency becomes especially clear if a value based pricing approach is applied.

In the case firm of this study a substantial part of the value created was customer specific resulting from adaptations and customizations of the generic products to customer and project specific requirements. Such adaptations could be far reaching and encompass hardware as well as software parts of deliveries through unique designs and redesigns. Most often these parts of deliveries involved working very closely with customers, sometimes at the customer site. The firm struggled with the pricing of these efforts and especially with making the value of them explicit and pricing them accordingly. In many cases the firm relied on cost-plus models based on the human resources involved, not unlike the setup in many consulting firms. But in several instances the inability of making value explicit and communicating it to customers led to the firm not charging for the efforts but giving it away as part of the generic product offering.

From a value based perspective, this case illustrates a business-to-business setting where uncertainty in value assessment is high due to the iterative and uncertain character of the final delivery. The setting is a prime example of shop logic value creation due to its high levels of customization and the iterative problem solving with customers. This setting makes cost estimation as well as value estimation difficult. Reference value assessment is especially difficult due to the absence of competitor deliveries for customer unique deliveries (Johansson and Andersson 2012). Rather the supplier has to focus on estimating future value in use for the customer. Such exercises will partly be estimates depending on the level of information available from the customer. They will also be estimates due to the future orientation of value as described by Hinterhuber (2008b).

Conclusions

The concept of pricing capabilities is highly important as it helps clarify the importance of organizational processes and routines of an organization in association with pricing. Thus, the concept also helps us make sense of and address the fact that pricing activities are associated with internal and external costs which need to be managed by the organization.

A common factor which influences the character of the pricing processes for both of the settings discussed in this paper is the reliance on value assessments. If the firm predominantly relies on cost based pricing, the pricing process may be able to act on data which to a larger extent is available *ex ante* (this of course depends on the reliability and variation over time of cost estimates). However, if a firm adds a value based perspective this influences the character of the pricing process significantly as the pricing process is intrinsically linked to value assessment (cf. Dutta *et al.* 2003 and Hinterhuber 2008b).

The two pricing settings discussed in this paper are different from the setting studied by Dutta *et al.* (2003) and this influences the nature of pricing processes. In the first price setting the pricing process is largely similar to that as described in Dutta *et al.* (2003), but it is more difficult to clearly separate the pricing process from the value creation process. In the first case discussed above it is shown how changes in pricing activities led to clearer establishment of future market value estimates. Thus, establishing future reference value is driven by pricing activities and pricing processes and routines. But such estimates also become crucial for value creation activities as they set the framework also for cost levels, given that a certain level of profitability is pursued. Therefore, the pricing process, with future reference value assessment as a core ability, is part in generating a key input to the value creation process. This is a matter which is not explicitly dealt with in Dutta *et al.* (2003).

In Dutta *et al.* we see how the process of establishing reference value and customer value is driven by the pricing function. These activities extend into sales and engineering and product development functions in order to collect and evaluate data. Thus, defining value levels is indeed driven by the pricing process and thus a part of the pricing capability. But, as the first case shows, in fast paced industries this capability will continuously set the framework for value creation processes. Value creation does not take place ahead of value definition. But rather, these two interact iteratively and pricing processes provide vital input to value creation decisions.

In the second pricing setting where the value creation process is iterative, the pricing process is also increasingly iterative and intertwined with the value creation process. Price setting authority is also more local due to the close relationships required for value assessment and creation. Thus, although Dutta *et al.* mention the iterative interaction between the internal and vis-à-vis customer processes, they also mention that the internal process precedes the vis-à-vis customer process in a price change sequence. In the second described pricing setting the two processes as proposed by Dutta *et al.* are very closely interrelated due to the focus being mainly on customer specific value creation and not on customer generic value creation. Thus, there is limited input to the pricing process *ex ante* (except for some cost bases, such as for instance labour costs for consulting services). And this is particularly the case for value estimates.

Practitioners should recognize that pricing should play a leading role in these settings. The pricing process must not only certify that the right price is set but also that value assessment provides the correct basis for value creation processes. Independent of whether value assessment is seen as part of the pricing process or not, pricing is likely (as shown in the above examples and the literature) to drive the development of value assessment. Still, it is not just value assessment which provides a framework for value creation efforts. Rather, several other aspects of the pricing process must be involved such as the overall pricing strategy and pricing policies in order to establish the revenue potential and thus the direction of value creation (see the emphasis on market strategy and tactics in association with value based pricing practice in Anderson *et al.* 2010). Therefore, a pricing process depending on value based pricing efforts must be initiated in advance of or closely interact with the value creation process from its beginning. It will in these settings have to be proactive vis-à-vis value creation in order to manage uncertainties related to value assessment.

Implications for the pricing field

Both of the pricing settings discussed in this paper require pricing processes that enable working proactively with pricing as well as in interaction with value creation processes. Thus, in the discussed pricing settings we need to challenge clear distinctions between value creation and value appropriation (cf. the distinction in Mizik and Jacobsson 2003), here with a particular focus on pricing. Furthermore the concept of pricing capabilities as proposed by Dutta *et al.* (2002, 2003) is highly important in order to put focus on the processes, routines and systems that the organization depends on for its pricing activities. However, it is also important to view pricing processes in relation to value creation processes in order to uncover various types of processes and to identify their interdependencies and interaction with value creation processes. Furthermore, in one of the pricing settings discussed the internally and customer oriented pricing processes were closely intertwined due to the single customer, high-level customization value creation character.

The findings in this study should be recognized by academics as an opportunity for future research. Future research should continue to study pricing processes from a capability perspective in various value creation settings in order to increase our understanding (1) of how pricing processes diverge between various settings and (2) what pricing process aspects can be considered as generic and contribute to creating a more consistent basis for the definition of pricing capabilities.

Implications for innovation in pricing

This chapter also illustrates the vital role of pricing processes in the organization. It shows how pricing processes must be proactive versus value creation and actively drive the incorporation of external and internal perspectives as a spanning process (cf. Day 1996). Thus, this chapter further emphasizes the strategic importance of a firm's pricing capability.

Practitioners should therefore recognize the need to build processes and routines which support a proactive role of pricing. As illustrated, this is crucial in fast paced industries in order to estimate future market value and establish pricing guidelines for future products (or updated products), and thus lay the foundations for future revenue estimates. It is also fundamental for firms that provide highly customized solutions in order to provide continuous assessment of value in use. Capabilities should be built so that pricing functions and activities are enabled to play a more active role in order to support value creation activities. This means that pricing must take a long-term view. Organizations should focus on the ability to assess future value and provide pricing guidelines at an early stage in relation to value creation activities, and on the ability to interact with ongoing value creation activities.

References

Akintoye, A. and Skitmore, M. (1992) Pricing approaches in the construction industry. *Industrial Marketing Management*, 21, pp. 311–18.

Alvesson, M. (1999) *Methodology for close up studies*. Institute of Economic Research Working Paper Series. Lund University.

Anderson, J. C., Wouters, M. and van Rossum, W. (2010) Why the highest price isn't the best price. *MIT Sloan Management Review*, 51 (2), pp. 69–76.

Bergen, M., Ritson, M., Dutta, S., Levy, D. and Zbaracki, M. (2003) Shattering the myth of costless price changes. *European Management Journal*, 21 (6), pp. 663–9.

Bernstein, J. and Macias, D. (2002) Engineering new-product success: The new-product pricing process at Emerson. *Industrial Marketing Management*, 31 (1), pp. 51–64.

Brown, S. L. and Eisenhardt, K. M. (1997) The art of continuous change: Linking complexity theory and time-paced evolution in relentlessly shifting organizations. *Administrative Science Quarterly*, 42 (1), pp. 1–34.

Brown, S. L. and Eisenhardt, K. M. (1998) *Competing on the edge*. Boston, MA: Harvard Business Review Press.

Brundin, E. (2007) Catching it as it happens. In: Nergaard, H. and J. P. Ulhoj (eds) *Handbook for qualitative methods in entrepreneurship research*. Camberley: Edward Elgar, pp. 279–307.

Cannon, H. M. and Morgan, F. W. (1990) A strategic pricing framework. *The Journal of Service Marketing*, 4 (2), pp. 19–30.

Christensen, C. (1997) *The innovator's dilemma: when new technologies cause great firms to fail*. Boston, MA: Harvard Business School.

Corey, R. (1989) *Industrial buyer behaviour*. Harvard Business School note, 9-582-117, April. Boston, MA: Harvard Business School.

Dawson, R. (2005) *Developing knowledge-based client relationships*. Woburn: Elsevier.

Day, G. S. (1996) The capabilities of market driven organizations. *Journal of Marketing*, 58, pp. 37–52.

Dean, J. (1950) Pricing policies for new products. *Harvard Business Review*, 1976 reprint.
DeVincentis, J. and Rackham, N. (1998) Breadth of a salesman. *McKinsey Quarterly*, 35 (4), pp. 32–43.
Dutta, S., Bergen, M., Levy, D., Ritson M. and Zbaracki, M. (2002) Pricing as a strategic capability. *MIT Sloan Management Review*, 43 (3), pp. 61–6.
Dutta, S., Zbaracki, M. and Bergen, M. (2003) Pricing process as a capability: A resource-based perspective. *Strategic Management Journal*, 24 (7), pp. 615–30.
Forbis, J. L. and Mehta, N. T. (1981) Value-based strategies for industrial products. *Business Horizons*, 24 (3), pp. 32–43.
Hinterhuber, A. (2004) Towards value-based pricing – An integrative framework for decision making. *Industrial Marketing Management*, 33 (8), pp. 765–78.
Hinterhuber, A. (2008a) Customer value-based pricing strategies: why companies resist. *Journal of Business Strategy*, 29 (4), pp. 41–50.
Hinterhuber, A. (2008b) Value delivery and value-based pricing in industrial markets. *Advances in Business Marketing and Purchasing*, 14, pp. 381–448.
Intel Tick Tock Model. Retrieved December 29, 2011 from http://www.intel.com/content/www/us/en/silicon-innovations/intel-tick-tock-model-general.html.
Johansson, M. and Andersson, L. (2012) Pricing practices and value creation logics. *Journal of Revenue and Pricing Management*, 11, pp. 64–75.
Løwendahl, B. (1997) *Strategic management of professional service firms*. Copenhagen: Copenhagen Business School Press.
Mizik, N. and Jacobsson, R. (2003) Trading off between value creation and value appropriation: The financial implications of shifts in strategic emphasis. *Journal of Marketing*, 67, pp. 63–76.
Moorthy, K. S. and Png, I. P. L. (1992) Market segmentation, cannibalization, and the timing of product introductions. *Management Science*, 38 (3), pp. 345–59.
Nagle, T. T. and Hogan, J. E. (2006) *The strategy and tactics of pricing: A guide to growing more profitably*. Upper Saddle River, NJ: Pearson Education, Inc.
Phillips, R. L. (2005) *Pricing and revenue optimization*. Stanford, CA: Stanford University Press.
Rutherford, D. P. and Wilhelm, W. E. (1999) Forecasting notebook computer price as a function of constituent features. *Computers & Industrial Engineering*, 37 (4): pp. 823–45.
Smith, G. E. and Nagle, T. T. (2005) A question of value. *Marketing Management*, 14 (4), pp. 38–43.
Spring, M. and Dalrymple, J. F. (2000) Product customization and manufacturing strategy. *International Journal of Operations and Production Management*, 20 (4), pp. 441–67.
Stabell, C. B. and Fjeldstad, Ø. D. (1998) Configuring value for competitive advantage: on chains, shops, and networks. *Strategic Management Journal*, 19 (5), pp. 413–37.
Thaler, R. (1985) Mental accounting and consumer choice. *Marketing Science*, 4, pp. 199–214.
Thompson, K. N. T. and Coe, B. J. (1997) Gaining sustainable competitive advantage through strategic pricing: selecting a perceived value price. *Pricing Strategy & Practice*, 5 (2), pp. 70–9.
Vogel, H., Bright, K. and Stalk, G. (2002) Organizing for Pricing. *BCG Perspectives*, September 2002.
Weiss, A. (2002) *Value-based fees: How to charge and get what you're worth*. San Francisco: Jossey-Bass Pfeiffer.

12

PRICING DUE DILIGENCE IN THE MERGERS AND ACQUISITION PROCESS

David Dvorin

Jered W. Haedt

Vernon E. Lennon

The case for change

Historically, the mergers and acquisition (M&A) process is undertaken primarily to grow inorganically or to achieve investment returns. A financial valuation of the target acquisition is completed by the acquiring business in order to determine an acceptable purchase price for the entity. The process used to develop the business valuation is meant to bring clarity and visibility into the expected financial synergies and strategic advantages of the new entity. However, failure to achieve the investment returns expected at the original acquisition event according to the financial valuation occurs frequently (Straub 2007; Pautler 2001). To make matters worse, a combination of incomplete, insufficient or incorrect assessments of the target business will increase the likelihood of missing investment expectations. Due to the frequent limits on time and data access during the due diligence process, along with the high level nature of the valuation, many acquiring firms miss their chance to investigate a potential arbitrage generated after a more detailed understanding of the target business's strategic pricing practices and organization. A more rigorous assessment of a target company's pricing capabilities and the associated improvement opportunities can substantially sharpen the enterprise valuation and the subsequent value capture from M&A.

Just as with company-to-customer transaction pricing, the M&A process positions buyers and sellers at opposite sides of the negotiating table. Successful deals are accomplished when common ground is found between buyer and seller, and both parties leave the process satisfied. Harnessing improved 'purchase price' information about the target company in an M&A process, through a comprehensive understanding of pricing capabilities, provides the seller with an improved position in the valuation discussions. The buyer, on the other hand, can achieve faster acquisition synergy realization using a complete pricing capability assessment.

Little research has been published on the assessment of a business's strategic pricing capabilities during the M&A due diligence process, and there is subsequently no detailed guidance on how the evaluation of a company's pricing capabilities should inform the financial valuation of the business. This paper will directly address both of these gaps with a clear and concrete pricing capabilities assessment process that effectively measures a company's strategic pricing capabilities and specifies how the results of the assessment affect the enterprise valuation of the entity. A brief review of the traditional M&A process will highlight specific information and process arbitrage opportunities. Then a detailed strategic pricing capability assessment will be elaborated including how the results of the assessment alter traditional cash flow entity valuations. Finally, recommended approaches for using the results of the strategic pricing capability assessment during the M&A process will be presented.

Typical M&A due diligence process

While specific due diligence does not occur until late in the acquisition process, it is arguably the most important part of the 'deal'. The due diligence process begins immediately following a Letter of Intent (LOI), and usually includes a large information and data request. The large information request tends to extend the due diligence beyond the typical 60-day timeline, but an unprepared seller can also produce data and reporting examples that are insufficient for the buyer.

The detailed analysis of the financial and operating levers of a target business leads to a valuation by both the acquiring company and the acquired company. In order for a deal to consummate, these two valuations need to be reconciled at the negotiating table. Buyers use their due diligence to produce an internally acceptable valuation for negotiations. Sellers build their valuation through their detailed understanding of the 'day to day' business. The 'day to day' operations, such as manufacturing, distribution, sales, marketing and, most notably in this discussion, pricing, can collectively provide tremendous insights for both buyers and sellers into operational efficiency and future earnings. The quick turnaround time in an M&A process, and the usual desire for rapid closure, often leave real information gaps in the buyer's analysis of the target's 'day to day' operations appropriately. This produces a potential arbitrage event in which the seller understands more about operational competencies than the buyer, but the arbitrage can be closed by the buyer if pricing capabilities are accurately assessed.

The major areas analysed during the traditional due diligence process are shown in Figure 12.1.

Due diligence
Existing process

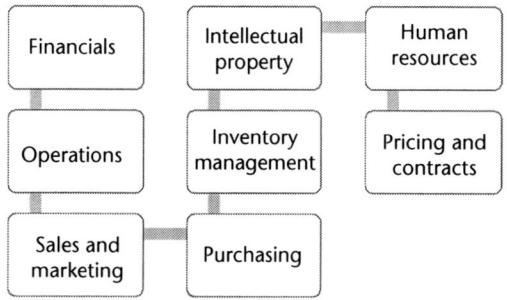

FIGURE 12.1 Due diligence – existing process

Several of the traditional due diligence areas yield potential questions to address for their impact on pricing strategy and realization.

- *Financials.* The perennial trio of financial statements (balance sheet, income statement and cash flow statement) and a detailed review of accounting practices are the first pieces of information passed between seller and potential buyer. Questions to address:
    o Is the financial data aggregated at too high a level?
    o Can underlying drivers of financial performance be clearly identified?

- *Operations.* Considered the next most important area, operations covers all of the major manufacturing and distribution processes of the target entity. Questions to address:
    o Is the operational information aggregated at too high a level?
    o Are the right operational metrics being monitored to understand the profit impact of manufacturing and distribution decisions?

- *Sales and marketing.* An in-depth understanding of the size and quality of the commercial team, along with marketing's ability to campaign appropriately, is necessary to predict future channel competencies. Question to address:
    o Are sales and marketing performance metrics being tracked at granular levels of individual offerings, sales personnel and customers?

- *Intellectual property (IP).* IP is critical to assessing competitive advantage and value extraction for an organization. It is also important to align IP with market value perceptions. Questions to address:
    o How does the existing and pipeline IP reflect future customer needs?
    o Does the existing and pipeline IP focus on specific function and service needs for which customers are willing to pay?

- *Contracts and pricing.* Price is the quantified and captured perception of value in the marketplace. Price capture goes far beyond just price setting. Questions to address:
    - How many full time employees in the organization are dedicated to pricing strategy, analysis and management?
    - How does this compare to the number of dedicated purchasing resources?

From the answers to the above questions, pockets of missed opportunity and limited information clarity often arise regarding pricing capability and pricing performance within the major areas of due diligence. Undertaking a due diligence approach more focused on pricing capabilities generates potential value arbitrage and enhanced synergy realization.

Revised M&A due diligence process

Recommended adjustments for each due diligence area and the addition of a strategic pricing capability assessment area together can collectively enhance the overall valuation of a business (Figure 12.2).

- *Financials.* While a significant amount of time during due diligence is spent analysing the financial information of a potential acquisition, often the level of granularity is not sufficient to truly reflect how well the company is operating. Hidden within the lower levels of product and customer specific activity, buyers will often find information suggesting that large amounts of capital (dollar, human, operational) are often spent chasing transactions providing negative or little return. With the proper analysis, such as the use of Price Waterfalls and Profit Leakage reporting, a buyer can understand where the 'bad' business is occurring, where proper resources are being used on 'good' business, and plan for a product and customer rationalization process to begin shortly after deal closure. Doing so will not only enhance the future value of the acquisition, but will

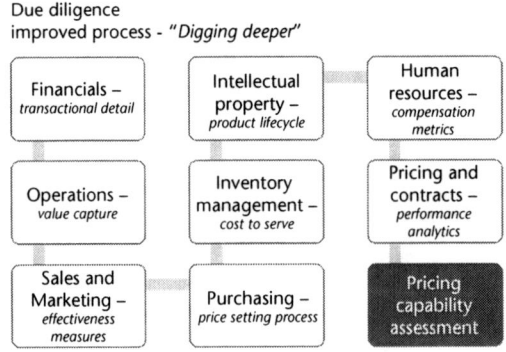

FIGURE 12.2 Due diligence – improved process: 'digging deeper'

also lead towards a better understanding of pricing captured during the product lifecycle and the impact of customer turnover.
- *Operations.* It is not enough for an investigating business to digest the portfolio of products or services, embrace new products in the pipeline, or fully understand the channels utilized in customer fulfilment. A true picture of the targeted 'go to market' approach is necessary in order to ensure that the right decisions are being made about 'what' to sell to 'whom' and 'when'. Buyers need to drive towards a full understanding of operational value capture and ensure that offer pricing is matched to the value within each situation. 'Churn' analysis is a great way to interpolate the influences of customer retention and price/volume into the reporting hierarchy, as a means to better understand operational efficiency.
- *Sales and marketing.* A key driver often missed in the due diligence dissection of the commercial team is sales force effectiveness.

    o Usually blunt performance measures, such as revenue dollars and gross margin per cent, are the primary yardstick for comparing regions, territories and sales person competency. While these are solid metrics to start the dissection process, they do not tell the buyer enough about the competency of the commercial team to truly affect the final valuation. First, no real measure of effective discounting is analysed to fully understand how relative behaviour is impacting top and bottom line results. Secondly, no profitability metric is measured that allows for a proper comparative analysis. Without this, regional pressures, product mix and competitive disadvantages can be lost in looking at the higher level metrics alone.
    o There is, however, a single metric that encapsulates both differential profitability and discounting behaviour, although it is infrequently used by buyers in the due diligence process. 'Price realization' is the measurement of a settled price compared to the initial target price for each particular pricing event. When strategic pricing is embodied by an organization, this metric can be used to derive an 'apples to apples' comparison across products, geographies and even salespeople, resulting in a true assessment of commercial competency. Of course price realization measurement is highly dependent upon an effective net price setting process.

- *Purchasing and vendors.* Given that the 'buy side' of margin plays as critical a role as the 'sell side', understanding the product management team's approach to the pricing process can tell a purchasing organization much about the transfer of value within a prospective target. This understanding coupled with how supplier pricing practices are paired with internal pricing practices provides a picture into future margin gaps and opportunities. Often lost in the due diligence process is an understanding of how product managers set price. Recognizing where different price methods are used (cost plus, market based, value based) along with understanding how they are managing the pricing of their full product spectrum, has a large impact on top and bottom line results.

- *Inventory management.* Transactional 'Cost to Serve' and 'Contribution Margin' are two key metrics that can enhance the dissection of inventory management practices at a potential target firm. Ascertaining initially if, and then if so to what degree, these two concepts are being employed can impact valuations by offering further insight into operational effectiveness.
- *Intellectual property.* Current and future intellectual property pricing is another area where a purchasing organization can find arbitrage in the due diligence process. The proper use of product lifecycle management along with competitive normalization (how to compare one product to competing offerings) reflects a firm's value management protocols. When done well, the higher margins early in the product lifecycle of one product can be replaced as newer and more advanced products come online. The management of this cycle not only maintains margin consistency, but also strengthens customer value perceptions and their 'willingness to pay'.
- *Human resources.* The key valuation area within human resources is the compensation criteria for all of the different operating areas of the firm. Variable compensation metrics that are based upon revenues and margins alone neglect the focus on profitability that is needed for all levels of the organization. Furthermore, these same profitability measures are often only enabled at the highest levels of a target firm and also tend to be aggregated. Offering these same drivers to lower levels of the organization and reflecting them through concepts such as 'target price' and 'price realization' measurement will influence all levels of an organization to focus on profit management.
- *Contracts and pricing.* Understanding a target firm's approach to price management at a tactical level is another way to influence valuations and find potential arbitrage. Analysing whether price changes have been made in broad sweeping cuts, based upon vendor cost increases only, or if a more strategic and tactical approach has been taken, once again offers insight into true value extraction. While the analysis here is of great value in the due diligence process, it is often neglected due to time constraints and resources required.

Sufficient data is needed to effectively complete a detailed pricing analysis and derive a proper understanding of price competency. Unfortunately, the due diligence process does not always allow for the time necessary to complete these protocols, and target firms do not always have the proper data prepared. A strategic pricing capability assessment process that generates quantifiable insight into a target firm's strategic pricing competency while not overburdening the due diligence process is described next. This approach reduces the time necessary to complete the transactional analysis, while simultaneously providing a tool with a high degree of correlation for prediction and understanding of a seller's capabilities.

M&A strategic pricing capability assessment – introduction

Practitioners undertaking a capability assessment during due diligence must conduct the assessment with limited data access and the time constraints previously referenced. As a result, the diagnostic techniques for use during M&A due diligence and elaborated below are intended to be objective, unequivocal and based on an arm's-length perspective of an enterprise's full pricing function and strategy.

A more data-intensive capability assessment is certainly recommended after a potential entity has been acquired. Although the outcome of an assessment for an owned-business is primarily the same – to identify, validate and quantify the pricing improvement potential for a business – the specificity of the outcome will increase when presented with full access to customer, offering and transaction detail. Pricing improvement opportunities for an owned-business will become customer-, market- and offering-specific while those for an acquisition target after due diligence are usually concrete but not as individualized.

The five components of the strategic pricing capability assessment for the mergers and acquisition due diligence process (Figure 12.3) are:

1. Overall strategic clarity
2. Market pricing intelligence
3. Transactional pricing management
4. Price performance measurement
5. Pricing organizational alignment

Upon completion, this capability assessment will highlight significant areas of improvement opportunity for the target and more importantly inform a better valuation of the enterprise.

Strategic pricing capability assessment
five components

FIGURE 12.3 Strategic pricing capability assessment

M&A strategic pricing capability assessment – (1) overall strategic clarity

The first component of the strategic pricing capability assessment is an evaluation of how well the business knows its own overall pricing strategy and how clearly it can articulate that strategy across the markets, customers, products and services it sells. This is an important foundation to strategic pricing execution because it sets the general direction for the business to follow for a wide range of areas including product development, sales force compensation, key performance indicators, account lifecycle management and customer communications.

General pricing strategy occurs typically in only three broad varieties – premium pricing, lowest price position or competitive parity. However, similar to other aspects of pricing execution, the tactical implementation of each flavour has a wide variability. A premium price provider, for instance, may at times need to be the lowest price provider to enter a different geography or industry segment. A lowest price provider may actually price a new technology or new service offering at a premium price level in order to specifically protect the value of its intellectual property or first-mover advantage. Best practice pricing does not require an unflinching single price position. On the contrary, best practice reveals that pricing strategy can be quite malleable in the presence of compelling market-based reasons to change. For example, wide and intended variation in the market price positions can be seen in the products from GE Healthcare, a typical price leader, across its developing markets. Also, targeted price promotions used to fill expected low yield periods can be seen from usual high price providers like Disney Resorts and many luxury cruise lines.

The assessment of a target's strategic clarity during due diligence does not therefore evaluate whether the business has selected the 'correct' flavour of pricing strategy. Instead, the assessment is how accurately a business can describe its pricing strategy. A company's leadership should always be able to explain, document and demonstrate the company's pricing strategy in total and the variation of that strategy by commercial segment. And once a pricing strategy is provided by management, it should match the offer positioning and commercial actions of the business under review.

For each component of the strategic pricing capability assessment, a series of diagnostic questions will be suggested. In addition, a recommended approach to conducting the assessment of each component will be offered.

Diagnostic questions for strategic pricing clarity:

1. What is the overall pricing strategy of the business?
2. How does the description of the pricing strategy vary across the senior team?
3. Is the pricing strategy specifically documented in the company's strategic plan?
4. Is the price position well defined for every offering by segment relative to competition?
5. How does this strategy vary across markets, products and services?

6. How is the pricing strategy reflected in the company's external literature?
7. Is strategic pricing a key component of both sales and product management's continuing education process?

Assessment process for strategic pricing clarity:

1. This component of the assessment is best undertaken in person with the target company senior leaders. The diagnostic questions should be posed and the answers documented during a meeting with the business. Ideally, this meeting includes the company's sales leader, the marketing or product management leader, the CFO or equivalent, the CEO or equivalent and the chief operating officer (COO) or equivalent.
2. A review of the company's external collateral should also be completed. This would include marketing brochures, company website collateral, company online social media postings, company press releases and any other published materials from the business.

An assessment of a company's strategic clarity during due diligence highlights improvement opportunities when there is ambiguity or inconsistency in the pricing strategy. In these cases, the commercial side of the organization lacks a coherent pricing position and will consequently price products and services inconsistently. The scatter plot of a company's net price versus volume that often show pricing 'all over the map' is one important symptom of a business with little strategic clarity. Articulated pricing strategy that is inconsistent from a strategic plan to the opinion of a senior leader to the printed collateral of business is another sure sign of limited strategic clarity.

Best practice for a company is to have a well-documented pricing strategy that is consistent in both its internal and external communication materials. For example, a premium pricing strategy should be reinforced by internal company documents that specify higher new product launch prices, more aggressive annual price realization targets and explicit competitive responses. A premium pricing strategy should also be reinforced by external collateral that highlights a company's high-end service reputation, its unrivalled financial returns for customers and the wide breadth of its offer selection.

Companies that are judged to have a high degree of strategic clarity in their pricing will not have any substantive improvement opportunities in this area, and there will be no impact from this assessment component on their valuation. Conversely, companies that are evaluated with little or no strategic clarity in their pricing should have their future enterprise value adjusted. Future value will be higher by an annualized 1 per cent improvement to sales if the strategic clarity can be improved. If there is no expectation to improve the strategic clarity for a business with a low assessment, then the future enterprise value should be discounted by 1 per cent to 2 per cent overall. The application of a valuation discount is particularly important for a business where the overall market historical average unit pricing trend has been negative.

M&A strategic pricing capability assessment – (2) market pricing intelligence

The second component of the strategic pricing capability assessment investigates how much data about the company's market is collected, analysed and utilized to make pricing strategy and tactical decisions. 'Market' here is defined as all of the factions external to the business that actively participate in the marketplace where the business manufactures and delivers its offerings. This wide definition of external parties encompasses end-use customers, resellers, competitors, suppliers, and channel partners such as distributors. There is a wealth of information available from these assorted players that can materially impact pricing strategy and execution. A business that effectively manages the collection and processing of the information from these sources and then proactively uses the insights to drive company pricing behaviour is a business poised for pricing success.

There is more often too much market information surrounding a business than too little. Even though perfect market price information is rarely found – competitor pricing exactly aligned by the business's own stock keeping unit (SKU) numbers or end user willingness to pay by transaction type – rich sources of customer, competitor and vendor pricing inputs abound. For instance, most companies have details embedded in their sales pipeline tracking systems, customer satisfaction surveys, quarterly account reviews and industry trade reports. Moreover, the collective institutional wisdom of the commercial teams is usually a rich source of information that is often not systematically mined. The amount of information is therefore not the metric to assess; rather, the sophistication with which a company collects, categorizes and then informs pricing decisions is the intended metric of merit during the due diligence capability assessment.

This component therefore focuses on the cataloguing and use of market intelligence data. It assesses an acquisition target's ability to strategically and thoughtfully weave the various market information sources into a coherent perspective on the pricing landscape.

Diagnostic questions for market pricing intelligence:

1. Does the business collect, store and analyse competitor pricing behaviours in a central electronic repository?
2. Are the reasons for won and lost deals/proposals collected and analysed?
3. Is quantitative end-user feedback about benefit and price perceptions used as an input to set prices?
4. Is there a quantitative assessment of the value provided by the business's products/services versus the next best alternative(s), e.g. return on investment (ROI) analysis?
5. Are commercial segments defined using customer buying behaviour distinctions?
6. Are suppliers regularly interviewed to identify early market trends?
7. Are raw material price changes a key component of price actions and are these changes made as feedstock spot markets move?
8. Does the business use pricing tests and pilots to validate opportunities?

Assessment process for market pricing intelligence:

1. Similar to the strategic clarity component, the assessment of market intelligence is best undertaken in person with the target company's senior leaders. This meeting includes the same participants as the strategic clarity discussion.
2. A review of the company's win/loss data should also be completed. If available, a review of the company's customer-facing ROI analysis or similar value analysis should occur.

Pricing improvements are available when a company does not collect and analyse their market data in a systematic way. A more effective use of market intelligence can lead to increased win rates, higher price realization in targeted segments and product development more suited to end-user customer needs.

The diagnostic questions from this assessment component are intentionally categorical so that they can be answered directly during due diligence. An overall improvement opportunity can be calculated based on the number of 'YES' answers provided to the seven diagnostic questions.

- 0–2 YES Answers = Significant improvement opportunities exist
- 3–5 YES Answers = Moderate improvement opportunities exist
- 6–8 YES Answers = Little improvement opportunities exist

Where significant improvement opportunities exist, the company's enterprise valuation should be adjusted higher by an annualized 1.0 per cent improvement to sales. Where moderate improvement opportunities exist, the company's enterprise valuation should be adjusted higher by an annualized 0.5 per cent improvement to sales. No adjustment should be made to the target company's valuation in the event that little improvement opportunities are identified by the market intelligence assessment.

M&A strategic pricing capability assessment – (3) transactional pricing management

The third component of the strategic pricing capability assessment examines how well the individual pricing and value variability of each customer and offering combination is executed within the company. Knowing exactly how much price is being realized by every transaction is paramount to knowing where the company can align pricing and ultimately improve profit. An evaluation of a target company's pricing capability during due diligence must include this component.

Transaction-level profitability is defined here as the return from the delivery of a specific product or service to a specific customer at a specific time. While the definition of returns will certainly vary – from simple gross margin to contribution margin to EBITDA (earnings before interest, taxes, depreciation, and amortization) – the concept of capturing the complete revenues and costs-to-serve for a defined product/service and customer combination is robust across segments, industry and geography. It holds for product- and service-based businesses, and also applies to both healthcare and information and business service sectors. From individual transactions, a business can determine the profitability for a particular product or service, a particular customer or larger aggregations like segments, product lines or locations.

The ultimate goal is to understand all transactional components and appropriate the costs and margin components correctly to each transaction. The appearance of high margins is often hidden by 'below the line' costs or the misappropriation of invoice level items. Furthermore, contracts with limited compliance discipline are often standard operating procedure for a business and customers can choose when to adhere to guidelines. This further dilutes margin management. This component of the capability assessment therefore focuses on the cataloguing, analysis and use of transactional data. It assesses an acquisition target's ability to build introspective analysis and achieve a clear perspective on their true margins. Without this diagnostic, true margins can be easily blurred and normal key performance indicators (KPIs) can be skewed and increase overall acquisition cost.

Diagnostic questions for transactional pricing management:

1. Are all direct and indirect costs associated by customer site (and customer master) tracked?
2. Do standard reporting tools offer the ability to drill down and track granular changes as a result of price-related functions (e.g. transaction P&L, waterfall analysis)?
3. Are customer discounts analysed in comparison to customer performance?
4. Are the total costs of support (call centre, technical, number of site visits) of each customer allocated to customer site?
5. Is the customer compared on a cohort basis for transactional costs?
6. Are salespeople, customers and products measured on price performance?
7. Are specific pricing analytics used to evaluate new sales opportunities (e.g. comparison to recommendation, comparison to average)?

Assessment process for transactional pricing management:

1. The assessment of transactional pricing management is best undertaken in person with the target company's sales leadership, finance leadership and the IT management team.
2. A review of the company's cost-to-serve approach and reporting examples, if available, should occur.

An overall improvement opportunity can be calculated based on the number of 'YES' answers provided to the seven diagnostic questions asked during the due diligence process.

- 0–2 YES Answers = Significant improvement opportunities exist
- 3–5 YES Answers = Moderate improvement opportunities exist
- 6–7 YES Answers = Little improvement opportunities exist

Where significant improvement opportunities exist, the company's enterprise valuation should be adjusted higher by an annualized 1.50 per cent improvement to sales. Where moderate improvement opportunities exist, the company's enterprise valuation should be adjusted higher by an annualized 0.75 per cent improvement to sales. No adjustment should be made to the target company's valuation in the event that little improvement opportunities are identified by the transactional pricing management assessment.

M&A strategic pricing capability assessment – (4) price performance measurement

The fourth component of the strategic pricing capability assessment is an evaluation of how well the business measures price performance, reports on the impact of price and reacts to the available tracking measures. The ability to accurately and granularly measure a business's pricing performance is essential to more sophisticated and strategic pricing actions. Assessing a company's price performance measurement proficiency is an important part of the due diligence discovery since having a detailed understanding of price capture is necessary for a business to make effective and enduring pricing adjustments.

A sound metric to measure pricing performance, such as price realization, is necessary to a business for several reasons. Businesses rarely pay attention to or improve on the things they do not measure. Pricing performance measurement through a small set of pricing metrics also allows for easier identification of improvement opportunities and required midcourse corrections. Finally, a good pricing performance metric can be a powerful organizing force for a business's value delivery. The voice of the customer can be heard in the improvement or deterioration of this quotient as a reflection of their value perception for the goods and services they procure.

Diagnostic questions for price performance measurement:

1. Are pricing performance metrics utilized and included in standard business reporting?
2. Is commentary on pricing performance regularly included in the standard business reporting package?
3. Is the impact of price on margin changes readily apparent in financial reports?
4. Are price performance metrics and reports distributed to pricing decision-makers, e.g. sales managers, product managers, contract approvers?
5. Is pricing variability regularly measured (e.g. price scatters or clouds, price bands)?
6. Are pricing performance metrics, forecasts and corrective actions regularly reviewed between finance, sales and marketing teams?

7. Is there a quantified pricing improvement metric included in the business's annual budget or operating plan?

Assessment process for price performance measurement:

1. The assessment of price performance measurement is best undertaken in person with the target company's finance and sales personnel. This meeting includes the same participants as the transactional pricing management and market intelligence discussions.
2. A review of the price-related reports (customer, product, geography, churn) should be completed.

Accurate price performance measurement helps a business highlight the fundamental drivers of its profitability. Isolating controllable price changes from turbulent mix changes is essential to focus appropriate attention on the company's effectiveness in selling value, negotiating price changes and positioning against competition. For the price performance measurement component, the number of 'YES' answers provided to the diagnostic questions during the due diligence process identifies the improvement opportunity.

- 0–2 YES Answers = Significant improvement opportunities exist
- 3–5 YES Answers = Moderate improvement opportunities exist
- 6–7 YES Answers = Little improvement opportunities exist

Where significant improvement opportunities exist, the company's enterprise valuation should be adjusted higher by an annualized 2.5 per cent improvement to sales. Where moderate improvement opportunities exist, the company's enterprise valuation should be adjusted higher by an annualized 1.0 per cent improvement to sales. If there is no expectation to improve the price performance measurement for a business with a low assessment, then the future enterprise value should be discounted by 1.0 per cent overall. This capability is particularly important in high price and long sales-cycle businesses where managing the customer lifecycle is of high importance.

M&A strategic pricing capability assessment – (5) pricing organizational alignment

The final component to the strategic pricing capability assessment appraises the degree to which pricing is cemented in the business as a way of life. The most effective pricing companies make pricing part of their DNA – pricing is explicitly reflected in the commercial team training programmes, the incentive structure, the financial reporting regimen and the product development process. The pricing literature supports the importance of organizational alignment to the success of any sustained pricing improvement initiative (Baker et al. 2010; Dolan and Simon 1996). This last component of the strategic pricing capability assessment determines to what degree price performance is an organizing force for the business as well as how advanced its pricing organization currently is by raising a series of questions during the due diligence process.

Well-executed pricing requires the delicate coordination across separate functions of a business. To align the sales, marketing, finance, manufacturing, customer service and R&D functions in the pursuit of pricing realization, a company must have a top-to-bottom commitment to effective pricing performance. There are simply too many places for pricing implementation to fail, too many systemic biases standing in the way of good pricing performance, and too many sources of profit leakage. A company must be properly aligned for its full price potential to be initially realized and then sustained.

Substantive pricing transformation at a company requires sustained management attention to the business's pricing strategy, execution and organization over time (Liozu et al. 2011). As businesses move through the stages of pricing transformation, their pricing function matures and becomes increasingly sophisticated (Hunt and Saunders 2008). Since the transformation stage and maturity state of the business are critical to pricing performance, the overall pricing improvement opportunity identified during due diligence is sensitive to the organizational starting point of the business. The assessment of the current level of sophistication for a business's pricing organization is therefore a vital factor in determining how much pricing may affect the company valuation.

Diagnostic questions for pricing organizational alignment:

1. Is there a defined pricing function in the organization?
2. Are pricing responsibilities not assigned to the pricing function clearly documented and assigned to specific individuals in the business?
3. Is there a pricing or margin component to sales compensation plans?
4. Is there an escalating approval process for net prices based on margin or price realization?
5. Is pricing included in sales training, both on-boarding and continuing education?
6. Is pricing included in product management training?
7. Is there a defined pipeline of pricing improvement initiatives categorized separated into short- and long-term opportunities?
8. Is there regular communication to the organization on the business's pricing performance?

Assessment process for pricing organizational alignment:

1. The assessment of pricing organizational alignment is best undertaken in person with the target company's senior leaders. This meeting includes the same participants as the strategic clarity and market intelligence discussion.
2. A review of the documentation about the pricing function including organizational charts, roles and responsibilities should be completed.

Pricing improvement opportunities will be limited without the presence of strong organizational alignment assessed during the M&A due diligence process. For this component, the number of 'YES' answers provided to the diagnostic questions listed provides insight into both the company's current pricing function and its ability to execute sizable improvement initiatives in the future. The measure of current organizational alignment along with the receptivity to future improvements together will drive the overall pricing improvement opportunity estimate.

- 0–3 YES Answers = Significant improvement opportunities exist
- 4–6 YES Answers = Moderate improvement opportunities exist
- 7–8 YES Answers = Little improvement opportunities exist

Where significant improvement opportunities exist, the company's enterprise valuation should be adjusted higher by an annualized 1.0 per cent improvement to sales. Where moderate improvement opportunities exist, the company's enterprise valuation should be adjusted higher by an annualized 0.5 per cent improvement to sales. No adjustment should be made to the target company's valuation in the event that little improvement opportunities are identified by the pricing organizational alignment assessment.

M&A strategic pricing capability assessment – aggregating the components

The five components of the strategic pricing capability assessment each generate potential adjustments to the overall enterprise valuation. At the conclusion of the assessment, the practitioner needs to total each individual adjustment to achieve an overall 'Price Premium'. As Figure 12.4 reflects, this premium is added to the traditional discounted cash flow valuation.

The Price Premium, in turn, is calculated as the sum of the individual component adjustments to the traditional enterprise valuation (Figure 12.5). Figure 12.5 also includes the range of potential valuation adjustments associated with each component of the capability assessment.

Valuation Equation

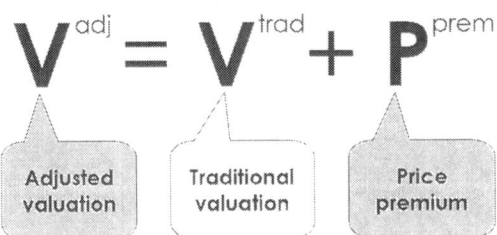

$$V^{adj} = V^{trad} + P^{prem}$$

Adjusted valuation · Traditional valuation · Price premium

FIGURE 12.4 Valuation equation

Price premium equation

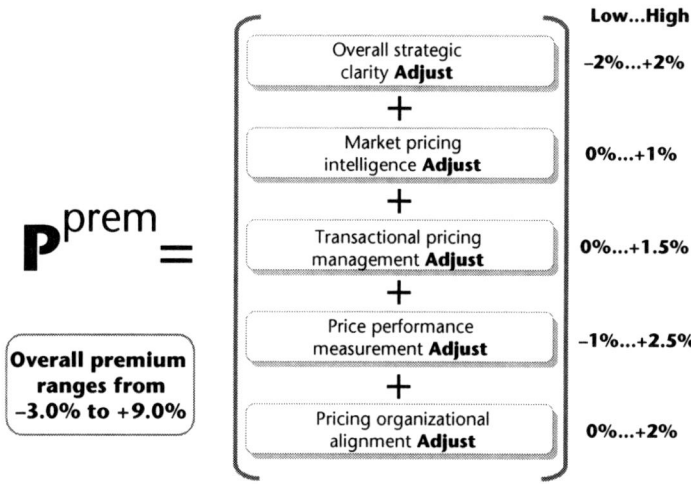

FIGURE 12.5 Price premium equation

Use of the results during M&A negotiation

There are two different perspectives to apply to the target company enterprise valuation after it has been adjusted based on the completed strategic pricing capability assessment. The first perspective is that of the potential buyer, and the second perspective is that of the seller.

The buyer's team leads the M&A discovery process, and so the adjusted valuation will result from that team's direct financial discounted cash flow analysis. Based on the total pricing opportunity adjustments, the buyer's view of the enterprise value may be as much as 10 per cent higher than a valuation conducted using traditional techniques. With a valuation that is adjusted higher as a result of the pricing opportunity assessment, the buyer has several new degrees of freedom to employ in the M&A process.

The buyer could simply include the higher valuation as the initial offer price to the seller. In effect, this approach presumes that other potential suitors have not conducted the same level of pricing opportunity assessment and therefore the buyer's valuation would surpass that of the other suitors in the first pricing wave. This 'first offer high' approach is suggested when the buyer believes that there are no strategically preferred buyers in the process according to the seller. In other words, if the buyer is on equal footing with other buyers and the expectation is that the target sale will go to the highest bidder, then the price-adjusted valuation should be included in the first pricing wave.

Another option for the buyer is to withhold the price premium, calculated as the difference between the price-adjusted valuation and the traditional valuation, during the buying process. In this circumstance, the price premium would serve as expected internal upside to the target purchase. The premium could be used to sell the acquisition internally to the buyer's stakeholders, but then not included in the offer price. This 'keep private' approach is suggested when the buyer believes that they are already one of the preferred buyers in the process and their traditional valuation is within the range expected by the seller.

A third option for the buyer is to use the price premium to measure the sensitivity of the expected returns from the traditional valuation and then only offer the price premium if the initial offer value needs to be increased. The sensitivity can be measured by comparing the key financial return metrics (ROI, internal rate of return (IRR) or net present value (NPV)) with and without the price premium. The premium can then be added to the offer price for the acquisition target only if needed. This 'use if needed' approach is suggested when multiple auction or proposal rounds are expected. This third option will most often occur, and so it will be most likely that some portion of the price premium will end up included in the eventual target company valuation.

From the buyer's perspective, a potential 10 per cent premium provides more negotiating room for the buyer to reach an accord with the seller. The salient characteristic of the enterprise valuation price premium is that it does not appear in the financial history or output of the target company. As a result, the price premium is not reflected in traditional valuation methodologies. It therefore provides real leverage to the buyer when calculated following due diligence because the seller and other suitors that follow the traditional valuation approach will not have the same insights about future profit improvement potential.

The second perspective on the adjusted valuation is that of the potential seller. A savvy seller of a business unit or portfolio company will conduct the same strategic pricing capability assessment that is suggested for the buyer. But the seller will complete this effort before putting the target business up for sale. In this case, the seller calculates an internal price premium for its business. The seller can then direct the discussions during management presentations to the potential pricing opportunity. The seller can also stand firmer on its asking price with the knowledge of this valuation adjustment.

A more impactful approach for the seller would be to include the price improvement potential in their financial forecasts. In this case, the seller would incorporate specific pricing improvements into the revenue and profitability projections for the business's future revenue and profitability performance. These projections would be based on the internal capability assessment and subsequent opportunity identification. The seller should include specific commentary on the expected actions and impact from pricing improvements in the management forecasts.

The seller's position is not nearly as strong as that of the buyer regarding the price premium on the valuation. The buyer identifies the price opportunity as a future potential while the seller's assessment is more accurately described as an opportunity lost – a revenue and profit improvement lever that has not yet been implemented. The strategic pricing capability assessment is nevertheless recommended for the seller to reduce the potential information inequality that might exist if the buyer conducts the assessment and the seller does not.

In summary, the adjusted target company enterprise valuation generated by completing a robust strategic pricing capability assessment provides the participants of an M&A deal process with a range of options for using the discovered value. As noted, since the valuation price premium does not appear on the company historical financial statements and rarely will appear on the management sales and profitability projections, the adjustment is not unlike an intangible asset of the company. And like other intangible assets, such as brand names or market reputations, the price premium will be subject to widely diverse interpretations. The preceding assessment approach is intended to reduce the diversity of opinion on the quantifiable impact of pricing improvement. However, participants in the M&A process who leverage the price premium for their enterprise valuation must be prepared to defend their valuation with the detailed findings of this capability assessment.

Implications to the field of pricing

In the final analysis, the mergers and acquisition process includes elements of both art and science. Final deal settlement prices are often predicated as much on the seller's ability to sell the concept of value in future returns as it is on the buyer's ability to dilute those claims with the information uncovered and analysed in the due diligence process. However, the very quality and quantity of information, or lack thereof, often plays more of a role in predicting future synergies and derived competitive advantages than any other part of the due diligence process.

Several areas within the current due diligence process that can be improved through enhanced information capture about the company's pricing capabilities have been highlighted. Recommendations were provided for what specific information to review and which specific questions to ask in order to uncover areas of arbitrage in the target company valuation. Using the strategic pricing capability assessment during the mergers and acquisition due diligence process will improve company valuation and provide more specific pricing improvement areas to validate after the acquisition is complete. The strategic pricing capability assessment is not intended to replace a more comprehensive and transaction-specific opportunity diagnostic after the company has been acquired. Rather, the recommended pricing addendum to the traditional due diligence process is designed to effectively evaluate the pricing opportunity environment for a specific business from the arm's-length distance of due diligence and thereby inform the final company valuation.

The strategic pricing capability assessment is a practice-proven appraisal framework that can be executed in a much shorter time and with a high degree of confidence. It fills an important gap in the pricing literature and provides a directly applicable solution for M&A practitioners to employ in their due diligence process. When embedded within the overall M&A framework, the strategic pricing capability assessment will not only provide a more thorough perspective of a company's pricing competency, but it will also produce greater clarity about the expected synergies and competitive advantages realized in the future cash flows of the acquired entity.

References

Baker, W., Marn, M. and Zawada, C. (2010) *The price advantage* (2nd edition). Hoboken, NJ: John Wiley & Sons, Inc.

Dolan, R. and Simon, H. (1996) *Power pricing: How managing price transforms the bottom line*. New York, NY: The Free Press.

Hunt, P. and Saunders, J. (2008) The journey to pricing excellence. *The Journal of Professional Pricing*, Fourth Quarter 2008, pp. 30–3. Retrieved from http://www.pricingsolutions.com/pdf/the_journey_to_pricing_excellence.pdf.

Liozu, S., Boland, R., Hinterhuber, A. and Perelli, S. (2011) *Industrial pricing orientation: The organizational transformation to value-based pricing*. Paper presented at the International Conference on Engaged Management Scholarship, Case Western Reserve University, Cleveland, OH.

Pautler, P. (2001) *Evidence on mergers and acquisitions*. Bureau of Economics, Federal Trade Commission, Working Papers. Retrieved from http://www.ftc.gov/be/econwork.shtm.

Straub, T. (2007) *Reasons for frequent failure in mergers and acquisitions: A comprehensive analysis*. Wiesbaden: Deutscher Universitäts-Verlag (DUV), Gabler Edition Wissenschaft.

13
BUSTING THE FOUR FATAL MYTHS IN PRICING

Nelson Hyde

Myth busters: four fatal pricing traps

If a firm lowers its price, will it sell more?

For years, Economics 101 has taught us that if a firm lowers its price, more people will buy and sales will increase. Yet much of the time this is simply not true.

Although individual products have price elasticity, at many stages of its life cycle a product is not highly price elastic. At these stages, lowering prices generates little new demand – and it can trigger a price war. Failure to understand clearly when and when not to lower price, or to factor in how competitors will respond, is at the heart of two of the pricing traps this chapter addresses:

- "If we lower our price, we will gain share."
- "We should drop our price to win this deal."

The price pressure in mature, commoditized industries can be excruciating. The antidote to price pressure is demonstrating real, solid financial value to the customer – showing how one's product's or service's differentiators will materially improve the customer's bottom line. This means going beyond describing features and benefits to demonstrating operational impacts and financial results. It is one thing to say that a product is more reliable (a benefit) because it is made of higher grade material (a feature). But it is another to show how the increased uptime from reliability (impact) adds $80,000 to the customer's bottom line (financial results). Using price rather than value to close deals is at the heart of the other two pricing traps this chapter addresses:

- "At the end of the day, customers only buy on price."
- "We have to set our prices at the market price."

In over 25 years, I have heard each of these statements at multiple Fortune 1000 companies in many different industries. I have heard them stated by sales VPs and CEOs, at conferences and in meetings. These statements have become a part of conventional wisdom. But each statement is true only in very narrow circumstances, a nuance that does not usually make it into the conversation. As a result, these statements are routinely misapplied.

These four traps are not so much about pricing strategy or tactics as they are about execution in the field. They are about competitive pricing dynamics at the most crucial moment that determines a firm's pricing success and margins: in other words, what the salesperson does next when the customer is banging on the table demanding a lower price.

It's been said that the definition of insanity is doing the same thing over and over again and expecting different results. Innovation in pricing means breaking the traditional mind-set and knowing when *not* to keep following the old rules.

Through principles and examples, this chapter shows how generalizing the four statements above to situations for which they were not intended only invites potentially fatal consequences. It identifies under which conditions these principles do and do not apply, and what to do as an alternative. It demonstrates what executives can do to break through the traps and seize a competitive advantage through innovation in pricing practices.

Trap Number 1: "If we lower our price, we will gain share"

Can a firm price its way to greater market share? Conventional wisdom says yes, but history does not agree.

Consider the wild ride of General Motors since this century began. The last year of the twentieth century was a good one for the North American light-vehicle market: the industry made $7 billion in profit in 1999. But signs of what was to come were already emerging. Despite the fact that more vehicles than ever were sold in 2000, the North American market lost money, and as a group that year the Big Three automakers – GM, Ford, and Chrysler – saw their market share drop for the seventh year in a row.

To protect their share, in 2001 the Big Three offered rebates averaging $2,300 per vehicle. But, according to CNW Marketing/Research, "These loan wars only reinforced the vicious cycle in which consumers stop buying as soon as the deals end, forcing carmakers to jump in with even bigger rebates. It's a nightmare." "It's almost like opium," said A.T. Kearney consultant James Mateyka in the *Detroit News*.

Seven years later, rebates were even bigger. By 2008, Ford's average rebate had crept past $4,000. Despite this, however, the industry's unit sales had not yet returned to their 2000 levels.

The North American car market had turned into a brutal fight for market share. In 2003, GM began an internal campaign to capture and retain a 29 percent market share; executives were seen famously sporting "GM 29" lapel pins. Yet from 2001 to 2008 the Big Three's market shares continued to slide, averaging a loss of more than 2 points a year. And they lost more than share: they lost money, too – a staggering $75 billion over that period (see Figure 13.1).

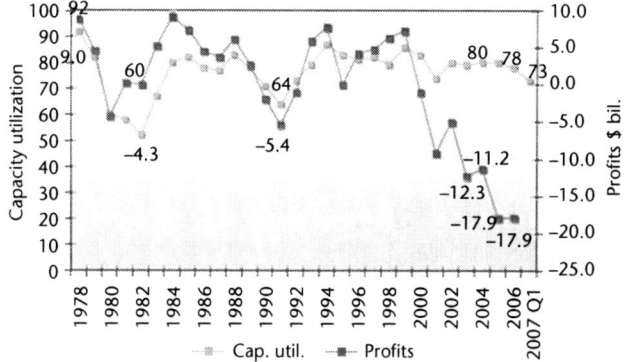

FIGURE 13.1 US car industry profit and capacity

Source: Centre for automotive research.

In 2007, desperate, GM completely reversed its course. It began to emphasize profitability over market share, and quality over quantity. It cut its low-profit fleet sales and reduced rebates.

Although these efforts were too late to prevent the bailout that was to come, GM's new price strategy is paying off in spades now. In the fourth quarter of 2011, GM reported its eighth straight quarter of profitability and predicted that it might reach $10 billion profit in 2012. Earlier in 2011, GM attributed fully half of its margin improvement to pricing, and it announced its third price increase of the year.

Why didn't the carmakers' price incentives increase overall demand, especially given that demand for cars remained somewhat positively elastic?

Rebates did increase demand a little, because they made cars more attractive for first-time buyers. But in this mature market, *most* of the market for new car buyers – the real engine that fuels growth and demand – had already been tapped. There were fewer first-time buyers. Most purchases were replacement purchases, and demand was not growing nearly as fast as before.

This shows how price elasticity changes over the course of a product's life cycle (see Figure 13.2). In a product's mature and declining stages, the market is mostly a replacement market, and demand is generated less by price than by other factors. For example, in health care, demand is driven much more by demographics, such as the growth in number of people over 50, than by price. If the price of an X-ray machine is reduced, it does not follow that more people will go out and break their arms. But if the number of people over the age of 70 increases, and if people in this age group are more likely to injure themselves in falls, there will be greater need for X-rays.

In a product's early-growth introduction phase, first-time buyers are not very price-sensitive because as early adopters they value the product for reasons other than its price – its new technology, for example, or the status it bestows on the

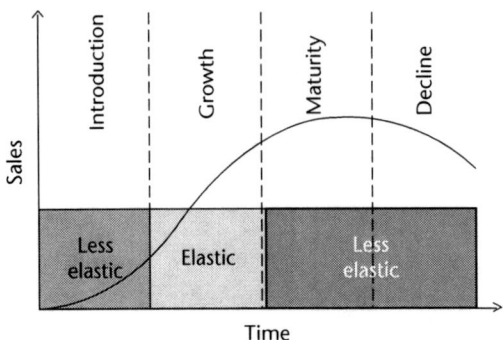

FIGURE 13.2 Price elasticity in the product life cycle

buyer. Of the four stages of a product's life cycle, only the growth stage is truly elastic; it is during this phase that lowering price can generate significant incremental growth in demand and rapidly increase the number of first-time buyers.

Demand aside, why didn't GM's strategy of lowering prices at least boost its market share? To be fair, lowering prices actually did influence its share – but only momentarily. The higher rebates boosted traffic to the dealerships and improved sales. But that lasted only as long as it took Ford and Chrysler to follow suit. After that, their respective market shares returned to the status quo; only now, the carmakers were earning less profit on each car.

It is tempting to lower prices to win a sale. And it *can* win the sale: every salesperson can tell stories about the deal won by beating the competitor's price. The problem is what happens next. Competitors will not roll over and play dead: they will match the price drops.

Taking a strategic view of market pricing means looking at the deal not in isolation but as one move of many in a chess game. If I make this price move now, what will my competitors do? What will happen then? Is that good or bad? Will I be better off, or worse off? If each of the Big Three had been thinking several moves ahead, there would never have been a price war, and Detroit probably would not have needed the bailouts.

My own company tried to increase its share in 2011. It succeeded. Now it is dealing with the significant fallout from missing its profitability targets. In situations like this the message needs to change from "any share is good share" to "grow profitably."

Trap Number 2: "At the end of the day, customers only buy on price"

If customers always bought on price, we would all be driving a Yugo. While most of us are concerned about price, we will also often pay more to get greater value. We will pay more *not* to get the Yugo.

FedEx figured this out early in its history. In 1981, FedEx began an advertising program with the tagline "Federal Express: When it absolutely, positively has to be there overnight." Its differentiator was a guarantee of reliability, not price. Unlike GM in the 2000s, FedEx's strategy was to maximize profit and *not* be the low-price provider. When UPS entered the express delivery market, it offered prices half those of FedEx's – but it could not provide the same level of reliability or service, and it struggled.

FedEx recognized that not all shipments are equal – that even though many shipments are urgent, some of those shipments really, really do need to get there by a certain time – such as parts that could otherwise hold up a production line. Anything with a drop-dead deadline. By assuming more of the risk, FedEx was able to charge more.

In other words, FedEx differentiated between those customers who buy based on price and those who are willing to pay more for greater value. One of the critical success factors for effective pricing is being able to tell which group one's customer is in. Trying to sell a jet to a customer who can only afford a propeller plane will result in one of two outcomes: either the supplier will sell the jet at a steep discount and devalue the jet for the rest of the market, or it will lose the sale because the discount isn't high enough.

Some customers are true pure price buyers – they cannot afford anything else, and they are relieved when a supplier can offer them a price that fits within their budget. But not all customers buy based on price alone, especially if they are niche and premium players who are not themselves trying to be the low-price provider. They are selling value and differentiation, and they rightly charge for this. As a result, studies show, they place a higher value on vendors who can provide a higher quality product, technical know-how, or service. They are more willing to invest time and money in their vendors, in exchange for customized product advantages not available to their competitors. It's not the case that they will pay any price; price is a factor, but it is not the main factor. They are relationship buyers.

It can be tough to tell which customer is a true price buyer and which is not, partly because of what Reed Holden of Holden Advisors calls "poker players." Poker players pretend to be concerned only about price, but they are in fact quite willing to pay more. They know that if they put up a fight, they can often pay a lower price for the same purchase they would have made anyway. So they bluff.

Companies with strong pricing offer products and services to price buyers that are different from those they offer to other buyers. Having a complete range of products in the portfolio – both the jet *and* the propeller plane – allows a seller to force clearer price-versus-value trade-offs. If a customer truly demands a lower price, the supplier can provide its lower-priced product. If the customer then complains that the prop plane is missing some important features, the supplier can offer a line of jets with the desired features – at a higher price.

Companies with strong pricing have also figured out how to tell which kind of customer they are talking to. There are usually some telltale signs; the key is to identify those that are specific to one's industry. For example, a freight transporter wanted to know which customers were bluffing on price demands and which customers really wouldn't pay more. This company shipped packages that were then amalgamated to fill a truck that goes to a specific destination. The business was highly commoditized, and price pressure was intense. However, some customers had a greater need for reliability or guarantees than others.

A salesman for the company was able to put his finger on the telltale sign: "Just go down and look at their docks." I thought – look at their docks? What is that going to tell you? But the salesman went on:

> If the docks are really clean and orderly, everything is in its place with a clear logic to the operations – that's a just-in-time inventory shop, and even if they pretend to scream and yell about price, they'll pay for guaranteed on-time delivery. If the docks are a mess, they usually won't pay as much – those are your price buyers.

Trap Number 3: "We have to set our prices at the market price"

Once upon a time, offering Internet connectivity was a selling point for hotels. Now, it's a staple. And customers expect it to be fast and free, and not just in the lobby.

Once upon a time, power-operated windows were a novelty in cars. When was the last time any of us hand-cranked a car window?

The evil twin of innovation is commoditization. As new innovations occur, good ideas get copied, and we move on to the next innovation. Gordon Moore captured this effect for technology industries in what became known as Moore's Law: the number of transistors in an integrated circuit doubles every two years.

What's the pricing corollary to Moore's Law for technology? Let's look at microprocessors. Over the five-year period ending in 1999, microprocessor chip prices fell at the rate of 60 percent a year. For every $100 worth of microprocessors sold in 1994, the price five years later was less than $8.

Companies of course must be able to anticipate this kind of headwind. However, once they do measure it, and then anticipate it, and then build it into their plans, it starts to become conventional wisdom. And then it's a slippery slope to believing that "that's just the way things are, there's nothing we can do about it." "You can't fight it." "It's what the market does." This is when "conventional wisdom" starts to become a self-fulfilling prophecy.

But that bogeyman we call "the market" is really a series of individual decisions made by individual companies. Push, shove, action, reaction. We saw above how carmakers' failure to anticipate competitors' reactions to price moves led to a destructive downward price spiral. But at each step, there was a decision point. Other than just blindly following your competitors, who in turn are probably blindly following you, what are the options?

The answer lies in "pricing power" (see Figure 13.3). Pricing power allows a company to withstand the forces of commoditization and the pressure of other companies' prices. Pricing power is created when a product or service (a) has differentiators (b) that customers value and will pay for. Even against the 60 percent price drops for microprocessors, for example, specialty processors for mobile phones

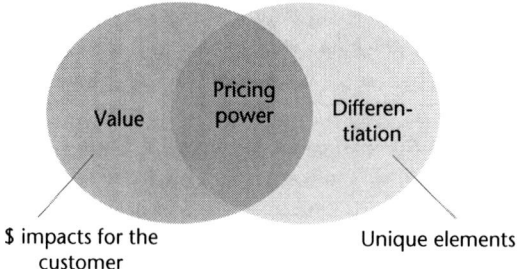

FIGURE 13.3 Pricing power defined

and gaming were able to command much higher prices and experienced less price erosion.

For pricing power to be successful, however, a company needs more than differentiation that customers care about. It also must be able to tell a convincing story about its added value. This means moving beyond talking with customers about features and benefits to talking about impacts – what impact the product has on the customer's own strategy, differentiators, and bottom line.

Without pricing power, or without a good way to convey it, a company will truly be buffeted by the "market." It will typically be forced to follow the market price, unless it has a cost advantage over its competitors and has room to undercut the competition.

Companies don't always have to be held hostage by "the market." Their costs plus a margin help set the floor price; their pricing power helps set their ceiling price. That leaves much greater latitude for setting price than what one's competitors charge.

Trap Number 4: "We should drop our price to win this deal"

Recently, my company was competing for a significant deal for large diagnostic-imaging equipment in Japan. Our Japan-based competitor was also trying to win the deal, and it offered a much lower price. So we did what a lot of companies would do. We lowered our price.

However, our competitor's equipment offered nowhere near the functionality or value that ours did. Theirs was a much lower-end version of a highly complex and innovative diagnostic machine. Yet when our competitor played the price card, we followed suit. We had pricing power, but we didn't leverage it. We let the competitor dictate the rules of engagement.

If that customer's budget could reasonably afford our more valuable equipment, then we should have been able to find a way to communicate that extra value and justify our price. If the equipment was too rich for the hospital's ability to pay, then why were we talking to them?

Effective targeting and good customer segmentation are central to strong pricing. This is where many companies' efforts to grow market share run into trouble.

Growing market share often means selling to new customers who are further "down-market." Yet the products we are selling haven't changed – and those products may be too rich for the new target audience. So we increase the discounts to close the sale.

Those heavier discounts effectively reset the market price – even for those customers who would gladly pay more to get more. Customers absolutely do talk to each other about what they've paid for something, and word gets around fast. In the diagnostic medical equipment industry, it's even worse: customers report what they paid to a third-party firm, who gladly publish the results.

The statement "We have to lower our price to win this deal" is often true. But that doesn't mean you always should. What are the alternatives?

Simple deal qualification can go a long way toward protecting price. And once a supplier knows that it's talking to the right audience, it still has to find compelling ways to tell its value story and highlight its differentiators. For this reason, many companies develop tools to quantify exactly how their offerings will impact the customer's bottom line.

But even that may not be enough. Customers need to believe they are getting a fair price. They are more convinced if they can negotiate the price down. Many purchasing agents earn commissions based on how much they save their companies – in other words, on how well they negotiate. They also take classes in how to wring the lowest prices from their vendors, and they study disingenuous but effective techniques:

- "You're close." (And then, when the vendor lowers the price, "You're getting closer." And then, "You're getting warm . . .")
- "We go way back. Is this how you treat your most loyal customers?"
- "We're a leader in this industry. Your customers do business with you because *I* do business with you."
- "You should be paying me a commission for all the work I've given you."

Effectively countering this is both an art and a science. When a customer says, "I need a lower price," the next words out of the salesperson's mouth are going to determine whether the company is about to improve or erode its margins. If the salesperson says, "Let me check with my manager," expect margin erosion. But there's a fighting chance if the salesperson is trained to ask for something in return, to negotiate some kind of give-get: "Sure, absolutely. I can make that happen. We can make that happen if you _____": fill in the blank. Maybe the customer needs to buy a service contract to get the lower price, or give the company a larger share of its business, or award the company the contract on a higher margin product.

Alternatively, the salesperson can remove something from the bid, reducing the product's costs and improving margin. Either way, the best salespeople anticipate the question and work out their response ahead of time in agreement with sales management to avoid being taken by surprise.

Pricing in the field

It is common to lower prices in order to grow revenue and market share. However, lowering prices can be a dangerous game, because it instantly lowers margins. Any gains in volume must be sufficient to compensate for the resulting margin gap. We have seen here examples in which neither additional volume nor margin materialized.

Sales is usually the keeper of volume and revenue; pricing and finance are often focused on profit. This chapter identified ways that *sales* can engage with customers to protect *price*.

The resulting price and margin improvements can be significant, as they were for GM. And the impacts are not limited to profitability. They can also include revenue growth. One high-tech company increased its quarterly margins by 37 percent while growing its revenues by 17 percent. Similarly, a software firm's 40 percent revenue growth over 18 months was accompanied by margin growth of almost 200 percent. It's time to change the way we think about the conventional wisdom. It's time to change how we apply accepted pricing principles.

Implications for innovation in pricing

This chapter identified ways in which commonly accepted pricing principles are misapplied, resulting in profit erosion, share loss, and even bankruptcy. We have an opportunity to innovate in our pricing by clearly identifying when business-to-business (B2B) pricing principles do *and do not* work, and where they need to be replaced by new, alternative principles.

Specifically, this chapter identified the pricing traps that result from applying four commonly accepted pricing principles to situations where they were not appropriate. It identified alternative practices that can be used in real time in the field, and the conditions under which they apply.

By taking into account two critical variables – how competitors will react to price changes, and how to shift the main value proposition from "look how good this price is" to "this is the value the product creates for you the customer" – this chapter presented new ways to use four conventional pricing principles:

- "If we lower our price, we will gain share."
- "We should drop our price to win this deal."
- "At the end of the day, customers only buy on price."
- "We have to set our prices at the market price."

Table 13.1 summarizes the opportunities to innovate on what have been commonly accepted but often misapplied pricing principles. It identifies four of those pricing principles, situations where they apply, conditions under which they will fail, and what to do if conditions ripe for failure exist.

TABLE 13.1 Capacity utilization and profitability in the US car industry

Pricing principle	Applies...	Does not apply when...	Practical application
If we lower our price, we will gain share	During growth phase of the product life cycle. When competitors choose not to respond	During early growth, mature, and declining phases of the product life cycle. When competitors respond by lowering their price	Quantify the financial value to the customer of one's differentiators. Price to capture a portion of the value one creates for the customer
We should drop our price to win this deal	When dropping price increases one's economic return over the life of the customer. When one can extract something of value from the customer in exchange (e.g. greater volume)	When customer is buying on the basis of one's value-add. When customer is a poker player who is only pretending to be a price buyer in order to get a lower price	Extract something of value from the customer in exchange. Link pricing to one's segmentation scheme. Create multiple price/product combinations with different value for the customer to choose from
At the end of the day, customers only buy on price	When customer is a true price buyer (cannot and will not pay the higher price)	When customer is buying on the basis of one's value-add. When customer is a poker player who is only pretending to be a price buyer to get a lower price	Identify telltale characteristics of true price buyers. Have different products for price buyers than for those who want added value
We have to set our prices at the market price	When one has no differentiators that produce economic value for the customer	When one does have differentiators that create economic value for the customer	Quantify the financial value to the customer of one's differentiators. Price to capture a portion of the value one creates for the customer

These new distinctions can empower salespeople to take new responsibility for margin, by improving price capture. Companies that have deployed these distinctions have not only improved margins, sometimes dramatically, but in some cases have also been able to do so while impressively growing their volume and revenue.

14

CREATING AND COMMUNICATING CUSTOMER VALUE

How companies can set premium prices that customers are willing to pay

Todd Snelgrove

Introduction

How does one get paid for value created? This question has been asked by every premium player in every market around the world. If a supplier creates value, and if that value requires investments, then it must find a way to obtain an equitable return on that investment, or the wheels of innovation will stop.

Successful companies allocate money to develop processes and cultures, and have the right people focused on finding innovation and on bringing that value to the market. The companies that are best in class in value-selling realize a 60 percent higher customer-retention rate, a 17.9 percent difference in year-over-year growth in company gross profits, and larger deal sizes (Aberdeen 2011).

So why is it that so many companies still adopt a market-share or cost-driven strategy rather than value-based pricing? Companies that employ a good value-based pricing strategy are 20 percent more profitable than those with weak execution on value pricing, and are 35 percent better off than those that follow a cost- or share-driven strategy (Monitor Group 2011).

Since the financial benefits of value creation and pricing are well known, why do so many companies fail to achieve the results they seek after they have done the work to create something that is of value?

Either they do not truly create customer value, and therefore cannot value-price for it; or they have not allocated the necessary resources to convert the value created into something that a customer is able and willing to pay for. Companies that choose a low-priced, commodity approach to their offerings will always be at the mercy of the next competitor to offer an "almost as good product at a lower unit price." For those that do invest and create customer value, it is time to do the work to capture that value.

We will delve into a case study of an industrial firm in a tough market. This firm has found a way to convert the value of its premium performance products and technical knowledge and to communicate it to customers so that they are willing and able to pay for it.

Current approach: total cost of ownership (TCO)

When a company is able to understand where value is created throughout the asset lifecycle, it can price for part of the incremental value created. But first it must understand what costs and values are incurred and generated, and where, when, and by whom. In general, the concept of *total cost of ownership* (TCO) is the best model to use to find these factors.

The existing literature and market consensus is that TCO is the "sum of purchase price plus all expenses incurred during the productive lifecycle of a product, minus its salvage or resale price" (Anderson and Narus 2004). TCO is exclusively concerned with the cost side of customer value and thus neglects the value of customer-specific benefits (Anderson and Narus 2004; Piscopo *et al.* 2008).

Future approach: total cost of ownership quantifying customer value along all relevant dimensions

To truly understand TCO, a supplier must ensure that all dimensions that affect the net profit generated for a customer are measured. The Gartner Group attempts to do this with a TCO variation called *total value of ownership*; however, the word "value" here refers to soft benefits such as ease of use, comfort level, or "happiness of a user." Although these soft values should be considered, a whole area of value creation has been missed: the revenue side. A true TCO analysis should explore all dimensions that affect the customer's net profit. Therefore, a wider explanation of TCO – one that looks at the difference between the next best alternative of an option, and that takes into account all increased or decreased revenue minus all increased and decreased costs over the life of an asset – allows one to determine which decisions are the most profitable.

Thus, suppliers that are able to help their customers increase revenue, expand margins, enter new markets, sell an "upgrade option," and/or enter into longer customer relations create a benefit for the revenue side of their customer's balance sheet that needs to be measured. A few real-life examples of an expanded TCO view follow.

The first example involves increased margin or sales for an original equipment manufacturer (OEM). When a supplier is able to help an OEM make a better piece of equipment, it can use that differentiated value either to sell more than its competitors or to value-price for it. However, if the supplier cannot help the OEM show its customer the value created, that value becomes "lost in translation" between the supplier, the OEM, and the product's final customer. In such cases it is incumbent upon the supplier to work with the OEM's product management, sales, and marketing teams to help them not only make a better application but also be able to sell that value to their customers.

A global OEM, after being pushed by field sales, decided that it needed to make a product that offered some customer features and benefits that were different than its competitors' rather than trying to make a good-enough, cheap product that everyone in the market was focusing on. The OEM worked with an established partner and added not only high-quality branded components but also a solution that lengthened their application's maintenance intervals relative to their competitors', because the bearings did not have to be greased. In this case, the value created for the OEM was the increased net margin they were able to obtain in the marketplace by having a differentiated product that they could show customers would have a lower operating cost, would require less maintenance and less lubricant, and would cost less to dispose of. In taking an expanded TCO approach, the OEM was able to realize higher profits by creating and selling value. If it had taken the existing TCO approach, it would have viewed the price premium for these greased-for-life bearings as a "cost increase" and not taken into account the increased price premium for which its application could be sold in the marketplace. To do this the OEM was shown the value via TCO reduction that its customers would obtain and given the sales, marketing, tools, and training to be able to articulate that to its customers.

A second example is the well-known "Intel Inside" designation. Let's assume that the Intel chip is better. Does it help the PC maker? Not really. It's the person who buys and uses the computer – who now has a machine that uses less energy, is faster, or crashes less – who benefits. That value would have been lost inside the machine if Intel did not find a way to either pull customer demand or support their computer manufacturers with "Intel Inside" market communication to push this "value." The marketing term *ingredient co-branding* describes this situation.

Let's consider another example, in which a firm helps a user operate a piece of equipment that is more reliable, that runs at higher production speeds, or that generates less scrap waste. In the existing TCO analysis, no value is taken into account for the profitability that is generated by the better running machine. In one case, an operator was able to increase the throughput of his process by 1.5 percent, which yielded a net profit of over $18,745,000 annually. The investment was justified only because the increased-profit side of the TCO model was included in the analysis.

What do customers really care about: total cost of ownership and net profit, or lowest unit price?

Before devoting the necessary time and investments to calculating the full TCO for a new product or customer, a supplier must first ask, "Do any of our customers still even care about value? Or in today's world, is it always about the lowest price?" Sales teams continue to send market reports back indicating that they've lost deals because the supplier's price was too high, and that the value it offers customers is not appreciated, so customers won't pay for it. In too many instances, people transpose the terms "cost" and "price." These are two completely different concepts. What customers want is the lowest total cost, since that will drive their profitability. However, if a company is unable to measure the values that it creates and how these either help increase revenue or reduce other costs, its customer will focus on unit price instead of total costs as they become conflated in the customer's mind.

Customers and procurement professionals do seek value as measured by TCO. Respondents to a 2008 *Purchasing Magazine* survey reported a continued decline in the importance of purchase price, whereas the importance of TCO remained flat. Not surprisingly, a 2007 study sponsored by the International Association of Commercial and Contract Management (IACCM) found that customers rank TCO as being nearly two times as important as unit price (Strategic Account Management Association and International Association of Commercial and Contract Management 2007). Procurement professionals and management teams are realizing that unit price is only a subcomponent of total cost, and that those price savings usually do not find their way to the company's bottom line.

Where costs and benefits exist in the four stages of an asset lifecycle

It is essential that a supplier know where the value and costs exist within the lifecycle of the asset that it is involved with – to know who obtains which benefit, and who is asked to make which investment. Sometimes an investment occurs in one stage and the benefit emerges elsewhere.

It all starts with the ***design phase***. For example, an OEM works with its component suppliers and aggregates these components into a functioning asset that has utility. Here is where decisions about operating and disposal costs for the user are made, such as what material to use, what tolerances the machine should be made to, how long the product will last, how expensive it will be to operate, and so forth. These operating attributes are intended to be trade-offs between what the customer wants and what they will pay. This phase is where miscommunication sometimes occurs. The constant reports from the field that customers don't want something better or that they do not value something lead product designers to reduce costs, usually by substituting *similar products* that have a lower unit price. People become confused about whether the customer seeks the lowest price, or the lowest cost. As the aforementioned research shows, they seek the lowest costs. Thus the supplier must ensure that it can demonstrate how the performance of its product(s) will reduce customer costs and/or increase revenue. If it is unable to demonstrate this, then the term *lowest price* becomes the discussion point.

The operating costs incurred by and benefits to the user who buys this product from the OEM can be broken down into the following three stages.

The approach starts with a close look at the *acquisition process*, including receiving costs, payment terms, holding inventory, and unit price. When asked whether they measure TCO, some procurement professionals will say yes. A follow-up question

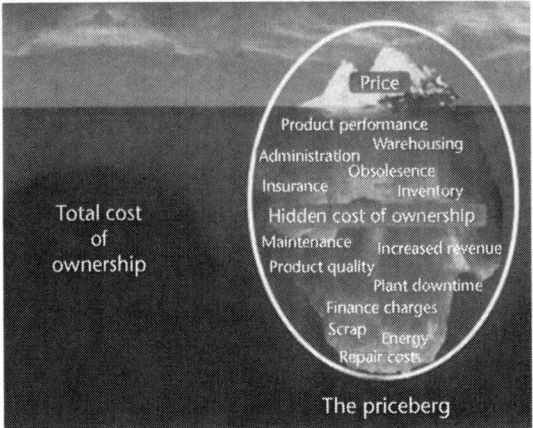

FIGURE 14.1 The priceberg

usually reveals that these are the indicators being measured. These are, of course, important measurements; however, in most cases they are just the tip of "The Priceberg" (Figure 14.1).

Next is the *operation phase*, during which the buyer uses what has been purchased, and in which the sometimes less visible costs below the water line come into play. Included here are factors such as how long the item lasts, how much energy it uses, and whether it can increase the throughput of what it is helping to produce, affect scrap rates, be easier and predictable to repair, and so forth.

Finally, the buyer needs to *dispose* of what has been purchased. Disposal can range from being almost free to very costly; the item may even have a residual value. For example, the cost to dispose of lubricants after their use can be as much as 2.5 times more than the cost to acquire them.

The breakdown of these costs into the different categories can vary as a result of many factors, but numerous studies show that the initial purchase price of an industrial application (such as a pump, fan, or gearbox) is 12 percent of its total cost (Accenture 2001). Simply put, should you focus on reducing the acquisition price of an asset, when it is only 12 percent of its TCO, or on buying a better asset that has the lowest operating and disposal costs, that covers 88 percent of its TCO? The better asset that is more "expensive" up front might just have a lower TCO.

Let's take for example an industrial asset, such as a pump, that follows the Accenture Study and 12 percent of its cost is the acquisition price while 88 percent is its operating and disposal costs. These pumps could have the same ISO specification. It should be noted that ISO is a conformance measurement, and all things that have the same ISO specifications do not have the same performance. We will assume two options exist: a $1,200 initial purchase price pump with $8,800 in operating and disposal costs, or a TCO of $10,000; versus a better pump that costs $1,500 to buy but uses $350 less energy, $250 less lubricant, enables you to predict its failure meaning it can be repaired for $235 less, saves one event of unplanned downtime which equates to 1 hour lost production at $7,500, and the pump lasts 20 percent longer. Its TCO is purchase price $1,500 + alternative operating costs of $8,800 − costs saved of ($350 + 250 + 235 = $835) + revenue increased ($7,500 × 10% operating margin = $750) plus the $1,500 pump has a 20 percent longer life meaning it has to be replaced less often saving 20 percent of its initial purchase price (20% × $1,500 = $300). By getting the supplier to help calculate the TCO, the low price product costs the company $10,000 and the better product doesn't cost the $1,500 + $8,800 costs that are assumed or $10,300, it actually costs almost $1,900 less: $1,500 + ($8,800 − $835 − $750 − $300) = $8,415 or a $1,585 saving. In this case, like most, the 25 percent more expensive pump actually ends up costing almost 16 percent less (Figure 14.2).

Looking at a far simpler example, what does the average person consider to be important when purchasing a car? Intuitively, once the specifications are chosen, such as a four-door family sedan, with automatic transmission, air conditioning, and a certain size engine, then one could assume the choice is made based on a unit-price comparison of the options that meet those criteria. However, the costs of owning a car do not end with the initial purchase. The operating costs such as fuel consumption, average cost to repair or service, financing, insurance, depreciation rates, and numerous other costs live well beyond the acquisition of the car. With this data, one might find that the car that initially appears to be expensive will actually provide the *lowest total cost*, and is therefore a better deal. In some cases the costs to insure different cars having the same features and specifications are very different. Since insurance is a mandatory cost, the cost differences should be included in a TCO analysis. Edmunds, a website for car buyers, has created their own TCO acronym, "true costs to own," which allows customers to calculate the differences

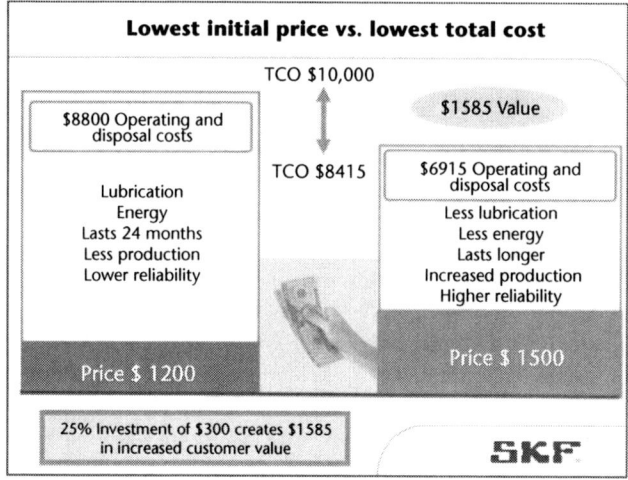

FIGURE 14.2 Price versus TCO

between cars (http://www.edmunds.com/car-buying/true-cost-to-own-tco.html). The Accenture (2001) report shows that for light-duty trucks, the initial purchase price is only 12 percent of its TCO, whereas for commercial aircraft it is 8 percent, and for Class 8 vehicles (large tractor trailers) it is 11 percent.

Because of the wealth of data that exists in the marketplace today, the ability to apply the concept to everyday purchases is now more feasible in the B-to-B and B-to-C worlds.

The key steps for successful value pricing and value selling

The first step is to determine what is of value to one's customers, creating products and services that deliver that value, quantifying that value, pricing for the value created, and then communicating that value so that customers are willing to pay for it.

Sales and marketing should spend their time understanding where they affect a customer's profitability – rather than arguing with their own management that their products are priced too high, or finding numerous creative ways to discount in the marketplace.

Creating the right products and services in order to price for value

The journey must begin with creating products and services that have customer value. This value needs to be compared with the customer's next best alternative. A company's customers always have a choice, whether it is to do nothing, to buy someone else's (different) option, or to buy the company's offering. Value is not realized in the mind of the engineer who creates a product; it is realized only when the customer uses that product and obtains something they value. By "value" we mean something the customer is willing to pay for. Numerous tools exist for helping companies in this area, from voice-of-the-customer analysis to value-mapping to simple surveys and the like. Simply put, customers are not in the business of buying products or services; they are in the business of making money. A company's offer had better help them accomplish this in some way.

Quantifying that value

Once a company has a solution that offers the customer a benefit, it must quantify the benefit that the user or users will receive versus the investment it is asking them to make. The term *investment* is used to denote the price differential between the company and the next best alternative, otherwise known as the price premium. If the company's marketing uses buzzwords such as longer, more, less, faster, quicker, better, or a list of hundreds of more generic benefit statements, then these need to be quantified. How many companies will allow their employees to buy something they want? A business case needs to be created. The question is, by whom? Is it the job of the supplier, or the person wanting to buy the solution? Presumably the company knows more about how its solution creates value, and has an interest in supporting the buyer in justifying the investment in its solution.

FIGURE 14.3 Documenting customer value

A recent study shows that 90 percent of buyers require a business case to change what they are doing and that 81 percent of them expect the supplier to deliver it (Alinean 2011).

A tool that allows the sales force to sit down with a customer and run the expected business case is what is needed. The tool should not just guess at some "maybe" benefits. Best-in-class tools have the following characteristics (see Figure 14.3).

- All inputs are changeable.
- Proof points are supported by references and technical reasoning.
- Ranges of expected numbers that help focus the discussion based on reference points.
- Database that shows where other users have obtained benefits, and what the impact was.
- Clearly understandable calculations. The goal is not to confuse one's customer into buying something. The logic and calculations should be obvious.

Now that the customer has a realistic business case, with the reasoning behind the case, references for the reasoning, support documentation, and an understanding of how the business cases was developed, a business discussion can occur. The premium value pricing can be seen as an investment. However, if the customer believes that the supplier is engaging in a value-pricing exercise (the more value he agrees to, the higher the price the supplier will charge), the supplier will encounter resistance. This exercise should be used to justify the supplier's price. We will later discuss how this value quantification helps in the initial pricing process.

All the customer can question now is whether the supplier will guarantee such performance, the probability that this will occur, whether the value created is aligned with the customer's goals, and the political question "Does the person investing in the solution belong to the department that will reap the benefit?" The supplier needs to have programs and answers for these reasonable questions.

At a 2010 Winning with Procurement conference, hosted by Huthwaite International in the UK, Paula Gildert, the head of R&D procurement at AstraZeneca, offered an interesting summation:

> Suppliers often don't come to us with a business case. But it's what we want. Sell your value in our numbers to get our attention. But if you can't quantify your value – don't be surprised at the failure of procurement to do so.

Pricing for the value created

Once a supplier has created value, and has quantified that value in terms of a comparison with the next best alternative, it is time to price so that the supplier and the customer each gain an equitable return for the investments that will be made or have been made.

Since different customers, different segments, and different groups within the value chain all have different value created for them, it is important to start with who obtains what value and where in the asset lifecycle. After a supplier runs numerous simulations, based on best available data, industry benchmarks it knows, and assumptions on improvements based on its test data, it can begin to obtain ranges of impacts for different customer segments. Whether it can support many different price points will then depend on its channels to markets and the type of product or service it is selling. For simplicity's sake, a supplier would choose a price for its new offering based on the average incremental value created versus the next best alternative, where the value surplus that the buyer receives is enough incentive for them to try the new offering. This ratio will change based on the hardness of the value created and the time frame. If the value is immediately recognizable and very hard in measurement terms, the supplier can charge a higher proportion of this value. However, if the payback is longer term, the hardness of the value less visible, and the certainty less, the supplier would and should retain less of the value surplus.

When the value is created through the OEM, the supplier must calculate the incremental value that the user of the products received and then work backward to value-price. For example, if a supplier's offering helps an OEM create a machine that lasts longer, uses less energy, and is less expensive to repair, the supplier would need to calculate how much value it creates for the user of the machine and then price for that as well as help the OEM explain that value to their customers.

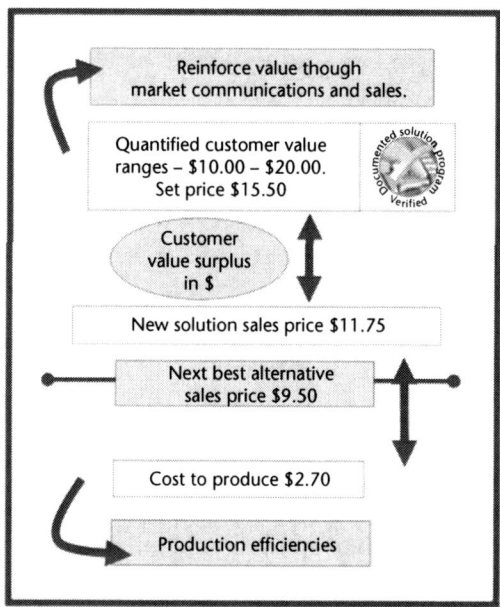

FIGURE 14.4 Quantifying customer value

The process

- Calculate ranges of customer value (Figure 14.4).
- Determine production cost.
- Determine whether there is enough profit to move forward. If not, STOP.
- Determine a sales price that maximizes one's profitability, with enough incentive for customer to move, versus next best alternative.
- Sales and marketing must work on increasing the understood customer value.
- Engineering, quality, processes focus on production efficiencies.

One option is pay for performance agreements, where suppliers are paid on their ability to increase the measurable value created versus the existing situation. Vitasek shows that companies engaging and rewarding their supply base around value created are more profitable than other companies (Vitasek *et al.* 2010).

Although value pricing is the usual and most visible way of capturing value, other options such as increased share of customer wallet, less discounting of overall business, longer customer agreements, and even a consulting fee for finding the cost-savings ideas might be more palatable and easier for the customer than a price premium alone.

Communicating the price premium

The supplier may have found value that its customer cares about, and may have created it, measured its financial impact, and priced appropriately for it, but if it cannot communicate that value in a way that the customer understands and appreciates, the whole exercise is likely to fail to yield the desired results. Let's discuss two main points: the use of the word *value* and what the customer hears, and the use of industry and technical jargon-laden pieces.

"Value" has begun to acquire a negative connotation in the marketplace. First, the word is constantly overused. However, and more important, "value" has come to be associated with low-priced offerings. Think of the advertisements one hears about store brands, low-frills airlines, low-priced knockoffs ... they all offer VALUE. The underlying message is that the only thing that creates value is a low acquisition price, that no other attribute creates a measurable or meaningful value. Even though that might be true for some of these product categories, it is not what I mean by value.

The word has also been used to encompass all the soft things we "enjoy" in a relationship. A value supplier is responsive, listens to its customers, and offers things it does not charge for. Basically, it creates *soft value*.

Finally, there is a term coined by Marco Bertini, an assistant professor of marketing at the London Business School, that I think sums up an issue I see in technical sales all the time. He calls it the "the curse of knowledge": "When we know something, it is difficult for us to imagine not knowing it or to understand why others also don't know it. As a result, we often find it hard to communicate and collaborate effectively with others" (Bertini 2011). In technical industries, we see communication material covered in industry language because we feel we are customizing our message. Even if a supplier's audience is a technical buyer, the supplier will need the commercial buyer's involvement. The supplier should not make the mistake of relying on the customer to translate its marketing message of longer, better, faster, more reliable, harder, or safer, into a business case for their company.

So let's not throw the word "value" around, unless we are willing to quantify it. It is more appropriate to speak of the financial impact that is created for the customer — and that impact must be expressed in dollars and cents, or euros, etc. (see Figure 14.5).

Implications for innovation in pricing

As has been suggested before, the pricing discussion must be part of the whole new-market development process, and it should provide that sober second thought that challenges the wild assumptions of engineers and product developers. Suppliers must keep asking "If value is really created versus the next best alternative, what can be charged for it?"

This discussion requires a true understanding of the TCO, including all profitability factors, and all costs and all revenues that have been created for each party along the value chain. If a supplier is trying to persuade an OEM to pay for value that will be realized by someone else in the value chain, then it must be able and willing to help the OEM communicate and capture part of that value. The theory of willingness to pay needs to be updated to a newer version — ability to pay — which

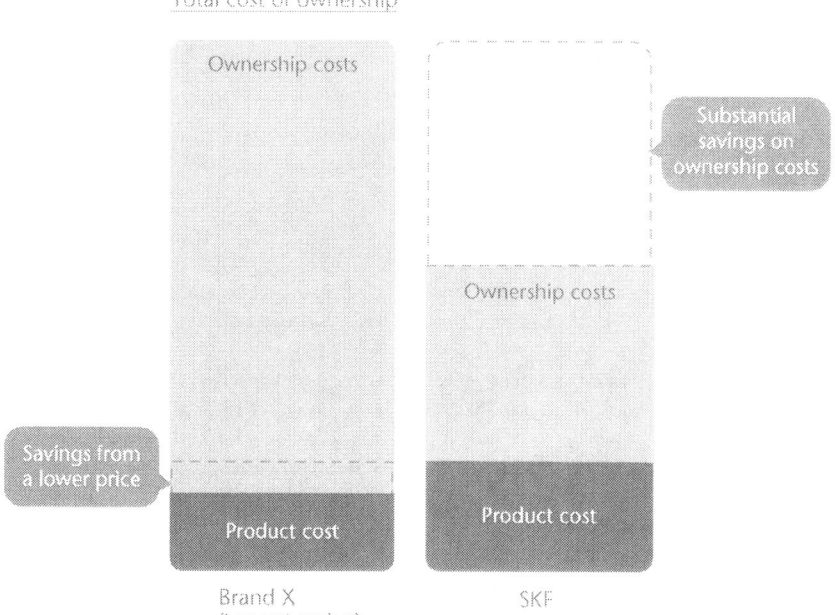

FIGURE 14.5 Price versus value

will be based on the soundness of the supplier's business case. At the extreme, a customer's willingness to pay will be based on their ability to pay. If it's a guarantee of performance and benefit, the buyer should be able to take the supplier's business case to their bank and use it as collateral to secure the investment needed to buy the supplier's solution. Willingness to pay increases as benefits are converted into hard, measurable currency, and ability to pay changes as the value created becomes a "currency" that can be traded internally for more funding or with a local bank.

Pricing professionals may need to offer customers many different ways to pay for the value created. A price premium supported by a business case that one's sales force customizes and can clearly articulate is only one way. Pay-for-performance relationships, in which a premium is paid as value is created, is the next evolution for some capital goods that can have clear measurement impacts.

A supplier that invests to create better products or services must ensure that it can capture part of the value created. It must equip its sales teams with the necessary tools, knowledge, skills to present, and market communication collateral so that they can explain why its price premium is an investment. In closing, let's consider a comment based on value-pricing research from Marco Bertini, of the London Business School,

> An interesting dynamic emerges when you compare the perceptions of most business customers and the reality. Lowest unit price is often assumed to be

desirable. In fact, firms that are convinced to buy on value exhibit higher repeat purchase rates, which suggests they are far more satisfied.

(SKF TCO Whitepaper 2010)

In using the term "convinced," Bertini means convinced by a business case, not by smoke and mirrors.

References

Aberdeen (2011) Sales effectiveness enablement. http://www.aberdeen.com.

Accenture (ed.) (2001) The total cost of ownership vision. In: Industrial equipment insight, 2. http://www.accenture.com.

Alinean (2011) The economic focused buyer reigns. http://www.alinean.com.

Anderson, J. C. and Narus, J. A. (2004) *Business market management: Understanding, creating, and delivering value*, 2nd edition. Upper Saddle River, NJ: Pearson Education, Inc.

Bertini, M. (2011) Marketing Programmes at London Business School.

Monitor Group (2011) *Operating profit relative to industry peers* [Diagram]. In: Pricing capability study. http://www.monitor.com.

Piscopo, G. H., Johnston, W. and Bellenger, D. N. (2008) Total cost of ownership and customer value in business markets. In: Woodside, A. G., Golfetto, F. and Gibbert, M. (eds) *Advances in business marketing and purchasing, Volume 14*. Bingley, UK: Emerald Group Publishing Limited, pp. 205–20.

Purchasing Magazine (2008) Purchasing survey. December 2008.

SKF TCO White Paper (2010) *The way to drive real sustainable profits to the bottom line*. Available at http://www.skf.com.

Strategic Account Management Association and International Association of Commercial and Contract Management (2007) *2007 Strategic customer–supplier relationships collaboration study* [Graph 6].

Vitasek, K., Ledyard, M. and Manrodt, K. B. (2010) *Vested outsourcing: Five rules that will transform outsourcing*. New York, NY: Palgrave Macmillan.

15

PRICING STRATEGIES FOR RECESSIONARY TIMES

Fernando Resende

The challenge

How to be profitable in a market with few but big opportunities, where the contractors push for the lowest price and the competitors' strategy is to win the deal, no matter what they need to do in terms of pricing.

The strategy

It's very common to hear customers asking for discounts to close a new contract or even to renew it, but there are some markets where the customers are in a very comfortable position to pressure the suppliers into low prices. Normally, these markets are clearly saturated in terms of growth or the number of new opportunities. In this type of market it is the norm to find one or more aggressive players that have as the only strategy to present the lowest price they can. The customer pressures the better technical players to present the same price level as the "low cost companies."

If the strategy of the company is to participate in these new opportunities, you can't play the game of low prices. You need to define a strategy to enter into business but using smart pricing. The company needs to define a strategy to drop down the "entry price level" and think about how to recover the money in the medium and/or long term. The main question in this situation is how to drop down the price and have a sustainable business.

The first and very important initial step is to make sure that the scope you are considering in your proposal is what the customer really needs and requests in the technical specifications. Below I present some topics you need to give careful consideration during proposal elaboration and negotiation.

Scope optimization

One of the main problems I faced in the past working in the pre-sales/pricing area is that sometimes the problem is not the pricing itself but the scope you are considering for the prices. I have already seen some cases where the pricing difference between two or three competitors could be reduced only by a revision of the scope together with the customer (or even with internal meetings reviews). If you don't realize that this work of scope review is necessary in some cases and you decide to go ahead with only pricing discounts, you may win the contract but with a margin smaller that you could have realized with a scope optimization.

When an RFP (Request for Proposal) is released, the scope and technical specifications are normally not so clear and sometimes this document doesn't bring enough information in order to build your solution. In these cases, what I normally recommend is to schedule a meeting with the customer to understand their needs if you have a good relationship with them. If the customer doesn't accept meetings during the RFP process, I recommend:

- Make a clear schedule that reserves you a good amount of time for a review of the scope. Normally the timing that the customer gives you to prepare the proposal is short, so plan all the activities from the beginning and convince all involved of the importance of following the schedule.
- Exclude anything extra from your scope. Make sure that the scope you're considering in your proposal is really requested by the customer. If it's not clear, consider this as optional, price it separately from the main scope, and inform the customer that it's not included in the basic prices.
- The best technical solution is rarely the most competitive commercial offer. There is no need to present the "state of the art" technical solution unless you're sure that the customer intends to pay extra money for that.
- What is not in the specifications or customer request, assume to your favour. Sometimes the customer mentions a technology or extra functionality only to know about the benefits of your solution but actually they are not asking you to include this extra scope into pricing. So, if these types of extra scope are not clearly defined as mandatory don't include them in your basic pricing.
- Utilize a roadmap fully to maximize cost efficiency. Consider the roadmap of your products and the customer schedule to build an optimized offer. Sometimes during the proposal elaboration you don't have the better cost solution but you can have it ready when the project will be implemented.
- If you are offering configurable equipment, utilize the minimum recommended hardware that meets the specifications and exclude redundancies unless requested.
- In the case of software, offer only the basic software and necessary additional software when required. Try to not price optional software/features. You can price it higher later once you have signed the contract.
- If services are part of the scope, offer only the requested scope. If the specifications are unclear, state clearly in your proposal what is part of the scope and what is not. Make sure that the seniority level of the resources you're considering are really appropriate to the service the customer has requested. For example, don't consider a Senior Engineer when a Technician is enough to execute the service

and meet the customer request. Often you have an overqualified team for the proposed service.
- Carefully analyze the service resources dimensioning; travel and living expenses, tools, cars, phones, etc. This can be a high cost.
- Regarding pricing of third party components, if the costs are relevant compared to total project costs, list the price of these third party components separately. Offer the customer the option to purchase these components directly from the third party.

Considering all the above mentioned, we can propose a better commercial offer with the scope appropriate for the customer needs. All extra scope can be priced with a comfortable margin that could bring you additional revenues in the medium to long term.

Recovery killers

Once you are comfortable that the scope of your proposal is optimized, you need to be careful with some points that I used to call "Recovery Killers." They are points that can destroy the margin of the project if you don't analyze them carefully.

- Be careful about discount applied to a unitary price list. Instead it is preferable to offer a special discount for the package, or special discount for the project, etc. If you decide to go with a unitary price list discount before the final scope definition, that sometimes could mean changes during the proposal/contract negotiation, you can discount items that have quantities different than forecasted in the RFP.
- Do not commit to price erosion. It's very dangerous to commit to future discounts if you don't have a clear visibility of your costs in future years. It is preferable to agree a new negotiation with the customer after a period of time or if there is huge change in the demand or quantities.
- Avoid extraordinary business models, such as pay-as-you-grow or revenue sharing, price per user/subscriber, unless careful analysis suggests otherwise. If you decide to go with a business model such as these, agree with the customer clear rules that they need to meet for the pricing to be valid.
- Avoid special discounts, such as percentage of sales, unless you have a clear commitment for the total scope/volume from the customer.

Checklist for smart pricing

There are also some basic rules that I like to follow during the pricing definition and during the negotiation phase with the customer. These can help you to define a pricing value for your products/solution instead of only price based on the cost plus margin.

- Always consider the previous prices that the customer has had. Do not give a discount without reason.

- Check if the customer has some link to another company (mother company, subsidiary) and align the prices.
- Think about where the scope of the project will grow in the following years and price accordingly. Price expansible items higher than one-off items.
- Price components that competitors don't have and the customer wants, with a higher price.
- Check out the market price level for similar deals or customers.
- Do not present prices for items customer don't ask for. You can price them higher later if you get the contract.
- Understand how the customer will negotiate the deal and how many "rounds" of negotiation there will be. If there is more than one round at list price, never offer your best price at the beginning.

The main idea of the process above is to reduce as much as you can the initial price for the customer to make the project viable from an investment point of view, avoid any extra discount that is not necessary, and maximize the gains for the medium to long term.

The results

Through a scope optimization you could drop costs and prices more than 30 percent depending on the case and also gain around 10 percent margin. Instead of giving discounts to the customers, you could optimize the initial scope, drop down the prices and keep the margins at a healthy level. Of course, there are some cases where you need to drop your entry margin anyway to win the business. But if you did a good job on scope optimization and smart unitary price lists, you can see your margin recover at the first expansion you have.

The unexpected findings

If you did a very good job with scope optimization and if you presented an aggressive price after the first bid, the customer can use your price and give it as a budget to the competitors. This may force you to give additional discounts in the next rounds of negotiation.

Key lessons

As part of a pricing team you're normally not in the sales or technical departments, or directly reporting to these structures. Be close to both these groups; they will be vital to you in defining a good strategy and ensuring the scope is optimized. Try also to be close to your customers wherever possible, asking the sales team to bring you to customer meetings in order to understand their goals better and also to be part of pricing negotiations.

16

A ZERO-BASED APPROACH TO THE PRICING STRATEGY

Roberto Bedotto

Introduction: the challenge

One of the many consequences of the "great recession" that started in 2008 has been to force businesses to rethink and adapt their strategy to the new conditions.

Among the main problems, which many businesses had to face, we number:

- market size shrinking fast (sometimes by double digits) and becoming more volatile
- customers suddenly having difficult access to credit, and delaying payments
- raw materials under pressure, with inflationary conditions.

These issues brought pressure to margins, and a change in the strategy and in part of the business model of the company was required.

In this framework, the top management acted swiftly and looked for responses, which could quickly gain traction in the organization.

The pricing area was an essential element of the response, obviously. Apart from bringing more attention and essentially more discipline to the transactional pricing area, a review of the long existing pricing strategy was required.

As a matter of fact, pricing strategy had long been untouched. It was mostly based on past history, and given relatively little attention during the annual operating plan process. However, the strategy of the company was changing, and the top management stated a requirement of leaving no stone unturned. The pricing team was tasked with securing alignment of the pricing strategy with the new business environment and the new strategy.

An important element of the revision was that it had to be easy to communicate within the organization; and that it had to happen in a relatively short amount of time (less than a couple of weeks, one if possible); finally, it had to happen with quite limited resources, both in terms of manpower and IT support.

The response of the pricing team was to develop a "back of the envelope" methodology, and support the management rethink and review the pricing strategy from scratch. This methodology is what we present in this chapter; it proved effective, so has been used ever since.

The strategy

The methodology we present here involves the following steps:

- a first half-day workshop to kick-off the methodology, and clarify the new strategy to all stakeholders. This exercise is run with top management, namely the managing director, sales directors, product management heads, finance, market intelligence, and of course the complete pricing team. This step is nicknamed the "polarization step."
- a data gathering exercise, carried out mostly offline by the pricing team.
- a second half-day workshop to review the conclusions and the numbers, with the same team as the polarization step.

The method proved to be efficient and effective and it was further applied multiple times.

The strategy, Step 1: Polarize

The aim of this step is to make sure that

- the pricing strategy is supporting the company strategy
- all stakeholders are very clear and aligned around the new strategy.

This step takes the shape of a workshop, run with those who have P&L responsibility: managing director, sales directors, product managers, with finance and market intelligence as support.

What we do in the first step is to outline the strategy by products and customers, or more broadly, what we sell/to whom we sell it.

"Outlining the strategy" means making the message of the strategy much clearer, *by polarizing it*. What the author does is to avoid talking about numbers here. Instead, he leads the audience into thinking about *resources utilization* or *focus areas*. Numbers come later.

He starts by considering that, by definition, the organization has 100 percent of resources available in any given year (say, 2011) and 100 percent in the following year (2012). The first step is about distributing resources by "what we sell."

The team outlines the strategy on a simple matrix. As column headers the reader can use, for example, the brands first, and then the products/services. Or – in case brands are not an essential driver of the pricing strategy – the reader can start from the products and services. In other words, what to use as column headers depends on the specifics of every business, so adaptation is needed here.

In the example reported here we start with the brands, and build a matrix as follows (see Table 16.1):

We input a "+" sign where next year we will put more focus (more attention, more time, more money, more resources) in an area. A "−" sign means that we will put less focus. An "=" sign means where we will put the same focus.

Again, let's be clear: a "−" sign does not mean that the company will not grow in that area, or that the company will disinvest. It means instead that the company does not need to focus resources there, as it may be that that area might be growing on its own, e.g. by a strong market pull.

The aim here is to polarize the strategy, and show clearly where the company needs to focus. Most important is that this polarization happens in a sort of closed system: if the management puts more focus (a "+" sign) somewhere, then it has to reduce focus (a "−" sign) somewhere else. Resources can not be focused everywhere.

As a second step, the team adds a further level of detail – in the case reported here, a split by product or service category, using the same methodology and principle (Table 16.2).

Note that within each brand, the "sum" of the categories is the "same sign" as in the previous matrix. So in Brand B, the sum of Category 2 and 3 is sum("+","− −"), that is, "−". This means that the company will focus less on Brand B overall, but still more on Category 2 within Brand B.

Note also that participants can re-order the matrix and see it first by category and then by brand, and it will still give the same message: Category 1 and 2 are "+", Category 3 and 4 are "−". This helps in adapting the message to the audience: brand managers will read about brand strategy here; and product managers will read about product categories strategy, as well.

TABLE 16.1 Brand growth matrix

	What we sell →		
	Brand A	Brand B	Brand C
TOTAL	+	−	=

TABLE 16.2 Brand growth matrix by product category

	What we sell →					
	Brand A		Brand B		Brand C	
	Category 1	Category 2	Category 2	Category 3	Category 3	Category 4
TOTAL	+	=	+	− −	+	−

The reader can complicate this step of "what we sell" as much as needed, depending on the strategy and the decision levels. The author suggests, however, to avoid overcomplicating the matrix, at first: adding too many details early in the exercise can strongly impact the analysis.

For the sake of the example, the author leaves it here and moves on to the other dimension of the matrix, that is, "to whom we sell."

This dimension depends, again, on the strategy of the company. In the specific case when this methodology was used for the first time, the author focused on distribution channels within a specific geographic area. Later that same year, he extended to a wider area and used geographic areas first, and distribution channels after. In following years, as a new customer segmentation was introduced, the same strategy was reviewed under the lens of market segments. The beauty and power of this methodology is that it is quite simple and adaptable.

In the specific example reported in Table 16.3, the author uses distribution channels.

By now it should be clear how to continue building up this matrix. If the reader needs to add some special customers, who are particularly important in the sales figures, he or she can do it, and add a second column to the left, right after the distribution channels. The author again gives a warning about avoiding overcomplicating the exercise, and suggests to leave it as simple as possible, especially during the first run.

The result so far has been to make the overall strategy focus much clearer. By polarizing the new strategy, every stakeholder is aligned around the same message. This is particularly relevant in a changing environment, where the effort of every stakeholder is to re-align the rest of the organization around the new objectives, and move the company in the new direction as fast and as effectively as possible.

The next step is to introduce the pricing strategy: the method used is to draft a high-level price waterfall within the matrix.

TABLE 16.3 Brand growth matrix by channel

To whom we sell ↓	What we sell →					
	Brand A		Brand B		Brand C	
	Category 1	Category 2	Category 2	Category 3	Category 3	Category 4
TOTAL	+	=	+	– –	+	–
Distribution channel 1	+	=	–	–	++	– –
Distribution channel 2	=	=	+	–	+	=
Distribution channel 3	–	=	+	=	– –	+

TABLE 16.4 Brand growth matrix by customer

To whom we sell ↓	Price waterfall strategy ↓	What we sell →					
		Brand A		Brand B		Brand C	
		Category 1	Category 2	Category 2	Category 3	Category 3	Category 4
Distribution channel 1	On invoice discounts	+	=	=	=	+	=
	Off invoice discounts	=	=	–	–	+	– –
	Total Channel 1	+	=	–	–	++	– –

For the sake of the example, the author focuses here on one distribution channel, say the first one; however all channels need to be represented, plus the total. It is obvious that it is of the utmost importance to keep the initial matrix quite simple and lean (see Table 16.4).

The reader can add another column to the right of the price waterfall, using major categories of price waterfall (e.g. brand discounts, channel discounts, year-end rebates on volumes, and so on).

The author suggests to keep it very simple during the first run; as the strategy and the methodology consolidated, the author led a deep dive in the different areas of the price waterfall, focusing on specific discounts, which needed tweaking.

All in all, at the end of this exercise, we have a clear, polarized sales strategy; and we link it to a clear, polarized pricing strategy.

The message can start being cascaded across the organization through a series of meetings with the relevant teams, and sponsorship and participation of most of the stakeholders.

The strategy, Step 2: Populate with data

After polarization, comes the financial side of the exercise: basically, add sales; and (at total level, per distribution channel) add profitability.

This step is run by the pricing department, in cooperation with finance and all other stakeholders, including IT.

The depth and width of analysis depends on data availability, and it is not uncommon to start with few numbers and a lot of guesswork. Numbers will, however, be directionally correct.

The strategy, Step 3: Review data – and ask the questions

The second half-day workshop is dedicated to reviewing the numbers, and finalizing the action plan. While populating the matrix with data, many stakeholders were already involved and became aware of the numbers as they were building up. Still, this workshop is relevant also in terms of project management, as a formal review of the action plan.

A series of questions need to be answered properly; the basic ones are:

- Is the pricing strategy aligned with the overall sales and profitability target? The author saw some very interesting discussions arising as a result of this exercise, in terms of either challenging too optimistic targets, or setting more ambitious ones.
- Is the pricing strategy making sense, namely:
  - From the customer standpoint: how much are we compensating trade for the job it is doing to bring our offering to the market, and assisting the market? This matrix might in some cases help ground some numbers. If the company's price list represents roughly the market price, then the amounts shown in the table are representative of the gross margin, which trade is making. In other less fortunate cases, the reader might be able to apply some guesswork and build the margin from the invoice price upwards, rather than from a list price downwards.
  - From the company's standpoint: is the way trade is compensated consistent with the strategy? A simple example will help illustrate this point. Let's consider cash. In these recessionary times, with a more complicated access to credit, it is quite possible that the company is focused on maximizing cash. Is the pricing strategy supporting this goal? This can happen if the price waterfall has a trade term, which helps bringing in cash, e.g. either by "sharing part of the cake" if a customer pays on time/in advance, and/or by punishing non-compliance.
  - If there is a proposal to change pricing conditions, this methodology helps to frame the discussion in an effective manner. Which distribution channels/product categories are most likely to be impacted, and how much of sales and profitability are at risk?
  - An interesting topic to investigate is also about the on-invoice vs. off-invoice discounts ratio. In the author's experience, it happened that some customers perceived prices as too high, having in mind the level of invoiced prices only. In their perception, year-end rebates played a minor role, even though they were sizeable in amount. In this case, and again, this structure helps to frame the company's answer.
- What is the action plan to make the new pricing strategy happen? In how much time can it be implemented? The answer depends on either legal constraints (contracts) and/or administrative constraints (IT system cannot cope with the new condition, or requires important investment in time and consultants to happen).

The results

The company implemented the majority but not all of the strategy as initially intended. The markets and competition reacted in a manner which made some of the actions obsolete and/or had to be changed.

Still, the methodology proved to be the best to plan quickly in volatile conditions, and it was used further on multiple occasions. In the eyes of the stakeholders, it proved quite effective in discussing and communicating quickly the strategic plan, including the pricing side.

Also, as stakeholders and management became accustomed with the method, they ran it at a much faster pace; eventually, it became part of the company's operating system. The fact that all major stakeholders were involved with the matrix contributed to polishing and sometimes adjusting the strategy overall, as well.

Communication around the new strategy was greatly improved by having a simple layout and methodology. Feedback around the new strategy and the adjusted pricing strategy became much quicker, direct, and effective.

Unexpected findings

The polarization side of the exercise, while always linked to pricing strategy, took on a sort of life of its own and eventually was also used to represent relevant market dynamics impacting our customers.

The methodology proved effective in eliminating doubts and misunderstandings about the strategy. It provided a crystal-clear view on the desired outcomes, and forced trade-off choices at a very early planning phase, which was very beneficial.

Another welcome side effect of this methodology was to demonstrate the need and usage of a pricing council, which was not formally established before. The pricing team further took the opportunity to use the pricing council in order to set additional central pricing guidelines.

Key lessons

- Start small and keep it simple and manageable. The level of detail can quickly become overwhelming and the important information lost in a sea of data and charts.
- Few data are OK for the first run of this exercise. Imprecision is also OK at this level, and being directionally correct is the essence here.
- Smaller workshops with the relevant stakeholders are best, as well as strong leadership of the meeting. More people around the matrix can mean that everyone feels compelled to add a piece, sometimes sidetracking the meeting.
- Involve top management. Do not even start if the highest level of management is not sponsoring this effort.
- Communicate, communicate, communicate. Every participant to the pricing council has a role in sharing the results with their teams.

Implication for innovation in pricing

This paper introduces a simple methodology to secure alignment of the pricing strategy around the overall strategy of the company.

This technique is born as a "back of the envelope" review of the pricing strategy, during the turbulent times of the 2008 economic crisis. It quickly evolved into a standard process to review and communicate the pricing strategy, and gain traction within the organization.

The methodology revolves around depicting the strategy of the company in terms of resources utilization.

The strategy is laid out in a matrix format, with the offer (product, service) as one of the dimensions, and distribution (geographies/channels) or segments on the other.

The pricing leader guides the pricing council to report the areas of focus of the strategy. By not using numbers in the first step, but mathematical signs (plus, minus and equal), it forces a polarization of the message of the strategy. It then introduces the pricing side and allows an easy review of the alignment between the two.

The process counts three main steps, and is normally run in a couple of weeks.

- a first half-day workshop to kick-off the methodology, and clarify the new strategy to all stakeholders. This exercise is run with top management, namely managing director, sales directors, product management heads, finance, market intelligence, and of course the complete pricing team. This step is nicknamed the "polarization step."
- a data gathering exercise, carried out mostly offline by the pricing team.
- a second half day workshop to review the conclusions and the numbers, with the same team as the polarization step.

The simple nature of the output enables a quick alignment with the strategy, and supports a quicker and more effective implementation of the new pricing strategy.

PART IV
Innovation in pricing tactics

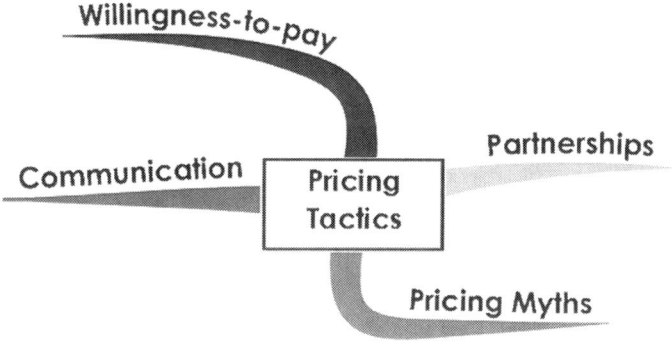

17

USING ECONOMIC VALUE COMMUNICATION TO BEND BUSINESS-TO-BUSINESS BUYERS' VALUE PERCEPTIONS

Christopher D. Provines

Introduction

Communicating value is a crucial element in making value based pricing work. Even the best offering, with a well thought out value based pricing strategy, will underperform its potential if the value communication strategy is not well designed and executed. In business-to-business markets, economic value communication is becoming more important as economic buyers play an increasingly influential role in the buying process and decision. Seller firms face margin erosion, pricing pressure and missed revenue opportunities if they cannot effectively deal with economic buyers who are unwilling or unable to acknowledge value.

There are a number of environmental and organizational forces causing the rise of the economic buyer in business-to-business markets. First, the great recession of 2008–9 has put pressure on businesses to take costs out and be more competitive. Next, there has been a strong move by many businesses to upgrade their procurement capability and become smarter buyers of goods and services. Finally, globalization has meant new competitors and broader transparency of prices across geographies and channels. Taken together, these drivers have significant implications for sellers and their pricing.

In response to these trends, many sellers have moved from selling a simple product or service to selling solutions. These solutions are generally more complex and require a different level of marketing communication and buyer involvement. Likewise, these complex offerings are usually more difficult to understand from an economic value perspective. So, sellers' own moves to differentiate offerings are creating the need to be more effective at economic value communications.

The focus of this paper is on economic value communication to the economic buyer in business-to-business markets. There are numerous people in the buying organization who influence supplier selection and purchase decisions in the business-to-business purchasing process. These people have differing roles, which can include the user buyers, technical buyers and economic buyers. Each of these buyer types can represent either individuals or groups of people (Miller and Heiman 1986). The primary focus of the economic buyers, as is used here, is on evaluating the economic consequences of selecting one supply alternative over another. These buyers are interested in the bottom line. They care about things like cost reduction, revenue growth, productivity improvements and return on investment. Usually these buyers are interested in not just price, but also getting good value for money.

One may assume that economic buyers are highly sophisticated in the application of analytical techniques to understand the bottom line impact of one solution as it compares to another. Surprisingly, research reveals that a large percentage of economic buyers lack the insights necessary to perform more sophisticated analysis of economic value – that is quantifying, in monetary terms, the differentiated benefits provided by alternative supply solutions (Ferrin and Plank 2002). Thus, there is an opportunity for sellers to 'bend' or shape the economic buyers' value perception by educating them through effective economic value communication.

Value communication is also generally an underappreciated area in many seller firms. For many firms and pricing practitioners, this author has observed that much of the focus of value based pricing is on setting the price and managing transactional prices. Much less relative focus is on developing a comprehensive, integrated economic value communication strategy and plan.

This paper is intended to help practitioners develop effective economic value communication strategies and tactics to bend buyers' value perceptions by answering the following questions:

- What are the types of economic value communication tools and tactics business-to-business firms use?
- How might the use of these tactics and tools vary based on different buying situations?
- How could a firm strategically assess a given buying situation and choose among the alternative economic value communication tools and tactics available?
- How can firms use economic value communication tools as part of a comprehensive economic value communication strategy and plan?

Background and theoretical foundation

Value in business-to-business markets

What is value? There is a diversity of opinion and a variety of definitions on what constitutes value (Day and Crask 2000). So, as a starting point, it may be helpful to define value. This paper proposes a slight adaptation of a commonly accepted definition from Anderson et al. (1993) of value in business-to-business markets. Value, as used in this paper, means the perceived worth in monetary terms of the economic, technical and psychological benefits received by a customer firm in exchange for the price paid for a product offering, taking into consideration competing alternatives and prices (Anderson et al. 1993). This definition brings together a number of important points:

- Value is perceived, thus implying the seller can influence the buyer's perception of value through effective communication.
- Value is expressed in monetary terms and is what the buyer firm receives in exchange for the price paid. This means that raising or lowering the price of the offering does not change its value. Changing the price only changes the buyer's incentive to purchase (Anderson et al. 2000).
- At a given price, all things being equal, a seller who excels at value communication could potentially sell more compared with a seller who does a poor job of value communication.
- Finally, value is relative to competing alternatives and prices. For buyer firms, this could include make versus buy decisions for manufacturers, and it could involve status quo versus making a change.

This definition of value assumes there are three types of benefits: economic benefits, psychological benefits and technical benefits. Economic benefits are measurable, differentiated benefits such as cost reduction, productivity improvements, revenue growth and rate of return (Nagle and Hogan 2006). As an example, a manufacturer of an x-ray machine used in the physician office setting may have a significant advantage compared with competitive x-ray machines in terms of routine user maintenance. This difference in user maintenance time can easily be quantified and translated into monetary terms for the buyer. This is an example of an economic benefit.

Another type of benefit is psychological. As used here in a business-to-business context, psychological benefits include things like trust, relationship, service and brand. These benefits do not directly translate objectively into economic value, but depend on each buyer's subjective assessment of value (Nagle and Hogan 2006). In business-to-business purchasing, the elements of risk and career consequences come together as an important driver of psychological benefits. The old saying 'nobody ever got fired for buying IBM' is an example of this psychological benefit. Buying IBM was considered a safe bet and, therefore, had a psychological benefit.

Finally, technical benefits include user friendliness, ease of use, quality levels and technical specifications. The assumption used here is that any technical benefit that can be objectively translated into an economic benefit is captured and communicated as an economic benefit. The previous x-ray machine example showed how a technical benefit, less routine maintenance, can be translated into an economic benefit. There may be other technical benefits remaining that are more perceptual, difficult to quantify or dependent on a subjective buyer assessment.

The focus of this paper is on economic benefit communications to economic buyers in business-to-business markets. Business-to-business consists of all organizations that acquire goods and services used in production of goods and services (Kotler 2003). For the purposes of this paper, this includes government organizations as well. The ability of sellers to bring convincing economic messages, tools and evidence is critical to influence buyers' value perception and willingness to pay. This does not mean that psychological and technical benefits are not important. Rather, the intent is to use economic benefits communication as the foundation for value communication in business-to-business markets. This assumes, of course, that the seller has a distinct advantage and some objective differentiated economic benefits.

Communication strategy

A well thought out communication strategy should include choices such as the objectives of the communication, the target audience, the key messages, communication tools to use, communication frequency, communication intensity and the economics of the proposed communication strategy. In business-to-business markets, there are a number of marketing communication channels that firms can use to reach target audiences such as advertising, sales promotions, public relations and publicity, direct marketing, and personal selling (Kotler 2003). Marketing communication mix, that is the tools firms use to communicate benefits and value, often varies based on industry norms, industry structure and other factors. For example, in healthcare markets, clinical trial data, scientific publications and health technology assessment studies play a key part in communicating value to various stakeholders.

In communicating value in business-to-business markets, the marketer will need to decide what element of value to communicate and which audience to target. In a buyer organization, there are different stakeholders involved in the purchase and supplier selection decision. These include the user buyer, the technical buyer and the economic buyer (Miller and Heiman 1986). Each member of the group has a set of individual preferences and a range of influence on the buying decision (Perdue and Summers 1991).

Figure 17.1 provides a summary of the intersection of the target audiences and the benefits communicated.

The focus of this paper is on the lower right-hand corner − communicating economic benefits or value to the economic buyer. This does not imply that communicating other benefits to the economic buyer is not worthwhile. On the other hand, this does not presume that communicating economic benefits to the other buyer types should be ignored. Rather, this assumes there is an opportunity for seller firms to get better at communicating economic benefits to economic buyers.

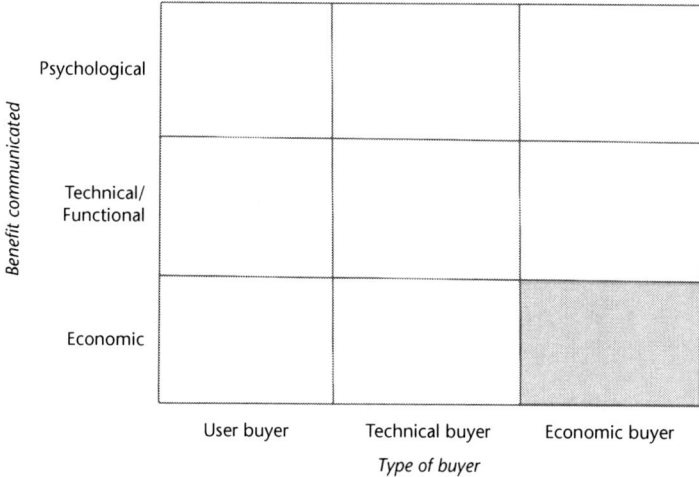

FIGURE 17.1 Intersection of benefits communicated and buyer type

Rise of the economic buyer

Webster and Wind (1972) defined a buying centre as the decision-making unit of a buyer organization. Organizational buying is often a complex process and involves multiple groups of people, differing goals and conflicting decision criteria. It is also a process that is influenced by other variables such as environmental, organizational, individual and social factors (Webster and Wind 1972). In recent times, two of these variables have had a significant impact on the role of the economic buyer in buying decisions. These two variables, which will be discussed in detail, are environmental and organizational factors.

Environmental variables, as described by Webster and Wind (1972), include political, economic, legal, cultural and technological factors that influence the buying decisions. A key environmental factor is economics. Economic factors include the general state of the economy and business conditions. The great recession of 2008–9 was a period of severe economic decline and uncertainty. One of the results of this period of economic decline was an increased focus on cost reduction and cost containment that seems to have carried on since the recession. This resulted in businesses turning to their supplier network to extract cost savings. Many suppliers felt the brunt of this cost reduction as pricing pressure.

The other key variable influencing buying that has changed recently are organizational related variables. Organizational variables include the organization of the buying centre and the purchasing function, technology relevant for purchasing, and the buying tasks (Webster and Wind 1972). Many businesses have invested in improving and transforming their purchasing function and processes in recent times. There has been a growing recognition of the role procurement can play in generating value for businesses. A survey of chief financial officers (CFOs) revealed that 73 per cent of CFOs believed that the procurement function has grown more strategic and nearly a fifth of chief procurement officers (CPO) now report to the president or CEO of their company (Aberdeen Group 2007).

Procurement has traditionally played a role in managing the buying process in many businesses. This included identifying vendors, creating specifications, initiating and managing requests for proposal, and negotiating with suppliers. In recent times, partly as a result of the economic environment, many businesses have used the purchasing or procurement function not just as an organization to initiate and manage the supplier selection process, but also as a lever to deliver significant business results. This means that procurement has evolved in many businesses from the task of just managing the buying process to actually being a key economic buyer in the supplier selection process.

The challenge with economic buyers

There is a problem with economic buyers, particularly procurement as an economic buyer. In general, purchasing managers are more knowledgeable about price but usually much less knowledgeable about value. There is also the issue of value ambiguity. This simply means that procurement either cannot translate different benefits into economic value or is uncertain about the reality of achieving the economic benefits.

This is a real life problem. From an economic value perspective, procurement traditionally thinks of economic value as total cost of ownership. This is the total cost to acquire, use, maintain and dispose of the supply item. Studies show that even the best procurement organizations do not consistently use total cost of ownership analysis when making purchasing decisions (All 2007). One study of purchasing managers showed that less than one third of respondents rated their company as good/excellent in even being able to identify cost drivers (Ferrin and Plank 2002). In using total cost of ownership in supply decisions, the following have been identified as key barriers for procurement organizations (Ellram and Siferd 1998):

- complexity: time consuming, difficult to understand, overall complexity
- cultural/organization issues
- proper use and relevance
- data availability.

In experiments with purchasing managers, one study found that purchasing managers usually chose a lower-value, lower-priced product over a higher-priced, higher-value product even if the two are monetarily equivalent to the reference. In general, there was a bias towards lower purchase price (Anderson *et al.* 2000). There are a number of logical explanations for this behaviour. It could be due to the rewards and goals of procurement. Most purchasing managers are rewarded for reducing supply costs. Alternatively, it could be due to economic value ambiguity. This means the certainty of achieving the economic value.

Finally, the purchasing managers' behaviour in this experiment could also be due to the type of supply item being purchased. In the experiment mentioned above,

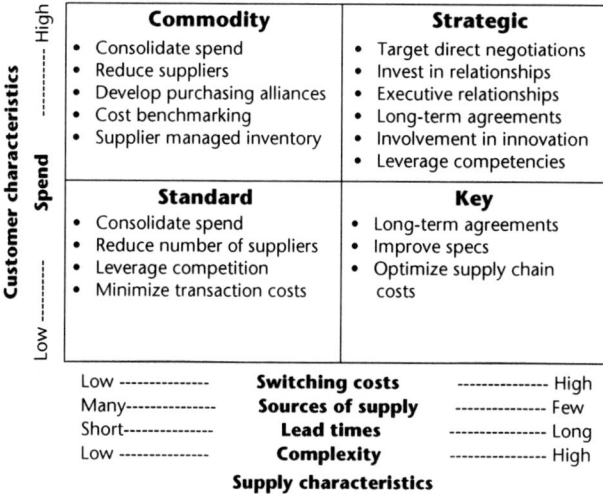

FIGURE 17.2 Supplier segmentation and procurement tactics

the item being purchased was a simple 10-hp replacement motor. This is a rather routine, non-strategic supply item. More sophisticated procurement organizations usually go through a process of segmenting supply items and suppliers into categories. The result looks something like what is illustrated in Figure 17.2 (Bueler 2006). It could be that the purchasing managers viewed the item as standard, and saw no reason to pay more for the item even if it offered more monetary value.

This leads to an important point. Professional purchasers in buyer firms get paid to drive business results. A big focus for professional purchasers is on taking costs out of the business. In the absence of compelling data, the professional purchasers will naturally use purchase price as a key benchmark and will work towards getting the lowest price possible, all things being equal. So, it is up to the seller to educate, provide compelling evidence and to convince the buyer of the economic benefits. Otherwise, it becomes a price game.

Evolving nature of procurement as an economic buyer

The modern procurement organization is under increasing pressure to deliver value from the supplier network in a number of ways. While reducing purchase price or costs have been the big area of focus of many procurement organizations, there are other areas that certainly cannot go neglected. For well-run procurement organizations, balancing a number of key objectives is critical.

Table 17.1 below presents a summary of the key objectives for the modern procurement organization. The degree of emphasis on each focus area will depend on the firm's industry, operating characteristics, business situation and procurement maturity.

TABLE 17.1 Focus areas and objectives for procurement

Focus area	Objectives
Supply costs	Reduce the purchase price as well as the total cost of ownership of supply items.
Supply chain risk	Reduce risk of supply disruption or supplier issues that may reflect poorly on company.
Innovation	Use supplier network to source product, process or business model innovation ideas and solutions to help grow and reduce costs.
Non-value added work	Eliminate non-value added work across the firm in supplier selection and management.

The reality is that while saving money is one of the key goals of procurement, particularly in tough economic times, most CPOs are also very concerned about supply continuity, quality or a supplier causing damage to the company's brand or image. A survey of top performing CPOs revealed that reducing supply risk scored almost as high as reducing costs, even in the midst of the worst recession in decades (Martindale 2009). For suppliers, this comes back to the idea of educating customers. Procurement organizations are rational and are interested in driving value in many different ways for their business. At the same time, these professional purchasers often lack the information and insights to make the best supply decisions. It is up to the supplier to educate these buyers and help them drive value.

Findings and practical applications

Economic value communication tools

Given the rising importance of the economic buyer in the purchasing process, sellers will need to decide what economic benefits to communicate and how to communicate those benefits. There are a range of tools and tactics available to communicate economic benefits. These vary from relatively simple to highly complex tools and tactics. Often sellers use a variety of these tools in combination to target buyers along the consumer response stages. These stages include awareness, interest, evaluation, trial and adoption (Rodgers 1995).

There is no standard definition for the types of economic benefit communication tools in use today. Depending on the industry, various terms are used to describe these tools. Based on the author's experience and an evaluation of case examples, definitions were developed. For the purposes of this paper, three categories of economic benefit communication tools will be defined. These include economic benefit claims, decision analytic models and workflow/business model studies. Each of these will be discussed in detail.

Economic benefit claims

First, there are economic benefit claims. Economic benefit claims are statements, messages and marketing collateral based on some evidence or data regarding the economic benefit of using the supplier's solution. These benefit communications can be delivered through numerous communication channels including websites, personal selling and advertising. These tools include customer self-reported data, observational studies and prospective studies.

A benefit claim is used to present facts and data, and is a non-interactive form of communication. Essentially, it is a one-way communication from the seller to the buyer and is usually intended to establish evidence and credibility regarding the economic impact of the supplier's solution. In choosing this type of communication tool, the seller will need to consider factors such as industry norms, the amount and type of evidence required to positively influence buyers, and the investment required to generate the claims.

As an example, consider eXmark, a manufacturer of lawnmowers. eXmark sells lawnmowers primarily to commercial landscapers. On its website, eXmark states 'our customers report a 20% improvement in productivity' (http://www.eXmark.com). The company also provides information about the economics and costs of running a commercial landscape business. This helps to put the 20 per cent productivity improvement into perspective for the landscape contractor. The economic claims are essentially based on customer self-reported data.

In some industries, such as medical device and pharmaceuticals, large-scale prospective economic studies are used to develop economic benefit communications. Consider the case of Cordis, the company that launched the first drug-eluting stent in the world. Drug-eluting stents are tiny metal scaffolds that are inserted into the patient's coronary artery to prop open a blocked artery. The metal scaffolds are coated with a drug that improves the effectiveness of the device. Cordis invested in economic studies across a large number of patients to collect and compare costs of treatment across hundreds of hospitals (Ryan and Cohen 2006). These types of studies measure the costs and benefits of using the new medical device in a controlled clinical trial and study results are usually published in peer review journals.

The final category of economic benefit claims is observational studies. These represent studies based on the supplier observing the impact of its solution on one or more customers in order to understand the costs and benefits. These studies are often referred to as value-in-use studies. Consider the case of Camfil Farr, a manufacturer of air filtration supplies. This company has completed numerous value-in-use case studies comparing the economic benefits of using its air filters to competitive alternatives. In one comparison in a single hospital study, the company reports a 400 per cent improvement in filter life and saving the customer $1,000 per air filter change-out per air handling unit (http://www.green-air-filters.com).

Decision analytical models

The next category of economic benefit communication tools is decision analytic models. The definition for these tools has been adapted from one that is used in the healthcare market. For the purposes of this paper, a decision analytic model will be defined as a logical mathematical framework that combines inputs, assumptions and data to help inform buyer decision makers (Weinstein *et al.* 2003). The value of the model lies not only in the results it produces, but also in revealing the causal logic between inputs and outputs (Weinstein *et al.* 2003). From a seller's perspective, the intent is to not only educate and inform, but also to persuade the buyer. Unlike economic benefit claims, these tools allow for an interactive exchange. Usually the tools allow the buyer to input operational variables and assumptions in order to understand the range of potential economic benefits.

In practice, across a variety of industries, these decision analytic models are often called varying names. There are no standard definitions or clear standards as to how to construct these models. The models range from simple web-based analytical frameworks to spreadsheets to other software. Table 17.2 below presents an attempt to define the variety of decision analytic models used.

Workflow/business model studies

The final category of economic benefit communication tools is workflow and business model studies. These are before and after studies that are performed by the seller in collaboration with the buyer. These typically occur when the seller is marketing a complete solution or a significant change in how the buyer will operate a major business process. It could also involve a major change to the business model of the buyer firm. In this case, it is difficult for the buyer to independently evaluate and understand the economic benefits of the seller's solution. Therefore, the seller needs to work collaboratively with the buyer to prepare a clear before and after picture of the economic benefits of making a change.

One example is studies that are completed in order to sell hospital laboratory automation solutions. Many hospitals are moving to automating their laboratories

TABLE 17.2 Summary of decision analytic models and examples

Tool	Definition
Interactive web-based economic benefit calculator	Website tool that allows potential customers to enter data and calculate economic benefits.
ROI tool	A spreadsheet or other software-based tool that is used to calculate a return on investment (ROI). ROI is typically used when there is some kind of upfront capital investment required by the buyer. These tools often rely on user input and assumptions as well as pre-defined algorithms to calculate economic benefits.
Value calculator	A spreadsheet or other software-based tool that is used to communicate economic benefits. These can include comparative analysis against next best alternative. These tools can range from simple to very complex.

for routine blood testing. In the past, hospitals operated numerous different types of instruments that perform blood tests with separate processes. Many of these instruments required hospital personnel to load and remove patient samples. With the advent of laboratory automation, robotics and automation technology is used to eliminate many manual processes such as loading, storing and moving patient samples. Automation results in lower labour costs, but also improved quality and timelier test results. This often requires a complete redesign of the hospital laboratory. Manufacturers such as Ortho Clinical Diagnostics sell automation equipment along with the service to redesign laboratory processes through lean six sigma (http://www.orthoclinical.com).

Another example is Xerox. Rather than sell just copiers or multifunction devices, Xerox is also selling managed document services. Presumably this is being done to avoid commoditization or to capitalize on a strategic advantage. In 2009, Xerox was awarded a $100 million, five-year contract to manage Procter & Gamble's worldwide print operations including print shops, offices and home-based work settings. The goal is to reduce P&G's document management costs by 20–25 per cent (Collett 2010).

As firms look to take costs out and become more focused, more and more they turn to suppliers who can help change the business model or completely reengineer major processes to improve costs, time and quality. This means that sellers will need to have the resources and skills to help these potential buyers understand the before and after picture as well as the risks associated with change. Many firms have already begun to outsource, reengineer or change major processes including business processes such as customer service, human resource processes, payroll and accounts payable.

Figure 17.3 provides a summary of the various economic benefit communication tools available to the seller. These tools are stratified by the complexity of the tool and the type of communication. The communication can be one way from seller to buyer, such as through a brochure. Alternatively, the communication can be two ways. An example would be a sales representative presenting a value calculator to a customer. The next section will discuss how to select the right tools for a given buyer situation.

Economic value communication strategy

In order to help facilitate selecting the right communication tool and tactics, a conceptual framework was developed. The framework proposes two factors that should influence the choice of economic benefit communication strategy and communication mix. The first factor is the complexity of the offering. The other factor is the buyer's perceived outcome risk.

From a definitional perspective, an offering was considered to be highly complex if it was a customized, integrative combination of goods, services and/or software to meet the customer's needs (Galbraith 2002). Often, complete solutions from sellers are viewed as highly complex solutions. The Xerox managed document services solution is an example. Complexity of an offering can also be driven by factors

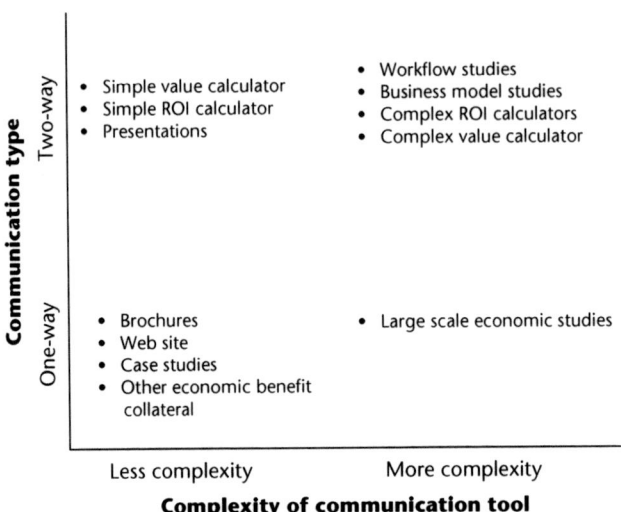

FIGURE 17.3 Summary of economic benefit communication tools

such as technical complexity, ease of installation and existence of after sales service (McCabe 1987).

Using complexity of the offering as a factor in determining the type of communication channel, tools and tactics is relatively straightforward. The more complex an offering is, the more difficult it is for the buyer to assess and understand value. Complexity of the product has also been associated with how buyer firms make the buying decision (McCabe 1987). In turn, this means that the seller needs to deploy different tactics to help educate the buyer in understanding the economic value. This concept is also consistent with findings from diffusion of innovations research. As the complexity of an innovation increases, it becomes harder to understand and the rate of adoption decreases (Rodgers 1995).

The notion of complexity as a driver is also aligned with the way economic buyers segment supply items (Kraljic 1983). Additionally, complexity is cited as a barrier in procurement organizations' ability to adopt total cost of ownership for purchasing decisions (Ellram and Siferd 1998). Consider the example of Xerox discussed earlier. The economic value messages and the communication tactics change significantly as Xerox moves from selling a product (copier) to a highly complex solution (outsourcing global print services).

The other factor that influences the communication strategy is the outcome risk perceived by the buyer. For the purposes of this framework, outcome risk is composed of four variables. The variables are potential business impact, trialability of the solution, observability of the benefits and compatibility with the buyer's business. The combination of these variables impacts the buyer's perceived outcome risk. This, in turn, should drive the seller's choice of the economic benefit communication strategy and communication mix.

Potential business impact is a fairly straightforward concept and an example may help illustrate. A manufacturer of analytical testing equipment would likely face more business risk in the decision of selecting a key raw material supplier than it would in selecting an office supplies vendor. A problem with the raw material vendor would have a much greater impact than a problem with office supplies. This concept also aligns with the way procurement views the supplier network from a suppler segmentation and purchasing strategy perspective (Bueler 2006; Kraljic 1983).

The other variables impacting perceived outcome risk are adapted from diffusion of innovation research. Rodgers (1995) determined that there are attributes of an innovation that drive the rate of adoption. In addition to complexity that was mentioned previously, additional attributes include trialability, observability and compatibility. In the context of perceived outcome risk for economic value communication, Rodgers' original definitions were adapted as follows:

- **Trialability** is the degree to which the buyers can trial the offering on a limited basis and measure economic benefits. The buyer will perceive more risk in offerings that cannot be trialed.
- **Observability** is the degree to which the outcomes are observable. The more transparent or observable the outcome, the less perceived risk by the buyer.
- **Compatibility** is the degree to which the seller's offering is seen as consistent with the buyer's existing systems, processes, organization, beliefs and behaviours. As the offering become less compatible, the buyer's perceived risk increases.

Combining the ideas of complexity of solution and the buyer's perceived outcome risk as two key factors that influence economic benefit communication leads to Figure 17.4, which provides a segmentation and categorization of communication tactics and tools based on the author's experience as well as a review of case examples. As outcome risk increases, there is an increase in the investment in economic communication required. Likewise, as the complexity of the offering increases, there is a need for a change in tactics to be sure that communication is effective. Regardless of the quadrant, there is a need for the supplier to 'teach' the customer new insights about the economics of the customer's business and show how the supplier's solution creates improved economic benefits relative to other alternatives.

The notion of teaching customers is consistent with recent research. Recent research on sales teams shows that the most successful sales representatives are those who challenge the customer and teach the customer something new about their business. The point of Figure 17.4 is that there is a variety of economic benefit communication tools available to the seller. In order to be successful, sellers will need to strategically assess the type of buying situation and choose the tool or combination of tools to best influence buyers. Each buying situation will be discussed in detail with an example.

Relative complexity of offering

		Lower complexity offerings	Higher complexity offerings
Degree of outcome risk	Higher risk	**Quadrant 1: Economic value communication tactics** • Value calculators • ROI calculators • Large scale economic studies • Case studies • Risk sharing or guarantees	**Quadrant 2: Economic value communication tactics** • Workflow studies • Business model studies • ROI calculators • Case studies • Risk sharing or guarantees
	Lower risk	**Quadrant 3: Economic value communication tactics** • Simple value calculators • Value selling collateral • Case studies	**Quadrant 4: Economic value communication tactics** • Case studies • Value calculators • Supplier scorecards

FIGURE 17.4 Economic value communication strategy framework

Quadrant 1: low complexity/high outcome risk

This is a quadrant where many new high cost technologies fall. Economic buyers are particularly concerned about investing in expensive new technologies and not receiving the benefit in return. Successful economic value communication tactics include large-scale economic studies, case or pilot examples, sophisticated value calculators and sometimes guarantees. Take the example of Genomics Health (GHDX). GHDX is a California-based, innovative diagnostics company. Oncotype DX Breast Cancer Assay is a multigene expression test, developed and marketed by GHDX, that physicians currently use to predict the likelihood of chemotherapy benefit and recurrence risk for patients with early-stage, oestrogen receptor positive breast cancer. Prior to this test being available, doctors relied on treatment guidelines that took into account inputs like the size and type of cancer tumour, to decide who should receive chemotherapy (Carlson *et al.* 2009).

In the traditional diagnostics testing industry, where a $50 test is considered expensive, GHDX set the price of its new diagnostic test at approximately $3,500. The value proposition to payers (government and private insurers) was simple. Based on existing treatment guidelines, some percentage of patients were receiving expensive chemotherapy (approximately $15,000) that the GHDX test suggested was not necessary. In order to persuade payers that the test was good value for money, GHDX developed economic studies and value models to prove that if physicians used insights from the new test, the test would be a fair value at $3,500.

However, for some payers, the evidence was not enough. A common challenge in the diagnostics industry is to prove not only that a test provides new clinical insights, but also that physicians would use insights from the test to change clinical practice. From a payer perspective, the payer is worse off if it pays for an expensive diagnostic test and the women and doctors do not follow the test results. So GHDX went a step further. They entered into risk sharing arrangements where they tracked, along with a payer, whether the test was having the intended impact on clinical practice. If the number of patients receiving chemotherapy exceeded an agreed upon threshold, even if the test suggested that the patients would not benefit, the insurer received a pre-negotiated lower price (Carlson *et al.* 2009). In this example, the supplier used multiple tools/tactics to create an integrated economic communication strategy including large-scale economic studies, value calculators and guarantees.

Quadrant 2: high complexity/high outcome risk

In this quadrant, there is not only high outcome risk for the buyer, but the offering is very complex. This makes economic value communication a challenge. Consider the example of suppliers who sell hospital laboratory automation equipment and services. Since each automation solution is customized for a given customer based on the customer's unique operating characteristics and needs, vendors develop different approaches to communicate economic value. Often the automation solution includes products, services and software. In this case, there is typically a detailed workflow study that is performed to develop a picture of the current state of the customer's operations.

Much like the Xerox example discussed previously, laboratory automation vendors try to identify operating improvements, which could include revenue growth, efficiencies and cost reduction opportunities. By teaching the customer about their current operating issues, the workflow studies open up the opportunity for the suppliers to highlight how their solutions could help drive improved economic value. In these complex selling situations, teaching the customer and highlighting economic opportunities is critical and requires a customized consulting-like approach.

Quadrant 3: low complexity/low outcome risk

In this quadrant, the solution should be relatively easy to understand and the outcome risk is low. An example is a manufacturer of air filters that has a superior filter, which requires less frequent changing. The filter is also more efficient because it causes fan motors to work less and has a lower loss of air pressure. Thus, it requires less electricity to operate. The air filter supplier communicates economic benefits around reduced labour for changing air filters and reduced energy costs. In order for the customer to achieve the outcomes promised by the air filter vendor, it simply needs to switch to the new filter.

In this example, the supplier uses simple economic value collateral to communicate the economic benefits. Since the filters fit the existing system (compatibility), can be used on a limited basis (triabability) and results measured (observability), economic value communication should be relatively simple. In this quadrant, typical communication tactics/tools include economic claims in the form of value-in-use studies and simple value calculators.

Quadrant 4: high complexity/low outcome risk

In this quadrant, the buying situation includes an offering that is relatively complex, but has lower perceived outcome risk. This could be due to the nature of the solution being purchased. An example of a relatively complex offering that has low outcome risk would be call centre outsourcing. Call centre outsourcing is not a new phenomenon. Business process outsource firms have been doing this for sometime. Additionally, outsourcing could potentially be done on a pilot or limited basis to 'trial' the outsourcing solution. Economic benefit communication tools for this quadrant would include case studies, ROI calculators and value calculators.

The conceptual framework presented in Figure 17.4 is meant to guide practitioners in thinking about an economic benefit communication strategy. Ideally, the economic benefit communication strategy should be an integrated strategy, which includes multiple communication channels, multiple tools and key messages to communicate. The communication objectives, investment required and the business case should be a starting point for the communication strategy. With this as a starting point, the seller will need to strategically assess the buying situation and choose the right mix of benefit communication tools and tactics to successfully influence economic buyers.

Conclusions

In business-to-business markets, value is perceived. It represents a combination of the economic, technical and psychological benefits received in exchange for the price paid, relative to alternative solutions. This means that sellers have the opportunity to shape or 'bend' buyers' value perceptions. Many buyers, even sophisticated ones, lack the tools and insights necessary to assess the economic benefits of suppliers' solutions. So, what do they know?

Being rational buyers, business-to-business economic buyers at least know and can evaluate one dimension of the offering. This, of course, is the price of the offering compared to other alternatives. In the absence of clear and convincing economic benefit communication, the seller risks a buyer who is focused primarily on price. This can lead to price competition and erosion.

One way to combat this price competition and erosion is to develop an integrated economic value communication strategy. This is not about simply developing a value calculator and handing it to the sales force. It is about developing a comprehensive communication strategy.

The complexity of the offering and the perceived outcome risk of the buyer are two key factors that should influence how sellers think about an integrated communication strategy. The greater the complexity of the offering, the higher is the need to communicate economic benefits. Similarly, the higher the perceived outcome risk, the more the seller will have to do to convince the buyer of the economic benefit of the solution.

Implications for the pricing field

- Much has been written about how to assess economic value and set prices based on economic value in business-to-business markets.
- However, a firm's investments in assessing value and setting value based prices will ultimately prove fruitless if economic benefit communication does not succeed.
- A company's economic benefit communication strategy is proposed to be dependent on two factors: (1) the complexity of the offering; and (2) the buyer's perceived outcome risk.
- Different value communication tools and tactics should be used depending on the complexity of the offering and the perceived outcome risk. These communication tools and tactics should come together in an integrated economic benefit communication strategy.

References

Aberdeen Group (2007) *The CFO's view of procurement: Same page, different language*. Report by Aberdeen Group, http://www.aberdeen.com.

All, A. (2007) Procurement must look beyond 'stuff' to strategy. *IT Business Edge*, November 16. Accessed January 16, 2010 from http://www.itbusinessedge.com/cm/community/features/articles/blog/procurement-must-look-beyond-stuff-to-strategy/?cs =17257.

Anderson, J., Jain, D. and Chintagunta, P. (1993) Customer value assessment in business markets: A state-of-practices study. *Journal of Business-to-Business Marketing*, 1 (1), pp. 3–29.

Anderson, J., Thomson, J. and Wynstra, F. (2000) Combining value and price to make purchase decisions in business markets. *International Journal of Research in Marketing*, 17 (4), pp. 307–29.

Bueler, D. (2006) *Supplier segmentation – The tool for differentiation and results*. 91st Annual International Supply Management Conference, May.

Carlson, J., Garrison, L. and Sullivan, S. (2009) Paying for outcomes: Innovative coverage and reimbursement schemes for pharmaceuticals. *Journal of Managed Care Pharmacy*, October, 2009.

Collett, S. (2010). Big businesses have a lot to gain from managed print services. *Computerworld*, 07:33.

Day, E. and Crask, M. R. (2000) Value assessment: The antecedent of customer satisfaction. *Journal of Consumer Satisfaction, Dissatisfaction & Complaining Behavior*, 13, pp. 52–60.

Ellram, L. M. and Siferd, S. P. (1998) Total cost of ownership: a key concept in strategic cost management decisions. *Journal of Business Logistics*, 19 (1), pp. 55–84.

Ferrin, B. and Plank, R. (2002) Total cost of ownership models: An exploratory study. *Journal of Supply Chain Management*, 38 (3), pp. 18–29.

Galbraith, J. (2002) Organizing to deliver solutions. *Organizational Dynamics*, 31, pp. 194–207.

Kotler, P. (2003) *A Framework for marketing management*, 2nd edition. Upper Saddle River, NJ: Prentice Hall.

Kraljic, P. (1983) Purchasing must become supply management. *Harvard Business Review*, 61 (5), pp. 109–17.

McCabe, D. (1987) Buying group structure: Constriction at the top. *The Journal of Marketing*, 51 (4), pp. 89–98

Martindale, N. (2009) Coping with crisis. *CPO Agenda*, Summer 2009. Accessed January 3, 2010 from http://www.cpoagenda.com/previous-articles/summer-2009/features/coping-with-crisis.

Miller, R. and Heiman, S. (1986) *Strategic selling*. New York, NY: Warner Books Inc.

Nagle, T. T. and Hogan, J. E. (2006) *The strategy and tactics of pricing: A guide to growing more profitably*, 4th edition. Upper Saddle River, NJ: Prentice Hall.

Perdue B. and Summers J. (1991) Purchasing agents' use of negotiation strategies. *Journal of Marketing Research*, 28 (2), pp. 175–89.

Rodgers, E. (1995) *Diffusion of innovation*, 4th edition. New York, NY: The Free Press.

Ryan, J. and Cohen, D. J. (2006) Are drug-eluting stents cost-effective? It depends on whom you ask. *Circulation*, 114, pp. 1736–44.

Webster, F. E. and Wind, Y. (1972) A general model for understanding organizational buying behaviour. *Journal of Marketing*, 36 (April), pp. 12–19.

Weinstein, M., O'Brien, B., Hornberg, J., Jackson, J., Johannesson, M., McCabe, C. and Luce, B. (2003) Principles of good practice for decision analytic modeling in health-care evaluation: Report of the ISPOR task force on good research practices – Modeling studies. *Value in Health*, Vol. 6.

18
VALUE

Distilling the essence

Harry Macdivitt

Introduction

Most businesses today are confronted with rapid technological change, intensive competition from existing competitors and new entrants, and ever decreasing lifecycles. These conditions have resulted, in many industries, in premature commoditization. In order to preserve their market share, companies often reduce their prices either voluntarily or as a result of insistence by customers exercising their buyer power. The result is declining revenue, margin erosion and business failure. Nevertheless, some companies manage to thrive. These companies identify and use customer value as a strategic tool.

What often present as pricing problems in reality are failures to come to grips with the underlying value issues. A deep understanding of customer value helps us to make much better business decisions. In one sense, every price accepted by a customer is a value-based price. If there were no value there would be no sale! But we can achieve much better prices by delivering much better value; or by making customers aware of the real value we deliver to them. This is true, whether we are pricing on cost or competition or deploying value-based pricing.

Value is tricky to define and conceptualize (Liozu *et al.* 2012) and, for this reason, can create difficulties both inside organizations and in communications with customers. Failure to identify the value created, and to present this compellingly to customers, reinforces commodity perceptions and fuels demands for further and deeper discounts (Hinterhuber 2008). It is a vicious circle. Effective practical solutions are elusive.

Businesses must learn how to define the value they offer in terms meaningful to customers, and to craft distinctive propositions which present this value compellingly and convincingly. This requires new and different thinking in which the focus of attention is moved away from product technology and specification to how products and services impact on customers at economic and emotional levels.

Our experience shows that when businesses make this transition, margins increase and market shares are protected.

In this chapter we present an innovative approach to defining and quantifying value. The model we describe, the value triad (Macdivitt and Wilkinson 2011), is a conceptually simple but powerful tool to help business managers focus on the value they offer. We describe two case studies in which the model has been applied with significant results.

The value triad in practice

Typical customer challenges

> All products in this market are exactly the same – including yours.
> automotive components manager in discussion with product manager

> This is a commodity market now.
> raised with sales executive by procurement manager buying speciality epoxy-based chemicals

> You'll have to drop your prices if you want to keep our business.
> asserted by purchasing executive in a UK hospital to a medical devices sales manager

> There is no way you'll get a penny more per litre than your competitors.
> opening gambit by chief buyer in an engineering company to industrial lubricants salesman

Every one of these assertions was made within the last few months of 2011 in the context of a sales interview. Every assertion was made directly to salespeople who promptly passed the problem 'upstairs' to product managers or other business managers. In every case the supplier's market share exceeded 50 per cent. And in every case managers were almost completely at a loss to know how to deal with the situation.

Academic studies have shown the impact of competitive intensity of pricing performance for new products (Ingenbleek *et al.* 2010). Continuing economic uncertainty has engendered a perception that the only solution to a pricing problem is to yield to customers' increasingly unrealistic demands, drop price and hope for the best. Because managers and salespeople do not know how to respond and lack critically needed confidence in pricing (Liozu *et al.* 2011), the only solutions are either to walk away or to discount – usually deeply. Deep discounts make things worse, not better, and sets up the discounter for more of the same. Walking away creates an opportunity loss.

There are alternatives. The above companies were not, and are still not, commodity suppliers. Each is still a leader in its segment with a market share between three and five times what one would expect in a genuinely commoditized situation. But their salespeople had been hoodwinked by their customers into believing that their prices were too high, that their products were commodities and not worth the prices being charged, and that they would lose out if they didn't drop their prices right now! Because these companies learned how to identify and use value, their customers are still buying, often at higher prices than before (Hill *et al.* 1998).

These companies use the value triad as part of their pricing methodology.

Most businesses today are seeking to protect the revenue, profits or share that they already have achieved. Developing a value argument for them is a strategy to reverse margin erosion. To achieve this, they must persuade their customers of their differential value (Hinterhuber 2004; Nagle and Holden 2002). These companies employ value as a means of fighting back against the torrent of demands for discounting.

The value triad

The value triad is an innovative approach to value identification and measurement (see Figure 18.1). It can help turn around the kinds of situations described above and provides an effective counter-argument to assertions that a particular vendor's products are commodities.

It can mean perception, an exchange or an economic enhancement. A simplistic definition cannot capture this completely. The value triad is a practical tool which helps managers capture as much as they can of the richness and variety of meaning encountered in value. By building a real focus on customer value into product development processes and service delivery, companies can have a solid basis for creating differentiation – doing something different in a manner that really matters to the customer. By clearly focusing on customers' needs and pain points, novel ways of serving can be uncovered (MacMillan and McGrath 1997).

By using the value triad it is possible to identify the factors critical to the customer's purchase decision, and how these can be met effectively. Value triad thinking helps users build powerful value propositions and construct value-based

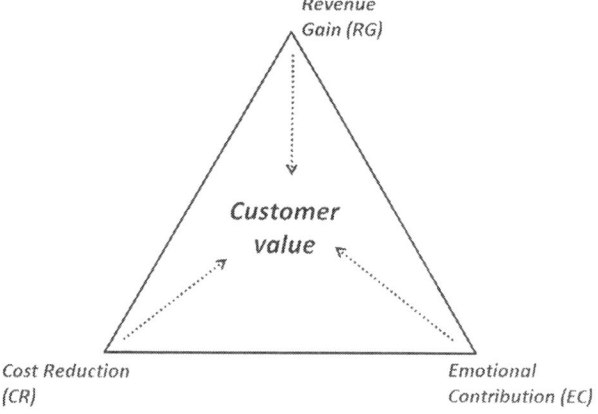

FIGURE 18.1 The value triad

prices founded firmly on how products can impact customers' businesses economically and customers' decision-makers emotionally. Value triad analysis lies at the centre of sales, marketing, product management and pricing. It is a unifying concept and can bring all of these important functions together (Macdivitt and Wilkinson 2011).

The three elements of the value triad are revenue gain, cost reduction and emotional contribution. Revenue gain and cost reduction focus on the functional, tangible, objective and inherently measurable elements of value. Emotional contribution, as its name implies, focuses on how less tangible, more subjective and somewhat less readily measurable factors contribute to the purchase decision.

Revenue gain (RG) refers to the increases in customer revenue resulting from the application of products and services. Cost reduction (CR) relates to how products and services reduce customers' costs. The key issue is that output value to the customer is not compromised. Finally, emotional contribution (EC) is in general linked closely to the 'feel good factor' – e.g. reduction of 'hassle', peace of mind, increased confidence, greater safety, aesthetic appeal, trust, self-esteem, reduction or elimination of psychological risk, etc.

Executives' opinions around tangible factors are generally closely aligned. The same executives, however, may have widely differing opinions about what affects them, personally, from an emotional perspective. Consequently, emotional impact is not absolute in the same way as are CR or RG. Different metrics apply to different people. Thus, EC intangibles can be difficult, although not impossible, to quantify (Hubbard 2010) supporting previous studies discussing the difficulty in assessing value (Anderson *et al.* 1993; Hinterhuber 2008). Notwithstanding this, emotional considerations have a profound but often covert impact on the overall attractiveness, or even acceptability, of a proposal. An important aspect of EC is psychological risk. Even when all the value elements are lined up in a row, risk factors may scupper the deal.

Customer perceived risk is manifested in many ways in practice. These include fear of criticism from superiors and colleagues, worry about causing an opportunity loss, uncertainty and lack of confidence in the supplier's ability to deliver, the supplier's inability to grasp the sensitivity of the customer's situation, and frank distrust of the seller or the salesperson.

In every situation, the analyst must scrutinize the risk factors – from the customer's perspective. This is one of the important functions of the pre-sales research and of the discovery process.

Value drivers and the 'So what?' question

Value drivers are those factors which ultimately lead a buyer to identify a preference and make a purchase decision. In a given context there may be several such drivers each with different 'weightings' in the choice process.

Table 18.1 shows (limited) lists of tangible and intangible value drivers. These, or a subset of these, ultimately are what most customers are looking to achieve

TABLE 18.1 Tangible and intangible drivers

Tangible drivers	Intangible drivers
Increased revenues	Improved aesthetics
Faster time to market	Reduction of risk
Decreased costs	Greater peace of mind/less worry
Improved operational efficiency	Improved comfort
Increased market share	Reduced 'hassle'
Decreased employee turnover	Reliability
Improved customer retention levels	Friendliness/absence of conflict

as the result of purchasing products or services. They are not hugely interested in technical specifications or even technology. The task of sales and marketing is to stimulate their interest. The best way to make this happen is to 'map' the clever parts of the product offer to the important parts of their customers' needs. This task goes well beyond the sales team and should engage the attention of marketing, product management, development, and design people at the very least. In short, value should run through the whole value chain, like a golden thread.

Illustrative example

A company sells lighting systems and assemblies to OEM (original equipment manufacturer) automobile manufacturers. The products are very clever. They can help drivers see round corners. They employ the very latest in halogen technology and are equipped with sensors that detect ambient light levels. They switch on automatically to the correct light intensity for the conditions and switch off again when not required. They are made with robust materials and employ designs that mean that the average time before failure is longer than other competitors, by a matter of months.

The first thing to consider is who might be even slightly interested in this list of product attributes? Clearly the end-customer/driver is one. These innovations might be quite interesting to him. Second, the OEM product designer who is looking to incorporate some kind of leading edge specifications in the product he is designing; he and other executives in the OEM may also be interested. A third group might be the dealer who sells and services the new vehicle after sales.

Let's eavesdrop on the conversation with one of these interested customers – the OEM warranty manager – the executive in charge of managing warranty claims through the dealer network.

Salesman: Our new lighting assembly is built with cutting-edge halogen lamp technology and equipped with sensors which can automatically adjust to ambient light conditions.
Manager: So what?

278 Harry Macdivitt

Salesman:	It's safer for the driver because she will have the right level of illumination at all times.
Manager:	What does that matter to me?
Salesman:	Well, it's made with state-of-the-art technology.
Manager:	So it is a new concept which can go wrong at any time?
Salesman:	Yes, it is new and innovative, but it's been fully tested.
Manager:	So you are guaranteeing it won't go wrong and cause my people all sorts of problems sorting it all out?
Salesman:	Well, no but it's really cool for the customer.
Manager:	What do I care?

This dialogue is going nowhere fast and it's pretty obvious what is going wrong. The warranty manager frankly does not care anything about the 'coolness' of the driver's experience. Why should he? He can't afford to own this car personally, so this assertion is completely irrelevant. He cares more about the leading-edge technology, but not in quite the way the salesman understands. The manager sees new technology as a source of real hassle, based on his years of experience repairing clever components that have failed after a few days' use. So this is not a really compelling value argument for him.

What salespeople frequently fail to recognize is that different people in the same organization have different needs, wants and expectations, partly driven by their job responsibilities and partly by emotional factors. We use the so what analysis and the value triad framework to examine things from the warranty manager's perspective (Table 18.2).

It is clear that of all the value drivers listed in Table 18.1, only five have any traction with this particular buyer:

- decreased costs (the warranty manager must work to a budget, after all)
- improved operational efficiency (this will be part of the pushback from his customers in the channel, associated with some level of hassle, too, no doubt)
- reduced hassle
- greater peace of mind (knowing that he has eliminated one important and recurring problem with the right purchase)
- reliability.

Some of these are economic in nature (cost reduction, improved operational efficiency) and others are more psychological/emotional in nature (reduced hassle and peace of mind). This set of drivers is quite different from those of the chief designer and different again from the end-customer's perspective.

So, what does the warranty manager really want? Let's try again.

Salesman:	Our new lighting assembly is built with cutting-edge halogen lamp technology and equipped with sensors which can automatically adjust to ambient light conditions. This means a great experience for the driver. It also means failure is almost unheard of within the first two years.

Value – distilling the essence

TABLE 18.2 So what analysis – warranty manager

Attribute	So what?	So what?	Decision
Innovative product design	Can help drivers see round corners	**Neutral for this stakeholder**	Don't care
Very latest in halogen lamp technology	Much greater illumination of road in dark conditions	New technology ⇒ teething problems ⇒ costs to replace ⇒ cost and hassle **Negative for this stakeholder**	Don't like – will cause me hassle and increase repair costs during warranty period
Ambient light sensors	Switch lights on when conditions warrant	Same as above **Negative for this stakeholder**	Same as above
Made with robust materials	More resistant to road use wear and tear	More durable ⇒ lasts longer ⇒ less replacement **RG, CR**	Like it but need evidence/proof
Plug-in design	Easy and quick to fit replacement unit	With competitive units usually hard to do in workshop ⇒ saves time, money, hassle **RG, CR, EC**	Like it but need proof
The average time before failure is months longer than competitors' products	Replacement during warranty period much less likely	Can reduce warranty repair incidents saving time, money, hassle. Also means time saved can be used for other things **RG, CR, EC**	Like it but need proof

Manager: How often does the lighting system fail?
Salesman: The chance of a system failing is less than 0.005 per cent within two years. So you could see 200 cars without a single warranty claim based on lighting system failure.
Manager: So what?
Salesman: Because of the way the system is designed, not only is the failure rate lower than any other supplier, but it is quick and easy to replace. Just pull out and plug a replacement component back in again.
Manager: [Thinking ...] So you are saying it can save my people time in dealing with warranty replacements and paperwork?
Salesman: Absolutely. Here are some independent studies ...

This is much better. Whether this imaginary conversation would play out this way in the real world does not really matter – there are obviously other factors at play. What does matter – and matters profoundly – is that a competent value analysis must be undertaken before making any client contact. Or, for that matter, before creating any value proposition or developing any marketing collateral.

Case studies

BOX 18.1 CASE STUDY 1 – MEDICAL SUPPLIES (LATE 2011)

A medical supplies company markets a range of wound dressings. Conventional wisdom in the health care industry, of which wound care dressings is a part, is to promote products primarily to clinicians on the basis that they are the principal players in an adoption decision. The sales arguments are backed up by a wealth of clinical documentation describing the results of clinical studies. The rather disturbing fact is that, for the most part, clinicians are rather uninterested in wound dressings. While they will listen politely to the salesman 'detailing' the proposition, little ever happens after the visit. Why? The clinician is not the most important person to be speaking to. The salesperson should instead be speaking to nursing staff whose day to day job, among a host of other things, is to use and apply these products. The adoption decision is based on practical patient comfort and ease of use considerations at ward level and on procurement costs at hospital level. Complex clinical arguments, important as these are in validating the product, do not constitute a compelling adoption argument to actual users.

It is interesting to look at the issues that do matter, and at the specific interests of 'stakeholders' in this application. Figure 18.2 relates to UK and Western European hospitals which are publicly funded and do not have a profit motive. In this case performance gain is substituted for revenue gain.

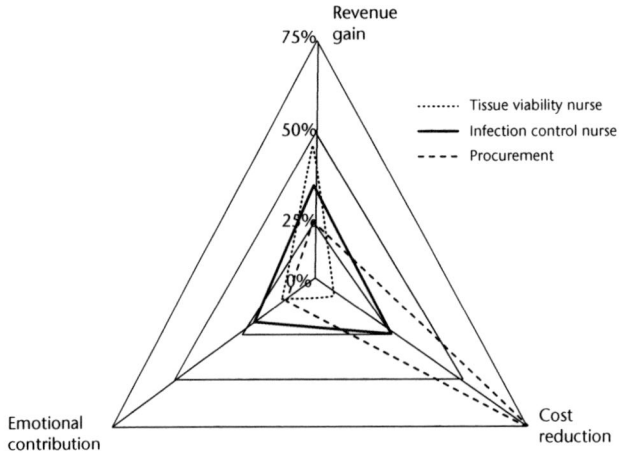

FIGURE 18.2 Importance of value triad factors to different stakeholders
Source: Discussions with product managers.

Continued

Notice the extent of variation in the importance placed by each stakeholder in the adoption decision on different triad elements. Notice also the shapes and orientations of each triangle are also quite different. It very clearly sets out the bases of the value arguments to each group. These arguments will be different in content or emphasis, or both. If there are more than three stakeholders, focus would only be on those with, on aggregate, the greatest influence on the adoption decision. As many of the influence factors as possible should be covered.

The next step is to examine minutely the full extent of the value being offered to each principal stakeholder. A 'copy–paste' from one stakeholder to another simply will not work. This is done using the 'so what' approach. Table 18.3 shows a partial 'so what' analysis for one category of decision-maker – tissue viability nurse. This is a specialist nurse who acts as an advisor to colleagues managing severe and chronic wounds at risk of serious infection. (The remainder of this table is withheld for reasons of commercial sensitivity.)

TABLE 18.3 So what analysis (tissue viability nurse)

Attribute	So what?	So what?
Highly effective in protecting high risk wounds	Improved clinical outcome	Wound looks much better ⇒ reduced patient anxiety **(EC)** Increased peer respect ⇒ enhanced self-esteem **(EC)**
	Reduces healing time	Eliminates additional costs of care from infections ⇒ saves staff and drug costs **(CR)** Reduced bed blocking ⇒ higher patient throughput ⇒ increased performance **(RG, CR)**
Safe	Reduced risk of complications	Reduced risk ⇒ greater 'peace of mind' **(EC)** Improved patient outcomes ⇒ reduced patient stay in hospital **(RG, EC)**

The company undertook an analysis for each principal stakeholder. Starting from the product attribute (left-hand column – 'Attribute'), the first 'So what?' question is asked. This leads to a general outcome statement, recorded in the middle column. The right-hand column contains responses to successive 'So what?' questions and will lead to the identification of one or more value drivers for each attribute. This provides an 'audit trail' of the analyst's thinking that others can challenge or accept as appropriate.

This is an essential step in creating a full statement of the value of a given product or service for each key stakeholder/purchasing decision-maker.

BOX 18.2 CASE STUDY 2 – INDUSTRIAL LUBRICANTS (MID-2011)

An international company supplying lubricants to a variety of engineering and manufacturing businesses initiated a strategic programme of change across its operating divisions. The main thrust of the strategy was to increase and intensify customer intimacy (Treacy and Wiersema 1993) as part of a move away from the aggressively price-competitive approach widespread in the sector. The initiative was about understanding deeply the real needs of their diverse customer base and positioning themselves across key segments as the natural first choice for both lubricants and machine maintenance solutions. The intention was that in the long term the company would move to a value-based pricing platform. In the short to medium term, the value initiative was seen very much as a part of their strategy to halt and reverse margin erosion.

The immediate priority was to move from a highly competitive cost-based approach, with its endemic 'nickel and diming', to one based on delivering real and sustainable customer value. The final 'building block' of this transition was to move the sales organization away from transactional selling towards a selling approach based firmly on identifying, creating and capturing customer value. The hope and the expectation was that this would reduce or eliminate the current practice of discounting (sometimes deep discounting) on demand. This necessitated a complete re-think of how their products were delivering customer value and a move away from simple, commoditized 'products' to integrated packages of product and services which offer more comprehensive 'solutions'. This is an important 'hygiene factor' for full implementation of value-based pricing (Macdivitt and Wilkinson 2011).

The company was delivering terrific value but was apparently unable to benefit from it! Great piles of money were being left on the table with no way of capturing it. The new thinking around value, and internal discussions between managers, led to the realization that there was widespread lack of clarity about what their value proposition really was both inside the company and also as delivered to customers.

The value triad precipitated a 'road to Damascus' moment for middle and senior commercial management because it provided for the very first time clarity in the company regarding what value really meant to the customer. Management fully understood that value was important but lacked a common language to articulate that value to the customer from the customer's perspective. Having been briefed intensively on the value triad, salespeople now have much more fruitful and structured conversations with customers. The focus of customer discussions has moved to how the supplier can impact on key performance areas. Time is no longer being wasted, and relationships eroded, on futile and stultifying arguments about price discounting. In the process, and almost as a by-product, customer intimacy is being enhanced!

The company made full use of the 'so what' analysis template but extended it in a way that enabled salespeople to identify and quantify value impacts interactively with their clients. An extract of a typical worksheet is summarized in Figure 18.3. The Excel model is installed on salespeople's laptops and used as part of the customer dialogue to identify and quantify economic impact of all the value triad elements on the client's organization. Much of the value calculator is pre-filled by the salesperson during their pre-sales activity. The model enables both buyer and seller to engage in an informed dialogue about the various tangible and intangible impacts. By employing the value calculator, the supplier was able to calculate the real economic impact of the solution on his customer's business – often very much greater than the price actually charged. The value triad methodology enabled him to succeed in his principal objective – to be able to halt price and margin erosion by demonstrating the economic superiority of his solutions to customers. This company is now well placed to develop and implement value-based pricing more comprehensively in this company.

This industry is intensely competitive and, in the case summarized in Figure 18.3, the buyer insisted 'there is no way you can supply us cheaper than our current supplier (at that time £1.47 per litre)' The salesman completely agreed and went on to demonstrate how much additional value he could deliver. Through the use of the value triad and the value calculator, the customer realized for the very first time the true economic impact of the service and readily agreed, after validation of the data, to a price of £2.26 per litre!

It is interesting that, as a result of this new thinking, salespeople now perceive customers no longer as adversaries but as supportive clients, and the sales dialogue as a means of jointly solving the client's issues rather than the combative relationship it had been previously. Even more interestingly, the new language of value has become part of the company's culture. Value, in this case, is truly being embedded into the value chain.

The nature of the relationship the sellers now have with their customers has also changed. The quality of the conversation has improved immeasurably and rather than trying to sell things TO the customer, they are now working WITH the customer to develop value-adding solutions. However, it would be untrue to say that this type of conversation can be undertaken with every potential customer. Not every customer wants to talk 'value' and some remain price driven. As a result of this the company is looking at segmenting its customer base not only by industry but, within each segment, on the basis of whether they are a price driven or a value driven customer. This has enabled them to start looking at exactly what their price driven customers are getting for their money – and if it's more than they have paid for, looking for ways of removing and redefining the package as another way of improving their margin.

Continued

Product attribute	Potential impacts	Revenue gain — So what?	$	Cost reduction — So what?	$	Emotional contribution — So what?	$
Effective lubrication	Extends machine life	More machine uptime		Reduction in scrap		Operator job satisfaction from higher bonuses and reduced hassle	5,000
	Better machining accuracy					Management reassurance on health & safety	
	Longer cutting tool life	More machine uptime		Lower spend on tooling capex	2,250		
	Longer roll life	More machine uptime		Lower spend on maintenance and capex	3,500		
	Better component tolerance and finish	Opportunity for premium pricing based on superior quality/appearance.	22,000	Reduction in scrap			
	Reduced energy consumption			Lower spend on energy	1,500		
Effective protection and cleaning	Reduced corrosion of components between process stages			Lower scrap rate			
	Reduced corrosion of plant and equipment	More machine uptime		Lower spend on maintenance and on new		Avoids cost and hassle of further processing	
	Better final component finish	Opportunity for premium pricing based on quality/appearance.					
	Fewer process steps required	Shorter process cycle time					
Durability	Long refill intervals	More machine uptime		Lower spend on fluids and waste disposal			
	Reliable and sustained performance in use			Lower spend on fluid maintenance	750	More confident production planning	
Total amount:			**22,000**		**8,000**		**5,000**

FIGURE 18.3 Extract from value calculator – lubricant company

Conclusions

The turbulent and demanding market conditions of late 2011 and early 2012 pose challenges which conventional approaches cannot handle readily. A new approach is required which allows us to identify every particle of value that we create and leverage it in the markets we work in.

- Executives are preoccupied with retaining the business they have won and with stemming margin erosion.
- Many businesses are confronted by customers who claim their products are commodities, despite gallant efforts to differentiate them.
- Traditional methods to retain share and preserve margin are disappointing and many are seeking a new approach.
- Customer value provides this approach but there is no clear, easy-to-use process for managers to follow.
- The value triad offers a robust and logical process to help managers identify customer value rigorously and to encourage deeper insight into pricing, product innovation, differentiation, marketing and sales strategies.
- The value triad can assist business leaders to embed customer value into their value-adding chains and culture by providing a common conceptual framework and language.
- The value triad can help facilitate more fruitful and structured conversations with customers by enabling all parties to focus on the customers' key issues.

Implications for innovation in pricing

In many businesses the most intractable pricing problems relate to presenting and defending vendor's prices. This is particularly acute in cost-based and competition-based environments in which the usual objection is that the given offer is a commodity and too expensive. Managers are hard-pressed to counter this because they have not assembled compelling evidence to make the customer believe otherwise. Their 'microscope' is turned inward on the components of their offer. This prevents crafting of usable rebuttal arguments without which they are obliged either to capitulate or walk away. Most companies in this situation do not know how to calculate, or to engage the customer's attention on, the critical customer value. The result is that they leave too much money on the table and enter into a dangerous vortex of discounting to retain the business they do possess.

Calculating the price is merely arithmetic, for the most part. The underpinning issue, which is the real cause of the problem, is value and getting this right in a given context. Much of the established literature on value focuses on the tangible aspects; in value triad terms 'revenue gain' and 'cost reduction'. Where there seems to be a relative dearth of thinking is in examining the impact of the psychological/emotional components of value. The emotional contribution factor can often be an enormous influence on the acceptability or otherwise of a proposed price. Because it is rarely articulated by the customer (at least in macho business-to-business (B2B) situations), it is also almost always forgotten or written off as unimportant. Yet in any given case the hidden emotional issues may dwarf the economic aspects. It may quite genuinely be the 'elephant in the dining room'! We would advocate that pricing people take serious stock of the emotional impact of their product or service offer on customers and to factor it in to the pricing equation – and the value proposition.

The value triad approach compels us to examine, minutely and explicitly, this aspect of the transaction. The value triad enables managers and customers alike to distil the problem down to its very essence – identifying the critical value drivers. In the companies in which this model has been applied the approach was completely new and led to changes in the vendor's value chain, the way in which the value proposition was created and presented and to the levels of prices realized. Margin erosion was halted and relationships with customers greatly improved. Through the lens of the value triad, businesses can transform their economics. But managers need to learn to turn the 'microscope' on customer value – and move to high magnification! A focused, assertive and single minded attention to this matter will help businesses justify their prices fully, reject the commoditization objection and halt margin erosion.

References

Anderson, J. C., Jain, D. C. and Chintagunta, P. K. (1993) Customer value assessment in business markets: A state-of-practice study. *Journal of Business-to-Business Marketing*, 1 (1), p. 3.

Hill, S. I., McGrath, J. and Dayal, S. (1998) How to brand sand: Contrary to popular opinion, it is possible to brand commodity goods. *Strategy and Business*, 11, pp. 22–34.

Hinterhuber, A. (2004) Towards value-based pricing – An integrative framework for decision making. *Industrial Marketing Management*, 33 (8), pp. 765–78.

Hinterhuber, A. (2008) Customer value-based pricing strategies: why companies resist. *Journal of Business Strategy*, 29 (4), pp. 41–50.

Hubbard, D. W. (2010) *How to measure anything: finding the value of intangibles in business.* Hoboken, NJ: John Wiley & Sons.

Ingenbleek, P., Frambach, R. T. and Verhallen, T. M. M. (2010) The role of value informed pricing in market oriented product innovation management. *Journal of Product Innovation Management*, 27 (7), pp. 1032–46.

Liozu, S., Boland, R., Hinterhuber, A. and Perelli, S. (2011) *Industrial pricing orientation: The organizational transformation to value-based pricing.* Paper presented at the International Conference on Engaged Management Scholarship, Case Western Reserve University, Cleveland, OH.

Liozu, S. M., Hinterhuber, A., Boland, R. and Perelli, S. (2012) The conceptualization of value-based pricing in industrial firms. *Journal of Revenue & Pricing Management*, 11 (1), pp. 12–34.

Macdivitt, H. and Wilkinson, M. (2011) *Value-based pricing: Drive sales and boost your bottom line by creating, communicating and capturing customer value.* New York, NY: McGraw-Hill.

MacMillan, I. C. and McGrath, R. G. (1997) Discovering new points of differentiation. *Harvard Business Review*, 75 (4), pp. 133–45.

Nagle, T. and Holden, R. (2002) *The strategy and tactics of pricing: A guide to profitable decision making*. Upper Saddle River, NJ: Prentice Hall.

Treacy, M. and Wiersema, F. (1993) Customer intimacy and other value disciplines. *Harvard Business Review*, 71 (January–February), pp. 84–93.

19

INNOVATIONS IN DETERMINING WILLINGNESS-TO-PAY FOR B2B COMPANIES

Neil Biehn

Craig Zawada

Introduction

The term 'willingness-to-pay' (WTP) is frequently used by pricing professionals to discuss the spending limit of customers for products they buy. Christoph Breidert, an author and PhD in business and economics (2005) defined it as the highest price an individual is willing to accept to pay for some good or service.

The concept holds promise for business-to-business (B2B) manufacturers and distributors when trying to estimate the right price for each of their products and markets. If you knew each of your customer's precise WTP for each product, you could simply charge that price. The result would likely be a huge increase in your profit *and* market share.

However, common business techniques to determine willingness-to-pay don't apply very well in the B2B environment. In 2006, researchers Breidert *et al.* (2006) reviewed the current methods for measuring WTP along with others such as Nagle and Holden (2002). These authors categorize methods for determining WTP into four key approaches: experiments, direct surveys, indirect surveys and market data (see Figure 19.1).

Can we use these techniques when estimating the willingness-to-pay of customers in B2B markets?

B2B pricing models

To start answering this question, we will examine the different types of business models commonly found in B2B. As seen in Figure 19.2, B2B pricing models include spot pricing, agreement or contract pricing, list or matrix pricing, subscription pricing and promotional pricing.

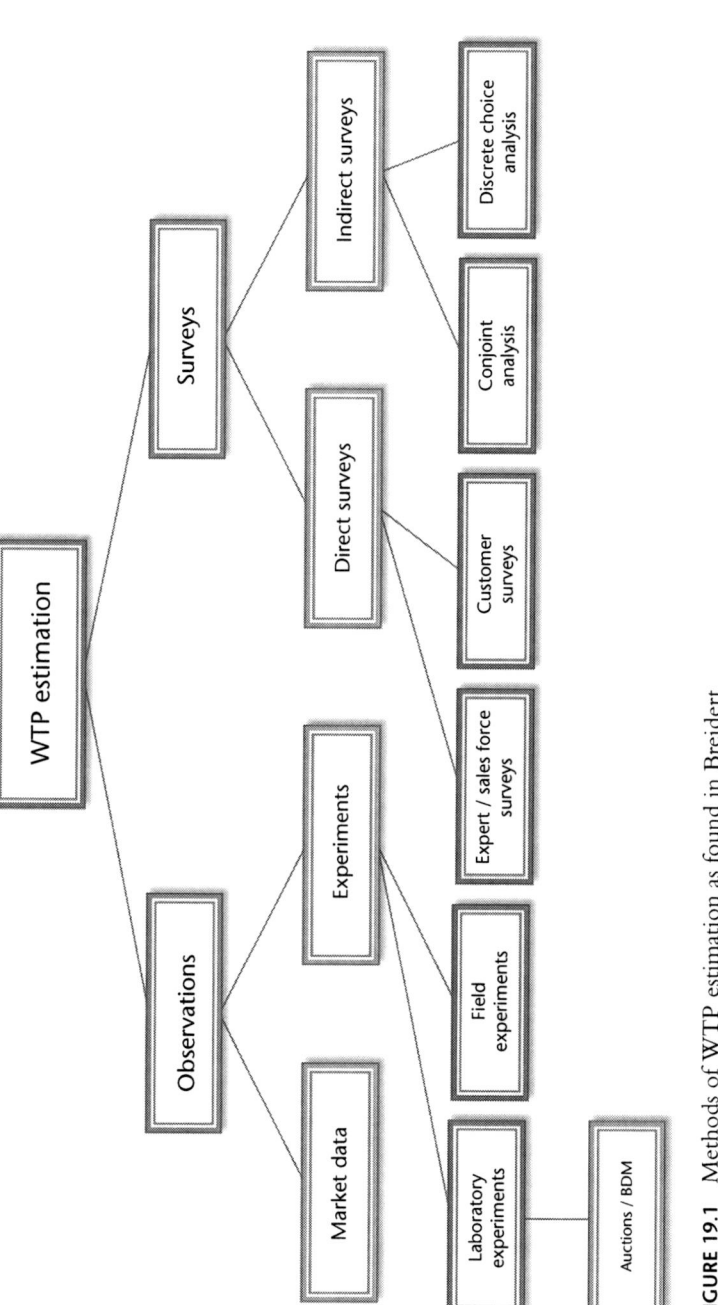

FIGURE 19.1 Methods of WTP estimation as found in Breidert

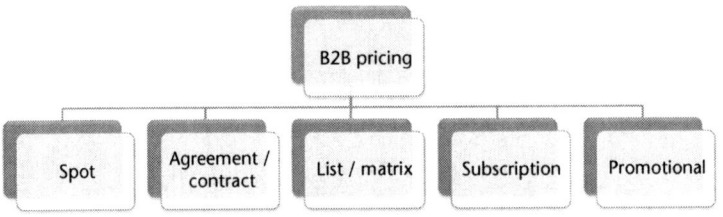

FIGURE 19.2 Common pricing models in B2B

Spot pricing: every transaction is priced individually

What makes spot pricing unique is that prices are subject to change at any time. Businesses that sell highly commoditized products are often spot because supply, demand and costs can change rapidly. Businesses that customize, or make to order, have a spot pricing model as requirements and product configurations are ever-changing. Companies that bid on projects can use a spot pricing model. Like make to order, each project has its own unique characteristics. Finally, companies that have agreement/contract pricing often receive special requests that require a one-time spot quote.

Agreement/contract pricing: pricing is set for a length of time

A large number of B2B customers have an agreement or contract pricing model. Special pricing agreements (SPAs) are set up because customers want special treatment beyond a standard price. Many businesses with agreements/contracts have customers that order frequently and don't want to negotiate every time they order. In other cases, contracts are sent out through a request for proposal (RFP) process to encourage competition. Under this pricing model, pricing is updated on a quarterly, semi-annual or annual basis where follow-up negotiation occurs upon contract expiration.

List/matrix pricing: non-negotiated pricing

Here, companies set non-negotiated pricing by product and/or customer tier. Special customers may get agreement/contract pricing, but the rest are subject to a list price which may include a set discount for different classifications of customers (e.g. based on annual purchases, region or channel). Companies with list prices have a catalogue or website that allows their smaller customers to order products without negotiation. Businesses with matrix prices segment customers into categories like bronze, silver and gold, and may also set list prices by region.

Subscription: per year/month pricing model with no expiration date

Companies that utilize a subscription pricing model are typically those that allow customers access to a service. In this model, a subscription price is set for as long as customers use the service – sometimes called an evergreen contract. These evergreen contracts may include yearly increases or fee changes as costs fluctuate. Subscription differs from agreement/contract pricing in one fundamental way – cost to serve. Those companies that employ a subscription pricing model usually have no way to estimate their customers' cost to serve – either because it is extremely difficult to determine or that costs are sunk.

Promotional: alternative pricing that incents behaviour

Almost every company has some form of promotional pricing or rebate programmes. Manufacturers incentivize resellers to sell their products, increase volume year over year, or increase the mix of more profitable stock keeping units (SKUs). Resellers may, in turn, have their own promotional programmes. Agreements/contracts are often negotiated based on volume commitments or market share requirements, where promotional actions create incentives to order more.

WTP estimation techniques for B2B

Now that we've outlined the different pricing models in B2B, let's examine how the different techniques for estimating WTP fit into those paradigms.

Surveys

Surveys can be a useful tool in B2B, but they are less useful in estimating elasticities for most of the pricing models outlined. For example, a survey completed by a chemicals distributor found that price was low on the list of why their top agreement/contract customers valued them as suppliers. Instead customers valued service, quality, product mix and communication over price. However, this provided little direction on determining the price sensitivity on any of the company's 100,000 SKUs that it carried.

Most business-to-consumer (B2C) companies find techniques such as conjoint analysis very valuable in estimating the willingness-to-pay of their consumers. However, the procurement departments of B2B companies hold their cards much closer to their chest and will often give unreliable answers to even the most well-crafted price-focused surveys. These techniques can be helpful for companies whose sales are concentrated in a few products, or for key new product introductions. And, the good news is that the costs have come down for doing this type of research. However, most B2B companies need a method to use across a disperse product or service line, and one that can be repeatable.

Experiments

All the B2B pricing models, except for list/matrix pricing, employ a sales force, pricing desk or price negotiators. Experimenting with price within a negotiated sales environment is extremely difficult. Sales people's commissions are at risk. Each negotiation is unique. The whole concept of experimentation is just difficult to make happen in practice. In addition, to account for all the potential variables to understand true cause and effect, often requires a very large sample to get reliable insights. This somewhat negates one of the potential benefits of an experiment which is the ability to test alternative price models with less risk than going to the market more broadly.

In the list/matrix and promotions pricing model, B2B companies can leverage the science of experiments to see how past price changes performed. By removing all outside influences to volume, a B2B aftermarket auto parts manufacturer identified over $3 million in recoverable profits simply by reverting price changes that decreased margin dollars. Even with that insight, only 4 per cent of the historical price changes yielded conclusive statistical evidence around their customers' willingness-to-pay.

Market data

Utilizing market data is the most promising and practical way for companies to get a handle on customer WTP. Unfortunately, as evidenced in Figure 19.1, there is very little research on how to use it. Nagle and Holden concede that 'if a researcher has a lot of historical data with enough price variation in it, useful estimates of price sensitivity are possible' (Nagle and Holden 2002). Here's the good news for companies in B2B markets:

> *Your transaction data has a wealth of information that can help isolate and identify your customer's WTP across your product portfolio.*

The key to unlocking WTP can be found in applying the science of pricing to your market data.

Willingness-to-pay: a constantly moving target

WTP in the B2B sales environment is an ever-changing, moving target. Consequently, it isn't simple or easy to quantify. Take this example: if you lose your car key, how do you put a price on its replacement? Your car dealer has a battery-powered key fob that can detect when you are in proximity and automatically unlock your car. Alternatively, you can ask for a mechanical key that opens only the driver side door. What is your willingness-to-pay for the added technology? Some 'traditionalists' would buy the mechanical key under all circumstances. Others would pay a significant price premium for the key fob convenience.

Consider another example: air conditioning. Is your willingness-to-pay different if you are replacing your old air conditioner during the winter months, compared to a breakdown during the dog days of summer? What if you live in Houston, TX or Seattle, WA? Here's the point:

> *WTP changes depending on the type of customer, product and transaction environment of the sale being executed.*

With customer behaviour, timing and environments constantly changing, a customer's WTP for a given product can be difficult to gauge. However, we have found that it is within reach of almost all B2B companies. The first step on the road to achieving WTP is the segmentation and normalization of market data.

> ## BOX 19.1 FULLY UTILIZING DATA KEY TO EVOLUTION FROM 'COST-PLUS' TO VALUE PRICING
>
> Many manufacturers today still use cost-plus pricing techniques as a general way to price products in a B2B environment. Example: price = cost plus 25 per cent of cost. Once prices are set, the effectiveness of that pricing is judged by the product's P&L statement. In contrast, applying scientific analysis to the data that already resides in a company's information systems provides a fact-based, practical alternative that determines each customer or customer category's willingness-to-pay.
>
> Scientific analysis of transaction data allows companies to understand which factors influence different willingness-to-pay and then feed that information into recommendations for future transactions. Our experience has revealed, for example, that sophisticated transaction analysis often shows the most potential for margin improvement exists among customers in the middle range of the profitability distribution. Many companies have taken tactical measures to find the extremely low or negative profit customers. Few have applied the science to identify average profit customers that could do a little better when comparing them to other like customers. This is where scientific segmentation improves the negotiating confidence of the sales force in pushing for increases in prices and margins when it makes sense. Operating at a highly granular level, customer by customer, product by product, pricing science makes a value-based pricing approach possible – estimating the value that customers actually put on products versus what they might currently be paying.
>
> Pricing tools can provide more accurate floor, target and stretch price guidance at the point of negotiation and empower the sales force while enforcing accountability. Such pricing insight is critical to assuring that manufacturers and distributors gain and sustain a competitive advantage through value-based pricing.

Segmentation and normalization: start with your own data

B2B companies typically possess plenty of data around their own products (cost, lifecycle, hierarchy, etc.), their customers (geography, size, industry, etc.) and their transactions, invoices and rebates (date, price, cost, discount, sales person, quantity, unit of measure, etc.). Do customers in different geographies have a different WTP? Does my customer base have a discount expectation based on the quantity ordered? Do customers react differently to a product that costs $4,000 than to a product that costs $20? Does my newest innovation get a value premium higher than its older version?

The science of segmentation answers these questions clearly and decisively by using your existing sales data. The process involves applying scientific algorithms using computer software to mine your data and analyse all combinations of attributes to determine the key variables that impact your customers' WTP. However, segmentation alone does not account for the dynamic nature of WTP discussed earlier.

Normalization is the principle that incorporates the variable of time to WTP that enhances the accuracy of future pricing products. Normalization works by looking at external factors (date, producer price index, inflation, etc.) that vary over time and then adjusts historical transactions appropriately. Economists use this technique all the time. For example, gold is at an all-time high but not when normalized against history. The early 1980s hold the price record when you adjust for inflation (Leonhardt 2010).

The science of segmentation puts different customers, products and transaction environments in separate WTP buckets. Normalization changes historical data inside each bucket to account for WTP changes over time. But you must go another step further by looking inside each segment and determining the unique WTP for each product through distribution analysis.

Using sales transaction analysis to estimate WTP

Once you've segmented and normalized your customer, product and transactional data, the next step is to examine the distribution of prices within each specific segment. How you proceed from here depends on the availability of *loss data*. If you know those price points in a segment where your customers walk away and where they buy, a clear distribution of WTP emerges. Research by Agrawal and Ferguson (2007) and Phillips (2005) explain how to use loss data to model win-elasticity across a specific customer segment.

Unfortunately, most B2B manufacturers and distributors do not have access to their loss information. Even if you could mine the data from RFPs or call centre transactions, it's almost impossible to know why someone *didn't buy your product because of price*. Therefore, a realistic yet robust WTP estimation for most B2B manufacturers and distributors must come from win-only data.

Estimating WTP using win-only data

Let's revisit the definition of WTP: *the highest price an individual is willing to accept to pay for some good or service*. Consider the price distribution for a specific product that sells between $1.00 and $3.00 as shown in Figure 19.3. If one of your customers buys that product for $1.45, then their WTP was greater than or equal to that price. Since we only have win data, that means the data distribution is *skewed* as it relates to the WTP of that customer or segment. Take a closer look at Figure 19.3 – a specific segment's win distribution. Prices cluster around $1.45. Does that mean $1.45 is your best estimate of the WTP of this segment? Answer: No. It means that your

Determining willingness-to-pay   **295**

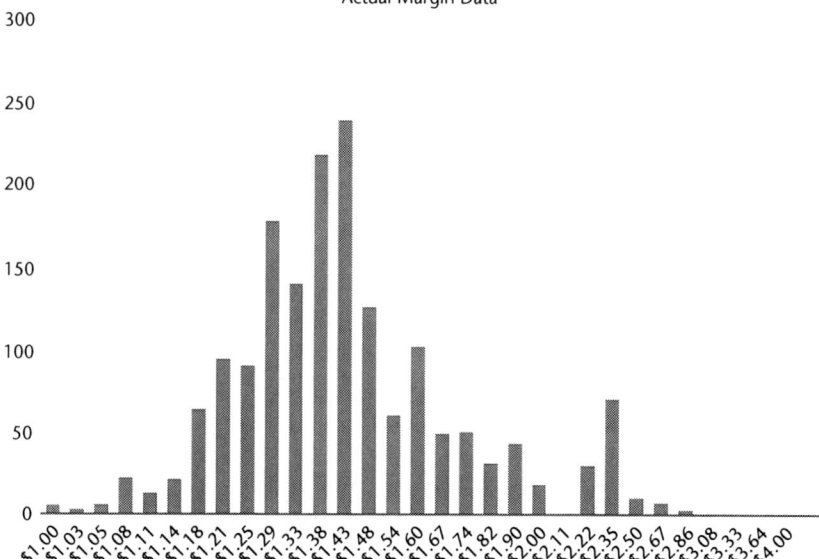

FIGURE 19.3 Histogram of volume versus price

sales force, pricing desk and category managers feel comfortable charging around $1.45 per unit. The true WTP of this segment is greater than $1.45. So what is the true WTP distribution of this segment? Applying proven science to pricing can give you the answer.

> *Pricing science can estimate the true willingness-to-pay even if loss data is unavailable.*

The ability of pricing science to unlock WTP depends on two key factors:

1. Lots of sales-win information – there must be enough data in each individual customer or segment to statistically support WTP estimates.
2. Flexibility in pricing – pricing cannot be uniform across all customers in the sense that contract, agreement, subscription or spot pricing decisions are customized though negotiations (e.g. by a salesperson or through some form of price approval process).

Prescriptive pricing based on WTP produces results

Prescriptive pricing means providing pricing decision makers with clear and concise recommendations on the price to charge. Other types of pricing analytics include (1) descriptive pricing – looking at historical and current trends and pricing errors/leaks, in order to make better pricing decisions and (2) predictive pricing – arming decision makers with estimates of future demand patterns, price response and what-if capabilities. In the case studies below, willingness-to-pay was used to generate prescriptive pricing actions that drove significant value in a short time frame.

BOX 19.2   PAPER COMPANY

Using internal win-only data to estimate WTP, a paper manufacturer generated an additional $18 million in revenue within six months. Some of the key variables in determining WTP included:

- Size of customer.
- Geography and location.
- Product category customers were buying from.
- Contract type and terms of contract – the inclusion of caps, payment terms, etc. greatly affected WTP.
- Product centricity – WTP of customers changed based on total spend of that product compared to the entire portfolio of products purchased. For example, if a customer's total spend is 100 per cent, then if one product takes up 40 per cent of portfolio, will be sensitive to price and WTP will be lower. But if spending only 1 per cent of portfolio, then WTP is higher.

BOX 19.3   ELECTRONICS DISTRIBUTOR

Using extensive data on tens of thousands of products, this company analysed and determined WTP by automating cumbersome manual processes and using statistical methods to segment its customer base into peer groups. Key WTP predictors included market share, customer type, volume and product cost. The company then developed scientifically generated target, floor and expert prescriptive pricing guidance for front line sales. Guidance increased margins of low-performing customers in each peer group, while ensuring that high performers continued to be highly profitable.

The approach helped reduce 'below-floor prices' by more than 10 per cent, while also increasing the number of invoices exceeding sales targets more than 10 per cent, resulting in a gross profit increase of over 230 basis points. Revenues increased by more than 2 per cent in individual segments.

Implications for the field of pricing

B2B manufacturers and distributors constantly customize and adjust their pricing for good reasons. Certain products demand a premium over others. Different regions have varying competitive landscapes. Contracts expire under varying circumstances. Yet most companies are missing out on a big opportunity. They do not possess what we call an 'institutional memory of pricing'. That is, the collective wisdom of pricing in the organization and in the market is not brought to each and every deal and each and every pricing decision in determining the true customer willingness-to-pay. This results in non-fact based rules of thumb and risk averse decision making. Companies are not able to respond as nimbly as they should to customer, cost, competitive or market changes.

Advances in computing power and data storage have made available to companies a virtual treasure of data relevant to pricing – both within their own transaction history, and from outside sources. Recent innovations for using this data and determining willingness-to-pay, as outlined in this chapter, are proven and practical and should be used by every B2B company.

Whether you rely on a centralized price matrix with customized exceptions, or a totally autonomous sales force, understanding the willingness-to-pay of your customers under various conditions gives you a significant competitive advantage.

References

Agrawal, V. and Ferguson, M. (2007) Bid-response models for customised pricing. *Journal of Revenue and Pricing Management*, 6 (3), pp. 212–28.

Breidert, C. (2005) *Estimation of willingness-to-pay: Theory, measurement, and application*. Doctoral Thesis, WU Vienna University of Economics and Business.

Breidert, C., Hahsler, M. and Reutterer, T. (2006) A review of methods for measuring willingness-to-pay. *Innovative Marketing*, 2 (4), pp. 8–32.

Leonhardt, D. (2010, November 10). The enduring myth of gold's record high. *New York Times*, p. B1.

Nagle, T. and Holden, R. (2002) *The strategy and tactics of pricing*. Upper Saddle River, NJ: Prentice Hall.

Phillips, R. (2005) *Pricing and revenue optimization*. Stanford, CA: Stanford Business Books.

20
CROSS-FUNCTIONAL COLLABORATION IN VALUE-BASED PRICING

Steven Forth

Introduction

Pricing can be a solitary and technical discipline. It requires mastery of concepts that are not always well known outside the profession, time needs to be spent gathering and analysing data from disparate and often incompatible sources, and in many companies pricing does not have the attention of the executive. A study by one of this book's editors, Stephan Liozu, has found that CEO's spend little of their time thinking about pricing issues (Liozu 2010) and pricing is sometimes referred to as 'the forgotten P of marketing' (Kolassa 2009). This is odd given the power of pricing as a profit lever (Meehan *et al*. 2011; Mohammed 2010). More importantly for this essay, pricing is a critical consideration when making decisions about the other three Ps: Product, Promotion, Placement. As E. Raymond Corey of Harvard Business School famously wrote in 1962, 'Pricing is the moment of truth - all of marketing comes to focus in the pricing decision' (Corey 1983). In some cases, pricing experts face active opposition and not just benign neglect. Sales has been known to refer to pricing as 'the sales prevention organization'.

The isolation of pricing from other business functions is emerging as an issue for the pricing community and for the businesses that rely on pricing experts to guide their pricing strategies and tactics. It is also a concern for pricing professionals as individuals, who can feel ineffective and alienated from the powers that be in their organizations. At the same time, companies are adopting powerful pricing management systems that are integrated with customer relationship management systems (CRMs). These software platforms are bringing pricing experts closer to other business functions such as sales. There is also interest in marrying pricing with product lifecycle management (PLM) and the enterprise systems that support it. Chief financial officers (CFOs) are getting into the game as well, as they come to understand the impact that pricing has on profitability and its power as a decision making framework (see Figure 20.1).

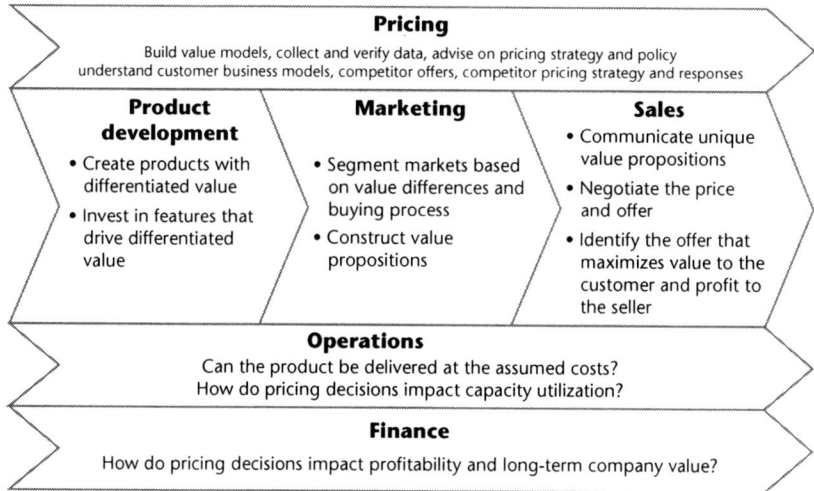

FIGURE 20.1 Internal participants in the pricing conversation

Increasing awareness of pricing as a profit lever, the rise of pricing management systems and the integration of pricing with other business functions is making pricing a more collaborative discipline, one that must interact with and support people in product development and management, marketing strategy, marketing communication, operations, finance and especially sales. And pricing must do this in the context of distributed organizations, where people work in different locations, even different time zones, and come from diverse backgrounds. Can the pricing function learn from the many years of research on computer supported collaborative work (CSCW) and by blending the concepts from CSCW with pricing can a new class of software applications be developed that support the integration of pricing across business processes? This paper discusses the approach taken by a software company as it went through the process of developing a new software application to support value-based pricing and iterating this development with customers. The author was a member of the management team of this company. The lessons learned are more generally applicable to business-to-business (B2B) pricing practices and the development of software to support collaborative business processes.

Theoretical foundation

Computer supported collaborative work (CSCW) deals with the class of applications between the enterprise data processing (systems such as those offered by SAP and Oracle) and individual productivity solutions that are used by teams to coordinate their activities (spreadsheets, presentation software, word processors and simple databases). For a good summary see Grudin (1994). These applications are meant to be used by groups to accomplish shared goals. In recent years, CSCW and groupware systems have been caught up in the wave of social media software, of which the best-known examples are Facebook and LinkedIn, although within companies solutions such as Jive are more common (Li and Bernhoff 2011). Unlike enterprise data management and enterprise resource planning (ERP) systems, collaborative work systems are meant to help groups of people to communicate, share information and make decisions together. They operate under different design principles. ERP systems are generally designed around a command and control metaphor and support transactional data that respects the ACID rules of atomicity, consistency, isolation, durability (Gray and Reuter 1993). Collaborative systems are based on a conversation metaphor where iteration and revision are part of the work flow (Englebart 1995). Additionally, a common visual framework has often been found to support conversations and mutual understanding (Tufte 2001).

The rise of social software has been accompanied by a more general acceptance of cloud-based Software as a Service solutions (Benioff and Adler 2009). Cloud-based software is software that is hosted on multiple distributed servers that are accessed remotely over the Internet. Some companies such as salesforce.com operate their own clouds, but most companies rely on third parties such as Rackspace or Amazon. Software as a Service (SaaS) is software that is hosted in the cloud and is paid for by subscriptions (generally monthly or annual) rather than through licences. Cloud-based SaaS solutions can be evolved and scaled much quicker than conventional on-premise software as there is only one instance to maintain and develop. Cloud-based SaaS applications are also easy to integrate with each other and work well with the distributed always being updated nature of the Internet.

In developing collaboration software for complex business processes like pricing it is important to have a formal model. Generic systems such as Microsoft SharePoint or 37 Signals Basecamp do not provide enough context to shape and direct conversations, to create a shared language system, or to organize and search the many types of data used in pricing decisions. A shared conceptual framework is needed. Ideally this framework should include a visual representation.

One obvious candidate for collaborative software systems to be used in pricing activity is economic value estimation or EVE, a framework for value-based pricing introduced by Tom Nagle and Reed Holden in the second edition of *The Strategy and Tactics of Pricing* and advanced in subsequent editions (Nagle and Holden 2002; Nagle et al. 2011). EVE is a powerful framework for collaboration as it requires information about the offer being sold, the competitive alternative and the customer's business model. It organizes these into a standard image that is well known to many people in the pricing industry and easy for people from other disciplines to understand (see Figure 20.2).

Offer

Features, benefits, value drivers of the offer are mapped. Value drivers (statement of the economic benefit of the offer for the customer) come in at least four flavours: revenue drivers, cost drivers, operating capital drivers, capital spending drivers. Each value driver is formalized as a mathematical formula (sometimes referred to as an algorithm in the literature) and this formula generally has a number of variables that depend on

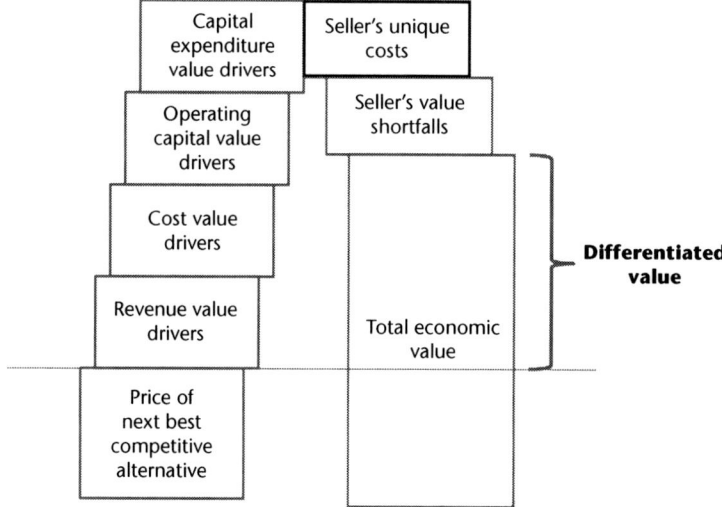

FIGURE 20.2 The canonical value model

the customer, competitor and offer. A very simple example of a value driver formula is (scrap costs savings) = (scrap costs) × (reduction in scrap costs using solution) − (scrap costs) × (reduction in scrap costs using competitive alternative). Value driver formulae can become quite complex, using many different variables, though the best practice is generally to keep them as simple as possible and when they get more than five variables to see if they can be separated into two value drivers. There are two classes of value drivers, positive and negative. Positive value drivers increase the differentiation value of a solution. Negative value drivers decrease the differentiation value. One type of negative value driver is any unique costs of using the seller's solution. These costs can come in many forms: training costs, inventory costs, new investments and so on. The other type captures shortcomings in the seller's solution compared to the next best competitive alternative.

Competitive alternative

With the exception of monopolies, pricing always takes place in a competitive environment. Even with many monopolies the buyer may have the option of doing nothing and not consuming. EVE requires pricing experts to identify the competitive alternative and the price of this alternative. Beyond that, the competitive alternative can create negative value drivers. In some cases, the competitive alternative will provide value that the seller does not. This value needs to be captured as negative value drivers.

Customer business model

Value drivers are always calculated as the impact of the seller's solution on the customer's business model relative to the competitive alternative. This information is captured in the value driver formulae. Additionally, value drivers are calculated in terms of the pricing metric, the unit in which price is quoted. It is much easier to build a value model when the pricing metric is one that maps to how the customer gets value. For example, the best pricing metric for an additive to a cement mix that reduces surface processing might be 'per square foot covered'. As this additive may actually be sold by the bag, the collaborative software supporting value-based pricing must make it easy to move back and forth between 'per bag' pricing and 'per square foot pricing' and possibly even 'per project pricing'.

Value-based pricing is widely acknowledged as the best practice in B2B pricing (Hinterhuber and Liozu 2012; Liozu et al. 2012) but in practice many companies have struggled to implement this approach (Toytari et al. 2011) or even to agree on its meaning (Liozu et al. 2012). A collaborative software platform may be able to give organizations a shared understanding of value-based pricing, a language system to talk about it, a virtual place for conversations to take place, and database for the many types of data collected.

An important part of collaboration is trust. Value-based pricing requires a great deal of data about customers and competitors. The people presenting the value model and using its outputs, such as value propositions and value messages to negotiate price, have to trust the data they are using and they need to be able to show the customer why they should trust this data. Research has found three key determinants of trust in collaborative software: transparency (the processes to generate the data and the use to which the data will be put is visible), provenance (one can track where the data comes from), security (data shared is secure and will not be shared beyond the intended recipients) (Botta et al. 2011; Braithwaite 1998) And of course honest conversations help to build trust. Success in value-based pricing requires the development of trust between product development, marketing, finance, pricing and sales. Another foundation for trust is the credibility of the data used in the models. Credibility is earned by making sure that data provenance is transparent, by validating the data through repeated conversations, and ensuring that unfavourable data as well as favourable data is presented.

Part of the power of EVE comes from its construction as a concept blend. Concept blending has been identified as a key approach to user design innovation across many disciplines (Imaz and Benyon 2006). For example, the common user interface metaphor of the Window is a blend of the concepts of physical windows and actions we take on them (open a window, look through a window) and the computer screen. It is also the way that apparently contradictory concepts can be combined into a more powerful syntheses (Fauconnier and Turner 2003). In the case of EVE, it resolves the apparent contradiction between the economist's view of pricing and that of marketing and sales. Most economists believe that efficient markets are the key to economic prosperity and accurate pricing. An efficient market requires transparent information about prices and products that can easily be substituted one for another. Price is set by market mechanisms and is assumed to trend towards the level at which supply and demand are balanced. Most companies have a very different view of the world. Product development and marketing generally

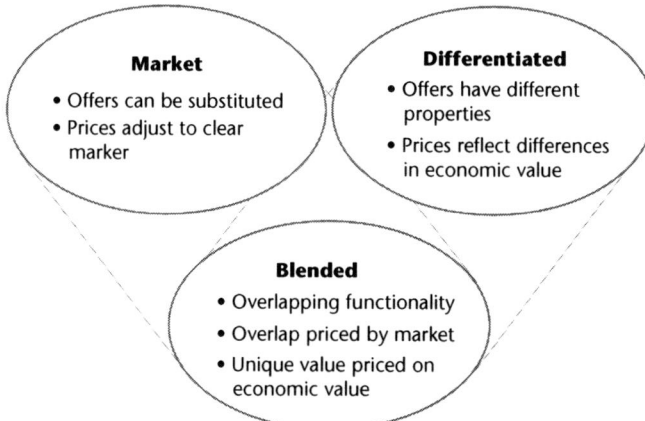

FIGURE 20.3 Conceptual blending of commodity and differentiation pricing

want to create differentiated offers, that can be branded, and where the differentiation and brand are rewarded with a price premium and higher market share. They try to create and shape markets, not just respond to supply and demand.

What about buyers? Some prefer commoditized products where they can easily substitute one vendor for another and drive prices as low as possible; in other words, they want to see the market at work. This is especially true of the procurement function in large companies. Other buyers are looking for a strategic edge for their own business, and want to buy the solution that will have the most economic impact and support their own differentiation. The business buyer, who is responsible for creating value at his own organization, often thinks in these terms.

This contradiction between commoditized market prices and differentiation is resolved by EVE because it blends market forces with differentiation in a way that combines the most important characteristics of each. When using EVE to implement value-based pricing one begins by recognizing that each customer differs in how much value they can get from a solution and by identifying the competitive alternatives. Buyers always have alternatives, and the price of alternatives is set by the market. But the alternatives are generally not identical. Each will have advantages and disadvantages for a specific customer and it is these differences that create differentiation, and with differentiation comes opportunity. In the real world of B2B selling, true commodities are rare, especially when the complete package of product plus services is considered (see Figure 20.3)

Findings

Value models evolve based on conversations – so does the software supporting value modelling

We developed a software platform iteration by working with users. Modern Software as a Service platforms (Fried and Hansson 2010) combined with Agile/Scrum

(Schwaber and Beedle 2002) development methods support this approach and make it easier to track how users are actually using the software. This approach led to important discoveries about how people develop and use value models in distributed environments. Some of the key findings are summarized below.

- People work on value models together.
- Value models evolve over time.
- Most value models start with a parent value model and are made using a 'save as' to create a new model that is then revised.
- Sales people want to be able to modify variables.
- Customer conversations give sales access to great insight into variables for specific customers.
- Customer conversations give sales insight into competitor offers.
- Variables are reused across value models.

Organizational issues in information sharing and control

The above findings about users helped uncover some critical organizational issues around information sharing and control. Many of these issues depend on company culture and its general approach to who should have access and edit privileges on pricing data. As pricing has such a direct impact on business performance the importance of these decisions and the emotions provoked are emphasized. The most important issues are given below in the form of questions that companies adopting value-based pricing will need to answer.

- How much control should sales have over which value messages are delivered to the customer?
- How much control should sales have over variables (unlimited, adjust within a prescribed range, none)?
- How much control should sales have over pricing and discounting?
- How much information should sales be given about costs and how granular should that information be?
- How should marketing and pricing inform sales about the use it makes of information gathered by sales?
- How much control should sales have over presentation formats?
- Can and should sales be able to construct value models for customers?

Initially we erred on the side of not giving sales enough control. But after observing sales people in selling situations using value models the software was revised and sales were given additional tools and control. Additional feedback and communication channels were also built into the software to improve transparency for sales.

A common language system is necessary but not sufficient – business functions, industries and customer all have unique vocabularies that need supporting

Product development, marketing, pricing and sales all have their own language systems that need to be supported. Part of the power of value-based pricing is that it gives people from different functions a common language system to discuss customers, competitors, value and pricing. But in practice each business function still needs to use its own frameworks and vocabularies. To accommodate this, we added modules specifically designed for marketing (value communication-marketing where marketing creates value propositions) and for sales (value communication-sales where sales people create unique value propositions that they can customize for specific customers) that provided a bridge from value-based pricing language to marketing language and to sales language. In the future this may need to be done for product development and management, operations and finance.

Transparency builds credibility and trust

People in all business functions and especially customers need to understand where data comes from in order to build trust and to be willing to share their own data. The first step towards this was to make it easy to document the source of each piece of data and for sales to access this data provenance information with customers. The next step was to provide methods to share data across value models so that data becomes more consistent and so that cases where different values are being used can be uncovered and investigated.

Data is refined in conversations with customers

One of the most common objections to value-based pricing is that the data needed to construct value models is not available. To some extent this is the result of a perceived need for precision. The underlying assumption is that data is more trustworthy and useful the more precise it is. Observing users, especially sales users, suggests a different approach. It is important to identify the most relevant value drivers for the customer and to be honest about the negative value drivers (acknowledging shortcomings helps to build trust). It is also important to have the value driver formula right; the maths must capture the key variables and their relationships. It is less important to have the actual values in the variables precisely correct. These can only be estimates and if they are at least 'in the ballpark' they can be refined in the conversation with the customer. This level of precision is enough to support value-based pricing and value-based selling. Collaborative software makes it possible to channel the values for variables uncovered by sales back to a database where they can be used in analysis of trends and to improve the value models.

Conclusions

Computer supported collaborative work (CSCW) and social software provide an alternative model to ERP in the development of software to support pricing professionals. The value-based pricing framework as exemplified by economic value estimation, or EVE, provides a compelling way to organize conversations between the stakeholders in B2B pricing: product management, marketing strategy, marketing communication, operations, finance, sales and of course the pricing function itself. By combining these two approaches a new class of pricing software can be developed that supports collaboration on pricing decisions and helps the sales force to negotiate prices based on differentiation value, rather than defaulting to price negotiation and discounting (see Geisman 2003 for a discussion of discounting practices in the software industry).

B2B pricing is the outcome of a series of conversations, both internal conversations between the various stakeholders and external conversations, primarily with customers, but also with analysts and the media. Software to support the pricing function must support these conversations. Conversations involve two or more parties and take place over time. Software for pricing must support multiple roles, create communications channels and provide a collective memory of the conversations. Effective conversations require trust between the parties. Trust is the outcome of credibility, transparency, provenance (the ability to track back the source of data and claims) and shared language systems. Pricing software needs to provide all of these if it is to be trusted by users and build trust between them.

Pricing requires data from many different sources: product development and management, marketing, operations and finance departments; open source data from the Internet and other publicly available sources; private sources such as market research surveys and closed data sources; and most importantly from customers. One can only execute B2B pricing in the context of conversations with customers. Pricing data goes well beyond historical records of pricing transactions. It includes data about one's own products and solutions, the customer's business model and the competitive alternatives. This is sometimes seen as a barrier to the adoption of value-based pricing and sales. It is difficult to gather precisely accurate data for each value driver and each customer. It can even be difficult to get accurate information on competitive alternatives. But this is why conversations are important. Conversations can support successive approximations that circle in to values that are 'good enough' for a customer to accept a price and make a buying decision.

The initial hypothesis behind this project was that pricing would benefit from a collaborative software system built using the framework provided by EVE. By building this software in an agile, iterative manner we are generating insight into pricing-related behaviours by pricing, marketing and sales organizations. These insights in turn support further development of the software in a virtuous circle of improvement.

Implications for the pricing field

The Cluetrain Manifesto made the provocative claim that 'markets are conversations' (Locke *et al.* 2000). The conclusion of this paper is that 'pricing is a conversation'

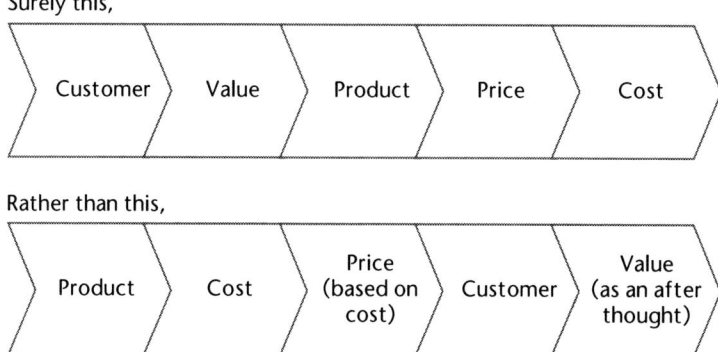

FIGURE 20.4 Order of conversations

and if the pricing function wants to play a larger strategic role within organizations and realize its full business impact then pricing professionals must get better at conversations. These conversations are both internal and external and are based on trust. Pricing experts have to learn to trust their colleagues in sales and their customers. In today's world many conversations take place through or are augmented by software. The path forward for pricing software is to support the conversations about pricing that need to take place within organizations and with customers, and to give pricing experts insight into the conversations that take place when they are not in the room.

Pricing starts with the customer and the customer's competitive alternatives. The pricing conversation has to begin with the customer and be focused on understanding how to create differentiated value for customers. Only then can one design a product that creates that differentiated value and set a price. Too often, products are designed and costs built in before pricing even gets to the table. And value, for the customer, well, that is an after thought (see Figure 20.4).

By getting involved in the conversation as products are developed, and staying with the conversation through sales, pricing can begin to realize its promise and transform business so that industries can support more differentiated offers and more profitable companies.

Thanks

Development of the LeveragePoint platform for Value-Based Pricing was led by Ed Arnold and Neil Davies of LeveragePoint Innovations Inc. Subsequent versions have benefitted from the insights of Jay Manson and many others on the LeveragePoint team, as well as users at LeveragePoint's customers. Dr David Botta and Dr Lee Iverson have taught the author many lessons about the development of collaborative software and trust-based systems. Stephan Liozu challenged my thinking and provided insights from a wide range of pricing research.

References

Benioff, M. and Adler, C. (2009) *Behind the cloud*. Hoboken, NJ: Jossey-Bass.

Botta, D., Muldner, K., Hawkey, K. and Beznosov, K. (2011) Toward understanding distributed cognition in IT security management: The role of cues and norms. *Cognition, Technology & Work*, 13 (2), pp. 121–34.

Braithwaite, V. (1998) Communal and exchange trust norms: their value base and relevance to institutional trust. *Trust Governance*, 1, pp. 46–74.

Corey E. R. (1983) *Industrial marketing: Cases and concepts*, 3rd edition. Englewood Cliffs, NJ: Prentice Hall, p. 93.

Engelbart, D. C. (1995) *Boosting our collective IQ*. BLT Press.

Fauconnier, G. and Turner, M. (2003) *The way we think: Conceptual blending and the mind's hidden complexities*. New York, NY: Basic Books.

Fried, J. and Hansson, J. H. (2010) *Rework*. New York, NY: Crown Business Publishing.

Geisman, J. (2003) *Discounting practices in the software industry*. Needham, MA: Software Pricing Partners.

Gray, J. and Reuter, A. (1993) *Distributed transaction processing: Concepts and techniques*. New York, NY: Morgan Kauffman.

Grudin, J. (1994) Groupware and social dynamics: Eight challenges for developers. *Communications of the ACM*, January, 37 (1).

Hinterhuber, A. and Liozu, S. (2012) Is it time to rethink your pricing strategy? *MIT Sloan Management Review*, 53 (4), pp. 69–77.

Hogan, J. (2008) *Building a world class pricing capability: Where does your company stack up?* Cambridge, MA: Monitor Group.

Imaz, M. and Benyon, D. (2006) *Designing with blends: Conceptual foundations of human computer interaction and software engineering*. Cambridge, MA: The MIT Press.

Kolassa, A. M. (2009) *The strategic pricing of pharmaceuticals*. New Jersey: Pondhouse Press.

Li, C. and Bernoff, H. (2011) *Groundswell: Winning in a world transformed by social technologies*. Cambridge, MA: Harvard Business Review Press.

Liozu, S. (2010) *Pricing orientation in industrial markets: The organizational transformation to value-based pricing*. Unpublished Qualitative Research Report, Doctor of Management, Case Western Reserve University, Cleveland, OH.

Liozu S., Hinterhuber A., Boland R. and Perelli S. (2012) The conceptualization of value-based pricing in industrial firms. *Journal of Revenue and Pricing Management*, 11 (1), pp. 12–34.

Liozu, S., Hinterhuber, A., Perelli, S. and Boland, R. (2012) Mindful pricing: Transforming organizations through value-based pricing. *Journal of Strategic Marketing*, 20 (3), pp. 1–13.

Locke, C., Levine, R., Searls, D. and Weinberger, D. (2000). *The Cluetrain Manifesto: The end of business as usual*. New York, NY: Basic Books.

Meehan, J. M., Simonetto, M. G., Montan, L. and Goodin, C. A. (2011) *Pricing and profitability management*. Hoboken, NJ: Wiley.

Mohammed, R. (2010) *The 1% windfall: How successful companies use price to profit and grow*. Hoboken, NJ: Harper Business.

Nagle, T. T. and Holden, R. K. (2002) *The strategy and tactics of pricing: A guide to profitable decision making*, 3rd edition. Englewood Cliffs, NJ: Prentice Hall.

Nagle, T. T., Hogan, J. and Zale, J. (2011) *The strategy and tactics of pricing: A guide to profitable decision making*. 5th edition. Englewood Cliffs, NJ: Prentice Hall.

Schwaber, K. and Beedle, M. (2002) *Agile software development with scrum*. Englewood Cliffs, NJ: Prentice Hall.

Toytari, P., Alejandro, T. B., Parvinen, P., Ollila, I. and Rosendahl, N. (2011) Bridging the theory to application gap in value-based selling. *Journal of Business & Industrial Marketing*, 26 (7), pp. 493–502.

Tufte, E. (2001) *The visual display of quantitative information*. Cheshire, CT: Graphics Press.

21

IMPLEMENTING EFFECTIVE PRICING STRATEGIES

Tools for tracking prices

Richard Coppoolse

Introduction – the power of price tracking

Most companies tend to think and speak about "markets," "economic situation," "competition," and "costs developments" as a way to explain sales and profitability moving up or down, and as a way to base business strategy on opportunities and threats, generated by these phenomena. So far all is fine.

Where things get tricky is when these phenomena start driving price decisions on both the strategic level and the tactical level. A far more detailed analysis is required for such decisions.

Price tracking sounds to many marketeers rather boring and more a role for controllers, yet it is the very backbone of any effective and successful price management structure. So spending ample time on this subject is a *must-do* for an organization. This is for many companies an innovative approach.

Current pricing by companies is often based on margin considerations, on historical price levels, or on what competition dictates according to purchase managers. When there is a change in one of the earlier mentioned phenomena, should we change our prices? It depends.

And if we change price, do we make a blanket change or a focused change? What should drive our decision making?

Quite often companies are lacking clear insight on the impact of a price change on their business. The well-known "price elasticity" is used as an argument to drive sales by lowering prices, often ignoring the information that is within reach: historical data on sales and price developments of the past years and lessons learnt from other products and categories, systematic price tracking will provide a serious insight improvement for a company to evaluate its strategic as well as its tactical decisions about how to move prices for the good of the company and its shareholders.

In this chapter, we will elaborate on the price reporting opportunity that a company can exploit to focus the business better on value capturing and thus on immediate and tangible profitability improvement.

Price reports: the power of price tracking

A well-known saying is: "what gets measured, gets done." This statement is also very true for pricing. As soon as it is clear what is happening to the price of products and services, the overall attention to price increases.

Looking at charts is a common way to quickly grasp what it is all about and to understand the trends. The same is valid for price reports. A simple representation of a few lines or Excel worksheets with conditional formats help you to quickly leaf through a pile of data and find where corrective action is required. In this chapter, we will discuss the various possibilities of data representation, its objectives, and suggested key users of the reports.

The report possibilities as shown in Table 21.1 will now be discussed.

Price reports versus margin reports

In this section, we will NOT discuss margin reports. These are fundamentally different: margin does not only take sales price into the equation, but also the cost

TABLE 21.1 An overview of price tracking tools

	Useful for	*Used by*	*Ideal frequency*
Price trends reports			
Price–sales charts	Price tracking	Sales, Marketing	Monthly
Price–mix charts	Price strategy	Gen.Mgt, Marketing, Finance	Monthly, Quarterly, Yearly
Price snapshot reports			
Price change vs. previous period	Strategy and tactics	Marketing, Finance	Monthly
Scatter charts	Price tactics	Marketing, Sales	Yearly
Price band charts	Price tactics	Marketing, Sales	Yearly
Bubble charts	Price strategy	Marketing	Yearly
Revenue causality reports	Price strategy	Marketing, Finance	Quarterly
Under floor price reports	Price tactics	Sales	Monthly
Advanced reports			
Top/bottom performers	Price tactics	Sales	Quarterly, Yearly
Sales vs. agreement	Price tactics	Sales	Quarterly
Price index reports	Price tactics	Sales, Marketing	Monthly
Price waterfall analysis	Price tactics	Marketing, Sales	Quarterly
Sales managers performance	Reward schemes	HRM, Sales, Mgt	Quarterly, Yearly

price. As a consequence, there are two variables in play, which can distort interpretations. Cost price has at least as many variants as the sales price, so margin is not a very clean instrument to steer your sales activity with. It also introduces an "inside-out" view culture in a company. This is fundamentally different from the focus on the sales price. In such a case the market is continuously in focus. The market defines what best to offer at certain price points and the cost price is then less relevant. There is nothing wrong with margin reports, though, but they serve a different purpose. They should not lead the price decision taking. If they are allowed to do so, you will end up with either too low or too high prices, leading to sub-optimal business results.

Who are your interest groups?

Amazingly, many companies generate reports that are often to be used by everyone. For pricing this is no different. An innovation is to distinguish target groups in the company.

The first and foremost user will be the **Marketing department** looking for trends to define strategy and to define corrective action where and when required. Price reports are a very useful tool to understand business trends of the market. They allow close monitoring of price development versus the market trend and versus the marketing strategy.

The second user group will be **general management** and **Finance**. The high-level insight provided by good price reports will help general managers and CFOs to keep the whole organization focused on the importance of price – and thus profit realization. It will prevent erratic decision taking on business strategy and will help define corrective action in the areas required.

The third group is **Sales**. Sales will use price reports in a very practical way: to find business opportunities and to correct prices which are out of line, or where customers do not live up to their promise. Here price reports are used as tactical market information.

Reports discussion
Price trends analysis
Price–sales charts

The price–sales graphs are widely used graphs indicating price as well as sales (Figure 21.1). They are easy to construct and give quick insight in both movements. It is also possible to add drill-down possibilities. Often these graphs plot in absolute value (with two separate y-axes). It is best to plot sales in quantity in such a graph, because one has implicitly the sales in value (quantity *price = value). There are different time periods possible: common are year-to-date, cumulative sales of budget year, monthly, quarterly, etc. The difficulty with these graphs is that the relation between the two values is not always obvious: the scales can be quite different, causing differences in up- and downswings. Secondly, the influence of market and market share growth/decline is hard to extract from such graphs. It is

Implementing effective pricing strategies **313**

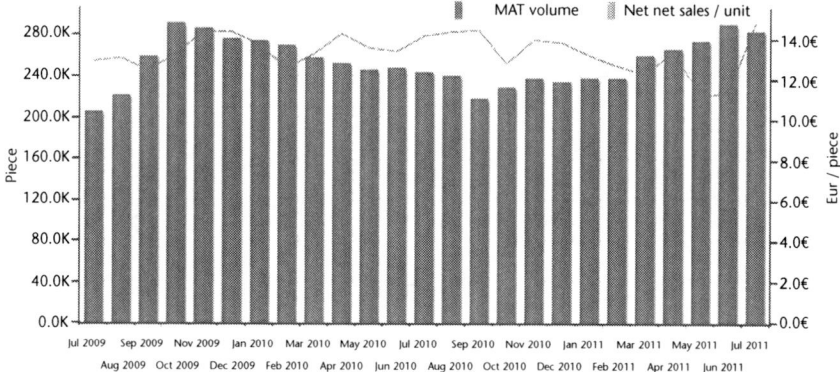

FIGURE 21.1 Price–sales chart

also difficult to make aggregate reporting as the price then also becomes an average, with even less explanatory meaning. Therefore, they have relatively low value in explaining price moves.

Price–mix charts

A more elegant graph is one where only "percent change" versus a previous period is plotted (Figure 21.2). Then the up- and downswings of each line is comparable and consistent over time, even years back. Explanation of each individual move can be sought through the other elements of the graph. Later, we will introduce the notions "mix" and "currency" as price elements. It is possible to plot everything in the same graph; this enhances the understanding of what is really changing. In this graph one can also apply different time horizons. These graphs are very powerful for aggregate reports as they can balance the different price effects into one overall index and allow for drill-down functionality.

A common problem is seasonality in data. If that is the case, you have to use moving annual totals (MATs) to evade the risk of letting this become visible in these graphs; this would lead to wrong decision taking. The downside of MATs is that the degree of change is substantially reduced due to the long average period. Preferably shorter periods should be used to analyze price trends. A downside of this kind of reporting is that it is quite heavy on calculations and modeling.

Price snapshot reports

The character of snapshot reports is that they do not show trend lines, but focus on differences, either in percent or in absolute value. The advantage of snapshot reports is that they give clear directional information about where the business is going. The disadvantage is that in a subsequent period the outcome might be considerably different (this also depends on the used time horizons).

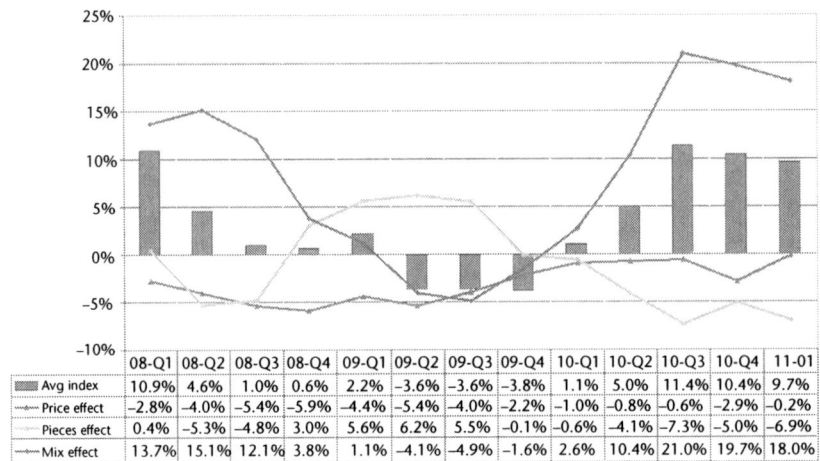

	08-Q1	08-Q2	08-Q3	08-Q4	09-Q1	09-Q2	09-Q3	09-Q4	10-Q1	10-Q2	10-Q3	10-Q4	11-01
Avg index	10.9%	4.6%	1.0%	0.6%	2.2%	-3.6%	-3.6%	-3.8%	1.1%	5.0%	11.4%	10.4%	9.7%
Price effect	-2.8%	-4.0%	-5.4%	-5.9%	-4.4%	-5.4%	-4.0%	-2.2%	-1.0%	-0.8%	-0.6%	-2.9%	-0.2%
Pieces effect	0.4%	-5.3%	-4.8%	3.0%	5.6%	6.2%	5.5%	-0.1%	-0.6%	-4.1%	-7.3%	-5.0%	-6.9%
Mix effect	13.7%	15.1%	12.1%	3.8%	1.1%	-4.1%	-4.9%	-1.6%	2.6%	10.4%	21.0%	19.7%	18.0%

FIGURE 21.2 Price–mix chart

	Price vs last year	Quantity vs last year
Product A	-1%	11%
Product B	-2%	-19%
Product C	-20%	108%
Product D	-3%	-2%
Product E	-6%	23%
Product F	-22%	14%
Product G	-5%	-1%
Product H	8%	-11%

FIGURE 21.3 Price change report

Price change versus previous period

This report can be very powerful to analyze price moves versus sales in quantity, especially when they are used in combination with the relative price–mix charts (see Table 21.1; Figure 21.3). A prerequisite is that the product or product group must be homogeneous in price over time, else the visual effect of a price change may be caused by mix effects. This chart can also be useful to analyze whether price and quantity are correlated, and if so, to what extent. It can trigger further research into the marketing mix as to why the effects are happening. The results of price and quantity can be compared with the marketing objectives and corrective action can be defined accordingly.

Scatter charts

Scatter charts are powerful charts where price (or price deviation, price index) can be plotted against sales volume or value, showing customer price levels (Figure 21.4). One can also plot the margin against sales per customer or margin per product turnover. In this case, margin equates to relative price. This only works when there is cost price homogeneity when aggregated product levels are

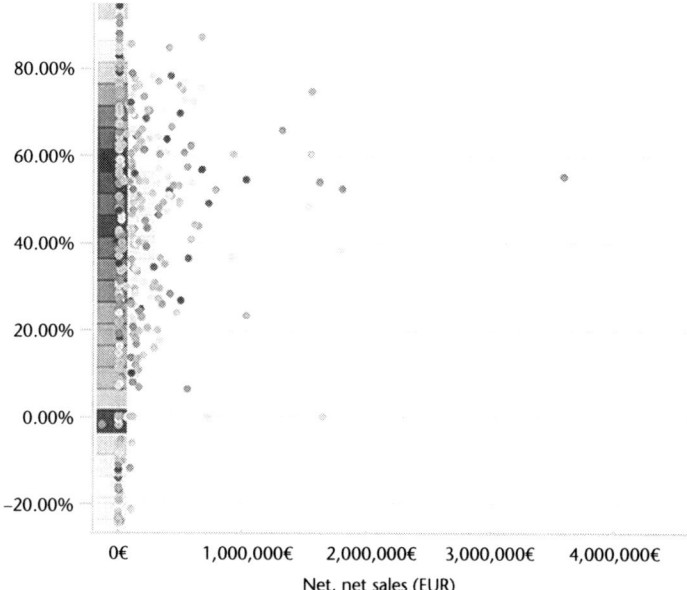

FIGURE 21.4 Price scatter chart

used. By comparing the weak scoring products or customers with the target or average, improvement objectives can be defined. Scatter charts are a perfect visual means to identify pricing that is not consistent with strategy. Often outliers are the cause of major disruption in companies: either the prices are too low and they are the cause of further price reductions to other customers, or prices are too high and are the cause of customers defecting to the competition. Such outliers should be carefully analyzed by Sales and corrective action should be monitored regularly. Using a scatter chart as the basis for price strategy should be avoided. This is a snapshot analysis without showing the direction of price movement, so predicting behavior is risky. It is more a tactical analysis to indicate corrective action.

Price band charts

A price band chart is actually comparable to a scatter chart, without the second (x-)axis with value or volume (Figure 21.5). This makes this a limited report in its usage. It only shows the spread between high–medium–low prices. To conclude that a certain spread is too wide is dangerous; it will depend on how homogeneous the products or customers within the band are. It may work though for a single stock keeping unit (SKU). It is a typical report for Marketing.

Bubble charts

Bubble charts are a specific kind of scatter chart where a third dimension in the bubble size (like margin) is added (Figure 21.6). This makes this kind of reporting interesting for marketing strategy purposes to analyze market attractiveness.

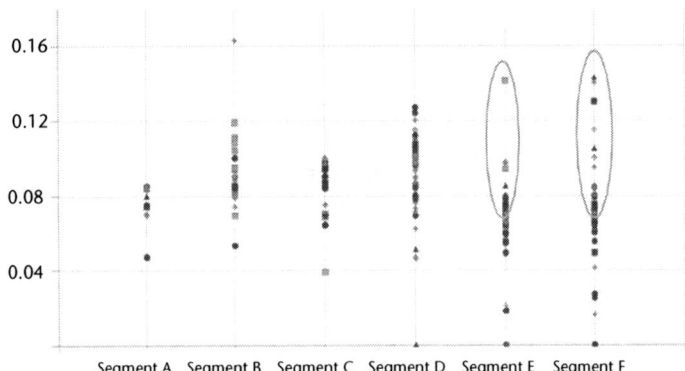

FIGURE 21.5 Price band chart

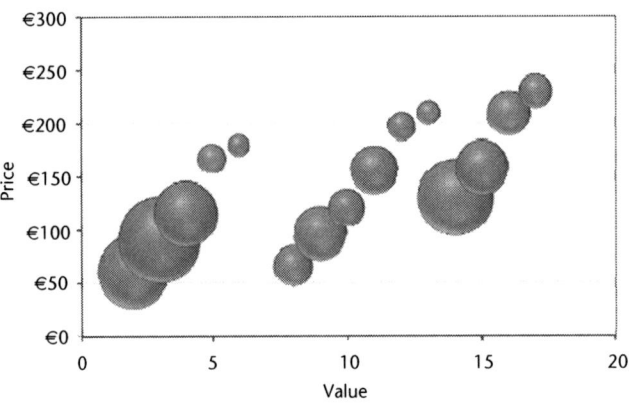

FIGURE 21.6 Price bubble chart

Revenue causality reports

A very interesting report is a revenue causality report (Figure 21.7). This report can show the "where got, where gone" of a business in parameters like: lost/won customers, price increase/decline, mix increase/decline, quantity increase/decrease at customer level, and the effect of exchange rates. This report requires a high level of data consistency, especially when products have short life cycles or when customers do not order certain products very regularly. By using advanced pricing software, drill-down possibilities will enable in-depth analysis and will drive corrective action by Sales and Marketing. Revenue causality reporting can be used to compare reality with strategy. Interesting analysis is a comparison of mix versus volume growth (a correlation of the quality of the volume growth) and price versus net customer growth (a correlation of price versus the customer base). Such analysis is input for corrective action. This report should be used with caution at aggregated business

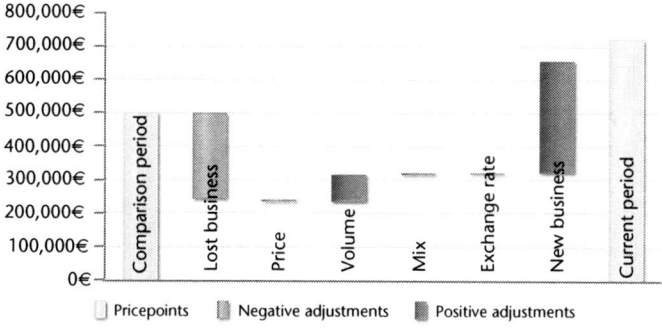

FIGURE 21.7 Revenue causality report

Product:	AV C/70	
Targetprice	€ 13.70	
Customer	Jan-March	Index
L.PS APS	€ 14.73	1.08
Parry group Ltd	€ 12.95	0.95
PG licht GmbH	€ 13.30	0.97
Luxeta GmbH	€ 15.12	1.10
Keenlight electrics	€ 17.24	1.26
Vau-lux GmbH	€ 14.27	1.04
ECLATEC STE	€ 17.21	1.26
IVELA SPA	€ 16.12	1.18
TURN LIGHTS SRL	€ 12.23	0.89
CINE PARTS	€ 17.16	1.25
HOLIGHT SA	€ 13.23	0.97
Neuco AG	€ 13.38	0.98

FIGURE 21.8 Target price analysis

level; at least a drill down in the major business areas is required, else the overall conclusion may be an amalgamation of deviating underlying effects.

Real versus target price

Price reports tend to focus on just that: giving the price for a certain product–customer combination. It becomes very useful when an assessment is being made whether the price is in line or not in line with strategy. This is reflected in a comparison with a target price (Figure 21.8). Snapshot reports especially allow for conditional formatting and thus a traffic light assessment within the report. Once a company has introduced a target price it becomes possible to measure against that. This is a major step forward compared to looking at margin targets.

Product:	AV C/70	
Floor price	€ 13.10	
Customer	Jan-March	Index
L.PS APS	€ 14.73	1.12
Parry group Ltd	€ 12.95	0.99
PG licht GmbH	€ 13.30	1.02
Luxeta GmbH	€ 15.12	1.15
Keenlight electrics	€ 17.24	1.32
Vau-lux GmbH	€ 14.27	1.09
ECLATEC STE	€ 17.21	1.31
IVELA SPA	€ 16.12	1.23
TURN LIGHTS SRL	€ 12.23	0.93
CINE PARTS	€ 17.16	1.31
HOLIGHT SA	€ 13.23	1.01
Neuco AG	€ 13.38	1.02

FIGURE 21.9 Floor price analysis

Under "floor price" reports

Once a company works with target prices, often floor or limit/stop prices are also introduced to give Sales guidance on how far they can go (down) with the price during the negotiations. This report makes it possible to track how the compliance is with the agreed floors (Figure 21.9). If a company works mainly with floor prices and not/hardly with target prices it is likely that skewing of deals against the floor price will occur. This is a signal for corrective action. Such corrective action could encompass the introduction of target prices in combination with a change in the compensation system for Sales, rewarding higher price capturing.

Advanced reporting
The notion of price indexing

The notion of price index or normalized price has already been mentioned. This index sets all products and aggregate levels against the average price or a forecasted target price. Since all products get the same target (100 or 1.00), it will be possible to compare a product of €0.10 with a product of €50.00 and to combine the two in one overall result. Weighing the two products can be based on turnover in value.

This price index is required to make a like-for-like comparison between high-priced and low-priced products in price setting toward customers. This is normally very hard for Sales. With price indexes, Sales will be able to assess quickly whether a requested price is possible or not.

Although it sounds obvious, and I have seen it used more than once in presentations of consultants, the reality is that often price indexing is not implemented during change processes, because it requires thorough thinking about how to set it up and how to introduce it in the company IT systems. Later on, other priorities take precedence and price indexing remains unused. The best moment for implementation is at the introduction of new pricing software or when the company adopts target pricing as the way to define pricing to customers.

Sales versus agreement tracking

Sales agreements with customers generally have conditional pricing aspects involved through conditional rebates. If all is well these are accrued by finance in the transactions and thus show up in the NN price. Yet few companies track whether customers live up to their agreements. A consequence is that generally too many rebates are paid out to customers. Although it is technically speaking not a pricing component, the result is: the customer does not pay the correct price for their purchases. So this report should be considered a pricing report.

Listing of top/bottom performing customers

A powerful report for Sales as well as for Marketing is the top/bottom customer price report. It shows where corrective action is required. Because normally customers buy a whole range of products it will be necessary to the normalized price or price index for this comparison. An alternative way is to use it for single SKUs or homogeneous products only.

Listings of top/bottom products per customer

This is a similar report as the previous one, only this time it is within a customer. This can be considered a drill down of the previous report. It will tell Sales why a customer is performing well or badly in price realization and will point at where corrective action can be made. A discussion with Marketing can take place whether the prices of a certain customer are justified. Both reports provide easy insight for Sales where things need corrective action and in combination with customer profitability reporting (where "cost-to-serve" is also involved) could result in overall profit improvement while letting go of some loss-giving business.

Price waterfall outlier reporting

An opportunity that remains often untapped is the analysis of deviation of conditions. First of all it requires that targets per waterfall condition type are established and secondly that the business warehouse allows for monitoring of the different conditions. The power of effective condition setting will steer customer behavior favorably; therefore, its monitoring is an important pricing element.

Sales managers performance assessment

Once price indexing is introduced this is not only useful to assess customer pricing and product pricing within customers. It can also be used to monitor how good your Sales team is in price setting and price preservation. An index per account manager can be calculated based on his or her customer portfolio (Figure 21.10).

If the resulting index is higher than 1.00 it will be interesting to observe what these people are doing to convince customers to buy at higher prices. Likewise, lower scores can be grounds for additional training.

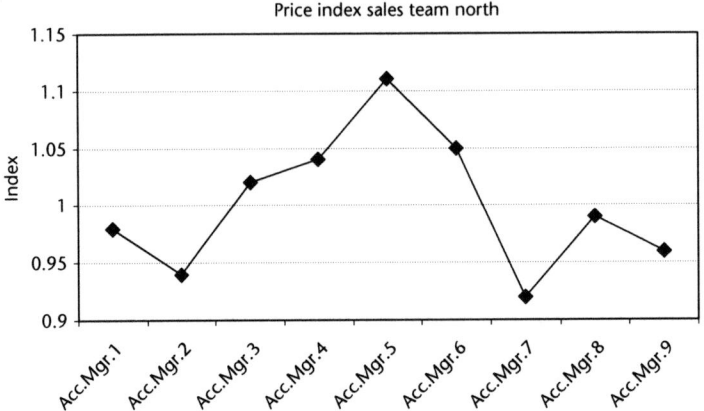

FIGURE 21.10 Price index analysis

Price performance indicators

Successful pricing by a company should result in higher margin, higher sales, and acceptable customer satisfaction scores regarding price. Price is by definition a dissatisfier for a customer: they have to sacrifice scarce funds to buy what they need. This is never done with joy. Customer satisfaction will rely on product performance and company performance. If a company gets a plus for pricing, it is either that the pricing scheme is transparent enough for the customer to do uncomplicated business with or it is because Sales is too relaxed about extra perks for the customer. Such a score always requires scrutiny, else you may leave money on the table.

Higher margin *can* be a result of better pricing, but is not necessarily so. It can also come from higher efficiencies; therefore, higher margin is not per se a good performance indicator for pricing effectiveness by a company.

Higher sales show that price is not hindering customer acceptance and purchase behavior, but can also be a result of market dynamics, competitive behavior, a product advantage, and a few other reasons; therefore, sales performance is also not a good indicator for pricing performance of a company.

Real pricing performance indicators focus on those areas where pricing has impact (Figure 21.11):

1. Performance against price strategy
2. Pricing control
3. Value capturing capabilities.

Most performance indicators responsibility should lie with Marketing and Sales as a shared responsibility. Senior management should have a performance indicator based on overall price performance development and mix development.

	Business deliverable	Measurable KPI (Smart)	Responsible
Performance against strategy	Improve usage of value based pricing (improve price index)	Realized price/target price	Senior management/marketing
	Continuous value capture focus	Mix development versus strategy	Senior management/marketing
Performance against strategy	Reduce low priced products	• % of sales with margin <x% (product axis) • Realized price increase versus target	Sales/marketing
	Reduce low priced customers.	% reduction of products under average price	Sales
	Reduce price/discount variance	% of manual prices in ERP system % of approvals (deviation from target price)	Sales
	Tail product analysis and slow movers analysis		Marketing/sales
Value capturing capabilities	Increase insight in value drivers by commercial people. Better negotiation position	Price development of price index vs. target	Sales

FIGURE 21.11 Pricing key performance indicators (KPIs)

Who is in charge?

There is always more than one owner for pricing. Actually, a distinction will have to be made between strategy and tactics.

Pricing strategy is clearly owned by Marketing and senior management. Not only is Marketing responsible for the connection with the overall marketing planning and the business objectives, they also have to feed back to senior management the results of activities and propose corrective action.

The pricing tactics are a different playing field requiring pricing specialists. Neither Marketing nor Sales have the know-how and (more importantly) the time to dive into the detail of pricing required to be successful in price management. More and more, companies are installing a Pricing Office that specializes in managing price in Commercial Operations and in supporting Marketing in the development and maintenance of pricing strategy. Price tracking and reporting is one of the prime tasks of the Pricing Office.

A recent study of the Professional Pricing Society shows that the Pricing Office typically reports into Marketing, Finance, the CEO, and only last to Sales. I consider it not a good idea to let a Pricing Office report into Sales. This is a conflict of interests and could lead to compliance issues.

A functional Pricing Office is an added-value investment for a company to capture more of the generated value.

Price definitions and structures

It is not uncommon that companies have difficulty in setting up bullet-proof price reporting. One of the key attention areas is the data itself: how they are booked in a business warehouse, how extractions can be made and even when this is done properly, there can still be a mismatch with what Sales perceives as "price." This has to do with a common language of what is meant by "price" and all its components. One of the first tasks for setting up price reporting is sorting this out. There can be in any company a multitude of definitions necessary in order to define all pricing activities. These should be reflected in the reporting system.

Pocket price

The base price level of all discussions should be the pocket price (also called net, or net net price). This is the price a company can calculate for its products or services after reduction of discounts, surcharges, rebates and adjustments, and other compensations, and can "pocket" at the end of the book-year. This is the real price that can be attributed to a product or service.

After this the **list price** and the **invoice price** define the base elements of a price waterfall.

Mix and currency effect

Apart from the change in price, two additional effects can be isolated from the sales data: the mix effect and the currency effect. The mix effect is the price effect that can be attributed to the changing mix of products in the total sales. Sales of higher priced products cause an average price increase although the individual prices may not change (this would be the price effect of the product itself). If companies work internationally there is a good chance of a currency effect due to the shifts in exchange rate. Both can be isolated from the total average sales through effective modeling and calculations.

Why is price tracking so innovative?

Price reporting seems so easy to do – just like any other sales or finance report. The reality is harder than that. It requires thorough thinking in setting up reports that make sense for its users: Marketing, Sales, Finance, and general management. This is one innovative part: think about your users!

Second, pricing projects start often like any other project: with a lot of enthusiasm and high hopes for quick wins. The reality can be harsh: internal resistance to change and no clear results will make your CEO feel uncertain about the project. The key question will pop up: "Where is the money?" Then the data throwing starts. By thinking at the start of the project about price tracking and KPIs, this can be avoided and the project leader can show through time the results in a consistent way. This generates trust and allows for corrective action when necessary.

The resulting pricing transparency will focus the whole company on price realization which is, together with the volume delivered, the most important profit driver. From there the next steps in a pricing improvement journey can be made.

Price reporting is tedious work, yet – just like finance reporting – it is one of the core activities for a modern – market oriented – company.

22
WINNING ON THE MARGIN

The B2B value imperative[1]

Mike Moorman

Today's business-to-business (B2B) Sales and Marketing executive faces a uniquely challenging selling environment. Rapid advances in buyer sophistication, Internet access to product information, and social media access to seller references and past performance have shifted power from sellers to buyers. These forces are further reinforced by continued product lifecycle compression, globalization, and vendor base consolidation.

The imperative to grow while protecting margins is forcing organizations to fundamentally transform their Sales and Marketing functions and the way they go to market. For many organizations the path to success includes significant advancement in their value-based selling capabilities.

Value-based selling (VBS) is not a new idea. It dates back more than 20 years. VBS is simple in concept: win and grow customers through product, service, and program offerings whose total value relative to price exceeds that of alternatives. By providing greater value the seller is able to win at a price premium.

The reality has proven more difficult. VBS requires a challenging shift in culture, strategy, operations, and execution capability. While most organizations have made steps in the right direction, few have yet achieved the degree of VBS capability required for sustained success in today's environment. Furthermore, as more organizations move to broad solutions selling, the degree of VBS difficulty increases. Solution selling typically involves broader coordination across the seller's business lines and an ability to sell at higher levels in the buyer's organization.

This article provides an introduction to the critical components that must be addressed to build world-class VBS capabilities. The insights shared derive from extensive VBS initiatives with more than 40 companies across 13 industries in North America, Europe, and Asia.[2]

The focus of this article will be on four success factors that have proven to be the most critical to VBS capability building:

1. VBS capability building requires a comprehensive and systematic approach that addresses the full sales and marketing system. Many organizations are falling short due to piecemeal approaches.
2. VBS requires a degree of Sales and Marketing alignment and integration that transcends that required by past models. Age-old division of labor practices that separate Sales and Marketing must be replaced by collaborative business processes.
3. VBS is a go-to-market strategy, not just a sales discipline. Segmentation strategy, value proposition strategy, sales process strategy, channels strategy, and sales force structure must come together to cost-effectively provide unique and compelling customer value.
4. Implementation of VBS requires skilled change management practices for transforming deeply entrenched sales force beliefs, behaviors, and skills. Top-down initiatives alone have failed.

The next section provides a brief introduction to VBS and is followed by sections that address each of the four success factors.

Introduction to value-based selling

Value-based selling capitalizes on the rational B2B buyer's goal to select and grant loyalty to the suppliers that provide the greatest economic benefit, or value, to their organization. "Buyer value" is measured in terms of the worth that a buyer perceives a supplier's offering will provide relative to price. "Supplier value" is the revenue stream the supplier is able to command minus the cost to provide the associated offering. VBS focuses on achieving greater value than alternatives for buyers while delivering attractive value back to suppliers.

Many organizations and sales people today remain entrenched in feature-, friendship- and price-based selling. The proliferation of purchasing committees and increased oversight of buyers is rapidly neutralizing this age-old sales practice. The buyer paradigm has shifted from "buy from the seller with a good product and competitive price that I most like" to "buy from the seller who presents the best total solution and terms that maximize the economic benefit to my company." Furthermore, because of the extensive product information now available on the Internet, buyers' expectations of sales people are changing. In particular, buyers are becoming less willing to meet with sales people who are essentially information providers. The entry chip is increasingly becoming the ability to bring new ideas and to prove economic value.

The financial stakes fueling VBS are underscored by a great deal of research conducted over the last 20 years. Three particularly relevant and compelling insights are the following:

- On average, a 1 percent increase in price translates into an 11 percent increase in profit (Marn and Rosiello 1992).
- New customer cost-of-sales is typically three to ten times as high as existing customer cost-of-sales.[3]
- Reducing unwanted customer defections by 5 percent can impact profits by 25 to 85 percent (Reichheld and Sasser Jr 1990).

In short, even small improvements in price and customer loyalty translate into significant contributions to company performance, and vice versa. Effective VBS is widely viewed as a means to positively impact all three of these metrics while also driving higher win rates, larger deal sizes, and reduced cycle times.

Four fundamental strategies exist for creating customer value:

1. *Lowest price accompanied by efficient purchasing and order-fulfillment.* This strategy equates to transactional "commodity-selling." Only the low cost producer in a given market can sustain this strategy – which typically negates the need for a sales force.
2. *Lowest total cost-in-use including acquisition, possession, and usage costs* (Figure 22.1). This strategy is a form of "value-based selling" that focuses on creating buyer cost advantages beyond just price.
3. *Higher value added to the buyer's own market offering.* This strategy is also a form of "value-based selling" and focuses on the upside revenue the buyer will attain by using the seller's offering.
4. *Multi-dimensional* strategy that combines elements of 1, 2 and/or 3.

Acquisition cost	Possession costs	Usage costs
Price	Interest	Field defects
Paperwork	Storage	Training
Shopping time	Quality control	User labor
Expediting	Taxes and insurance	Product longevity
Mistakes in order	Shrinkage and obsolescence	Replacement
Pre-purchase product evaluation	General internal handling	Disposal

FIGURE 22.1 Total cost-in-use components

The optimal VBS strategy is situation specific and depends on four factors:

- customer needs and preferences
- supplier capabilities
- the value of the customer to the supplier
- the competitive alternatives,

Because these four factors vary across the customer universe, many organizations are best served by hybrid VBS strategies. These strategies customize value propositions, sales processes and sales channels by customer segment or groupings of segments. Much of the challenge in VBS strategy design is determining the most cost-effective hybrid strategy that provides optimal effectiveness, efficiency, and flexibility, and that enables world-class execution.

The sales effectiveness system

At a fundamental level, VBS is best viewed as a continuous "customer value management cycle" (Figure 22.2).

End-to-end excellence in the customer value management cycle is the hallmark of exceptional VBS organizations. Gaps at any step result in value leakage in one of four forms: value given away, lost opportunity to create value, incomplete customer perception of value offered, or incomplete customer perception of value actually delivered.

Effective VBS has a specific and recognizable signature. Market offerings are developed according to customer-specific needs, buying processes, buying preferences, and addressable potential. These offerings are communicated and proven in terms of functional and economic benefits and worth. Meaningful differentiation

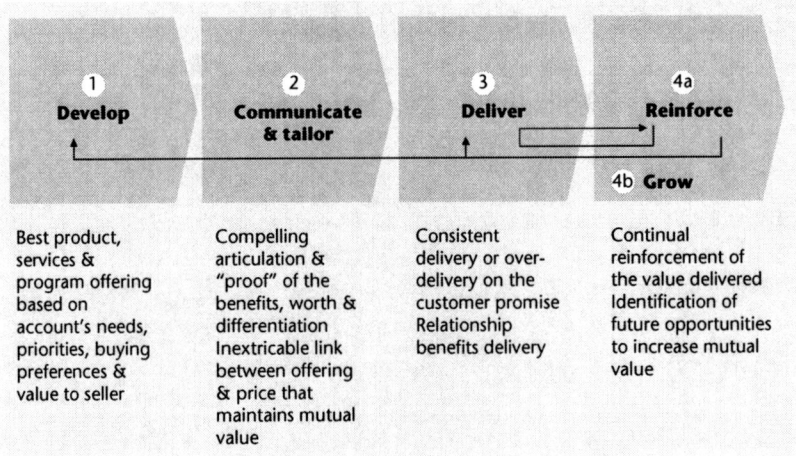

FIGURE 22.2 VBS customer value management cycle

from the next best alternative is clearly established. Pricing is based on value, and price reductions are always accompanied by reduction in the overall offering. The customer promise is kept or exceeded. Value delivered is quantified, reinforced, and leveraged to build the relationship to the next level. Both the buyer and seller benefit.

When successfully executed, VBS removes the burden from the buyer to "figure out" worth, and reduces the risk to the seller that the buyer will fail to do so. It provides buyers with the business case needed to justify the purchase decision within their own organization, based on terms that are meaningful to the spectrum of decision influencers. It also provides the seller with the business case needed to command a value-based price premium. VBS elevates the relationship from a friendship to a business relationship, predicated on mutual and verified benefits that over time result in strong trust and loyalty.

There are no silver bullets or short-cuts to achieving competitive VBS capabilities. The landscape is littered with leaders who have over-relied on training, new compensation plans, and updated brochures. In many cases, all three were pushed top-down with little consideration to addressing the barriers associated with truly changing sales person understanding, beliefs, behaviors, and skills.

Meaningful advances in VBS capability require a comprehensive, systematic, and integrated approach to strategy design and capability building. Sales and Marketing is a dynamic system – and is arguably one of the most complex functions in any business. Each of the key components in this system must be addressed and aligned to accomplish end-to-end excellence in the customer value management cycle. A detailed overview of these components is depicted in Figure 22.3.

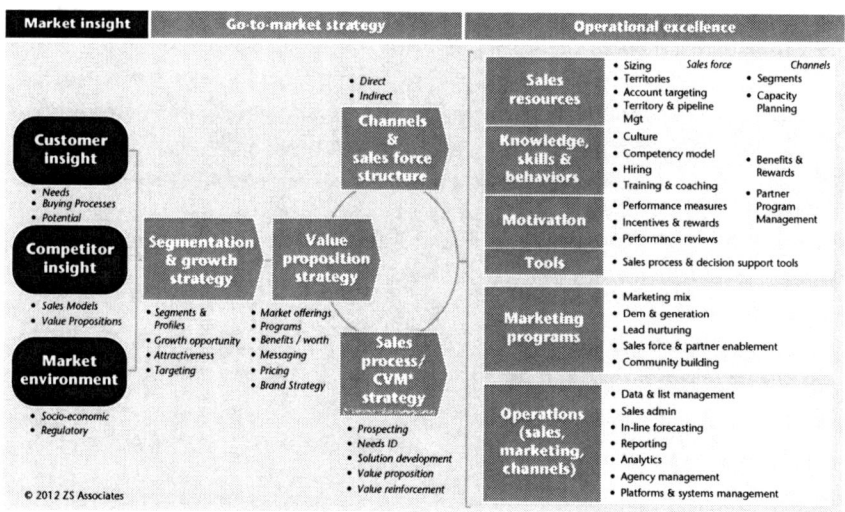

FIGURE 22.3 Sales effectiveness system

The sales effectiveness system has a strong left to right hierarchy. Organizations frequently undermine their VBS efforts by investing in downstream components before they have sufficiently addressed those upstream. Effective and detailed customer insight, competitor insight, segmentation, value propositions, sales processes, and sales force structure and roles are a precursor to sales force implementation. Otherwise, individual sales persons are left to their own devices to develop their own value propositions and sales processes in the face of sophisticated and demanding buyers. Past experience suggests that the top 10–20 percent of the sales force could do this well, but that the remainder will falter.

Alignment of the operational elements is equally important. Team sizing and individual account assignments have to ensure appropriate sales force capacity to cover target segments. New VBS knowledge, skills, and behaviors must be fostered through competency evaluations, training, coaching, and hiring. Performance measures and incentive plans must be aligned to motivate performance focus and accountability. And new tools must be put in place to enable the sales force to execute VBS.

Failure to address any one of these critical components, as well as other marketing program and operations elements, will reduce VBS effectiveness. When it comes to VBS, the sales effectiveness system is a recipe, not a menu.

Sales and Marketing alignment

The sales effectiveness framework helps underscore the criticality of Sales and Marketing collaboration to VBS capability building. Customer insight, competitor insight, segmentation strategy, and value proposition strategy (including pricing) are the domain of "strategic marketing." Furthermore, it is Marketing that should assume the responsibility for maintaining and providing the detailed value proposition content critical to effective VBS.

The traditional division of labor between Marketing and Sales has failed to accomplish the coordination between strategy and execution required for VBS. In many companies the relationship between Marketing and Sales is designed to be more or less a "baton hand-off." Marketing creates the strategy and then hands off the baton to Sales to execute.

This model has failed to lead to strong VBS for at least three fundamental reasons:

1. In many B2B companies, Marketing is predominantly focused on marketing communications. These companies may not have a strategic marketing capability.
2. The strategies that have been developed may not reflect market realities or may not lend themselves to effective execution.
3. The sales force is not confident in the strategy and is therefore unwilling to take the personal financial risk associated with implementation (e.g. vis-à-vis their variable incentive compensation plans).

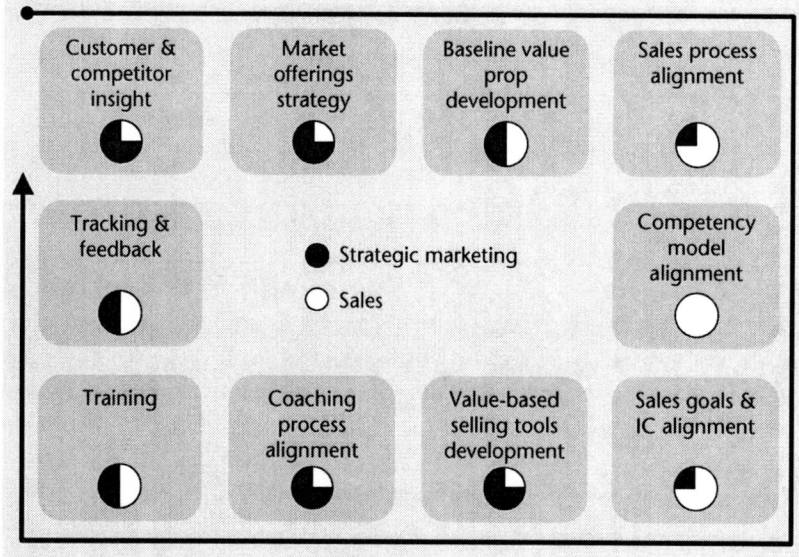

FIGURE 22.4 Sales and Marketing "three-legged race" collaboration (case example)

Overcoming these barriers requires Marketing and Sales to move from a "baton hand-off" to a "three-legged race." Each function has unique information and skills critical to many aspects of both strategy and implementation. Both are major stakeholders in the success of VBS. New "collaborative business processes" hold promise for achieving the alignment between Marketing and Sales necessary for VBS (Moorman *et al.* 2007). As a case in point, Figure 22.4 shows the mutual roles that Sales and Marketing played in a recent and highly successful VBS effectiveness transformation at one Fortune 200 company.

Marketing's and Sales' shared imperative to develop VBS capability is likely to be the "burning platform" that finally leads to more effective collaboration between these two mutually dependent functions.

VBS go-to-market strategy

Many practitioners narrowly view VBS as a sales practice. The reality is much different. VBS is as much a go-to-market strategy as it is a sales methodology. Segmentation strategy, value proposition strategy (including pricing), sales process strategy, channels strategy, and sales force structure take on unique characteristics under VBS.

Account segmentation strategy

Value-based selling requires B2B segmentation strategies comprised of at least two dimensions, as illustrated in Figure 22.5. The horizontal dimension partitions the

			What is valuable to them			
			Needs segments (primary marketing research)			
			Solution seekers	Relationship oriented	Best of breed	Price buyers
How valuable they are to us	Potential segments (secondary data analysis)	Quintile 5 ($15–7M)	149 (accounts)	61	250	462
		Quintile 4 ($6.9–4M)	217	112	493	845
		Quintile 3 ($3.9–2.5M)	127	237	982	1,295
		Quintile 2 ($2.4–1.0M)	198	192	2,031	4,754
		Quintile 1 ($0.9–0.1M)	72	450	3,972	7,463

FIGURE 22.5 Two-dimensional B2B segmentation (case example)

account universe into "needs-based" segments. These segments group accounts based on common needs, buying preferences, and buying processes. The vertical dimension partitions the account universe into "potential based" segments. These segments group accounts based on similar total opportunity to the seller.

Together these two dimensions provide an actionable picture of the account universe based on (1) what buyers in the segment value, and (2) how valuable the accounts in the segment are to the seller.

Segments are the building blocks around which value proposition strategy, sales process, channels strategy, and sales force structure are designed. Effective segmentation strategies rely on deep customer insight.

To be useful to strategy design, customer insight must be available in a way in which it can be collectively evaluated and considered. This implies a business process that is led by Marketing and that captures and integrates information from many sources. Common customer insight sources include the following:

1. Primary marketing research.
2. Acquired account-specific data (e.g. D&B, Info Group, Hoovers, etc.).
3. Internal customer relationship management (CRM) systems.
4. Sales, customer service, customer support, and engineering feedback.
5. Customer loyalty and satisfaction tracking studies.
6. Win/loss assessments.
7. Syndicated studies.
8. Internet searches.
9. Social media.

Many companies underinvest in customer insight at the expense of their VBS aspirations. Exceptional customer insight is a strategic advantage when it comes to VBS.

Market offering element	Benefit	Economic worth
Through our inventory management service, we will staff your supply room with our employees (a feature).	Our inventory management service will lower your labor costs because our workers do not belong to a union	With our inventory management service, your firm will lower its annual inventory costs by $225,000

Example for a complete market offering

Market offering elements (features)	Benefits	Economic worth
Expertise in customer's business • Provide team with business & technical expertise explicitly focused on your industry • Thought leadership in emerging issues & solutions • Knowledge management tools for reps • Account specific web page	• Don't have to repeat myself or train the next person when I call • Don't get handed off to the next person • Get provider who knows me & my business	
Tailored solutions • Flexible solutions developed specifically for your needs & priorities (list products, services, programs, systems) • On-site technical expertise & customized configurations • Simplified pricing structures	• Client team who understands my needs • Cost-effective solutions that meet my needs • No unnecessary "extras"	• Save $3M per month thru increased labor productivity • Increase revenues by 5% through increased manufacturing capacity • Reduce product disposal costs by 3% per year • Reduce installation & operation risks (contractual guarantees)
Productivity improvements • Applications for streamlining resource requirements & minimizing total cost-in-use • ROI analysis tools	• Value-delivered reporting (proof) • Proactive issues identification & alerts	
Service excellence • Seamless customer experience across all touch points • Second level response team • Response time contractual standards	• Rapid response • Single point of contact	
Purchase efficiency • Streamlined contracts • Service charge transparency • On-line purchasing for repeat & simple orders • Integrated electronic invoicing	• Easy to work with (responsive) • Transparent pricing • Streamlined invoicing	

FIGURE 22.6 Marketing offerings and value proposition (case example)

Value proposition strategy

Value propositions are the detailed communication of the benefits and worth the customer will realize from the market offering being proposed to them (Figure 22.6). The opportunity to create customer value extends well beyond the functional benefits of a seller's product. Companies also create customer value through the services, programs, and relationship benefits they provide their customers.

A frequent challenge that organizations struggle with is the difference between a value proposition, a positioning statement, and brand strategy (Figure 22.7). Marketers often talk about "the 30 second elevator speech" that the sales force needs. This view is flawed, and based on a lack of understanding of a sales person's actual operating environment and role.

As was shown in Figure 22.6, value propositions are a detailed articulation of the company's proposed market offering – and the economic benefits and worth associated with that market offering – in relation to a buyer's needs and opportunities. While the sales force can benefit from a succinct 30-second version of the value proposition, the conversation that they have with buyers is much more involved. This is another example of a situation where a collaborative business process can overcome a disconnect that can occur between Marketing and Sales.

Development of compelling value propositions can be viewed as a step-wise process (Figure 22.8).

The process begins by inventorying all of the ways the company already does, and could, create customer value. Defining the potential "market offering

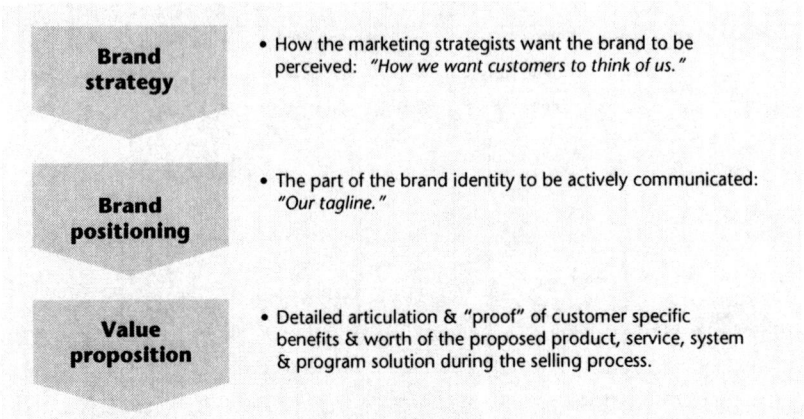

FIGURE 22.7 Brand positioning versus value proposition

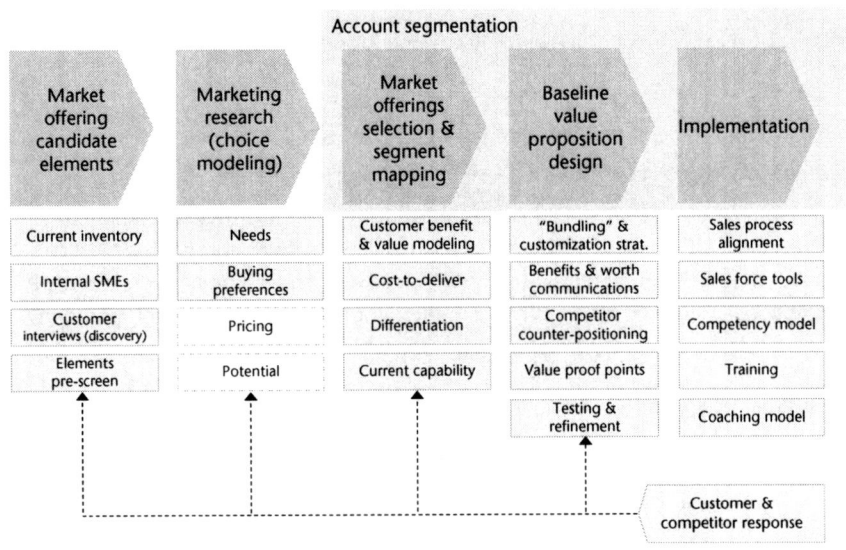

FIGURE 22.8 Value proposition development roadmap

inventory" requires consideration of the customer value chain – both in terms of total cost-in-use and customer revenue generation.

The second step is to conduct broader primary marketing research to explicitly evaluate customer needs and priorities relative to the specific set of market offerings that are in question (i.e. those being debated). A critical success factor in this research is to understand the relative degree of importance that different customers place on each potential market offering. Research that poses the question "what is important to you" will usually get the response "everything and at a low price." Choice-models that force the respondent to communicate relative priorities amongst possible market offering alternatives are the most effective techniques for establishing relative importance.

Selection of market offering elements for each customer segment should be based on a number of attractiveness dimensions. Some of the most important include degree of value created for the customer, cost to deliver, degree of competitive differentiation achieved, current capability, and customer willingness to pay. In some cases, impact on the customer's total cost-in-use and revenue generation must be modeled to fully understand the extent of customer value created.

Once market offerings have been designed and mapped to segments, the challenge is to translate those offerings into specific customer benefits and worth. Benefits should be communicated in the customer's language wherever possible. Depending on the value proposition strategy, worth is communicated in terms of acquisition cost savings, total cost-in-use savings, and increased customer revenue associated with using the solution. In most selling situations, the specific worth an individual customer will realize must be refined as part of the selling process itself. Best-in-class value sellers collaborate with the customer during the estimation process to ensure accurate data and strong buy-in to key assumptions.

There can be complex interactions between a given market offering and a buyer's total cost-in-use and revenue synergies. For this reason, and because the data required may be excessively difficult to access or highly confidential, it is not always possible to fully quantify the economic impact of every component of a given value proposition. In such situations the focus should be two-fold:

- Priority should be placed on quantifying the economic impact of the value proposition elements that are most differentiated from those of competitors and also highly important to the buyer.
- Where economic values cannot be estimated for these components, other performance parameters should then be quantified. For instance, these might include specifics on delivery times, defection rates, or a host of other quantifiable factors important to the buyer's success.

In all cases, it is critical that the seller be able to "prove" the value being asserted. VBS companies use many techniques to substantiate their value claims. Common examples include quantitative modeling using customer data, case studies, side-by-side trials in conjunction with the buyer, third party trials, and customer testimonials.

The degree to which value propositions will be tailored to specific customers is an important aspect of the value proposition strategy. A wide spectrum of value proposition strategies exists. Figure 22.9 summarizes the fundamental options ranging from completely standardized to highly customized.

As the degree of customer customization increases, the role of the sales force in developing the value proposition becomes more prominent. In highly consultative sales situations the seller may develop unique customer solutions that draw

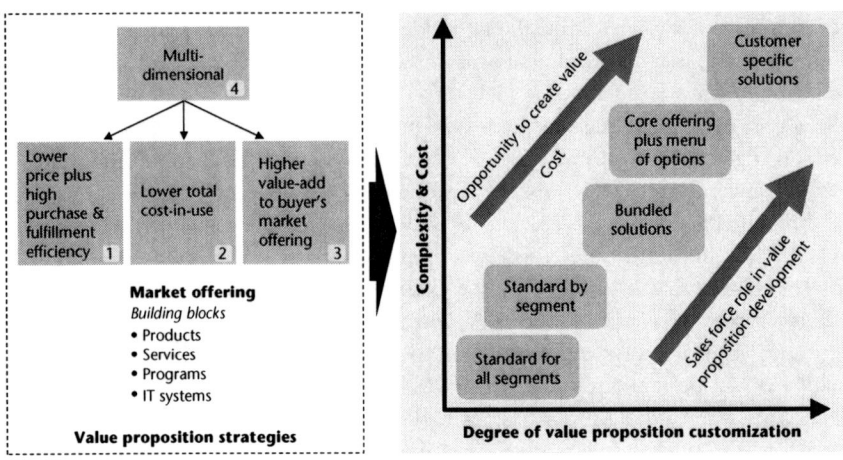

FIGURE 22.9   Value proposition strategy continuum

on a broad cross-section of the company's capabilities. In some cases the proposed solution may even require changes in the seller's and buyer's operations, or partnership with other vendors or business partners. High customization provides the greatest opportunity to create customer value. It also increases cost of sales and operations. Mutual value creation for both buyer and supplier is achieved when the VBS strategy balances customer benefits with willingness to pay. Providing benefits that a customer will not pay for, through either price or volume, equates to giving away value and profit.

Hybrid value proposition strategies often present the greatest opportunity to profitably maximize value creation across target customer segments. Such approaches employ a mix of value proposition strategies based on customer segment or account-specific profile. For example, more standardized value propositions may be targeted at lower value segments or those that have simpler needs. Customized value propositions may then be targeted at higher value customers with more complex needs. Hybrid value proposition strategies lead directly to hybrid sales channels and more complex sales force structures. The reason is that different channels and sales structures vary considerably in their ability to cost-effectively deliver specific value propositions and sales processes.

Best practice VBS marketers create a "baseline" value proposition for each target segment regardless of the degree of customization that will ultimately take place. Baseline value propositions provide the market offering and associated customer benefits and worth starting point. For segments receiving no customization, the sales force can leverage baseline value propositions "as is." For segments receiving customization, sales persons tailor the baseline value proposition based on the specific account's needs, priorities, and value to their own company. Even for enterprise and large "segment of one" accounts where significant customization may be required, it is beneficial to provide Sales with a starting point from which to work.

Editing allows sales persons greater sales efficiency and effectiveness than creating from scratch.

The role of pricing within the overall value proposition is of special criticality to VBS. The difference between economic value delivered by the seller's solution and the seller's price represents the net benefit to the buyer. When this net benefit is greater than that of alternatives, the buyer has a strong business case for selecting that seller. Obviously, one way to increase the net benefit is to reduce price. However, as has been pointed out, even small decreases in price have significant negative impact on profit.

Cost-plus pricing and match-the-competitor pricing are relatively common approaches used by many B2B sales organizations. Neither are tied to actual value creation and often lead to value and profit shifting from the seller to the buyer. VBS calls for "value-based pricing." Under "value-based pricing," pricing is linked to the actual economic worth of a given solution. The idea then is to set price such that two conditions are achieved:

1. The net benefit to the buyer is slightly greater than that of alternatives.
2. The commensurate net benefit to the seller achieves the seller's margin requirements or better.

When these two conditions are not simultaneously met, one of two conditions exists:

1. The solution and associated price need to be further tailored to provide greater net benefit relative to the customer's needs and alternatives.
2. The seller does not have a competitive solution or cost of goods sold (COGS) (and/or needs to reshape the buyer's understanding of their needs and solution requirements).

VBS and value-based pricing are inextricably linked. One does not exist without the other.

Sales process

The sales process is in many ways the backbone of VBS. Sales processes, such as the example shown in Figure 22.10, provide the roadmap by which account-specific value proposition development, communication, proof, tailoring, delivery, and reinforcement are consistently and effectively accomplished.

Sales processes are not recipes for success to be followed to the letter. For instance, they do not prescribe customer needs, the value proposition, or the negotiation strategy to be employed. Rather, sales processes provide a logical progression of activities that maximize success at each stage in the customer value management cycle. Sales processes greatly improve sales discipline. Examples of the benefits highlighted by the sales managers of a large financial services organization are provided in Figure 22.11.

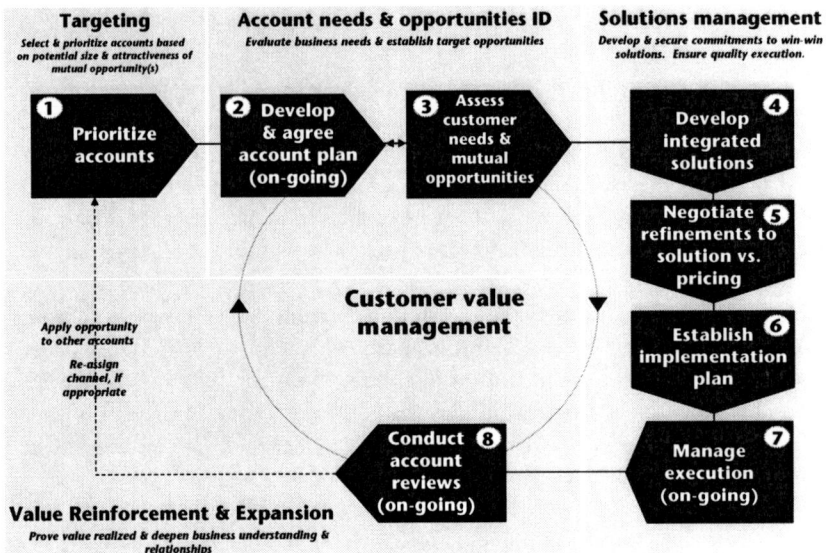

FIGURE 22.10 VBS sales process (case example)

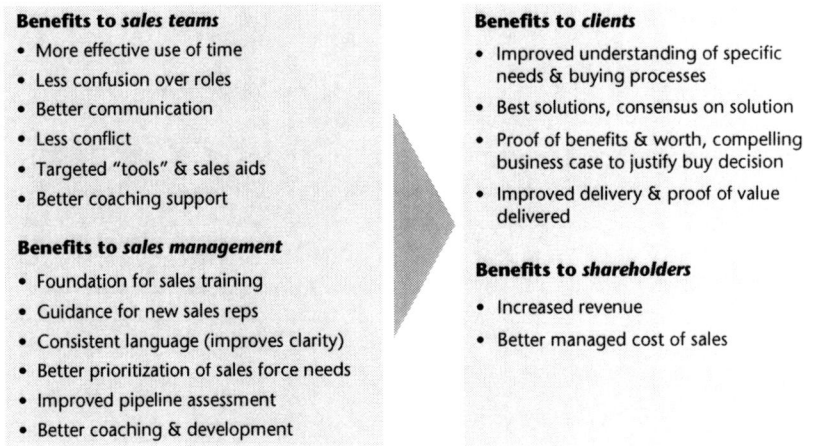

FIGURE 22.11 Sales process benefits (case example)

VBS sales processes dive deeper than just the top-level phases exemplified in Figure 22.10. The best sales processes incorporate a number of elements under each phase including: critical activities, advance objectives and metrics, roles and responsibility definitions for all functions engaged, and key enablers available to support that phase. When developed in this way, the sales process provides the playbook for the company's customer value management strategy.

VBS sales processes tend to have a number of common traits:

- They seek to identify and confirm customer needs *before* engaging in discussions about the seller's products and services.
- They seek to explicitly link the seller's proposed solution back to the buyer's needs and priorities. Often times the seller contributes "consultative" value through this process alone.
- They seek to gain agreement that the seller's solution addresses the buyer's needs *before* addressing price.
- They link price to the specific value that will be contributed by the solution. They also seek to ensure that changes in the solution are accompanied by corresponding changes in price and vice-versa.
- They ensure that value actually delivered vis-à-vis the original customer agreement is tracked and communicated. In this way, they ensure that value perception does not trail off over time, and establish an ongoing interaction that reveals new opportunities.

Sales channels strategy and sales force structure

Sales channels strategy and sales force structure dictate the type of sales resource that will be deployed against different activities, offerings, and account types. The primary objective of sales channels strategy and sales force structure is to determine the most cost-effective approach for delivering the value proposition strategy and sales process to each of the company's target customer segments.

A diverse range of sales channels are being employed by today's B2B organizations. Common examples include the following:

- global account management
- key account management
- field sales
- inside sales
- business partners
- e-channels.

There are literally hundreds of permutations on these basic approaches. With the evolution to hybrid value propositions and the proliferation of sales channel options, sales force strategy design has become complex. Many factors must be considered in their design. The factors that we have found to be the most significant are summarized in Figure 22.12.

Assigning the right accounts to each sales channel is as important as the design itself. VBS organizations develop and manage centralized business processes that ensure objective account to channel assignment on a periodic basis. These business processes address both current customers and prospects. And they mitigate "land grabs" or other politically driven processes that create mismatches between sales resource and what is actually required. These same business processes tend to ensure optimal sales resource sizing and allocation across channels. Inaccurate sizing leads

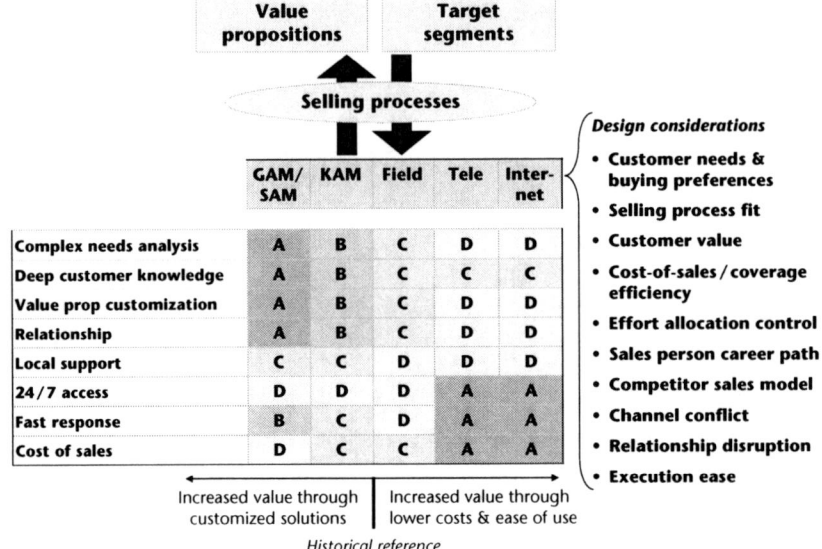

FIGURE 22.12 Sales channels and sales force structure design considerations

to coverage gaps and inability for the sales force to fully execute the required sales process with target accounts.

VBS implementation and execution

Transforming a sales force from a friendship, features, and price focus to a value focus is always difficult. Tailoring and communicating value proposition benefits and economic worth requires strong business acumen and deep knowledge of their customers' business models. In many cases VBS sellers must be able to model the impact of their offering on the buyer's total cost in use; or help forecast the increased revenue the buyer will achieve in the sales of its own product. They need to speak the language of finance while being able to address the unique needs and issues of diverse decision influencers. VBS requires knowledge, skills, effort, support, and tools well beyond those necessary for friendship, features, and price-based selling. This challenge provides one explanation for why so many selling organizations have not been able to break free of their old selling habits, even though they realize the imperative to do so.

Three downstream components in the sales effectiveness framework play a particularly critical role in driving VBS implementation and execution:

- VBS specific competency models
- VBS selling tools that support each stage of the sales process
- Expert VBS coaching and apprenticeship.

For most sales forces, a majority of sales persons will have been selling for many years. During this time they have developed deeply entrenched work styles and viewpoints on how to succeed. Convincing and motivating these individuals to re-invent themselves, and enabling them to do so, is perhaps the single greatest challenge associated with large-scale VBS initiatives.

An important tool in this regard is the sales force competency model and evaluation process. The competency model paints a picture of "what is expected" and "what success looks like" under VBS. A new approach to competency models and evaluation is typically required for VBS. In particular, VBS competency models tend to be organized around the VBS sales process. In this way they provide context for competencies that are meaningful for the sales force, and that provide the template against which meaningful performance reviews and coaching can be conducted.

A well-designed VBS competency model sets the foundation for a number of downstream elements including: (1) the sales force's understanding of the new expectations; (2) the evaluation and placement of sales people in new roles; (3) the accuracy and relevance of future individual performance evaluations; (4) the quality and specificity of coaching; and (5) the quality of future hiring decisions.

Quality VBS sales tools also play an essential role in both motivating and enabling the sales force to adopt and perfect VBS. Figure 22.13 summarizes some of the most critical tools and demonstrates how they fit into the sales process. These tools should not be confused with sales force automation (SFA) or CRM tools that the sales force may already be using. VBS tools are largely a new phenomenon and meant to enable the sales force at each stage of the selling process. Such tools allow the sales force to more effectively and efficiently identify needs, develop solutions, communicate and prove solutions, negotiate price versus solution trade-offs, and reinforce value. Furthermore, since the tools sequentially align with each step in the VBS sales process, use of the tools indirectly helps sales people to learn and adopt the process.

Of particular criticality to VBS transformations is winning the hearts and minds – and building the expertise – of the first-line sales managers. Their understanding, buy-in, and expertise in value-based selling will strongly shape those of the representatives reporting to them. A first-line sales manager who is opposed to the company's VBS strategy, or who lacks VBS expertise and skills, can undermine the success of an entire district, or more.

Winning hearts and minds of the first-line sales managers – and of the sales representatives – can only be achieved to a limited degree through logical argument and leadership mandate. Top-down approaches alone are prone to fail. Sales force buy-in and engagement requires that four gates be opened. First, managers and sales people must fully "understand" how the new behaviors and skills are actually different than the current. A pervasive belief that "we already do that" has derailed many VBS initiatives. Second, they must "believe" two things: (1) that IF I adopt those behaviors and skills that I will be more successful, AND (2) that I have the aptitude to achieve those behaviors and skills IF I so choose. Third, they must feel

340 Mike Moorman

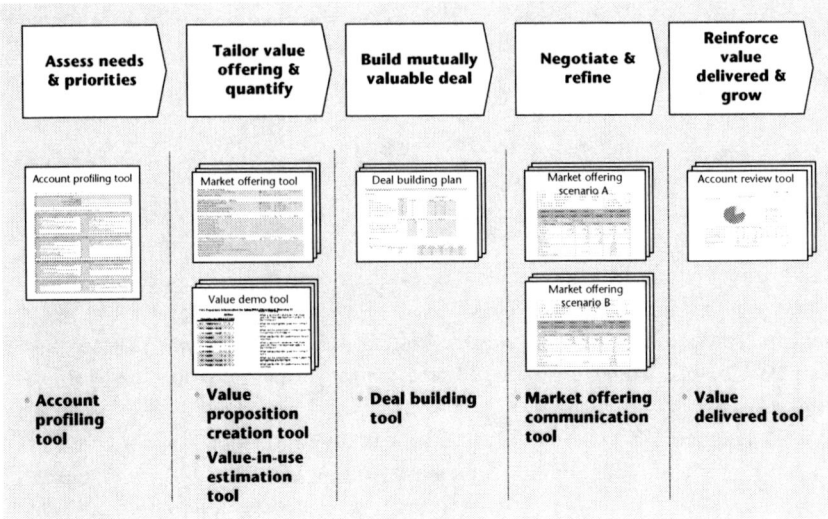

FIGURE 22.13 VBS software tools requirements (case example)

motivated to make the effort and to take the risk associated with change. Fourth, they must experience positive aspects from the change early enough in the trial period to stay committed.

Two approaches in combination have proven particularly effective in winning sales force hearts and minds. Part 1 is a compelling case for change that clearly communicates why change is imperative, the specifics of the change relative to the present situation, a believable path to get there, ways in which the organization will assist individuals in the change, and what's in it for the company, the customer, and the sales persons. Part 2 offers compelling proof points that the desired change is feasible and will deliver. The best proof points typically derive from early-experience teams that trial the approaches and tools, or from individuals that are on an adoption fast-track relative to the rest of the sales force. Testimonials and case examples from these teams or individuals carry significant weight with their peers. Failure to adopt these types of bottom-up approaches to implementation and change management places VBS initiatives at high risk of sales force rejection.

Assuming that hearts and minds have been won, the quality and rigor of first-line sales manager coaching is in many ways the "secret sauce" for VBS capability building. This is particularly true when large shifts in mindsets, behaviors, and skills are being sought. Training is an important and necessary aspect of developing VBS knowledge. However, value-based selling is predominantly an apprenticed skill. Training is good for conveying concepts, frameworks, and methods. Value-based selling is a skill requiring complex problem solving, business acumen, and adaptability. It is developed over time through practice and coaching from a VBS expert. Coaching also plays a critical role in motivating sales reps to trial and to

High impact:

- **Sales process**
  - Needs assessment & validation
  - Solution development & validation
  - Negotiations
  - Communication / proof
  - Value reinforcement
- **Planning**
  - Account planning
  - Call planning
  - Account targeting
  - Pipeline management

Hygiene:

- **Basic sales skills**
  - Communication
  - Cold calling
  - Closing
  - Dealing with concerns
  - Time allocation
  - Tools

FIGURE 22.14 VBS sales managers focus heavily on advanced coaching elements

stick with value-based selling behaviors during the uncomfortable period of new behaviors and skill building.

At steady state, world-class sales managers spend upward of 50 percent of their time coaching. During VBS implementation this allocation can be even higher. The primary focus of VBS coaching is depicted in Figure 22.14.

First-line sales managers must be expert in VBS to be effective VBS coaches. This requirement presents a dilemma during large-scale transformations. Many of the first-line sales managers may themselves never have been apprenticed in VBS, and are not VBS experts. In such cases, carefully designed programs are required to rapidly build manager expertise in VBS. Such programs typically include a combination of extensive training and reinforcement, outside hiring, frequent sharing of issues and best practices, coaching by senior leadership, and enlistment of outside advisors.

Of course the other components in the sales effectiveness framework are also mission critical for VBS. The measures, incentive systems, and reporting have to motivate VBS. The organization has to hire and place the right kind of people. Performance reviews have to reinforce the right behaviors, skills, and accountability. Marketing operations and sales operations have to help enable many aspects of execution. IT has to build and support the right information and tools. In this regard, VBS is a business initiative, not just a sales force initiative.

Conclusion

VBS capability increasingly will be a differentiator between winners and losers in B2B markets. As VBS strategies become the norm in B2B markets, the strategic advantage will shift from strategy to quality of execution. The relative complexity of building and executing VBS strategies ensures that meaningful and sustained differentiation will be achievable for some time to come.

While there are many organizations that have minimal VBS capability, there are also many that have made great progress. This latter group provides an important proof of feasibility. Successfully transforming the Sales and Marketing organizations of today to avert commoditization and to compete with value-minded competitors takes strong leadership skills. A comprehensive, purposefully orchestrated approach to capability building that systematically addresses all sales effectiveness drivers is required. Sales and Marketing has to adopt collaborative business processes. Customer segmentation, value propositions, selling processes, channel strategy, and sales force structure have to be carefully designed and aligned. Special attention to competency models and the decisions they support is necessary. Strong coaching and VBS tools are required to motivate adoption, improve capability, and sustain momentum. And the job is never finished. Sustained VBS leadership will result from focused continuous improvement.

Implications for innovation in pricing

The point has been made in this article that "value-based selling" and "value-based pricing" are inextricably linked. When they are not, sellers will nearly always give away value or, alternatively, be viewed as too expensive by the buyer.

Value-based selling organizations rigorously link their pricing strategy to the market offering options. Pricing strategy for these organizations is dictated by three factors: the economic worth of the solution to the customer, the economic worth of the next best alternative, the cost to deliver.

With VBS, price is not negotiated independent of solution. "Too high a price" implies that there are elements included in the market offering that the buyer does not value. Negotiations are then oriented around price-offering trade-offs that optimize value from the buyer's perspective. By approaching the selling process in this way, the VBS seller maintains their necessary margin and win rates, and avoids the value and profit shifting so common in many organizations.

Value-based selling and value-based pricing place certain demands on the selling organization and individual sales persons including the following:

1. The selling organization must have deep knowledge of the buyer's business model and the ways in which their offering will impact the buyer's total cost-in-use and the buyer's sales of their own products.
2. The selling organization must be able to quantify and prove the value relative to alternatives. In many cases, this will actually require the sales person to have the business acumen necessary to tailor the quantification and proof to individual buyers. Marketing will typically need to play a significant role in establishing proof points and enabling the field with the information and VBS tools they require.

3. Individual sales people will have to learn and apply a new level of discipline in their sales processes. They must resist the urge to jump into product or service discussions in advance of understanding and validating customer needs. They must also resist the urge to discuss price prior to presenting the proposed market offering. Price and market offering are inextricably linked.
4. Finally, leadership must have the courage to "walk away" from customers who reject a value-based solution and price once all solution/price combinations have been exhausted. Unprofitable customers are best left to the competition to suffer.

Notes

1 An earlier version of this paper has been published as ZS Associates White Paper in 2007.
2 Source: ZS Associates B2B VBS engagements.
3 Source: ZS experience based on hundreds of sales force strategy studies.

References

Marn, M. V. and Rosiello, R. L. (1992) Managing price, gaining profit. *Harvard Business Review*, Sep–Oct, pp. 84–94.

Moorman, M. B., Rossman, J. and Zoltners, A. A. (2007) Redefining the relationship between marketing and sales: The frontier of B2B marketing and sales effectiveness. *ZS Insights B2B*, December 2007.

Reichheld, F. F. and Sasser Jr, W. E. (1990) Zero defections: Quality comes to services. *Harvard Business Review*, Sep–Oct.

23

THE THICK AND THIN TAILS OF PRICING

Darren Huxol

The challenge

In significant business-to-business (B2B) transactions there is a substantial amount of benefit and risk transferred between the seller and the buyer. This transfer initially occurs through the pricing and contractual agreements associated with the transaction. As the product and/or service performance is demonstrated, the ramification of the actual benefit and risk transferred is understood. This transfer can happen immediately, over many years or even decades. See Figure 23.1 for examples.

Key industries applicable to this paper:

- large engineered solutions
- large software deployments
- long cycle durable goods
- insurance products
- financial service products.

This paper will explore the following key fundamental assumptions associated with these transactions: economic value, sustainability of competitive advantage, cost of market share, and cost of goods sold (CGS) variation driven by product utilization and scope of deliverable.

Seller implications

The seller's first assumption is how much incremental economic value can be derived in price from the sale of a new product vs. the customer's next best alternative. The seller should price their product equal to current market pricing or any new competitive product price points plus a portion of the incremental economic benefit generated to the buyer from the product. The next assumption should be to understand the sustainability of the economic benefit advantage in the context of

The thick and thin tails of pricing 345

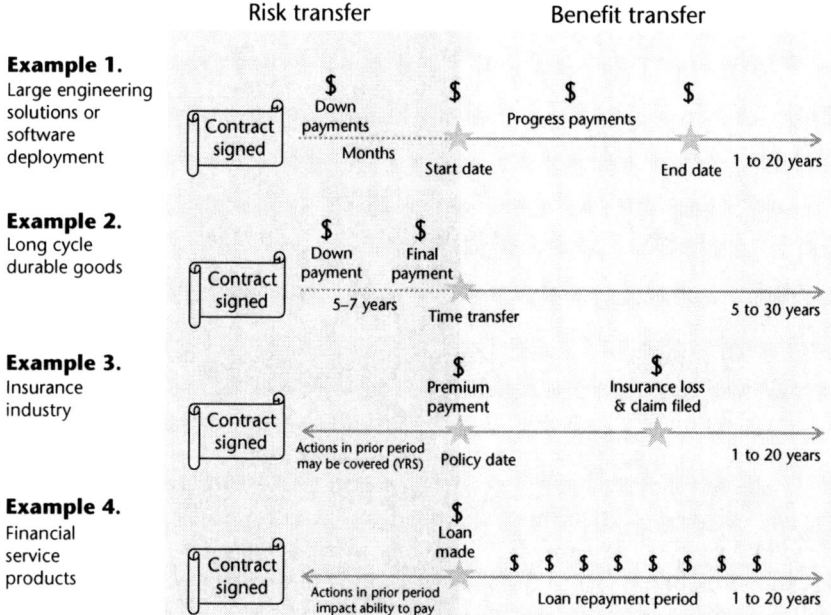

FIGURE 23.1 Risk and benefit transfer in different industries

competitive actions. This assumption will translate into market share targets and a required expense to obtain this target market share. The expense can be categorized into the following categories: branding, product promotion, amount of economic benefit shared, warranty, and performance guarantees/liquidated damages. Market share and the resulting volume will drive CGS assumptions. The CGS assumption should be divided into two types: one that is somewhat controllable (manufacturing), and one that is less controllable and will vary by customer. The less controllable CGS assumptions can be attributed to customer product utilization and scope of deliverable. Differences in product utilization will drive a variation in cost in long-term service agreements or where warranties extend over long periods. Scope of deliverable will drive cost in that in many of these transactions there are many unknowns intrinsic to the transaction.

Buyer implications

The buyer has a similar if not somewhat opposite set of challenges and assumptions. The first challenge is to not overpay for under performance or a product that does not provide the economic benefit promised. The second challenge is to ensure that there is a good competitive supply side environment, and that potential suppliers are progressing technologies and new products that develop more economic value to the buyer. The next set of challenges relates to the actual transactional negotiation: How much economic benefit should be given to the seller? What are the buyer's remedies for future performance issues? How does the buyer obtain the widest possible set of scenarios for product utilization or unknowns around scope requirements? In terms of a longer relationship, how does the buyer ensure that suppliers make a reasonable (not outstanding) return and stay in business for future needs?

Relating examples to key assumptions

The concept of **economic value** is probably most pronounced in **long cycle durable goods** transactions. For discussion purposes, let's take the purchase of an all-new, white paper designed airplane. The buyer may be required to make a decision five years before the actual product can be delivered. Therefore, the buyer must choose between a few alternatives which can only be understood via the review of drawings, engineering-based arguments, and promises/historical performance of the supplier. If the economic benefit is NOT delivered via the airplane chosen and delivered by an alternative not chosen, the buyer may be jeopardizing the entire airline's viability, given the airline may not be competitive to their customer base vs. an airline which chose the alternative over a long period of time. **Large engineered solutions** may have similar significance to the buyer and **large software deployments** can affect the efficiency of the buyer and thus impact the buyer's competitiveness. The concept can also be seen in **insurance** and **financial service products** via the cost of money arbitrage.

Sustainability of competitive advantage is a huge concern in the **large software deployment** industry which is a driving force in determining a software company's pricing strategy. Pricing can range from free (given away to drive adoption) to extremely expensive (which includes increasing switching cost to the buyer). Both strategies attempt to drive sustainability in an industry which has shorter and shorter technology to commercialization cycles and large amounts of capital inflow driving intense competition. This concept is also applicable to **long cycle durable goods** industries where market position can change dramatically if a competitor develops a disruptive technology that drives more economic value. Ultimately, the ability to continually develop new proprietary technology to meet current and future needs will drive a sustainability of competitive advantage.

Cost of market share is easily highlighted in **financial services products** and the **insurance** industry which require large promotional budgets to obtain sales volumes big enough to use the "Law of Large Numbers" to help mitigate or diversify the inherit risk in the products. The management of these branding and product promotional/distribution incentive costs is a huge part of the pricing equation. This concept is also very valid in **long cycle durable goods** where there are large performance guarantees or liquidated damages (cost to win) that incentivize buyers to accept the risk of potential future product performance issues.

Product utilization is a significant concept in the **insurance** industry. The **insurance** industry has developed large underwriting departments to understand how the insurance product is going to be used, and to ensure that pricing is commensurate with the risk associated with the specific utility. **Long cycle durable goods** original equipment manufacturers (OEMs) who provide long-term service agreements to support their products will want to understand how their product is going to be used, given that service cost can vary by type and amount of utilization.

Scope of deliverable is a huge part of the commercial negotiation in **large software deployments** and **large engineered solutions**. Given that the deliverable is usually customized for the buyer, there is a significant amount of unknowns to the seller which can drive cost significantly.

Thick and thin tails

Given the preceding points, opinions will be made by both the seller and buyer; thus, there will be by definition a range of possible outcomes to the transaction. If you plotted the outcomes on a graph, you could develop a histogram or scatter plot and derive an associated distribution curve. The difference between the seller's and buyer's expectations of the shape of this distribution curve (in regard to a specific transaction) is at the core of the issue.

This paper will focus on two distribution curves: (1) a tight distribution curve with a limited set of outcomes (more certainty), and (2) a wide distribution curve with many outcomes (less certainty). The more the product performance is predictable, the tighter the distribution curve and the "thinner the tail." Less predictable outcomes result in a "thicker tail." Both types of distribution curves provide challenges to effective pricing strategies; this paper will focus on the thick tail distribution curve (see Figure 23.2).

The strategies

1. Portfolio price optimization: The goal of this strategy is for the seller to find a point of optimization of revenue via the intersection of the accumulated market share or risk assumed (X axis) and revenue received (Y axis). This has also been referred to as the efficient frontier of capital utilization. The seller must also switch from viewing the management of price through each single transaction to looking at the aggregate of price over the portfolio of all transactions. The **insurance** and **financial services** industries depend on this strategy to diversify risk and ensure optimal leverage of their capital (see Figure 23.3).

    The risk involved generally can be characterized as one of the following: under-pricing for the value generated, loss of market share and lower overall absolute margin, or the assumption of a disproportionate amount of exposure to risk. To effectively deploy this strategy there must be a critical mass of core long-term customers which represent a diversified set of opportunities and or risk. **Long cycle durable goods** OEMs will also use this strategy in their service business to find price elasticity and defend against non-OEM parts.

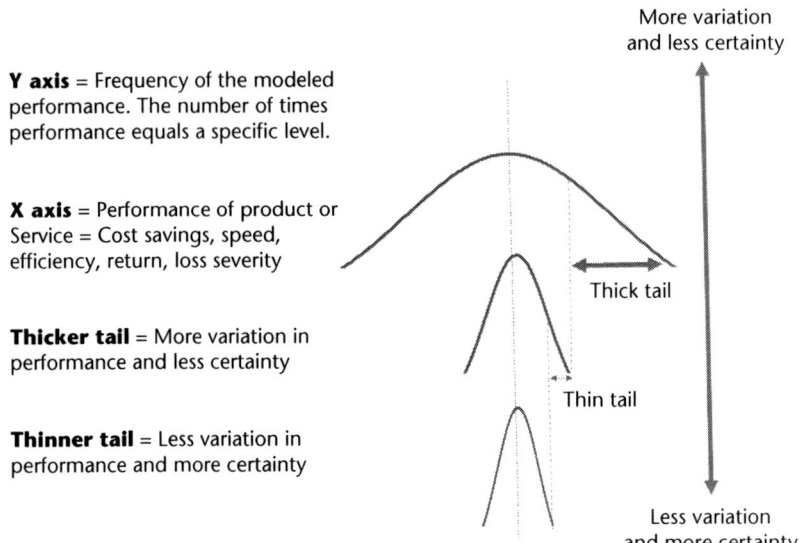

FIGURE 23.2 The thick and thin tail in pricing

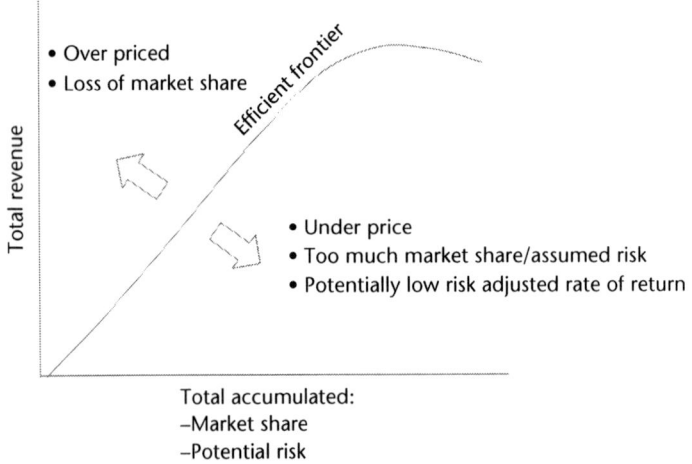

FIGURE 23.3 The efficient frontier

2. Premium branding and value selling: The goal of this strategy is to obtain a price point commensurate with the customer value (benefit) provided and a price premium compared to the competition's price or the customer's next best alternative price.

The point of premium branding and value selling is to influence the buyer to adopt a position of willingness to pay for value to be received in the future.

Understanding how much the customer is willing to pay vs. the next best alternative is critical. The customer will not pay for 100 percent of the value they receive; otherwise they would be indifferent to either product. It is very important to understand the drivers of value, what drivers will be recognized, and what percentage of value will be realized through price. The **financial services industry** uses this strategy to differentiate pricing between an A rating company (good) and a below investment grade company (poor). In other words, you are more willing to pay for an interest stream from a highly rated company than from a lower rated company. In the **long cycle durable goods** industry this strategy is used to test viability of business plans (should new technology investments be made) and to obtain a price premium when a company feels that their performance will be better than the competition (before and after actual product delivery) (see Figure 23.4).

3. Variable pricing structures: The goal of this strategy is to mitigate uncertainty (non-planned work, scope changes, and the associated increase in cost) through a contractual pricing structure which both the seller and buyer co-create to frame large variations in outcomes (wide tails) so both the seller and buyer are willing to enter into the contractual obligation. The pricing structure will define both the benefit and risk transfer and risk mitigation remedies. Commercial transactions in which there are technology maturation requirements, unique and specific fulfillment requirements, low confidence levels of success, and solutions requiring multiple partners will likely deploy these structures.

There are generally three types of pricing structures: (1) firm fixed price; (2) time and material (T&M); (3) hybrids that have some level of fixed price,

Competing product value comparison

	Competitor A value	Competitor B value	
Value A		▬▬▬	
Value B		▬▬▬	
Value C	▬▬▬		$ NPV of value advantage
Value D		▬	
Value E	▬▬		
Value F		▬	
Value G		▬	
Total value advantage		▬▬▬▬	

FIGURE 23.4 Value comparisons for competing products

Note: NPV, net present value

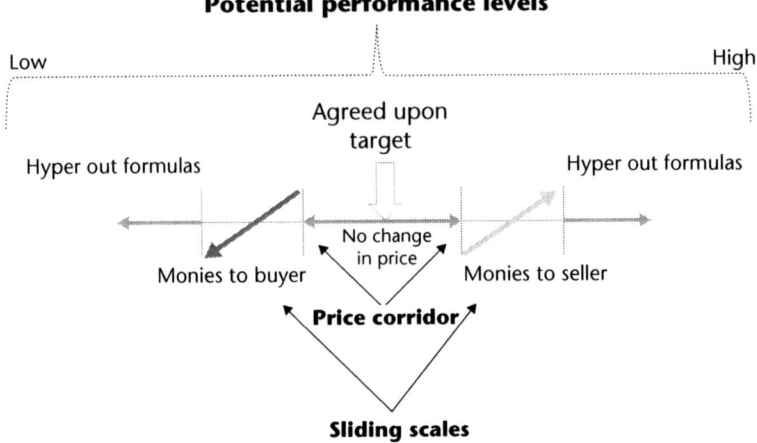

FIGURE 23.5 Price and performance corridors

but also allow for price to increase or decrease based on predetermined variables (see Figure 23.5).

The more certain the seller is of the scope requirement, and the higher the confidence level regarding fulfillment of the obligations associated with the commercial transaction, the more firm fixed pricing structures should be used. As scope, time, resources, cost, and probability of success become less known, the more the selling company should deploy variable pricing structures. Both **engineered solutions** and **large software deployment** industries use this strategy to mitigate risk and re-capture unforeseen cost.

The result

The efficacy of these pricing strategies depends on the ability of the seller to influence the buyer and usually is backed by a track record of long-term execution of product or service performance and meeting financial obligations. Ultimately, if benefits are not delivered, risk cannot be transferred to the buyer, and the pricing power will move away from the seller. Willingness to pay is also highly impacted by timing of the marketing message, the transparency of the benefit/risk transfer, and the credibility of the seller's promise.

To deploy price optimization a company must develop core competencies in forecasting demand, understanding customer buying behavior, and predicting competitive responses. Companies seeking price optimization should invest in capabilities to monitor demand drivers, use metrics for revenue, marketing share, and risk at the transaction level and at the portfolio level, focus on the development of channels to enable a constant rebalance of the portfolio of customers and/or offerings, and finally become excellent in testing for price elasticity. These companies will be focused on managing both the short term and long term and will be thought leaders in their industry space.

Value selling requires a longer pre-sale relationship, product promotion, and educational efforts. When a buyer is window shopping there is more willingness to accept a marketing message regarding product benefits, so their willingness to pay for the brand or specific product is subconsciously positively impacted. If the value sell is done at the time of the transaction, there is a significant risk of failure to capture price given that buyers will be in a negation mindset. If new technologies are involved, the seller must ensure they win the technical evaluation as a foundation for the commercial negotiation. The seller must also ensure that to obtain this level of influence, the cost of influence does not outweigh the price point and margins targeted. The cost to influence can be defined in terms of the following: branding, product promotion (commercial and technical), warranties, guarantees, liquidated damages, and the monetization of future seller obligations. Lastly, segmentation is an exceptional marketing tool to be deployed to target customers with more "willingness to pay" and to tailor unique value sell messages to different decision making stakeholders.

Variable pricing structures have worked well in many industries to mitigate risk, but are not failsafe in eliminating risk. There will always be situations when the seller and buyer find that the contract agreement is lacking in applicability.

Hybrid structures can also become very complicated and can include multiple contract clauses including price corridors, sliding scales, incentives, trigger or multi-trigger points, and hyper outs. This complexity can be problematic when competing against more simply structured offerings.

When competing against suppliers that use fixed pricing the outcome has been mixed, with fixed pricing normally winning share, at least at first. Suppliers that have advantages in work scoping, customer insight, and execution excellence who use fixed pricing against a variable pricing structured competitor can win in the long term; that said, suppliers without these capabilities can find themselves in Chapter 11 quickly. Variable pricing structures are also usually more transparent as to cost and resources, which can invite challenges from the buyer, so companies using these structures should prepare for this discussion.

Tenure of relationship matters with sellers over the longer term able to capture prices commensurate with the value transferred to buyers. Over long periods of time with multiple commercial transactions, sellers and buyers are able to true up differences in expectations. The shorter the relationship, the more pricing inertia there exists to overcome, and the more pricing must rely on branding and performance remedy strategies.

The unexpected findings

Thick tails can polarize an organization and can freeze commercial activity. There should always be a healthy debate between those that own controllership and those that drive the ongoing commercial actions. When these relationships fail to devise methods to translate and communicate, emotions can enter decision making which can introduce unintended outcomes. Emotions can drive the need for financial analysis of the unquantifiable which can stifle a business, and at the same time a business can be put in jeopardy by not transferring enough risk fueled by the desire to compete. Consequences include: losing key opportunities which may not be available again for a long time; technology obsolescence; and poor implementation of risk mitigation strategies.

Early adopters will always pay a discounted price for taking risk. These buyers thrive on taking risk and some have very solid business strategies around being an early adopter. Sellers need to understand when their product is moving from the early adopter stage to the mainstream and change their pricing strategy appropriately. Predicting the tipping point to the mainstream and being prepared to change course proactively can be hugely rewarding.

Excel is a wonderful tool that can deceive you. Excel makes you feel confident that you have a great understanding of the issue, by allowing you to model and quantify the reward and risk of a transaction. Excel can drive organizations to adopt a decentralized pricing practice as individuals, not the organization, start to make more assumptions on the reward and the risk. With thick tail products, this quickly becomes problematic, as assumptions are part of modeling and modeling is always going to be wrong; the question is just how wrong.

Key lesson

Pricing is a team sport when it comes to thick tail industries and products. Pricing leaders are not just pricing practitioners; they are business and product leaders, sales and commercial leaders, and even your branding team. The seller also needs both its customer facing team and controllership heads in the game to win. Even with thick tails, the seller needs to be able to quickly pivot from offense to defense. Having a great cross-functional engagement will facilitate speed in the execution of a strategy shift. Lastly, and hopefully this paper has demonstrated the point, pricing for thick tails is both a discussion on price and risk.

Implications for innovation in pricing

To be an innovative pricing leader in a think tail industry, one cannot think like the traditional pricing practitioner (relying on detailed spreadsheet management and the manipulation of internal price and cost numbers). These industries require the pricing leader to be part-coach and part-psychologist, be a great team leader, and have excellent domain knowledge.

Innovative pricing leaders need to know when to play offense or defense. Playing offense means more price for more risk transfer, where a defensive strategy transfers less risk and uses other mechanisms to obtain the same amount of price. Leaders should push offensive plays when the entity has domain knowledge of risk involved, investments in knowledge management have been made, the right metrics are used, the entity has a history of successful execution, current design principles are applicable, and the organization is aligned. A good defense is called for in situations when the seller is not the incumbent, execution requirements are beyond core capabilities, one-off opportunities and new risk elements are introduced, decentralized decision making using Excel is the norm, and the organization makes decisions in silos vs. teams.

Innovative pricing leaders should know how to leverage the smarts of the organization. Pricing leaders should develop a non-formal network of domain knowledge and subject matter experts. These individuals can give the pricing leader key insights on green/red flag signals. This network will know when divides within core competency functions (product, technical, operational) are becoming problematic, when excessive risk assumption is taking place, when obligations are straying from core competencies, and when the threat of disruptive technologies are being introduced. The use of the network should be to determine when the tail is getting thicker.

Innovative pricing leaders should have the branding and product promotional leader as their best friend. Truths about tails can be found in the intensity of a company's branding and associated message. For one, branding does more than get the seller in the door, it drives price through product positioning. If a company is hesitant to be definitive and bold it could be the sign to play defense, and vice versa, an intense bold and specific message can signal the need for playing offense. Investigating your company's message vs. the competition's should provide excellent insight on the size of the tail.

Innovative pricing leaders should develop objective third party relationships. Third parties with credibility can play a huge role in the amount of price and risk transferred. Third party examples include trade organizations that perform benchmarking reviews, reference customers, prime contractors who measure tier one and tier two suppliers, and finally organizations like financial rating agencies, although lately they have been in question. The more a seller can provide a buyer with objective third party affirmation of results, the more willingness to pay will increase.

PART V
Psychological aspects of pricing

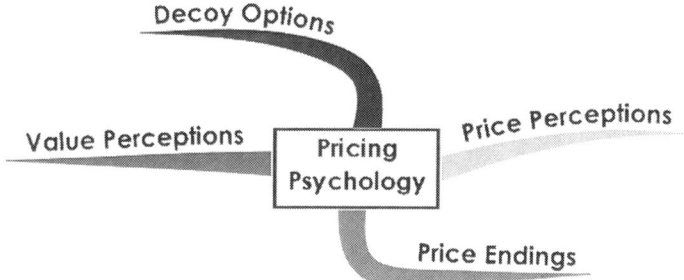

24
BEHAVIORAL ASPECTS OF PRICING

Ben Lowe

Julian Lowe

David Lynch

Introduction

Getting the right price can build company value more than almost any other business action, yet buyer behavior with respect to different prices is still not well understood and the use of "rules of thumb" continues to dominate business practice (Cespedes et al. 2011). A study by McKinsey & Company suggests that around 90 percent of products are underpriced (Marn et al. 2003), and this has significant implications for business performance.

In a rational world where everyone has good information one might expect that consumers will buy when total perceived value is greater than price charged. The greater the difference, the greater is their "willingness to pay" (WTP). In determining WTP, many other behavioral factors can disturb the rational analytic perspective of buyers. For instance, the notion of fairness might be important. This is illustrated by the launch of Radiohead's new album, *In Rainbows*. Fans were asked to name their own price for the album. Interestingly many consumers paid for the album and the average price paid was around £4 (BBC 2007).

Marketers try an increasingly broad range of approaches to "hide" prices. They partition prices, they trade-off price for quality or volume, they set prices that price discriminate across segments, psychological needs, geography and urgency of need. According to a recent report of the UK's Office of Fair Trading, over 20 percent of advertisements including prices were deemed to be deceptive in some way or another (Ahmetoglu et al. 2010). Price is also an important signal; when Phillips, the electronics manufacturer released the Philips Intimate Massager and set the price at £89.99 – it was set at that level "to be seen as respectable" (Mortishead 2008), reflecting the role of price to signal product legitimacy.

Hyper-competitive markets, globalization, online auctions, new purchasing and retail formats, provide an increasingly complex array of contexts in which price has to be managed. The sellers need to understand the "value" the customer is searching for, when price might itself be one of the most important attributes for consumers (e.g. Severin et al. 2001). Recent research suggests mood and environment can deliver major benefits in encouraging consumers to increase their WTP. Thus, price is multifaceted. While it is about "what price do I charge," it is also "how," "where," and "when."

This chapter will explore key behavioral aspects of pricing. Specifically, the chapter will begin by contrasting traditional perspectives on price with more contemporary perspectives on price; it will then examine the notion of perceived value and its multifaceted nature. The chapter will then outline the key behavioral aspects of price including internal and external reference prices, pricing and consumer perceptions of fairness, price endings, decreasing and increasing price, price–quality perceptions, and consumer price knowledge.

Perspectives on consumer response to price

The essence of effective marketing is to create value for customers and capture that value for the firm through current profits and longer-term reputation and image. Value is created through a product that meets customer requirements, is available for them to access, and is communicated effectively. These three Ps of marketing are complemented by the fourth P that involves the effective use of price as it is set to capture the value the rest of the mix has created. A pricing strategy involves setting a price that creates an incentive for consumers to buy a product or service and generate sufficient revenues to encourage the firm to sell that product. In short, consumers buy when perceived value from a product exceeds price. Perceived value represents their WTP; any price less than that, subject to a budget constraint, should lead to a purchase. Sellers need to understand WTP and competitor offerings when setting prices.

Some economic models assume that customers are perfectly aware of product features and competitive offerings and that all that is needed is to understand the demand–price relationship. Monroe and Lee (1999) list other restrictive assumptions of an economic model. This (rather narrow) economic perspective is sometimes contrasted with a marketing perspective, which explicitly sees price as an integral part of the marketing mix that signals as well as captures value. The manipulation of all four Ps together may create a difference between marketing and economic approaches to pricing, although such a perceived difference might involve a misinterpretation of textbook models of business behavior that merely seek to explain, in parsimonious fashion, the relationship between price, revenue, output, and profit. Some empirical research on price–quality relationships confirms that more often than not, long-term prices reflect differences in products and attributes (Murray and Sarantis 1999), and maybe there is less difference in economic and marketing approaches than is sometimes thought.

Fundamentally, consumers are expected to purchase an item whenever the perceived value of that item exceeds its actual price. The greater this gap, the greater the incentive to buy. Much marketing strategy is aimed at influencing behavioral factors that increase perceived value and thus the size of the gap. Gourville (1999) suggests the behavioral factors that disturb the simple relationship between price paid, WTP, and cost of goods and services, including the perceived fairness of price, the relative incentive to buy (e.g. value of consumer surplus relative to the price of the product), the difference between actual price and a consumer's reference price, and price compared to perceptions of costs.

The economic notion of incentive to buy is when perceived economic value > price. This gap is sometimes referred to as acquisition value or consumer surplus. The behavioral notion is that economic value + psychological value needs to be > price. The marketing notion combines these approaches but recognizes that consumers often have less than perfect information and that price itself is a signal of quality and that savvy consumers might also consider the ease of purchase and use of a product as important creators of customer value and therefore WTP.

Economic, marketing, and behavioral factors influence WTP and therefore value to buyers. In addition, buyer knowledge of prices is affected by their past experience, search behavior and their ability to disentangle complex deals. Increasingly the view is that complex offers that surround products are sometimes interpreted poorly by buyers who deliberately bound or restrict their search for information or who are unable to disentangle competitive claims. Unit pricing, ethics, regulation, and competition affect the consumer's response to the different factors affecting WTP and the pricing strategies of sellers. Most importantly, the nature of perceived value to buyers is complex and influenced by a myriad of subjective factors.

Perceived value

The preceding section identified the delivery of value to customers as a fundamental element of the marketing concept that builds and sustains competitive advantage. By delivering value, companies try to satisfy customers, resulting in improved customer loyalty, sales, and profits. To this end, managers need to understand the nature of customer value and where they should focus their efforts to enhance the value they create for customers.

The concept of perceived value is defined above as the psychological and economic value gained from consuming a product or service. The difference between perceived value and price is the incentive to buy and is referred to as consumer surplus or acquisition value in the economics and marketing literatures respectively. Perceived value may be confused with other similar marketing and economic terms, such as utility, price, and quality (Sánchez-Fernández and Iniesta-Bonillo 2007).

The economic view of value as instrumental, task-related, rational, functional, and cognitive (Sweeney et al. 1999), is criticized by some authors with the view that perceived value is a multidimensional construct that consists of several inter-related attributes (e.g. perceived price, monetary and non-monetary costs, quality, utilitarian and hedonic benefits). Such studies posit that perceived value incorporates a hedonic component, which reflects the entertainment, experiential, and emotional (affective) worth of consumption. This has led to greater interest in the cognitive-affective components of perceived value.

The notion of perceived value suggests that subjective judgments of value, whether they be cognitive or affective, are what influences consumer decision-making. These evaluations are based on more than experience or knowledge relating to the benefits of the physical product but also a customer's individual perception relating to the purchase. Previous research has highlighted how such judgments of value are influenced by the context in which consumer decision-making takes place. Perceptions of value have been found to differ between product types, individuals, and circumstance (over time and in different environments). Consumers can also differ in the value they associate between both different and the same products. Even a consumer's value of the same product may vary over time and the types of values that are most salient are likely to vary with circumstance. In some research, four different types of value have been identified (e.g. Grewal et al. 1998; Woodruff 1997):

1. acquisition value: perceived benefits relative to perceived costs
2. transaction value: the pleasure associated with a perceived fair price
3. in-use value: benefits derived from using the product
4. redemption value: the residual benefit after a product has been consumed.

The dynamic nature of perceived value means that the importance placed on each different value is likely to change over time and in different contexts. For durable products, acquisition and transaction value are likely to have a stronger influence on purchase decisions, with in-use and redemption value becoming more important during latter stages of usage. In such cases, the decision to trial a product is more likely to be influenced by perceived acquisition and transaction value, whereas re-purchase behavior and customer loyalty may be more strongly related to in-use and redemption value (Parasuraman 1997; Slater and Narver 1994).

Whether a simple or complex view of perceived value is used, recent developments in the field have shifted the emphasis away from a utilitarian and economic conception to a behavioral conception based on psychological theories that attribute consumer choices, in part, to simpler heuristics. An important heuristic identified in research studies into how buyers perceive the fairness or appropriateness of a price is that of the reference price which can be defined as the price against which buyers compare the offered price of a product or service. This concept is considered in the next section.

Internal and external reference prices

The notion of transaction value can be closely linked to a product's reference price (Urbany *et al*. 1997). The Nobel Prize winning work of prospect theory, whereby individuals evaluate their decisions based on losses and gains, rather than absolute magnitudes (Kahneman and Tversky 1979), has had important implications for our understanding of consumer response to price, and specifically perceptions of their transaction value. In applied consumer behavior studies empirical research for fast moving consumer goods (FMCGs) generally suggests that consumers make decisions about price by referring to some of kind of reference price, whereby the gap between what one thinks a product's price *should* be (e.g. a normal price, a fair price – its reference price) and the actual price of the product is a better predictor of behavior than the price alone (Mazumdar *et al*. 2005). In other words, if a consumer's reference price is higher than the actual price, then the consumer is more likely to frame the purchase as a "gain" and view the product as a good deal. However, if the reference price is lower than the actual price, then the consumer is more likely to frame the product as a "loss" and think the product is not such a good deal. Therefore, an important part of the behavioral perspective on pricing focuses on this gap between the actual price and the reference price. This has been coined transaction value (Thaler 1985) or "sticker shock" (Winer 1986). Thus, in studies concerning consumer response to price, researchers typically study acquisition value, and also transaction value (Grewal *et al*. 1998; Lowe and Alpert 2010; Thaler 1985; Urbany *et al*. 1997). The implication is that longer-term price management and its impact upon these value perceptions is a more important objective than short-term price management because past prices signal a product's worth to consumers – it is the price history as well as the current price which consumers use to make purchase decisions (Winer 1986). These past prices provide consumers with a reference price and the reference price is used to judge the expensiveness of a product.

For new products, the implication is that setting the right price for a product early on in its lifecycle is especially important, because it will set the standard against which the expensiveness of that product is judged in later periods. Therefore, reference price management is important to products in existing categories, but especially important to products in new product categories where consumer price perceptions have yet to be framed (Lowe and Alpert 2010; Marn *et al*. 2003). Thus, not only is price management important but, relatedly, so is *reference price management* (Nagle and Hogan 2006).

Marketers try to influence our reference price, and therefore transaction value, through external reference price claims (e.g. "Was $109.99, now $59.99"). Such promotions are often accompanied by time limited cues (e.g. "Hurry, before sale ends"). The most recent research in the area provides evidence, based on a series of field experiments, that reference price advertisements are generally more effective when consumers are shopping for a product, and that such advertisements are more effective when accompanied by a time limited promotion (Howard and Kerin 2006). This contrasts to some degree with prior work on reference price advertising which seems to suggest that reference pricing alone is effective in influencing shopping intentions (e.g. Biswas and Blair 1991).

Pricing and fairness

The concept of a reference price has been shown to be multifaceted and context specific. For example, Lowe and Alpert (2007) show that different reference prices are used for new products as opposed to existing products. However, one commonly used reference price is a fair price (Mazumdar et al. 2005). Gourville (1999) identifies a variety of factors that influence the buyer's perception of the fairness of a price. Earlier Scitovszky (1944–5), observed "the normal or fair price is contrasted to the actual price whenever they are different, and it is only when they are different that judgments of cheap or expensive occur." This relates again to the notion of transaction value. A large perceived margin is unfair and dissuades buyers from purchasing. Thus, a price hike in the context of current shortages might similarly be seen as unfair, as would a small sale reduction on a high price compared to that same (absolute) reduction on a low price.

In these cases, it might be argued that individuals are effectively deciding their response to a price change judged on its fairness. Perceptions of fairness impact WTP by consumers being less willing to pay a price they feel is "unfair." This might be extended to a long-term depreciation of a seller's reputation and marketability of its products because of its perceived lack of "fairness." Fairness is also an ethical issue that society in general might have a view on and this might influence the control or pressure to control its prices by regulators. The pricing of medicines in developing countries is a case in point (Dolan and Gourville 2009).

The main managerial issue is how to deal with customer perceptions of unfairness. That is, how does the seller encourage them to disregard "unfairness" in their decision-making? Gourville (1999) recommends actively managing price expectations and actively managing perceptions of cost of goods sold. The counterpoint to ensuring customer perceptions of fairness is that many firms pursue pricing policies that are considered "fair" as in equitable between product lines, but that such pricing mismanages potential profits. Cost plus pricing is an example, as is averaging prices across groups of very different consumers. Cespedes et al. (2011) note that,

> Many executives celebrate a sort of pseudo-democracy in their pricing policies. For years, UPS charged one price to all customers ... When it entered the market, FedEx became the fastest U.S. company to reach $1 billion in sales in part because its pricing recognized inherent value differences between customers.

The notions of fairness come from customers, not pricing formulas. Fairness is important and can be managed, but it is not about equity *per se*. A key issue in fairness is the extent to which prices move away from some reference point. The behavioral effect of increasing and decreasing price is now considered.

Increasing and decreasing prices

If managing consumer price perceptions is important, then understanding how price increases and price reductions affect consumer perceptions of value can be critical. It is quite common for marketers to reduce prices, usually through some kind of sales promotion, to stimulate demand for a product. To this end, marketers have a range of tools at their disposal, including price discounts, coupons, bonus packs, contests, free gifts, introductory prices, etc. One issue that is important when assessing consumer reaction to sales promotions involves the depth and frequency of sales promotions. For instance, for FMCG products discounts of greater than 5–10 percent are generally necessary before consumers notice that there is even a discount (Gupta and Cooper 1992). This is known as the just noticeable difference (JND) (Monroe and Lee 1999) and suggests that marketers should reduce prices by an amount that is noticeable to consumers. It is likely that the JND level changes as a function of the product category under consideration, consumer involvement with the purchase decision, knowledge about the product category, and the magnitude of the product's cost to the consumer. Conversely, consumer response to discounts of different levels is not necessarily linear, such that larger and larger discounts have smaller and smaller marginal effects. For example, some research shows that discounts higher than 30 percent do not evoke a large marginal change in preference, as consumers tend to "discount the discounts" (Gupta and Cooper 1992). Therefore, those managers responsible for setting discounts should carefully consider the level of the discount that is being set so it achieves its objectives in an optimal way. Managers need to also consider the frequency of discounting too. Discounts which are too frequent may lead consumers to perceive that a sale is not a real sale. For example, Alba *et al.* (1999) show that a small but frequent discounting strategy may be most suitable for stores wishing to present a low-price image, rather than infrequent but heavier discounting.

Another issue that is important to consider when selecting a sales promotion is the kind of sales promotion to use (e.g. monetary versus non-monetary) and its differing effect upon consumer value perceptions. Consumers react differently to different types of sales promotions. For example, Chandon *et al.* (2000) broadly distinguish between monetary promotions (e.g. a discount) and non-monetary promotions (e.g. a free gift), and show that sales promotions techniques have benefits other than a monetary saving. These benefits include utilitarian benefits such as monetary savings, enhanced value for money through increased quality, and increased convenience, and other hedonic benefits such as increased entertainment and enhanced exploration ability.

Taking a somewhat different approach other research contrasts the differences between monetary and non-monetary sales promotions based on their impact upon consumer reference prices. For example, Diamond and Campbell (1989) show that monetary promotions such as discounts lead to lower reference prices than non-monetary promotions, and this has consequences for transaction value. However, Sinha and Smith (2000) show *one-off* price promotions may not affect reference price. Intuitively, and based on prior research, it might be expected that introductory low prices or monetary discounts may downwardly bias a consumer's reference price (e.g. Diamond and Campbell 1989), whereas for extra free product offers, the reference price is more likely to remain unchanged (Sinha and Smith 2000). This is important because if an introductory low-price promotion leads to a lower reference price than an extra free product promotion, then one might expect the gap between the product's reference price and its actual price to increase. As the gap increases, this reduces transaction value, which in turn reduces purchase likelihood. Based on a similar premise, Lowe and Barnes (2011), using a national sample of UK consumers, show that introductory low price promotions are more (less) effective than extra free product promotions when the product is perceived as newer (less new). This seems to be because newer products are seen to be more risky and monetary promotions can reduce perceived risk relative to non-monetary promotions.

On the other hand marketers sometimes wish to increase prices. Again, drawing on prospect theory (Kahneman and Tversky 1979) this is most likely to be viewed as a loss by consumers, and in some cases consumers will perceive this to be unfair. Price increases are sometimes unavoidable due to increased input costs. Nonetheless these increases must be framed in a way that consumers feel is fair. For example, Campbell (1999) shows there are two key causal influences on our judgments of price fairness. These are the inferred motive of the firm (e.g. whether the motive is judged to be negative or positive – as in whether or not the profits will be allocated to the firm or a good cause) and the inferred relative profit of the firm (e.g. a normal profit or a *more than* normal profit). This relationship is moderated by a firm's reputation (e.g. socially responsible or not socially responsible with other stakeholders – staff, the community, etc.). Bolton *et al.* (2003) extend this research and show that consumers' knowledge (measured subjectively – e.g. their perceptions) of prices, profits, and costs lead to changes in their perceptions of price unfairness. Therefore, based on this data it appears that consumers are skeptical toward a firm's motives and tend to assume price changes and price differences are unfair based on some kind of perceived motive for firms to take profit, even when they are actually beyond the firm's control. They conclude that price increases deemed to be most fair are deemed to be fair as a result of quality differences – so perceived differences in quality are an important cause of price fairness perceptions and should be an integral part of marketing communications. Thus, when increasing prices marketers should "nibble" not "bite" (Kalyanaram and Little 1994: 416), the opposite of when decreasing prices.

Price endings

Consumer response to prices also exhibits some peculiarities in relation to an offering's price ending. The study of price endings and odd-even pricing tactics (e.g. $19.99 or $20.00) is not new to the field of marketing. However, relatively little empirical research has provided conclusive evidence of the nature of the effect, and its moderating conditions. This is despite the fact that the practice remains widespread. For example, Schindler and Kirby (1997) show that the digits 0, 5 and 9 are over-represented in a large sample of newspaper advertisements, consistent with many similar studies. The practice has also been shown to transcend different cultures (Simmons and Schindler 2003; Suri et al. 2004). Because of its prevalence, and ability to influence consumer choice, the topic is important for marketers and consumers alike.

The main proposition that has been tested in price ending research is that small one-penny price changes can have large effects upon sales, if prices are changed from an even number such as $20.00 to an odd number (and in particular a number ending in 9) such as $19.99. Thus, in some cases consumers could be highly price sensitive to price changes which are extremely small, and otherwise unnoticeable, leading to spiked demand curves at prices ending in 9 (Anderson and Simester 2003). There are three main theoretical arguments for such effects. One argument is that price ending effects are most likely to be seen when associated with cheaper products. However, Schindler and Kibarian (2001), based on a survey of market prices, show that 9-endings were not commonly associated with the cheapest products. Relatedly, there is evidence to suggest that 9-endings are typically associated with the presence of low-price appeals (e.g. a reference price or some kind of claimed saving, rather than cheaper products *per se*). Thus, a second explanation is based around retailing folklore, whereby managers who want sale prices to appear cheaper use 9-ending prices because they believe consumers will see these as being cheaper (Schindler 2006). A third argument advanced in the literature is based on the premise that consumers read prices from left to right and that right-hand digits are less important than left-hand digits. Either left-hand digits are recalled better by consumers (e.g. see Guéguen and Legoherel 2004), or, if the left-hand digit changes, then this change is most salient to consumers, leading to a left-digit effect (Thomas and Morwitz 2005).

In general, there is no widespread consensus about how price endings influence consumer choice, and because of limited systematic empirical research in the area, generalizations about price ending effects are not empirically verifiable. For example, some studies find that odd prices ending in 9 increase consumption relative to even prices (e.g. Anderson and Simester 2003). Other studies find inconsistent effects or that odd prices *reduce* consumption relative to even prices (e.g. Bray and Harris 2006). These findings point to a variety of conditions that moderate the effect of 9-ending prices.

Some research shows that the price magnitude of the product (e.g. low-priced versus high-priced products) is important in research on price ending effects. Anderson and Simester (2003) show that $9 price endings (as opposed to 9 cent) can increase sales by as much as 40 percent relative to other price endings. This effect was stronger for newer products than for existing products, providing some rationale for the inconsistent effects found by Bray and Harris (2006). More recent research points to the importance of the left-digit effect (Thomas and Morwitz 2005) as an important moderating condition. The left-digit effect suggests that

9-ending prices are only effective if the left digit changes as well (for example, from $20.00 to $19.99, rather than $21.00 to $20.00). This effect is shown by Thomas and Morwitz (2005) to be greater (smaller) when the difference between the two prices is smaller (larger). Therefore, the left-digit effect will be greater for a promotion such as "Was $20.00, now $18.99" (versus $19.00) rather than a promotion such as "Was $20.00, now $11.99" (versus $12.00).

Therefore, in summary, the evidence suggests that price endings are important and that small price changes can have a dramatic influence on sales. However, this is not a universal truth, and based on the majority of research the effectiveness of price endings seems to depend upon a variety of different factors including association with other low price cues, price magnitude, product newness to customers, changes to the left digit, and managerial interpretation of consumer response to price endings. While price movements and price endings need to be managed effectively, often the greatest challenge to sellers is how to price the quality or attributes of a product that influence whether something is considered a good or poor buy. These price–quality perceptions are considered in the next section.

Price–quality perceptions

Price is usually assumed to be inversely related to demand. This is illustrated in Dolan and Gourville's (2009) "Value-pricing thermometer" in Figure 24.1. Conventionally, a seller tries to increase the difference between price and cost of goods sold (profit) while consumers are more incentivized to buy, and the greater is the gap between perceived value to them and product price. The expected price–quality relationship is for higher prices to be linked to more attributes and better quality, because these lead to higher *perceived* and *objective* value. Research referred to earlier suggests that over time there is often a correlation between prices charged and the quality or attributes of a product or service. However, some research as well as extensive anecdotal evidence, suggests that there might be a positive relationship between price and perceived value in some circumstances – even though objective value and product attributes remains unchanged. Some pricing research shows consumers may infer quality from price when they lack the ability or motivation to process product-related information (Suri and Monroe 2003). Thus price *can* serve as a heuristic which provides information to consumers.

There are a number of circumstances when this price–quality relationship is likely. Higher prices may signal better quality to the consumer without adequate information; when product attributes are difficult to measure except through experience; or where there is high uncertainty on the part of the consumer about what to buy. Price might also be used as a quality signal where information search is difficult or there are few sources of available data (e.g. cars and electronic equipment versus perfume, clothes, or wine). The assumption underlying these perceived positive price–quality relationships is that as well as uncertainty and lack of information, price is also determined with reference to another or expected price point. The buyer's receptiveness to price is about what s(he) expects. Buyers also have

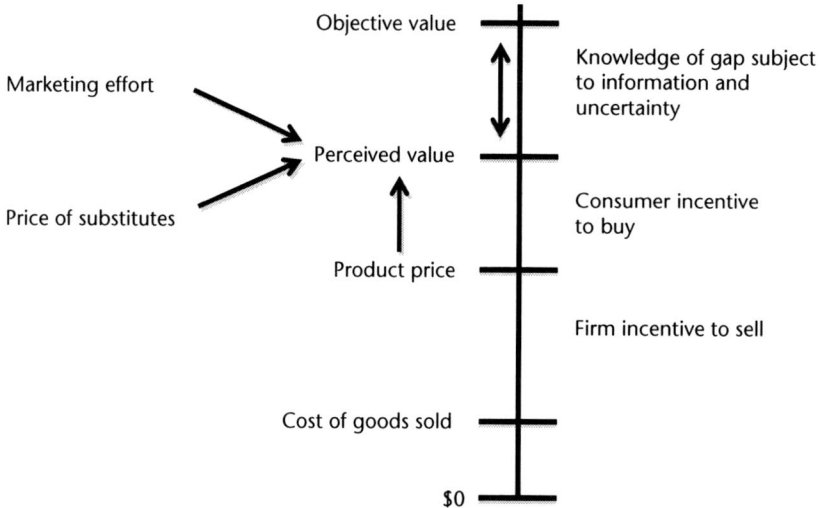

FIGURE 24.1 The value pricing thermometer (adapted from Dolan and Gourville 2009)

some notion of perceived quality that can be different to objective quality. According to Zeithaml (1988), perceived quality involves a higher level of abstraction than specific attributes, and resembles attitude. Judgments about quality are made within a buyer's evoked set; comparisons with reference prices are critical. Such judgments about the superiority or excellence of a product or service is essentially user-based, rather than product- or manufacturing-based (Garvin 1983). This abstract view of quality is coupled with a view that buyers do not always know or remember prices paid, but encode prices in ways meaningful to them. This is parallel to the emotional and intuitive decision-making processes that Kahneman (2011) contrasts with more deliberate and cognitive approaches.

Recent research by Bornemann and Homburg (2011) suggests that with increasing psychological and temporal distance, price–quality relationships are more likely. People are more likely to construe price as indicating quality and less likely to focus on price as a cost, the more distant they are from the purchase. Thus when a product is less part of a consumer's regular experience or when its purchase and consumption is for some time in the future, price–quality relationships are likely to be more pronounced. There is evidence that price–quality effects have decreased over the last three decades but still remain potent. Völckner and Hofmann (2007: 194) in a meta-analysis of price–quality relationship research conclude that over the period 1989–2006 the incidence of inverse price–quality relationships identified in the research literature declined. However they comment that:

> consumers still use price as an important indicator of quality .... Managers must be aware that price–quality inferences remain important aspects of consumers' behavior and (should) consider them when setting prices ... setting a

low selling price or lowering a price with a discount not only lowers consumer costs but also threatens to lower their perceptions of product quality through negative signaling effects.

Thus, price–quality relationships are pervasive in many markets. However, there are limits to the extent that perceived value can be positively influenced by price. With the growth of social media, the buyer's ability to call-up data on price and quality comparisons has increased. Quality signaling using price may in the future require other strategies such as bundling and product augmentation to achieve increases in demand.

Consumer price knowledge

The extent to which consumers use different heuristics might depend upon the accuracy of their price knowledge. Consumer price knowledge has long been a subject of interest for practitioners and academics alike. Conventional neoclassical microeconomic models assume that consumers *know* the prices of the products they are purchasing. However, a wealth of research suggests that this might not be the case (Dickson and Sawyer 1990; Gabor and Granger 1961). If so, this has important implications for what is known about price, and about how consumers use price in their purchasing decisions. For example, reference pricing studies that use scanner data to model consumer reference prices based on past prices consumers have been exposed to may not be accurate, if this is the case. Likewise, how reference prices are formed must be subject to some kind of systematic bias that is not yet well understood. More recently, Monroe and Lee (1999), in reviewing contemporary and emerging perspectives on pricing, argue that initial research in this regard is limited because it relies on the ability of consumers to *recall* prices. Instead, they argue, consumers may have knowledge about prices in a relative sense (e.g. being able to rank from cheapest to most expensive), even if they cannot recall exact prices. Using a sample of French supermarket shoppers, Vanhuele and Drèze (2002) provide an explicit test of this and tap into recallable price knowledge (e.g. whether or not the consumer can recall the price), price recognition (e.g. whether or not they can recognize if they paid a particular price), and the ability to spot deals (e.g. whether or not they can tell if something is a good deal). Like Monroe and Lee (1999) they conclude that consumer price knowledge is more pervasive than the ability to recall a particular price. This may account for the findings of reference price research using scanner data. Therefore, while shoppers cannot recall past prices accurately, they have the ability to spot good deals and bad deals. Estelami and De Maeyer (2004) expand existing research by examining consumer price knowledge for durable goods. They find that price knowledge varies considerably across a range of durable goods (e.g. higher for essential goods and lower for recreational goods). They also find that purchase frequency and amount spent on advertising are important variables that can explain consumer price knowledge, whereby more frequently purchased products and heavily advertised goods are associated with higher price knowledge. More recent research shows how the number of low-priced items in a store can affect the degree to which the store has a low price image, and how different customers rely on different heuristics to make judgments in arriving at their perceptions. Specifically, they show that stores with greater numbers of low priced products are more likely to have a low-price image. However, this seems only to be the case for high-knowledge consumers; low-knowledge consumers associate a low-price image with the ease to which low prices can be recalled (e.g. the salience of promotions and other low price cues). Therefore, consumer price knowledge is an important variable for marketers to understand. Its link with other psychological concepts within the domain of pricing is important for theoretical and practical reasons, not least because marketers' actions can influence this rather malleable and subjective variable.

Behavioral pricing concepts in non-market settings

So far the discussion has centered around market goods, but how are goods and services valued (and implicitly priced) when there is no market? In a free market economy, goods and services are sold for prices that reflect equilibrium between supply and demand, that is the costs of production and what people are willing to pay. Non-market goods or services (non-market goods) are not bought or sold directly and do not have a directly observable monetary value. Examples of this include nature-based recreation activities such as visiting public parks and gardens, wildlife viewing, or rock climbing. A basic purpose of government is to provide citizens with non-market goods and to place values on such goods so that investment can be prioritized. Such decisions require governments to have an accurate understanding of the values attributed to such goods by society. To estimate the value of non-market goods, several economic tools have been developed, including: contingent valuation surveys; attribute-based methods, and travel cost methods (Brown 2003). However, recently an alternative tool for valuing non-market goods — happiness economics — has been proposed.

In neoclassical economics, utility is not a psychological experience that occurs during or after consumption. Instead, utility is defined by revealed preference: preferences (i.e. utility) are revealed from behavior (i.e. choices) (Stigler 1950). Proponents of revealed preference argue that information about utility is captured by choice, assuming that consumers act as rational agents (Kahneman and Thaler 2006). The reliance on measuring value through economic measures of utility (e.g. revealed preference and stated preference methods) has recently been criticized (e.g. Kahneman and Thaler 2006). The field of behavioral economics refers to the attempt to develop economic theory by providing it with more psychologically plausible foundations (Johnson 2006). Much emphasis in behavioral economics concerning valuation of both market and non-market goods focuses on subjective well-being (happiness) as an experience-based measure of utility (Diener 2009; Kahneman and Krueger 2006).

The term subjective well-being refers to "a broad category of phenomena that includes people's emotional responses, domain satisfactions, and global judgments of life satisfaction" (Diener *et al.* 1999: 277). There are two distinctive components of subjective well-being: an affective part and a cognitive part (Diener *et al.* 1999; Kahneman 1999). The affective component refers to the presence of positive affect (i.e. emotions) and the absence of negative affect. The cognitive component of subjective well-being relates to an information-based appraisal of a person's life as a whole (Schwarz and Strack 1999).

Behavioral economists argue that experienced utility can be measured and is distinct from decision utility (Kahneman and Thaler 2006). In response to criticisms concerning the measurability of experience utility, Kahneman *et al.* (1997) nominate how the concept can be operationalized through instant (hedonic and affective experience during consumption), predicted (beliefs about the experienced utility of future outcomes), and remembered (past hedonic and affective experience) utility. Following these major advances in the field of subjective well-being, much work is underway that evaluates the contribution it can make to informing policy decisions (Loomes 2007). In particular, experienced-based utility, by providing measures of subjective well-being, can provide an alternative to estimating prices.

Implications for innovation in pricing

The first and most important thing managers need to recognize is that getting the "right" price is critical for both revenue and profitability. Gourville and Soman (2002) note that an average price increase of 1 percent could boost the net income of the typical large US corporation by about 12 percent. Clearly, what is "right" depends as much on customers' differential response to different prices as it does on organizational objectives. But how can a manager gauge the "right price"? One way is through field experiments testing different price/promotion levels (Almquist and Wyner 2001), an area in which the direct mail industry leads the way. Yet another part of the solution is the acknowledgment that the value of a product or service sets the upper limit for how high a price can be raised, and that value is made up of psychological and objective or utilitarian value. Managers must understand what this psychological value is and the attributes of their products and services which relate to it. The psychological value of a product is not only determined by its brand, rarity, and social norms, but is also affected by perceived fairness or "rightness" of a price. These issues of fairness may be influenced by how, when, and where prices are charged, and involve both affective as well as cognitive decision processes.

Gourville and Soman (2002) assert that consumers typically tend to look at price differences in terms of the saving as a proportion of actual price and as an indicator of the size of the incentive to enter the transaction. Similarly, they may resent prices that are not a reflection of the costs of a good and sellers may need to add features that justify the perception of higher costs. For some goods, a reference price might be used to identify what is "fair," while what is a fair price might be the subject of more intensive introspection for utilitarian goods compared to luxuries. These insights suggest buyers make various judgments about perceived value and a fair price that, in common with decision-making generally, suffer from extensive biases.

The manager needs to understand these processes and the reference points most salient to their customers in order to be able to tweak price most effectively. Once these reference points are understood, managers must manage price expectations through establishing clear reference prices, avoiding major and discontinuous price hikes, invest in establishing some product uniqueness to avoid price comparisons, and establish benchmarks for good value by outlining favorable price comparisons with *different* products known for being good value. Finally, managers can avoid cost of goods sold comparisons by bundling, adding abstract features and focus cost comparisons using absorption costing.

In the end, WTP is driven not only by the "economic utility" of the transaction, but also by the "psychological utility" of the transaction. There are many levers that managers can use to increase psychological utility or reduce dissonance. For example, adjusting price endings is one way where small price changes have been shown to lead to large changes in demand in some circumstances. However, these findings are based upon a variety of different factors including the product's price magnitude, its relative newness, changes in the left digit, and accompanying promotional material with other low price cues. Managers must consider these moderating influences when setting price endings. When managing price, adjustments and sales promotions should ultimately be based on a longer-term pricing strategy, not just a knee-jerk reaction to competitors' promotional offerings. Maintaining pricing discipline through active management of reference prices and other salient consumer reference points will lead to more favorable price comparisons. However, reference price is multifaceted and managers must understand their individual customers and the reference prices those customers use in different circumstances, and their attributions of fairness. For example, non-monetary sales promotions have been shown to take the focus off price and assist in maintaining reference price perceptions.

Ultimately consumers make apparently irrational decisions and bound their search behavior; sellers should be able to improve profitability by understanding these decision processes. In summary, sellers must understand how WTP is influenced by objective value and psychological factors. They need to be able to estimate price sensitivity by customer, outlet, context, and use, and through establishing clear reference prices they need to integrate price decisions with the rest of the marketing mix.

Conclusions

This chapter has described how research into pricing, using behavioral concepts, represents a significant source of marketing innovation for alert sellers. Buyers without adequate information might make a number of seemingly conflicting purchasing decisions. Sometimes these are the result of time-saving heuristics or sometimes they are the result of apparently irrational behavior. Consumers often behave in somewhat counter-intuitive ways (e.g. using price as an indicator of quality, purchasing more with trivial price changes) and do not always have accurate information (e.g. low price knowledge) on which to base their decisions.

These decisions might be thought of as irrational but stem from the key driver of behavior – perceived value. Price, a seemingly objective variable, may be interpreted by consumers in a *seemingly* subjective way. In order to understand how consumers might respond to price, managers must understand the reference points and heuristics that consumers use.

The research into consumers' behavioral response to price presented here tends to be based on consumer settings, and is usually based around conventional channels, rather than online channels. Therefore, future research and innovation within the field should seek to understand and establish the nature of these cognitive biases in business-to-business settings and in online markets, where some of the assumptions underlying consumers' boundedness and access to information are relaxed. Future research should also consider better measurement of WTP, given it is a key construct in the field – current research is often limited by directly questioning customers about price and this increases its salience to the respondent and perhaps overstates its effect. Other indirect approaches have their limitations too. Further research could also take advantage of the lack of research in online settings and couple this with advances in experimental techniques and dynamic pricing capabilities of the online environment.

References

Ahmetoglu, G., Fried, S., Dawes, J. and Furnham, A. (2010) *Pricing practices: Their effects on consumer behaviour and welfare*, report prepared for the Office of Fair Trading, London, March 2010.

Alba, J. W., Mela, C. F., Shimp, T. A., and Urbany, J. E. (1999) The effect of discount frequency and depth on consumer price judgments. *Journal of Consumer Research*, 26 (September), pp. 99–114.

Almquist, E. and Wyner, G. (2001) Boost your marketing ROI with experimental design. *Harvard Business Review*, 79 (October), pp. 135–55.

Anderson, E. T. and Simester, D. I. (2003) Effects of $9 price endings on retail sales: Evidence from field experiments. *Quantitative Marketing and Economics*, 1 (1), pp. 93–110.

BBC (2007) Yorke paid nothing for own album. Retrieved from http://news.bbc.co.uk/1/hi/entertainment/7103071.stm.

Biswas, A. and Blair, E. A. (1991) Contextual effects of reference prices in retail advertisements. *Journal of Marketing*, 55 (July), pp. 1–12.

Bolton, L. E., Warlop, L., and Alba, J. W. (2003) Consumer perceptions of price (un)fairness. *Journal of Consumer Research*, 29 (March), pp. 474–91.

Bornemann, T. and Homburg, C. (2011) Psychological distance and the dual role of price. *Journal of Consumer Research*, 38 (October), Pre-published March 18 2011.

Bray, J. P. and Harris, C. (2006) The effect of 9-ending prices on retail sales: A quantitative UK based field study. *Journal of Marketing Management*, 22 (5–6), pp. 601–17.

Brown, T. (2003) Introduction to stated preference methods. In: Champ, P., Boyle K., and Brown, T. (eds) *A primer on nonmarket valuation (the economics of non-market goods and resources)*. New York: Springer, pp. 99–110.

Campbell, M. C. (1999) Perceptions of price unfairness: Antecedents and consequences. *Journal of Marketing Research*, 36 (2), pp. 187–99.

Cespedes, F. V., Shapiro, B. P., and Ross, E. B. (2011) *Pricing, profits and customer value (Note 9-811-016)*. Boston, MA: Harvard Business School.

Chandon, P., Wansink, B., and Laurent, G. (2000) A benefit congruency framework of sales promotion effectiveness. *Journal of Marketing*, 64 (4), pp. 65–81.

Diamond, W. D. and Campbell, L. (1989) The framing of sales promotions: Effects on reference price change. In: Srull, T. S. (ed.) *Advances in consumer research, Volume 16*. Provo, UT: Association for Consumer Research, pp. 241–7.

Dickson, P. R. and Sawyer, A. G. (1990) The price knowledge and search of supermarket shoppers. *Journal of Marketing*, 54 (July), pp. 42–53.

Diener, E. (2009) *Well-being for public policy*. New York: Oxford University Press.

Diener, E., Suh, E., Lucas, R., and Smith, H. (1999) Subjective well-being: Three decades of progress. *Psychological Bulletin*, 125 (2), pp. 276–302.

Dolan, R. J. and Gourville, J. T. (2009) *Principles of pricing (Note 9-506-021)*. Boston: Harvard Business School.

Estelami, H. and De Maeyer, P. (2004) Product category determinants of price knowledge for durable consumer goods. *Journal of Retailing*, 80 (2), pp. 129–37.

Gabor, A. and Granger, C. W. J. (1961) On the price consciousness of consumers. *Applied Statistics*, 10 (November), pp. 170–88.

Garvin, D. A. (1983) Quality in the line. *Harvard Business Review*, 61, pp. 65–73.

Gourville, J. T. (1999) *Note on behavioral pricing (Note 9-599-114)*. Boston: Harvard Business School.

Gourville, J. and Soman, D. (2002) Pricing and the psychology of consumption. *Harvard Business Review*, September 2002. Reprint R0209G.

Grewal, D., Monroe, K. B., and Krishnan, R. (1998) The effects of price-comparison advertising on buyers' perceptions of acquisition value, transaction value, and behavioral intentions. *Journal of Marketing*, 62 (2), pp. 46–59.

Guéguen, N. and Legoherel, P. (2004) Numerical encoding and odd-ending prices: The effect of a contrast in discount perception. *European Journal of Marketing*, 38 (1/2), pp. 194–208.

Gupta, S. and Cooper, L. G. (1992) The discounting of discounts and promotion thresholds. *Journal of Consumer Research*, 19 (December), pp. 401–11.

Howard, D. J. and Kerin, R. A. (2006) Broadening the scope of reference price advertising research: A field study of consumer shopping involvement. *Journal of Marketing*, 70 (October), pp. 185–204.

Johnson, E. J. (2006) Things that go bump in the mind: How behavioral economics could invigorate marketing. *Journal of Marketing Research*, 43 (3), pp. 337–40.

Kahneman, D. (1999) Objective happiness. In: Kahneman, D., Diener E., and Schwarz N. (eds) *Well-being: The foundations of hedonic psychology*. New York: Russell Sage Foundation, pp. 3–25.

Kahneman, D. (2011) *Thinking fast and thinking slow*. New York: Farrar, Straus and Giroux.

Kahneman, D. and Krueger, A. B. (2006) Developments in the measurement of subjective well-being. *Journal of Economic Perspectives*, 20 (1), pp. 3–24.

Kahneman, D. and Thaler, R. H. (2006) Utility maximization and experienced utility. *Journal of Economic Perspectives*, 20 (1), pp. 221–34.

Kahneman, D. and Tversky, A. (1979) Prospect theory: An analysis of decision under risk. *Econometrica*, 47 (March), pp. 263–91.

Kahneman, D., Wakker, P., and Sarin, R. (1997) Back to Bentham? Exploration of experienced utility. *The Quarterly Journal of Economics*, 112 (2), pp. 375–405.

Kalyanaram, G. and Little, J. D. C. (1994) An empirical analysis of latitude of price acceptance in consumer package goods. *Journal of Consumer Research*, 21 (3), pp. 408–18.

Loomes, G. (2007) (How) can we value health, safety and the environment? *Journal of Economic Psychology*, 27, pp. 713–36.

Lowe, B. and Alpert, F. (2007) Measuring reference price perceptions for new product categories: Which measure is best? *Journal of Product & Brand Management*, 16 (2), pp. 132–41.

Lowe, B. and Alpert, F. (2010) The formation and evolution of reference price perceptions in new product categories. *Psychology & Marketing*, 27 (9), pp. 846–73.

Lowe, B. and Barnes, B. (2011) Consumer perceptions of monetary and nonmonetary promotions for new product. *Journal of Marketing Management*, Pre-published April 21, 2011.

Marn, M. V., Roegner, E. V., and Zawada, C. C. (2003) Pricing new products. *McKinsey Quarterly*, 3 (July), pp. 40–9.

Mazumdar T., Raj, S. P., and Sinha I. (2005) Reference price research: Review and propositions. *Journal of Marketing*, 69 (4), pp. 84–102.

Monroe, K. B. and Lee, A. Y. (1999) Remembering versus knowing: Issues in buyers' processing of price information. *Journal of the Academy of Marketing Science*, 27, pp. 207–25.

Mortishead, C. (2008) Philips changes the mood with warm intimate massager. *The Times*, 6 September 2008. Retrieved from http://www.timesplus.co.uk/tto/news/?login=false&url=http%3A%2F%2F www.thetimes.co.uk%2Ftto%2Fbusiness%2Findustries%2Ftechnology%2F.

Murray, J. and Sarantis, N. (1999) Price-quality relations and hedonic price indexes for cars in the United Kingdom. *International Journal of the Economics of Business*, 6 (1), pp. 5–27.

Nagle, T. T. and Hogan, J. E. (2006) *The strategy and tactics of pricing: A guide to growing more profitably*, 4th edition. Upper Saddle River, NJ: Prentice Hall.

Parasuraman, A. (1997) Reflections on gaining competitive advantage through customer value. *Journal of the Academy of Marketing Science*, 25 (2), p. 154.

Sánchez-Fernández, R. and Iniesta-Bonillo, M. Á. (2007) The concept of perceived value: a systematic review of the research. *Marketing Theory*, 7 (4), pp. 427–51.

Schindler, R. M. (2006) The 99-price ending as a signal of a low-price appeal. *Journal of Retailing*, 82 (1), pp. 71–7.

Schindler, R. M. and Kibarian, T. M. (2001) Image communicated by the use of 99 endings in advertised prices. *Journal of Advertising*, 30 (Winter), pp. 95–9.

Schindler, R. M. and Kirby, P. N. (1997) Patterns of right-most digits used in advertised prices: Implications for nine-ending effects. *Journal of Consumer Research*, 24 (September), pp. 192–201.

Schwarz, N. and Strack, F. (1999) Reports of subjective well-being: Judgmental processes and their methodological implications. In: Kahneman, D., Diener N. and Schwarz, N. (eds) *Well-being: The foundations of hedonic psychology*. New York: Russell Sage Foundation, pp. 61–84.

Scitovszky, T. (1944–5) Some consequences of the habit of judging quality by price. *Review of Economic Studies*, 12 (2), pp. 100–5.

Severin, V., Louviere, J. J., and Finn, A. (2001) The stability of retail shopping choices over time and across countries. *Journal of Retailing*, 77 (2), pp. 185–202.

Simmons, L. C. and Schindler, R. M. (2003) Cultural superstitions and the price endings used in Chinese advertising. *Journal of International Marketing*, 11 (2), pp. 101–11.

Sinha, I. and Smith, M. F. (2000) Consumers' perceptions of promotional framing of price. *Psychology & Marketing*, 17 (3), pp. 257–75.

Slater, S. F. and Narver, J. C. (1994) Market orientation, customer value, and superior performance. *Business Horizons*, 37 (2), p. 22.

Stigler, G. J. (1950) The development of utility theory. II. *Journal of Political Economy*, 58 (5), pp. 373–96.

Suri, R. and Monroe, K. B. (2003) The effects of time constraints on consumers' judgments of prices and products. *Journal of Consumer Research*, 30 (June), pp. 92–104.

Suri, R., Anderson, R. E., and Kotlov, V. (2004) The use of 9-ending prices: Contrasting the USA with Poland. *European Journal of Marketing*, 38 (1/2), pp. 56–72.

Sweeney, J. C., Soutar, G. N., and Johnson, L. W. (1999) The role of perceived risk in the quality-value relationship: a study in a retail environment. *Journal of Retailing*, 75 (1), pp. 77–105.

Thaler, R. (1985) Mental accounting and consumer choice. *Marketing Science*, 4 (Summer), pp. 199–214.

Thomas, M. and Morwitz, V. (2005) Penny wise and pound foolish: The left digit effect in price cognition. *Journal of Consumer Research*, 32 (June), pp. 54–64.

Urbany, J. E., Bearden, W. O., Kaicker, A., and Smith-de-Borrero, M. (1997) Transaction utility effects when quality is uncertain. *Journal of the Academy of Marketing Science*, 25 (December), pp. 45–55.

Vanhuele, M. and Drèze, X. (2002) Measuring the price knowledge shoppers bring to the store. *Journal of Marketing*, 66 (4), pp. 72–85.

Völckner, F. and Hofmann, J. (2007) The price-perceived quality relationship: A meta-analytic review and assessment of its determinants. *Marketing Letters*, 18, pp. 181–96.

Winer, R. S. (1986) A reference price model of brand choice for frequently purchased products. *Journal of Consumer Research*, 13 (September), pp. 250–6.

Woodruff, R. B. (1997) Customer value: The next source for competitive advantage. *Journal of the Academy of Marketing Science*, 25 (2), pp. 139–53.

Zeithaml, V. A. (1988) Consumer perceptions of price, quality, and value: a Means–end model and synthesis of evidence. *Journal of Marketing*, 52 (3), pp. 2–22.

25
RESEARCH ON ODD PRICES
Dead end or field of potential innovation?

Carmen Balan

Introduction

Half a century ago, the literature on pricing topics included several terms used as synonyms, respectively 'odd prices', 'just-below prices', 'magic prices', 'charm prices', 'irrational prices', 'intuitive prices', 'rule-of-thumb prices' and 'psychological prices'. There was no formally accepted definition of these terms and of the content of such strategies. In essence, 'odd pricing' consisted in setting prices just-below an even denomination. The usual examples were the prices ending in '9', '.99' or '.95'.

The first signs of odd pricing practice date back to the late nineteenth century in the United States. After many decades of debate about odd prices, one may think that knowledge in this field reached a maturity stage. Are odd prices a domain of study about which no new insight may be added? Is the influence of odd prices on consumers fully understood and measured?

Criticism relative to this research field is not uncommon. The main problems are the inconclusive, and sometimes contradictory, character of the findings as well as the overall limited evidence about the consumer perception of odd prices. For instance, Gendall *et al.* (1997) stated that 'Overall, the findings of research into the effects of odd pricing on demand have been mixed and inconclusive ... Clearly, the efficacy of odd pricing remains unproven.' After a review of empirical studies about odd prices, Gendall *et al.* (1998) concluded that these represent 'an inconsistent and sometimes contradictory picture. Some studies appear to provide evidence of odd-pricing effects, while others do not.' Harris and Bray (2007) noted that 'Many authors have acknowledged that empirical evidence conclusively proving or disproving the theory that price endings affect sales volumes is extremely limited'. In addition, a gap between the research priorities and the managerial practice evolved, as Wagner and Beinke (2006) underlined: 'Overall, the academic discussion of odd pricing focuses mainly on the verification of odd-price effects rather than offering effective decision-making support'.

Is the research on odd price topics at a dead end or is it a field open for potential innovation? To answer this question, the present paper analyses major contributions to the research on odd prices and provides a systematic view of some of the most prominent findings.

Overview of the research on odd prices

This section discusses the origin of odd pricing, the explanations for the effect of odd prices, the first research strides and the scope of the research on odd prices.

The origins of odd pricing

In the late nineteenth century, in the United States, currency standardization acted as a facilitator of odd pricing. The imported British goods often had odd-price endings due to the currency conversion from pound sterling into dollars. The favourable image of these products among Americans enticed retailers to apply odd pricing to domestic products.

Another explanation of the odd pricing could be the use of cash registers (Landsberg 1992). For the items priced one or five cents just-below a round figure, each time the vendor had to return change to a customer he had to open the cash register which rang up the sale, making it less possible to put money in their own pockets.

The practice of high-awareness retailers promoted the use of odd prices and subsequently was considered new and positive by consumers. Such an example consists in the 99 cent sales introduced by Macy's New York department store, at the beginning of the twentieth century. The main reason was also to issue change and record sales at the cash register. By 1885, Macy's — prominent retail chain in the USA — reached annual sales of $5 million (Hower 1943 as cited in Stigler 1956). Competitive retailers did not hesitate to adopt the odd pricing.

Between psychological bias and rationality: explanations for the frequent use of odd prices

The wide spread of odd prices was often explained based on the hypothesis of 'price illusion', according to which consumers systematically underestimate prices with just-below endings. For instance, a price of $399 may be perceived as '$300 and something' rather than 'almost $400'. Similarly, a price of $3.99 is perceived as below $4. Many retailers considered that odd prices may sometimes generate lower-price perceptions.

Consumers are considered to ignore the rightmost digits of the price (Nagle and Holden 1995; Kotler 2000). Thus, the behaviour of consumers facing odd prices is marked by irrationality.

Huston and Kamdar (1996) confronted the 'price illusion' hypothesis and tried to reconcile just-below pricing with consumer rationality. They examined the prices of garments from women's clothing catalogues. The two authors concluded that consumers face small but real costs when recalling and processing price digits.

The disregard of the rightmost digits becomes a rational option for some consumers, because considering more digits increases marginal costs. Sellers may yield profit from this behaviour by charging prices ending in 9. The study did not support the traditional argument that 9-ending prices signal low-price items to consumers.

To explain the frequent use of prices ending in the digits 99, Stiving and Winer (1997) have used consumer choice models and scanner panel data for two brands of each of two frequently purchased product categories (tuna and yoghurt). Their findings support the taking into account of the price digits in consumer choice models and provide a rational explanation for the frequent use of odd prices. Consumers trade off the low likelihood of making a mistake against the cost of mentally processing the price digit corresponding to pennies. They prefer a good purchase decision with the least amount of mental processing. In addition, the research results showed the existence of both level effects and image effects associated with odd prices. The level effects refer to the underestimation of the value of the price and the image effects to the meanings inferred by consumers from the rightmost digits.

The prospect theory formulated by Kahneman and Tversky (1979) states that decision-makers assign value to gains or losses rather than to final assets. Their findings showed that 'the value function is normally concave for gains, commonly convex for losses and is generally steeper for losses than for gains'. Boyes *et al.* (2007) relied on this theory to answer the question 'Why odd pricing?' Their experiments showed that consumer behaviour relative to odd prices is rational and informed. These odd pricing tactics reflect the preference function, as consumers dislike losses more than they value gains relative to a reference price.

Another approach in explaining the reaction of consumers relative to odd prices is based on the analogue model of numerical cognition. Thomas and Morwitz (2005) obtained empirical evidence that supported the model, reflecting the way the human mind converts numerical symbols to analogue magnitudes on the mental scale. Their findings demonstrated the left-digit effect, respectively the way consumers encode and compare multi-digit numbers. The 9-ending prices influence the magnitude perceptions of consumers only in specific situations: (i) when the leftmost digit of the compared prices differ (e.g. $2.99 vs. $3.00); (ii) when the numerical and psychological distances between the target price and the price of a competing product are short.

The explanation for the wide spread of odd prices should be identified in relation with both consumers' behaviour and retailers' reasoning. Gedenk and Sattler (1999) underlined that the pricing behaviour of retailers is based not only on tradition, but also on economic reasoning. Based on their research results, they concluded that setting 9-ending prices is a rational way of dealing with uncertainty. More precisely, a retailer assuming the existence of price thresholds will not incur a huge loss in case he is wrong. If thresholds exist and they are ignored, the losses may be significant.

The explanation of the usage of odd prices remains a topic open to further debate.

Research on odd prices: the first strides

One of the first studies relative to the impact of customary prices on demand was presented by Ginzberg in a one-page report published in 1936. The goal of the experiment conducted by a large American mail-order company was to study the effects of odd and even pricing on demand. The company hypothesized that the effectiveness of its odd pricing resulted from consumers' habit/inertia and from 'universal indulgence'. The company applied even prices for a representative sample of items in several regional issues of the spring catalogue (6,000,000 copies), while it maintained odd prices in other catalogues. The even prices diminished by half the sales of some items, increased disproportionately the sales of some other products and left unchanged the sales of the rest of the items. The results were inconclusive relative to the impact of odd prices and to the attachment of consumers to odd prices. The company was not interested in further testing because costs exceeded benefits. In the case of one item, 'a change of one cent a yard led to a loss of $50,000'.

In 1967, Hollander mentioned that few studies attempting to measure consumer attachment to 'customary prices' were reported until that moment. In 1972, Georgoff noted the absence of a clear definition of 'odd pricing'.

The research on odd prices has a long history. After 75 years since the first study endeavours, theorists and practitioners use a wide array of terms and do not share a common viewpoint relative to the concept of odd pricing.

Scope of the research on odd prices

A significant number of studies were designed to investigate the effects of odd prices on consumers. The major directions of study are presented in Figure 25.1.

From a chronological perspective, the first direction focused on the effects of odd prices on the demand size. Further, a new direction evolved and referred to various aspects that may be labelled 'salience of odd prices', even if not all researchers used this terminology. Lately, several researchers started to explore the effects in specific sectors, customer segments, cultures, etc.

Effects of odd prices on demand

One of the first research directions referred to the type and size of the impact of odd prices. Some of the studies provided empirical evidence for an increased demand.

The results of a mall intercept of 300 household shoppers organized by Gendall et al. (1997) supported the assumption of the positive impact on demand. The effects of odd prices on respondents' purchase probability were studied for six products: block of cheese, frozen chicken, box of chocolates, hair dryer, electric kettle and food blender. Two criteria were used to select products: the broad appeal and the existence of four critical price levels identified by retailers (under $10, $20, $50 and $100). According to the results, an odd price (e.g. $9.99) generates greater demand than a slightly higher even price (e.g. $10). The effect was more visible for lower-priced food items and for price endings in the digit 9.

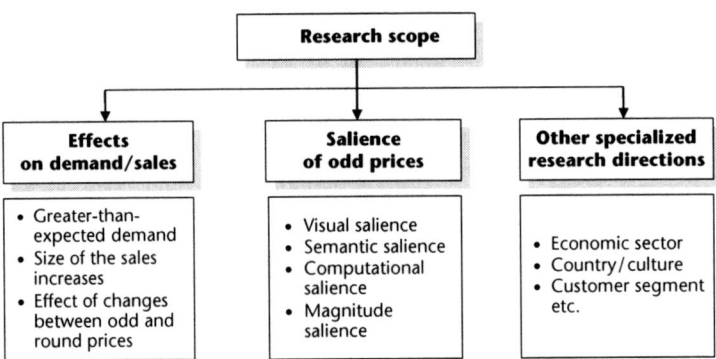

FIGURE 25.1 Scope of the research on odd prices

A study designed by Gendall et al. (1998) also provided support for the assumption that odd endings like 95 and 99 cents produce greater-than-expected demand, at least at the individual brand level. Three brands of three products were considered: a $4 can of fly spray, a $7 block of cheese and a $50 electric kettle. The experimental model assumed that consumer choice depends on the relative utility of the alternatives offered. For the electric kettle, the results showed a 6.4 per cent increase in sales for a 0.1 per cent reduction in price from $50 to $49.95. The increase was almost in the same range (between 8 and 10 per cent) as in studies designed by Blattberg and Wisniewski (1987) and Schindler and Kibarian (1996). For the fly spray and the block of cheese, the equivalent relationships were less attractive, but provided empirical support for higher sales increases when applying 99-ending prices rather than slightly higher even prices.

Three field experiments organized by Anderson and Simester (2003) led to the conclusion that $9 price endings increase demand. However, the effect is stronger in the case of new products for which customers have less relative price information compared to established items. The experiments demonstrated that $9 price endings are less effective at increasing demand when items already have 'sales' signs.

In contrast, the study of Bray and Harris (2006), revealed that 9-ending prices do not always lead to optimum sales. The two authors organized a large-scale trial in 12 stores with the support of a retailer with 400 stores across the UK that applied 9-ending prices on all non-promotional prices for more than 50 years. Prices were increased by one penny (from the retailers' traditional 9-ending prices to the pound-round prices) for a selection of ten shopping products with broad appeal and relatively low cost (under £15). The results of the trial showed sales increases for nine out of the ten products. These suggest a statistically significant link between price endings and sales, but not necessarily in favour of the 9-ending prices.

Manning and Sprott (2009) found that changes between odd prices and round prices influence the product choices of consumers at the point of purchase. More specifically, the evidence provided by three experiments demonstrated the following: (i) choice share of a lower-priced alternative was maximized when it had a just-below price (i.e. $1.99) and the higher-priced alternative had a round price (i.e. $3.00); (ii) price endings that minimized the difference in the leftmost digits of the prices (i.e. $2.00 and $2.99) produced the largest share for the higher-priced alternative compared to all other price endings; (iii) just-below prices shifted the share of choices towards the lower-priced option in the case of expensive products (e.g. a gift).

This research direction focused on the effects of odd prices on demand has not always led to conclusive results.

Salience of odd prices

Salience is a term found in various fields of research such as pricing, consumer behaviour, cognitive psychology, policy making, etc. However, the use of the term did not lead to a clear and generally accepted definition of the concept of price salience.

According to Kim and Kachersky (2006), there are two major perspectives of salience in the research literature focused on other fields than pricing. The former is focused on attention (respectively a person's attention is captured by one aspect of a situation, which is more prominent and noticeable than others). The latter is centred on memory (the salience of a topic being related to the amount of information a person holds about that topic, salience being a process that increases the probability of storing a piece of information in memory).

Relative to the multi-dimensional prices, four dimensions of price salience were identified: visual, semantic, computational and magnitude (Kim and Kachersky 2006). Hereinafter, these dimensions are analysed (not necessarily from multi-dimensional perspective).

Visual salience of odd prices

A visually salient price attracts consumers' attention. Such a price will not be ignored by them. An example of research on the visual salience of odd prices is the study of the direction of price digits. The concept of digit directionality consists in the left- or right-facing orientation of the price digits. The perception of digit directionality refers to the consumer perception that these numbers are 'pointing' or 'facing' a particular direction.

According to Coulter (2007), the use of truncation encoding strategies depends not only on the left-to-right processing of the price digits, but also on the direction of digits and the resulting eye-movement bias. He tested the digit-directionality assumption (that digits 1, 2, 3, 4, 7, and 9 face to the left, digits 5 and 6 face to the right, and digits 0 and 8 appear symmetrical and may be considered 'neutral'). The hypothesis of the directionality of the digits 2, 3, 6, 8, 9 and 0 was confirmed. In another experiment, subjects were exposed to six advertisements for a fictitious snowboard brand. Each ad contained one of the following prices: $888.98, $888.58, $855.88, $899.88, $887 or $886. The price $888.98 was more likely to be rounded down than $888.58. The subjects were significantly more likely to round down a price of $887 to $880, than a price of $886. According to the findings, greater (lesser) degree of attention paid to a price digit results in more (less) accurate recall of that digit and consequently decreases (increases) the likelihood that consumers exhibit a price truncation behaviour (the right-facing digit 5 facilitated accurate price encoding and recall, while the left-facing digit 9 led to a price truncation strategy).

There is a lot of room for further study of the visual aspects of odd price salience.

Semantic salience of odd prices

Consumers' perceptions and symbolic signals of odd prices were studied by researchers. In essence, according to the theory of consumer behaviour, perception consists in the process by which stimuli are selected, organized and interpreted (Solomon et al. 2010). Through information processing, consumers assign meanings to the price stimuli.

In 1991, Schindler noted both the perception of deception by the seller and the perception of the presence of discounts. On one side, consumers may realize that odd and even prices are equivalent and may consider that sellers tend to mislead them by means of odd prices. On the other side, odd prices may signal the presence of discounts and cost savings, while even prices may signal higher levels of product quality.

Practice shows that prominent retailers with a relatively classy image such as Neiman-Marcus, Nordstrom and Macy's tend to use round-number prices that end for instance in the digit 0 and to avoid the digit 9. In contrast, retail chains such as Wal-Mart and Target which are more focused on the mainstream buyers show a propensity towards odd-ending (Stiving 2000).

Numerous research studies explored the association between price and quality. Pricing experts consider that a buyer tends to use price as a cue for quality when he does not have information on other salient attributes of the offering.

The quality-price inference was also identified among young buyers (18–25 years old) from Taiwan, in the case of mobile phones and notebooks (Tsao et al. 2005). According to the research findings, there is a positive relationship between the perceptual belief and the inferential belief about the price–quality association. This link is stronger when the perceptual belief is based on direct purchase experience (the case of mobile phones) rather than on advertising. In the absence of a direct purchase experience (the case of notebooks), buyers tend to rely on advertising to form their inferential belief.

The findings of a controlled experiment organized by Schindler and Kibarian (2001), make retailers aware of the two-fold effect (positive and negative image) of odd prices presented in advertisements. The study focused on the reactions of middle-income women from the suburban environment to a set of advertisements that prominently displayed a price with either 99-ending or 00-ending. The results underlined that the 99-ending may communicate a favourable image that products are on discount without any unfavourable association of low quality. In the case of retailers with a higher-perceived quality, advertisements that display 99 price endings may decrease the image of customers relative to the merchandise quality and retailer's classiness.

Further research by Schindler (2006) explored the 99 price endings as a signal of a low-price appeal for consumers. The findings based on 2,292 price ads indicated the existence of a quite strong relation in the marketplace between the use of 99-ending prices and the presence of cues for a low-price appeal. According to the research results, this appeal is determined by the tendency of retailers to supplement a low-price claim with any available means to make the price actually appear low and get the attention of consumers. Due to repeated exposures to such ads, consumers learn the association between 99-ending prices and cost savings.

The computational dimension of salience

Computational salience increases with the decrease of computational complexity. Estelami published the results of two studies relative to the computational effect of price endings in multi-dimensional-price advertising (1999). There are goods and services advertised with a variety of dimensions that require computation in order to know the final price. Mail-order companies advertise separately the product price and the shipping/handling costs. Prices are often multi-dimensional in the financial sector or in the retailing of durable goods.

The research findings showed that computation difficulty is a function of both price endings and arithmetic operations required to compute the price. The computational effort reflected by the response time may increase up to ten times in the case of non-rounded endings (e.g. $154), compared to the round format (e.g. $100). When consumers have to make multiplications, the computational effort may increase four times compared to the situations when only addition is needed to calculate the final price.

The use by sellers of non-roundable endings in multi-dimensional prices and calculations with a higher degree of complexity may result in lower accuracy of consumer's price perception. Consumers may perceive as more fair and attractive the prices presented in a simple manner.

The magnitude dimension of salience

Magnitude is another dimension of price salience. The prices which exceed the top of the reference range could be salient.

The practice of 9-ending prices pushes the upper limit of the price range (Kim and Kachersky 2006). However, research carried out by Schindler and Kirby (1997) provides evidence that supports the underestimation effect rather than the perceived-gain effect. The research was based on 1,415 sampled selling prices ranging from $.34 to $3,900,000, included in print newspaper advertisements from major US metropolitan areas.

Findings showed that consumers underestimate the actual price as they spare the effort of processing the last digit. A price of $799 may be truncated to $790 and thus may fall within the reference price range. A rounding to $800 will surpass the upper bound of the reference price range. Consumers tend to translate non-round numbers into round numbers if round-number prices are not provided by retailers. This information processing results in the underestimation effect, according to which the price perceived by the consumer is lower than the actual price. The high cognitive accessibility of the round numbers leads to an overrepresentation of the 9-endings in price advertisements and explains the overrepresentation of the 0- and 5-ending prices.

Due to the underestimation effect, prices become salient as consumers perceive them as lower than the displayed prices. Several questions may be added relative to the potential impact of the product, brand and competition over the consumer information processing.

Other specialized research directions

Besides the study of the effects of odd prices on demand and the odd price salience, research efforts were also deployed in several specialized research directions. Examples are the use of odd prices in sectors such as restaurants and tourism, the effects of odd prices in specific countries/cultures and the application of odd prices to specific customer segments.

Research on the use of odd prices in specific economic sectors

Lately, the perspective about consumer response to odd prices was enriched with research findings that refer to the intangible services offerings. Besides retailing, odd prices may be found in the hospitality sector, in restaurants and hotels.

A relevant example is the study of Parsa and Naipaul (2007). The results of a mail survey on a sample of fine-dining restaurants and quick-service restaurants provided empirical support that restaurant operators intentionally use odd-even pricing to send pre-purchase signals of quality and value. The authors formulated the price endings and consumer behaviour model (PCBM) with hypotheses confirmed by research. Thus, fine-dining restaurants signal quality by means of 00 price endings, while quick-service restaurants signal high value with 99 price endings. These price endings provide an equilibrium solution in the restaurant sector.

An analysis of restaurants from France, Spain and Italy, and a subsequent comparison with US and Taiwanese restaurants, showed differences in terms of odd-pricing tactics (Hu et al. 2006). The researchers classified the restaurants in three categories: (i) high-end, fine-dining restaurants with menu prices of €18 or higher; (ii) mid-priced, casual-dining restaurants with menu prices between €7 and €17; (iii) quick-service restaurants with menu prices of €6 or less. As regards the rightmost single digit, 0-ending prices dominated the menus of the European restaurants (99.66 per cent of the menu items in the high-end restaurants, 92.38 per cent in the casual-dining restaurants and 85.98 per cent in the quick-service restaurants). The 5- and 9-endings had a lower occurrence. Price-ending practices in Europe differ from those applied in the USA and are more similar to those in Taiwan. Relative to the two rightmost digits of the price, the researchers identified that in the high-end European restaurants, the 00-ending prices were predominant (80.48 per cent of the menu items). The 50-ending and 80-ending were also used (11.52 per cent and respectively 3.37 per cent). In the mid-price restaurants, 00, 50 and 80 were the most applied endings (25.36 per cent, 16.77 per cent and respectively 10.47 per cent). In the quick-service restaurants, the most commonly used two-digit price endings were 50 (20.48 per cent), 00 (15.63 per cent) and 80 (9.86 per cent).

Another study that opens a specialized perspective of the odd-ending prices is the research designed by Kleinsasser and Wagner (2011). The study refers to the impact of odd prices on consumers in the hotel sector and the moderating effects of personal involvement and price interest in this relationship. The research findings showed that price endings influence price perceptions. The part-worth utilities of different price endings decrease with increasing prices. The survey evidence supported the hypothesis that highly involved consumers are less sensitive to the image effects induced by price endings, compared to less involved consumers. The respondents highly interested in price seemed to prefer prices ending in 9, while respondents less interested in price did not prefer 9-ending prices. Thus, findings demonstrated that consumer involvement and the price interest have a moderating effect on perceptions of price endings.

Odd prices in specific countries and cultures

Most empirical research relative to odd prices focused on the practice of companies in western countries, especially in the USA. During the last decade, the interest of researchers was also directed towards other markets, for example Europe and Asia.

An example is the study of Suri et al. (2004) that contrasts the effectiveness of 9-ending prices in the USA with Poland. The findings revealed that 0-endings were the most popular in the Polish ads and 9-endings in the US ads. Odd prices were perceived as a gain by a higher percentage of the US respondents compared to the sample of Polish respondents (89 per cent compared to 55 per cent), the difference being statistically significant. As regards the fair price estimate, Polish consumers tend to associate odd prices with an overall loss, while US respondents associate them with a small gain. Polish respondents perceive odd prices as less fair, sales offers with such prices being less valuable and more likely to deceive them.

Holdershaw et al. (2005) explored the effects of odd pricing on demand in China. A stated-preference choice modelling experiment was organized for three commonly used products: detergent, thermos bottle and peanut oil. Research findings were consistent with results of studies carried out in western countries. The 9-ending prices generated greater-than-expected demand for each of the three products, while 5-ending prices generated this effect for two products (thermos bottle and peanut oil). From the researchers' perspective, the effects of odd prices on demand have a biological rather than a cultural explanation. The experiment showed that the higher the odd price, the greater the effect on demand.

Another direction of research refers to the analysis of odd pricing within a cultural framework. Nguyen et al. (2007) explained the variances in the practice of odd and even pricing in western versus non-western countries, on the basis of high context (HC)/low context (LC) culture constructs. Their approach was based on the theory of the anthropologist Edward T. Hall (1976), according to which LC cultures attach more importance to the explicit message and to the meaning of the message, rather than to the context in which the message is conveyed. On the opposite side, HC cultures care about the implicit, non-verbal cues of the message. Nguyen et al. conducted a survey of prices posted on the web mainly in local online shopping malls, for a sample of ten countries (China, Hong Kong, India, Japan, Brazil, Argentina, USA, Australia, Norway and Italy). The research findings showed that consumers in HC non-western cultures are less inclined to associate odd prices with cheaper items or gains, compared to consumers from LC western cultures. In HC non-western cultures, odd prices may very likely offend consumers. In these cultures, 9-ending prices may be less successful than even prices ending in 0 or 8 (for the Cantonese Chinese, the number 8 means luck and for the Japanese consumers it symbolizes prosperity). Western companies should not transpose the odd pricing tactics from their country of origin to markets with HC culture. If they still intend to use odd prices, conveying a gain that is more real is recommended (e.g. 3.90 instead of 3.99).

Odd prices and specific customer segments

Most studies have considered consumers as a homogeneous mass. A relatively new field of investigation is related to the perception of odd prices by specific consumer segments.

One of the few attempts to investigate the response of market segments to odd prices is the research of Harris and Bray (2007). The goal of the study was to identify in the UK the consumer groups that are more likely to choose odd-ending prices versus round-ending prices. The research findings revealed that men are more likely to respond to round-ending prices and women to odd-ending prices. However, respondents are not exclusively focused on one type of ending. Consumers over 60 years old preferred round-ending prices.

Damay et al. (2011) examined how children between 6 and 12 years old attribute and select product prices according to their presentation (price format and ending). The research findings revealed that children tend to prefer round prices. These preferences are expressed especially for high-priced products and increase with the education level and age. When required to select prices from a predefined set, the propensity to round prices extends to all products, not being limited to high-priced items. Children also prefer to choose 0-ending prices when prices are presented in a decimal form. The level of price knowledge does not affect children's preference for 0-ending prices.

Conclusions

The effects of odd prices were investigated by researchers during almost eight decades. However, the findings of the empirical research on odd prices are sometimes considered inconclusive, contradictory and scarce. The opinions of researchers are split.

A significant feature of this overview is the focus on the diverse and dynamic body of knowledge consisting in odd-pricing research results. The paper is not substantiated on 'carved-into-stone' statements about 'already-known' aspects usually presented in marketing textbooks. The aim was to explore research endeavours that are sometimes limited in terms of approach and findings, but which contribute to academic and managerial advancement.

This paper provided a systematic analysis of major research contributions and introduced three building-blocks of the scope of the research on odd prices: effects on demand/sales, salience of odd prices and other specialized research directions.

This analysis answers the question raised in the introduction. Even if odd pricing practice is more than one century old, research on odd price topics has a long way to go in the clarification of major aspects of interest to practitioners and to an increasing number of researchers.

Managerial implications for innovation in pricing

Researchers still study the effects of price endings on consumers and sales. Clear dos and don'ts for marketing professionals have not emerged. Additional empirical evidence is required because the possibility to generalize the results of the available research studies is limited. However, several aspects to be considered when setting prices are presented hereinafter.

Odd-ending prices may positively influence buyer behaviour, generating greater demand than a slightly higher even price, at least in markets such as the USA. Managers and professionals might consider applying such prices that are common practice among retailers. Consumers could more positively react to odd prices in the case of lower-priced food items. The prices ending in 9 or .95 or .99 are widely applied. However, 9-ending prices generate sometimes lower sales than the immediate upper round-ending price.

To increase the effectiveness of odd prices, managers and professionals must think about the visual, semantic, computational and magnitude salience of these prices. From the visual salience perspective, consumers may more accurately recall right-facing digits (like 5) and may round down the prices with left-facing digits (such as 9). From the semantic perspective, the symbolic signals of odd-price endings may impact consumer demand. The 99-endings could generate cues for a low-price appeal to potential buyers. However, for retailers with a classy image or high-quality positioning, the display (at least in the advertisements) of 99 price endings may be negatively perceived by consumers. As regards the computational salience of odd prices, rounded endings and less arithmetic operations make prices more salient. However, if the objective is to make comparisons with competitive offerings more difficult, higher complexity may lead to lower accuracy in consumers' perceptions of multi-dimensional prices. With regard to magnitude, prices that overpass the top of the reference range could be salient.

The use of odd prices evolved not only in retailing, but also in the hospitality sector. Managers and professionals from this field must consider the existing mental associations of odd prices with a specific level of quality and value, perceptions that were probably forged by the price setting practice itself. In the USA, the managers of fine-dining restaurants that want to project a high-quality image could use 00-ending prices, compared to the case of quick-service restaurants that could use 99-ending prices which convey a high-value image. The price-ending practice differs in Europe from the USA. In almost all categories of restaurants from European countries such as France, Spain and Italy, zero is often the rightmost single digit of the menu prices. The two rightmost digits of prices that predominate in high-end European restaurants are 00, while in mid-price restaurants they are 00 and 50 and in quick-service restaurants they are 50 and 00. As regards the tourism sector, for example in Austria, companies that focus on customers that are less involved in the buying decision could apply 9-endings that are preferred by such consumers which are very interested in prices.

The decision-makers from companies with an international presence should be aware of the differences in business practices and consumer perceptions among countries. For example, 0-ending prices are more suitable in Polish ads, compared to 9-ending prices in the USA. In Poland, it is advisable not to apply odd prices because consumers perceive them as less fair and deceptive, compared to the USA consumers that associate odd prices with a small gain. In addition, odd prices are not recommended in high-context non-western cultures where most consumers feel offended by odd prices and where there is no image effect of cheaper items or gains. However, instead of 9-endings, managers may use 8-ending prices for the products addressed to the Cantonese Chinese consumers (that associate the digit 8 with luck) and to the Japanese consumers (for which the digit 8 means prosperity).

The preference for odd prices differs by age groups. A manager targeting primary school children cannot achieve positive results with odd prices, as they prefer round prices. There is evidence that consumers over 60 years old prefer round-ending prices.

Is odd pricing a relevant and profitable strategy for companies present in business-to-business markets? The empirical evidence refers to the impact of odd prices on consumers rather than on businesses. In principle, in business-to-business markets, odd prices could not impact significantly the organizational buying behaviour as companies are rational rather than emotional in their purchasing decisions. Nevertheless, organizational decisions are made by individuals and one may hypothesize that their consumer behaviour and mental associations could transgress the 'corporate boundaries'.

When balancing the pluses and minuses of odd prices, managers and professionals should be aware of 'the other face of Janus'. There are multiple warnings not to be overlooked. First, the use of odd prices by many brands within a category may deter the impact upon consumers. Second, the impact of odd prices on sales volume is rather difficult to quantify in a market characterized by various competitive influences. Third, odd prices are associated by several groups of consumers with low quality or with misleading retail practices and could negatively affect high-end brands focused on performance and service or with a classy positioning.

Recommendations

A distinctive feature of the paper is the formulation of recommendations for further innovation in research on odd prices. The agenda for future investigations may be centred on two pillars – the scope and the design of the research. For the former, two areas may be considered: (i) consumers' perception of and response to odd prices; (ii) supplier's odd pricing practices. For the latter, new choices of methods and approaches are possible.

First, the analysis of the odd pricing tactics of vendors is important considering the hypothesis of the potential of such practices to shape the purchasing behaviour of consumers. Not only marketing managers, but also macro-policy makers and consumer protection decision-makers might be interested. The following aspects may draw the attention of researchers:

- occurrence of odd prices in different economic sectors;
- specific features of odd pricing in various countries/cultures;
- types of price endings applied to various product categories;
- range of effects on sales generated by odd prices in the case of retailers of fast moving consumer goods and of service providers;
- managerial beliefs relative to consumer behaviour and natural cognitive tendencies;
- perceptions of managers relative to the effectiveness of odd prices;
- reasons why managers apply/avoid odd prices etc.

Second, most of the future innovation in the research on odd prices might be related to the study of consumers' perceptions and response. The following directions could be considered:

- magnitude of the demand increases generated by odd pricing in the case of various price endings and demand curves;
- insights into the information processing of price endings by consumers (also in relation to various factors such as the time pressure on purchasing decisions and the multi-sensory stimuli from the retail environment);
- odd prices and the effect of complexities in multi-dimensional prices on consumers' computational effort;
- perception of consumer segments (based on age, familiarity with the brand/product, lifestyle, involvement in the purchase decision, price sensitivity, etc.) relative to odd prices and reasons of specific behavioural responses;
- influence of cultural values and norms on consumers' reaction to price endings and symbolic meanings of price endings in different cultures;

- effectiveness (in terms of consumers' response) of odd pricing by products/categories, quality level, brand image and market status.

Third, another area of innovation in research on odd prices is the identification of research methods able to enhance the validity of results. Experimental designs consisting in real buying decisions could bring additional clarifications compared to controlled laboratory experiments. However, both have limitations. Field trials may lead to inconsistent results due to the numerous marketing factors that are not controlled by researchers within the market environment. Such factors are competitive actions and marketing communication. The results of face-to-face interviews about the propensity to buy and about the preferences relative to price endings may be questionable due to the pressure placed on consumers and because the statements of consumers may not lead to actual purchases. The often-used laboratory studies have as the main drawback their inability to accurately reflect the real purchasing situations. More sophisticated research methods may be considered. An example could be the hybrid approaches of the conjoint analysis, in order to estimate the utility of more attributes and attribute levels in relation with the odd pricing tactics.

Fourth, besides research methods, the innovation in further studies may target research approaches. Cross-category, cross-brand and cross-cultural analyses will provide additional insights into the research scope. Comparisons among product categories relative to odd pricing effects may guide the decisions towards increased effectiveness. Analysis of similarities and differences between the effects of odd prices on the brands within a specific product category may lead decision-makers to better choices and lower losses caused by inappropriate pricing tactics. Approaches based on contrasting the effects of odd prices in high-context and low-context cultures may provide support to managers for the adaptation of their pricing tactics to the local markets or for the extension of the pricing decisions from the country of origin.

The above-mentioned directions of innovation in the research on odd prices are only some of those that will evolve in the near future. It is not innovation for its own sake. Finally, the utility of all the future endeavours in this field will be validated by marketing practitioners interested in enhancing business profitability and in expanding the presence of their companies on the global market.

References

Anderson, E. T. and Simester, D. I. (2003) Effects of $9 price endings on retail sales: Evidence from field experiments. *Quantitative Marketing and Economics*, 1 (1), pp. 93–110.
Blattberg, R. C. and Wisniewski, K. J. (1987) *How retail price promotions work: empirical results*. Working Paper No. 42. Nielsen Marketing Science Conference, Chicago, IL: University of Chicago.
Boyes, W. J., Lynch, A. K. and Mounts, W. S. Jr. (2007) Why odd pricing? *Journal of Applied Social Psychology*, 37 (5), pp. 1130–40.
Bray, J. P. and Harris, C. (2006) The effect of 9-ending prices on retail sales: A quantitative UK based field study. *Journal of Marketing Management*, 22 (5–6), pp. 601–17.

Coulter, K. S. (2007) The effects of digit-direction on eye movement bias and price-rounding behaviour. *Journal of Product and Brand Management*, 16 (7), pp. 501–8.

Damay, C., Guichard, N. and Clauzel, A. (2011) When children confront prices: an approach based on price presentation. *Journal of Product & Brand Management*, 20 (7), pp. 514–25.

Estelami, H. (1999) The computational effect of price endings in multi-dimensional price advertising. *Journal of Product & Brand Management*, 8 (3), pp. 244–56.

Gedenk, K. and Sattler, H. (1999) The impact of price thresholds on profit contribution – should retailers set 9-ending prices? *Journal of Retailing*, 75 (1), pp. 33–57.

Gendall, P., Fox, M. and Wilton P. (1998) Estimating the effect of odd pricing. *Journal of Product and Brand Management*, 7 (5), pp. 421–32.

Gendall, P., Holdershaw, J. and Garland, R. (1997) The effect of odd pricing on demand. *European Journal of Marketing*, 31 (11/12), pp. 799–813.

Georgoff, D. M. (1972) *Odd-even retail price endings: Their effects on value determination, product perception and buying propensities*. East Lansing, MI: Michigan State University.

Ginzberg, E. (1936) Customary prices. *American Economic Review*, 26 (2), p. 296.

Hall, E. T. (1976). *Beyond culture*. New York, NY: Doubleday.

Harris, C. and Bray, J. P. (2007) Price endings and consumer segmentation. *Journal of Product & Brand Management*, 16 (3), pp. 200–5.

Holdershaw, J., Gendall, P. and Gou, Y. (2005) The effects of odd pricing in China. *Journal of Asia Pacific Marketing*, 4 (1), pp. 76–84.

Hollander, S. P. (1967) Social pressures and retail competition. In: Cateora, P. R. and Richardson, L. (eds) *Readings in marketing: The qualitative and quantitative areas*. New York, NY: Meredith Publishing Company, pp. 343–52.

Hu, H.-S., Parsa, H. G. and Zhao, J. L. (2006) The magic of price-ending choices in European restaurants: a comparative study. *International Journal of Contemporary Hospitality Management*, 18 (2), pp. 110–22.

Huston, J. and Kamdar, N. (1996) $9.99: Can 'just-below' pricing be reconciled with rationality? *Eastern Economic Journal*, 22 (2), pp. 137–45.

Kahneman, D. and Tversky, A. (1979) Prospect theory: An analysis of decision under risk. *Econometrica*, 47 (2), pp. 263–91.

Kim, K. M. and Kachersky, L. (2006) Dimensions of price salience: a conceptual framework for perceptions of multi-dimensional prices. *Journal of Product & Brand Management*, 15 (2), pp. 139–47.

Kleinsasser, S. and Wagner, U. (2011) Price endings and tourism consumers' price perceptions. *Journal of Retailing and Consumer Services*, 18, pp. 58–63.

Kotler, P. (2000) *Marketing management: The millennium edition*. Upper Saddle River, NJ: Prentice Hall.

Landsberg, S. E. (1992) *Price theory and applications*, 2nd edition. Fort Worth, TX: The Dryden Press.

Manning, K. C. and Sprott, D. E. (2009) Price endings, left-digit effects, and choice. *Journal of Consumer Research*, 36 (2), pp. 328–35.

Nagle, T. and Holden, R. K. (1995) *The strategy and tactics of pricing*, 2nd edition. Englewood Cliffs, NJ: Prentice Hall.

Nguyen, A., Heeler, R. M. and Taran, Z. (2007) High-low context cultures and price-ending practices. *Journal of Product & Brand Management*, 16 (3), pp. 206–14.

Parsa, H. G. and Naipaul S. (2007) Price-ending strategies and managerial perspectives: A reciprocal phenomenon – Part I. *Journal of Services Research*, 7 (2), pp. 7–26.

Schindler, R. M. (1991) Symbolic meanings of a price ending. In: Holman, R. H. and Solomon, M. R. (eds) *Advances in consumer research, Volume 18*. Provo, UT: Association for Consumer Research, pp. 794–801.

Schindler, R. M. (2006) The 99 price ending as a signal of a low-price appeal. *Journal of Retailing*, 82 (1), pp. 71–7.

Schindler, R. M. and Kibarian, T. (1996) Increased consumer sales response through use of 99-ending prices. *Journal of Retailing*, 72 (2), pp. 187–99.

Schindler, R. M. and Kibarian, T. M. (2001) Image communicated by the use of 99 endings in advertised prices. *Journal of Advertising*, 30 (4), pp. 95–9.

Schindler, R. M. and Kirby, P. N. (1997) Patterns of rightmost digits used in advertised prices: implications for nine-ending effects. *Journal of Consumer Research*, 24 (2), pp. 192–201.

Solomon, M. R., Bamossy, G., Askegaard, S. and Hogg, M. K. (2010) *Consumer behaviour: A European perspective*, 4th edition. Prentice Hall, Financial Times.

Stigler, G. J. (ed.). (1956) *Trends in employment in the service industries*. UMI. Retrieved December 10, 2011 from http://www.nber.org/chapters/c2824.pdf.

Stiving, M. (2000) Price-endings when prices signal quality. *Management Science*, 46 (12), pp. 1617–29.

Stiving, M. and Winer, R. S. (1997) An empirical analysis of price endings with scanner data. *Journal of Consumer Research*, 24 (1), pp. 57–67.

Suri, R., Anderson, R. E. and Kotlov, V. (2004) The use of 9-ending prices: contrasting the USA with Poland. *European Journal of Marketing*, 38 (1/2), pp. 56–72.

Thomas, M. and Morwitz, W. (2005) Penny wise and pound foolish: The left-digit effect in price cognition. *Journal of Consumer Research*, 32 (1), pp. 54–64.

Tsao, H.-Y., Pitt, L. F. and Caruana, A. (2005) The formation of a 'high price-high quality' inferential belief: A study among young buyers of mobile phones and notebooks. *Asia Pacific Journal of Marketing and Logistics*, 17 (1), pp. 50–60.

Wagner, R. and Beinke, K.-S. (2006) Identifying patterns of customer response to price endings. *Journal of Product & Brand Management*, 15 (5), pp. 341–51.

26
APPLYING CONSUMER PSYCHOLOGY TO SOFTWARE PRICING

Anshu Jalora

The challenge

Product versioning enables software companies to tap into customers' differential willingness to pay (Lehmann and Buxmann 2009; Shapiro and Varian 1998), while value-based pricing allows them to identify customer value drivers and the perceived worth of different features and functionalities by the customers (Muller 2011; Raghunathan 2000). If we look at the pricing of some of the popular consumer software products available in the market, we can notice that these products are being offered in multiple versions, with substantially differentiated prices. For example, check the prices of Microsoft Office in Figure 26.1, Norton Anti-Virus in Figure 26.2, McAfee Anti-Virus in Figure 26.3, Adobe Acrobat in Figure 26.4 and SPSS in Figure 26.5.

Consider the prices shown in Figure 26.5 for different versions of IBM SPSS Statistics. The Standard version is priced at $5,120, while the Professional version is priced at $10,300. Here the customers can easily associate the price difference between these two versions with the additional features in the Professional version. That is, by paying $5,180 ($10,300 − $5,120) extra, customers will get access to the Categories, Data Preparation, Decision Trees, Forecasting, and Missing Values modules. Customers will probably make a decision based upon their specific functional needs. Notice that the difference in the marginal costs of production of the Professional version versus the Standard version is negligible. Here, IBM would like to persuade its standard version customers to buy higher priced Professional or Premium versions. The same situations hold for the other software products mentioned above. To some extent, customers can be incentivized to buy higher-end version products by keeping the price difference between the lower-end versions and the higher-end versions low. However, this approach runs the risk of undervaluing the additional features in the higher-end versions, and therefore can be applied to a limited extent!

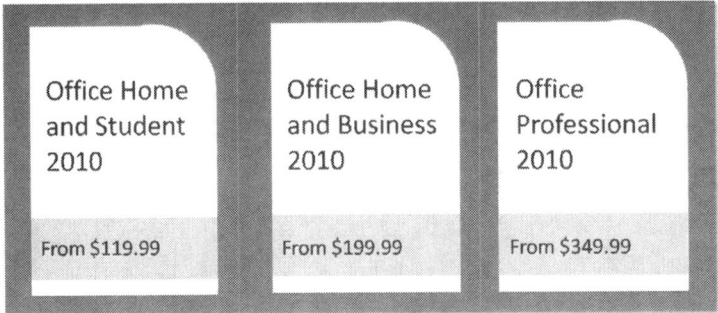

FIGURE 26.1 Microsoft Office prices (http://office.microsoft.com/en-us/)

FIGURE 26.2 Norton prices (http://us.norton.com/products/)

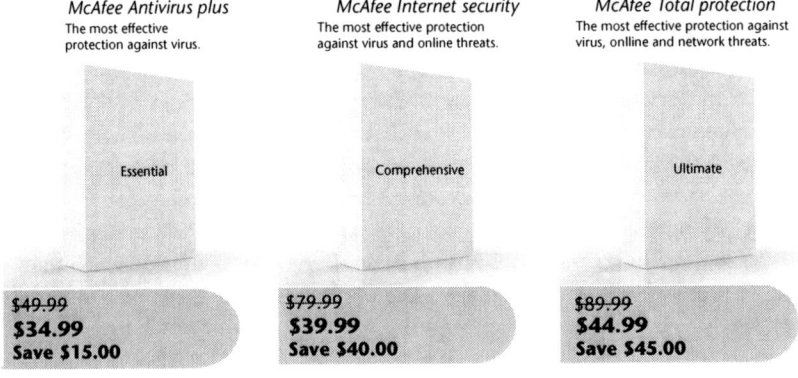

FIGURE 26.3 McAfee prices (http://home.mcafee.com/store/)

Microsoft Windows 7 situation

Microsoft is offering Windows 7 in Home Basic, Home Premium and Professional versions in India. Their prices are shown in Figure 26.6. The price differences between the different versions can be attributed to the additional features in the

FIGURE 26.4 Adobe Acrobat prices (http://www.adobe.com/products/acrobat.html)

FIGURE 26.5 IBM SPSS Statistics prices (http://www-01.ibm.com/software/analytics/spss/products/statistics/)

higher versions, as highlighted in Figure 26.6. Similar to the SPSS case described earlier, there is a substantial price difference between the Professional version and the other lower-priced versions (Home Basic and Home Premium), while the difference in the marginal costs of production of these products would be negligible.

Microsoft would prefer its customers to buy the Professional version. Let's assume that Microsoft has already optimized Windows 7 prices for maximizing profits, and has already explored opportunities for temporary price reductions and freebies for getting short-term lift in sales of the Professional version (Chandon et al. 2000; Raghubir 2005). The challenge for Microsoft is to further influence customer behaviour and motivate them to purchase the Professional version without changing the prices or the composition of the different versions.

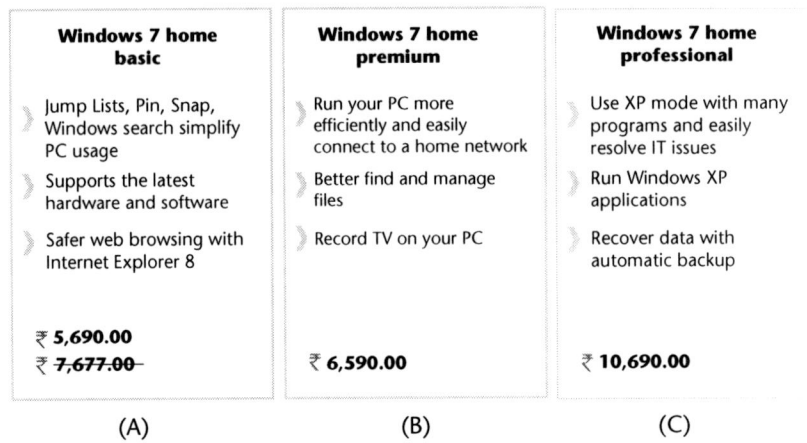

FIGURE 26.6 Microsoft Windows 7 prices (http://www.microsoftstore.co.in/)

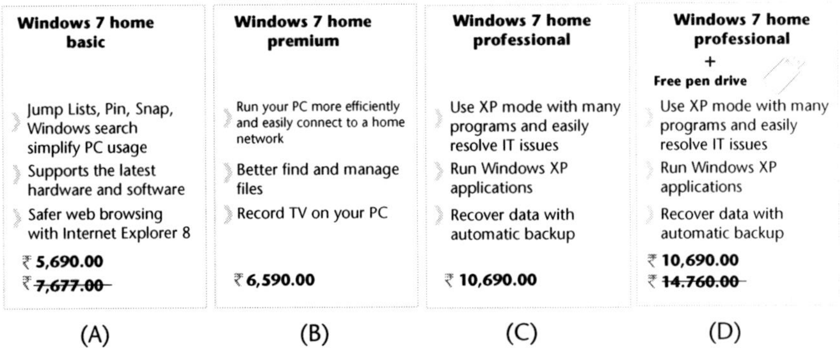

FIGURE 26.7 Options offered to test group (http://www.microsoftstore.co.in/)

The strategy

In response to the challenge identified in the previous section, Microsoft explored opportunities with adding a 'decoy' (Huber *et al.* 1982) to its portfolio of Windows 7. Microsoft created a new version of Windows 7 Professional bundled with a 4 GB Pen Drive (Option D in Figure 26.7), and priced the bundle at Rs 10,690. To make this new version attractive, Microsoft priced Windows 7 Professional (decoy, Option C in Figure 26.7) also at Rs 10,690. If we compare these two options, we can notice that Option D dominates over Option C, by offering more (4 GB Pen Drive), while charging the same price.

Notice that since Option C is a decoy, no one will buy this option; however, it will set a reference price against which customers will compare the price of Option D. Ariely (2010) highlights an important aspect of consumer psychology that while making purchase decisions, consumers, instead of absolute assessment, perform a relative assessment of prices of different options available to them. Since Option D offers more for the same price as Option C, Option D appears as an attractive deal.

The image and the price presentation for Option D are also intended to reinforce the positioning of Option D as an attractive deal. Microsoft is displaying the keyword 'Free' next to the Pen Drive in the image for Option D. Poundstone (2010) discusses the power of this keyword and how it drives customers' interest in the product, and we can expect the same to happen here too. The image being used with Option D is blowing up the size of the Pen Drive, and therefore is an attempt to get customers more focused on the free item. Option D's price is being displayed with a much larger price struck out. This might give an impression to the customers that the price being displayed is a limited time discount price, and will create a sense of greed and fear in the minds of customers, and is likely to get them interested in Option D.

To the best of our knowledge, there is no empirical evidence on whether the use of decoy options in the consumer software industry has been successful. In the following section, we'll empirically quantify the impact of decoy options on consumer behaviour with respect to selecting Windows 7 versions, and overall revenues with Windows 7.

Results

To quantify whether the decoy option (Option C in Figure 26.7) makes the dominant option (Option D in Figure 26.7) appear more attractive, we created two survey groups of 200 members each. The members in both the groups were students enrolled in the MBA programme at NMIMS, and were randomly assigned to the groups. All these students were regular users of laptops and well aware of the different versions of Windows 7. Members in one of the groups were shown the four options in Figure 26.7 (Home Basic, Home Premium, Professional and Professional with Free Pen Drive) and were asked to select the option they would be interested in buying. We call this group the 'test' group. In the other group (called the 'control' group), the members were shown the three options in Figure 26.8 (Home Basic, Home Premium, Professional with Free Pen Drive) and were asked to perform the same exercise as the members in the test group.

Tables 26.1 and 26.2 summarize the selections made by the members in the test and control groups respectively. We can notice that in the test group, 20 per cent of the respondents selected Option D (Windows 7 Professional + Free Pen Drive), while in the control group none of the respondents selected this option. The expected revenue in the test group (Rs 7,158) is 15 per cent higher than the expected revenue in the control group (Rs 6,230). A 15 per cent increase in the top line revenues with Windows 7 will lead to an enormous lift in the bottom line numbers. Thus, we can say that the presence of Option C (the decoy) makes Option D a lucrative one and has the potential of increasing the overall revenues by 15 per cent.

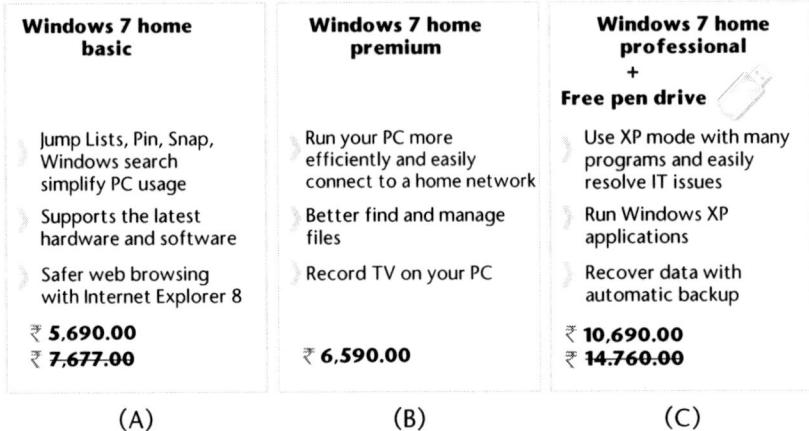

FIGURE 26.8 Options offered to control group (http://www.microsoftstore.co.in/)

TABLE 26.1 Results – test group

Option	Description	% Responses
A	Windows 7 Home Basic	28
B	Windows 7 Home Premium	52
C	Windows 7 Professional	0
D	Windows 7 Professional + FREE Pen Drive	20

TABLE 26.2 Results – control group

Option	Description	% Responses
A	Windows 7 Home Basic	40
B	Windows 7 Home Premium	60
D	Windows 7 Professional + FREE Pen Drive	0

Unexpected finding

The change in the response mix over the three options, with and without the decoy option, reveals something unexpected. Notice that when the decoy option was present, the share of response for Option A dropped by 12 per cent, while it dropped by 8 per cent for Option B. Option B is more expensive than Option A; therefore, the additional spending in buying Option D is lower for the customers who would have bought Option B, vis-à-vis those who would have bought Option A. Therefore, we would expect more Option B customers than Option A customers to opt for Option D. However, our results are contrary to this.

One way to explain this finding is customers are opting for Option D only when an incentive has been created for them. This suggests that those opting for Option D might be deal hunters who will opt for the lowest price option in the absence of deals.

Key lessons

The key learning from this chapter can be summarized as follows:

- Even when a product is not contributing to sales, it can still help create reference prices for the customers.
- Product versioning and value-based pricing approaches can be made more effective by exploring the psychological elements in the consumer decision making process.
- Sales mix shift between different versions of a product can have substantial impact on both the top line and the bottom line numbers, and can be induced by pricing.
- A small incentive offered to customers can be exaggerated in their minds by price presentation techniques.

Implications for innovation in pricing

In this chapter, we investigate the impact of adding a decoy version to a portfolio of versions of a software product. A decoy version is a marginally inferior version of an existing version ('dominant' version) – in terms of product features – and is priced at the same level as the dominant version.

Ariely (2010) highlights an important aspect of consumer psychology that consumers, instead of absolute assessment, perform a relative assessment of prices of different options available to them. Our approach, of adding a decoy to a portfolio of versions offered to customers, taps into this aspect in making an existing product version at its existing price appear more attractive. Presence of a decoy version is effective in shifting the sales mix in favour of the dominant version. When the dominant version is the highest priced version in the portfolio of versions, presence of the decoy version leads to a lift in overall revenues.

References

Ariely, D. (2010) *Predictably irrational, revised and expanded edition: The hidden forces that shape our decisions*. Rev edition. New York, NY: HarperCollins Publishers.

Chandon, P., Wansink, B. and Laurent, G. (2000) A benefit congruency framework of sales promotion effectiveness. *Journal of Marketing*, 64 (October), pp. 65–81.

Huber, J., Payne, J. P. and Puto, C. (1982) Adding asymmetrically dominated alternatives: Violations of regularity and the similarity hypothesis. *Journal of Consumer Research*, 9 (1), pp. 90–8.

Lehmann, S. and Buxmann, P. (2009) Pricing strategies of software vendors. *Business and Information Systems Engineering*, 1 (6), pp. 452–62.

Muller, J. (2011) Value-based portfolio optimization for software product lines. *Proceedings of the 15th International Software Product Line Conference, Munich*, pp. 15–24.

Poundstone, W. (2010) *Priceless: The myth of fair value (and how to take advantage of it)*. New York, NY: Hill and Wang.

Raghubir, P. (2005) Framing a price bundle: the case of 'buy/get' offers. *Journal of Product & Brand Management*, 14 (2), pp. 123–8.

Raghunathan, S. (2000) Software editions: An application of segmentation theory to the packaged software market. *Journal of Management Information Systems*, 17 (1), pp. 87–114.

Shapiro, C. and Varian, H. R. (1998) Versioning: The smart way to sell information. *Harvard Business Review*, (November-December), pp. 106–14.

PART VI
The next frontier

27

THE NEXT FRONTIER OF THE PRICING PROFESSION

Kevin Mitchell

Introduction

Over the past fifty years, pricing has evolved from a topic purely related to economics and academic research to a very practical and powerful instrument to drive profitability in firms. The pricing function has also evolved especially in the last two decades with the development of a strong marketing discipline and the creation of the 4Ps in which price, the only "P" that is not an initial marketing expense, plays a critical role. Today, as pricing becomes a more published topic in economics, marketing, and management literature, we also experience some barriers to making the pricing function and the profession as a whole a true managerial discipline. Compared to other disciplines such as innovation, continuous improvement, and supply chain management, the pricing function is not fully breaking through to the next level. The pricing discipline stands at an existential crossroads. Trade organizations, such as the Professional Pricing Society, and academics have been strong and passionate contributors to bring the pricing discipline to the forefront of the marketing and finance field, but these groups cannot do this alone.

In this concluding chapter, we will reflect on where we come from as a profession as well as where we need to go to bring pricing where it deserves to be. We will examine the next frontier of pricing and call for much innovation in the pricing field to generate excitement and interest for the discipline and profession as a whole.

Where we come from

The pricing discipline has come a long way. There has been a series of evolutionary changes in the last few decades. The most critical change has been the role that pricing has played within the firm: from what was a "gut decision" made by a vocal senior manager in marketing or finance, to a more specific clerical or bookkeeping function who maintained a written price list (strictly on a "cost-plus" basis, most likely), to finally become a more strategic function with decisions made at the highest level of the organization.

Pricing as a clerical function

An early pricing practitioner may not have even known that she or he was exercising the pricing function or was in charge of pricing activities in their firm. Perhaps this person was an outcast in the marketing or accounting department with limited upward mobility or gravitas within their company. As no pricing-specific classes were offered in colleges and universities beyond perhaps a few chapters in Introductory Marketing courses, skill sets and training were difficult to define or locate. Limited power and limited information would mean that our proto-practitioner's work would exist only at the mercy of a cross-functional menagerie that likely had very different goals and ideas. Corporate desires for market share or sales volume targets would (and often still do) greatly outweigh aims to improve specific margins or profits, so pricing goals would have been nebulous. Our proto-practitioner would quickly learn about situations where higher ups would decide that big deals would not be lost because of price.

This administrative employee probably had very little interaction with customer purchasing departments and would have been at a supreme disadvantage in the rare situations when there was customer contact. Then (and now, to a smaller extent) buyers would have had better data, better systems, stronger motivations, and better training at a minimum. If price became a sticking point, a customer could rely on the sales department to pull rank and make the deal outside of pricing targets.

One evolutionary step: becoming tactical

Increased focus on pricing's potential as a profit lever for the firm led to greater knowledge of and emphasis on our practitioner's goals. Those within the pricing discipline were gaining a framework of the importance of their jobs and had opportunities to increase their skill sets. Pricing managers could block some unprofitable deals (leading to the common joke of the pricing department being the "sales prevention department") and perhaps even had options to move up in their firms, although still lacking the career progression of more glamorous fields. Some industries had pricing software options available to further level the field in dealings with customers' purchasers. Marketing research used tools like conjoint analysis to provide better data and estimate elasticity. There were even whole textbooks (Monroe 1990; Nagle and Holden 2002) on pricing – first and foremost, not just subsets within other marketing books.

As the pricing discipline advanced, practitioners learned the value of their daily tasks and could communicate gains made by advising senior management about bottom line gains. Consulting companies created pricing practices whose primary concern was to help clients improve their pricing structure and processes. Eric Mitchell began publishing *The Pricing Advisor* newsletter in 1984 and *The Journal of Professional Pricing* in 1991. Pricing conferences, networking options, and literature began to grow and flourish.

Pricing as a strategic function

Further advances came as corporations looked to leverage pricing power and value propositions to improve profitability. Many companies expanded pricing departments and created vice president level positions in pricing. Some practitioners (Reid 2010) have called for the further expansion of the CPO – Chief Pricing Officer – position and Wall Street analysts began to look beyond same-store sales and other volume measures in favor of pricing metrics. In 2010, billionaire investor Warren Buffett even placed pricing power above management acumen in evaluating the worth of a company. Along with management focus, special pricing projects and longer-term corporate goals became commonplace and organization charts and reporting structures elevated pricing's status within the firm.

Several top business schools (Wharton, Stanford, University of Chicago, and others) have made pricing education a cornerstone of their executive education programs and some business schools (notably, University of Rochester) have developed concentrations in pricing. Advanced training options and professional designations, such as the Certified Pricing Professional, have allowed pricing practitioners to escalate their skills and demonstrate extra learning within the discipline. Pricing has become a topic of discussion in many board rooms, executives' suites, and team meetings in medium and large enterprises.

So pricing has made some great progress in becoming a function that is now more and more accepted in the organizational fabric of firms. In the last 20 years, pricing has been placed on the map and has demonstrated its potential impact with best-in-class marketing organizations. Our question becomes: Where do we go from here? How do we bring pricing to the next level and to reach its next frontier?

The next frontier

Our reflections at PPS have led to the identification of six critical elements for the future of the pricing profession.

Greater use of technology

As with other professions, pricing is benefiting from great advances in technology. From powerful computers to the more advanced version of analytical software, the pricing function has gained in analytical skills, speed of execution, and quality of team interactions. Pricing decisions are taken with more scientific support, more team interactions via video conference or other collaboration tools, and a greater ability to be tested in the field with customers. Feedback and data can be received in real time via enterprise resource planning (ERP) or customer relationship management (CRM) platforms. In short, it is just the beginning. The technological developments we have witnessed in the last few years can only offer immense possibilities for pricing experts. Working closely with IT departments, pricers can have access to the best communication and analytical tools to make the best decisions.

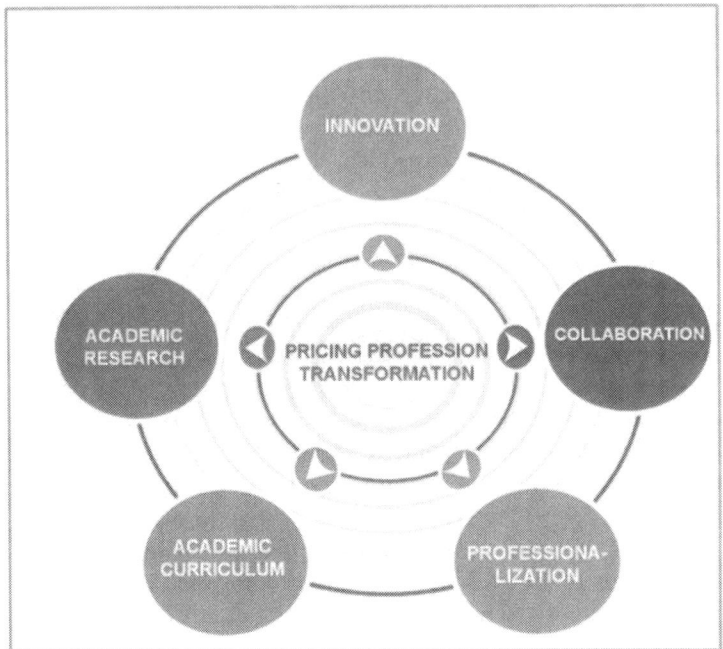

FIGURE 27.1 Framework for transformation

The increasing importance of pricing software

Over the past 10 years, we have witnessed the emergence of robust and modern pricing software that allow firms to systematize and optimize their pricing activities. These software platforms have made great inroads with Fortune 500 companies and are very relevant in the pricing sphere. The next generation of pricing software is being created as we speak. The cloud computing environment offers many opportunities for smaller firms to benefit from pricing software at a fraction of the costs without a long and difficult implementation process. Companies will be able to rely on proven, systematic, and robust platforms instead of Excel-based, internally designed, static tools and methods. The increased adoption of software also benefits the pricing profession as skills and competencies can be transferred from firm to firm creating opportunities for advancement.

More coordination and professionalization of the pricing function

The transformation of the pricing profession in firms requires the combined positive impact of the five elements which are shown in Figure 27.1 (Liozu and Hinterhuber 2011).

More academic research

Generally speaking, there is a need for more robust and systematic academic research in the areas of value and pricing management to support the proliferation of new pricing knowledge in the marketing construct. Recent academic research undertaken at Pennsylvania State University's Institute for the Study of Business Markets and at Georgia State University's Center for Business and Industrial Marketing (Ulaga 2001) is critical for the pricing profession to create knowledge, to bring documented and tested evidence of their positive impact on firm performance, and to educate practitioners.

Systematic academic curriculum

Tomorrow's marketing leaders should be equipped with the most relevant and rigorous academic knowledge on pricing. Pricing should become an integral and systematic part of the marketing curriculum: currently, only about 9 percent of business schools offer a course that has a significant emphasis on pricing (McCaskey and Brady 2007).

Greater levels of innovation in pricing

Pricing is evolving in certain areas such as revenue management, yield management, and mostly in the service, e-commerce, and software sectors. We need to see more innovation, experimentation, and new training methodologies in business-to-business (B2B) pricing. Experimentation is an important requirement for the internalization of new pricing concepts, strategies, language, and overall theories. B2B pricing may be more static in nature. By creating more excitement in the pricing field, we can attract the best minds and researchers in the field.

Collaboration among academia and practice

The profession requires a coordinated and collaborative profession-wide transformation process which involves academia, practitioners, consultants, and professional associations such as the Professional Pricing Society. This dialog and collaboration among these parties leads to the definition of a research agenda and common goals for the profession.

Professionalizing the pricing function

Joe Podolny, former dean of the Yale School of Management states: "An occupation earns the right to be a profession only when some ideals, such as being an impartial counsel, doing no harm, or serving the greater good, are infused into the conduct of people in that occupation" (Podolny 2009). The professionalization of the pricing function requires: the establishment of a code of ethics for the pricing community; the development of capability matrices and of formal entry requirements for pricing professionals; pricing governance mechanisms and dedicated career paths for pricing professionals in companies; and emphasis on continuous formal learning. Some of these activities are already underway; much, we feel, remains to be done for pricing to become a true profession.

Pricing in the C-suite

The next frontier for the pricing profession also involves the elevation of C-suite positions such as Chief Pricing Officer and Chief Value Officer representing the pricing and value management functions. The Chief Marketing Officer (CMO) and Chief Commercial Officer (CCO) positions have been more widely accepted over the past decade. While the role of CCO is relatively new, about 200 CCOs have been appointed worldwide since the role emerged (Abele and Stevenson 2009). Similarly, the number and presence of CMOs is accelerating around the world. In 2006, Spencer Stuart identified more than 30 CMOs in FTSE top 50 companies. In the USA, among Fortune 100 firms, 23 had a CMO as the head of marketing in 2008 (Grewal and Wang 2009). The acceptance of the role of Chief Pricing Officer (CPO) and Chief Value Officer (CVO) have a long way to go. First of all, in most companies, the pricing and value management function receives limited attention. Data from the Professional Pricing Society, the world's largest organization dedicated to pricing, reveal that fewer than 5 percent of Fortune 500 companies have a full-time function exclusively dedicated to pricing (Mitchell 2011).

The mid-market opportunity

Who manages pricing in the millions of small and medium business around the world? The Small Business Administration reports that 99 percent of businesses are small in nature and create the vast majority of GDP. As a profession, how do we carry the pricing and value messages to the millions of marketing, sales, and finance professionals involved in pricing strategies and tactics? One opportunity to reach them is to start publishing pricing knowledge in mainstream media and to partner with larger associations such as the American Management Association or the American Marketing Association. Here the frontier might be difficult to reach. But we have to start somewhere and create an "army" of pricing evangelists spreading the good word on the power of pricing excellence.

The skills of the future

Last but not least, we project that the pricing skills of the future are going to evolve. With the advent of pricing software and greater access to technology, pricing professionals will have to show a combination of hard and soft skills. Pricers will be required to gain organizational and behavioral skills to accompany firms through their transformational activities. Soft skills, such as change management, emotional intelligence, and communication intelligence, will be needed more and more. How then do we equip pricing professionals with these skills? Firms will have to create more balanced profiles to be able to speak with computers and software for data analysis but also to lead humans through tough and sometimes tenuous transformational journeys.

Conclusions

The pricing professional is evolving and will continue to do so with the increased role of technology. The Professional Pricing Society is staying ahead by embracing megatrends and by preparing the way for the next transformational steps. We are planning for the future by embracing technology in our training programs but also during our numerous industry meetings. We are embracing academic research and have welcomed thought leaders in our future thinking. The road ahead is bright and challenging. We can achieve great things as a profession as long as we all work together and lead the profession to reach this new frontier. Join us in this journey!

References

Abele, J. M. and Stevenson, J. M. (2009) *The rise of the chief commercial officer*. Heidrick & Struggles White Paper, pp. 1–4.

Grewal, R. and Wang, R. (2009) The chief marketing officer: New vintage, or just old wine in a new bottle. *The Chief Marketing Officer Journal*, 1, pp. 29–33.

Liozu, S. and Hinterhuber, A. (2011) The pricing function in industrial markets. *Journal of Professional Pricing*, Q1, pp. 20–4.

McCaskey, P. H. and Brady, D. L. (2007) The current status of course offerings in pricing in the business curriculum. *Journal of Product & Brand Management*, 16 (5), pp. 358–61.

Mitchell, K. (2011) *The current state of pricing practice in U.S. firms (opening speech)*. Paper presented at the Professional Pricing Society Annual Spring Conference, Chicago, USA.

Monroe, K. (1990) *Pricing: Making profitable decisions*. Burr Ridge, IL: McGraw-Hill Companies.

Nagle, T. and Holden, R. (2002) *The strategy and tactics of pricing: a guide to profitable decision making*. Upper Saddle River, NJ: Prentice Hall.

Podolny, J. (2009) The buck starts (and stops) at business school. *Harvard Business Review*, 87 (6), p. 62.

Reid, W. (2010) Consider this – Why companies need a chief pricing officer. *Industry Week Newsletter*.

Ulaga, W. (2001) Customer value in business markets an agenda for inquiry. *Industrial Marketing Management*, 30 (4), pp. 315–19.

INDEX

5-endings 376, 384–5, 387
9-endings 11, 365–6, 376–88

acquisition price 231–2
acquisition value 188, 360
advanced reporting 318–19
advertising 357, 368
agreed-upon price 141
agreement/contract pricing 288, 290
AMOS (Analysis of Moment Structures) 78
analytics (in pricing systems) 121
ASP (average sales price) 121
ASV (average shared variance) 39
attitude (in LACEY framework) 111
AVE (average variance extracted) 39, 78–9, 81

B2B (business-to-business) markets: alternative pricing methods 131–7; and communicating value 255–8, 270–1; and cross-functional collaboration 299, 302–3, 306; and risk/benefit transfer 344–5; and ROI 119–26; and value chains 135–7, 147, 149–50; and value creation 183–4, 187, 189–94; and VBS 323–4, 329–30, 335, 337, 341–2; and WTP 288–97
B2C (business-to-consumer) markets 11–12, 74, 123, 135–6, 291
'baton hand-off' system 328–9
benchmarking 173–4
benefit/risk transfer 344–5, 350
Bertini, Marco 238
brand awareness 170
brand growth matrix 247–9
brand positioning 331–2
brand value 136
Breidert, Christoph 288
bubble charts 311, 315–16

Buffet, Warren 68, 305
buyer behaviour: and consumer price knowledge 368–9; and fairness 362; and increasing/decreasing prices 363–4; and perceived value 359–60, 372; and price endings 364–6; and price–quality perceptions 366–8; and price setting 357–8, 370–1; and reference prices 361–2; and response to price 358–9; and WTP 357–9, 362, 371
'buyer value' 324
buying influences 167–8
buying-decision criteria 168–70

CA (Cronbach's alpha) coefficient 78
callable revenue management 9
CBE (pricing champion behaviour) 75, 78–80, 82–4, 90
CBP (cost-based pricing) 36–8
CCO (Chief Commercial Officer) 109–10, 116, 408
centralization: definition of 29, 30–1; and expertise centralization 38; and hybrid organizational design 30; importance of 28; and organizational change 29–30; overview 10; practical variations 30–3, 42; research carried out 27–8; and sales force price delegation 56–61; success measurement 32
centre-led pricing 30–2, 34–5, 38–42
centre-supported pricing 30–2
CEOs (Chief Executive Officers): and building VBP 179; and championing 10, 67–8, 71–2, 85–6; and CVOs 111, 116; and price tracking 322; research interviews 12–14, 68, 74; and strategic clarity assessments 205
CFA (confirmatory factor analysis) 39, 77–81

CFI (comparative fit index) 80–1
CFOs (Chief Financial Officers) 259–60, 298
CGS (cost of goods sold) 344–5
championing: effectiveness of 67–8, 85; overview 10; research hypotheses 68–74; research methodology 74–82; research results 82–6
change management 11
cloud-based software 300
cluster analysis 154, 158
CMB (common method bias) 77–8
CMO (Chief Marketing Officer) 109–10, 114, 116, 408
coaching (in VBS) 340–1
COBP (competition-based pricing) 37–8
COGS (cost of goods sold) 144–5, 335
collective mindfulness (CM) 68, 72–3, 75–6, 78–80, 82–4, 91
commitment (in LACEY framework) 111
commoditization 222, 273–5, 303
compatibility 267
compensation criteria 202
competency models 338–9
competitive alternatives 301, 303, 306–7
competitive price positioning 58–9
competitor performance 173–4
competitor pricing 123, 133, 190
complexity of offerings 265–6, 267–70
compromise effects 12
computational factors 383
conceptual blending 302–3
confirmatory factor analysis 78–81
conjoint analysis 132, 141, 168–70
connectivity 149–50
consulting industries 191–2
consumer price knowledge 368–9
consumer response to price 358–9
contingent pricing 9
contracts and pricing (in due diligence process) 200, 202
'contribution margin' metric 202
convergent validity 78
COOs (Chief Operating Officers) 205
Corey, E. Raymond 298
'cost of production' theory 100–1
cost reductions 124
'cost to serve' metric 202
cost-plus pricing 52–3, 108, 134–5, 147, 178, 293, 335
CPO (Chief Pricing Officer) 105, 109–10, 116, 405, 407–8

CPP (Certified Pricing Professional) program 180–1
CR (composite reliability) 39, 78–9, 81–2
CR (cost reduction) 275–6, 279–81, 284–5
Creative Pricing (book) 3
credibility 305
CRM (customer relationship management) systems 119, 298, 405
cross-functional collaboration 298–307
CSCW (computer supported collaborative work) 299–306
cultural differences 385–6, 388
currency effect 322
customer benefits 48–9, 153–4, 181, 234–6, 257–9, 333–4
customer business models 301–3
customer conversations 305–7
customer discounts 47, 50, 56, 61, 62, 224, 363
customer interviews 173
customer loyalty 324–5
customer value management cycle 326–7
customization 190–1, 333–4
CVMA (customer value map analysis): and defining customer value 48–9; implementing 52–60; and organizational barriers 47, 50, 60–1; and sales force price delegation 47, 52–61; and VBP 46–7
CVOs (Chief Value Officers): emergence of 99–100, 106, 407–8; framework for 108–13; job description 113–16; lessons of 107; and value creation 113–16; and VBP 108

data analysis 33–4, 51–2
data collection 33, 51, 74–5
data elements (in pricing systems) 122–3
'day in a life' study 173
'day to day' operations 198
debundling 135
decentralization 27–31
decision analytic models 263–4
decision-making distribution 167–8
decision-making rationality 68, 73–4, 76, 78–80, 82–4, 86, 88
decoy options 12, 396–9
defining price 321–2
demand 103, 379–81
design phase (of asset lifecycle) 231–2
diamond–water paradox 100, 102–3
'digging deeper' (in due diligence process) 200
digit directionality 381–2

412   Index

diminishing marginal utility, law of 101
disposal phase (of asset lifecycle) 232
distribution channels 248–50
distribution curves 347–9
division of labour 104–5
documenting price agreements 145–7
Drucker, Peter 104, 106
due diligence: and pricing capabilities 197–8, 202–15; revised process 200–2; and target company information 197–8; typical process 198–200

EBITDA (earnings before interest, taxes, depreciation, and amortization) 59
EC (emotional contribution) 275–6, 279–81, 284–6
economic benefits 257–8, 262–6
economic buyers 258–62
economic crises 178–9
EDI (electronic data interchange) 119
EFA (exploratory factor analysis) 39
'entry price level' 241
environmental variables 259
ERP (Enterprise Resource Planning) 120, 300, 305–6, 405
escalation policies 161–2
EVE (economic value estimation) 300–3, 306
even prices 364–5, 379, 382
evolution of pricing 403–5
execution (in pricing systems) 120–1
experimentation (in LACEY framework) 111–12
experiments (in WTP estimation) 291–2
expertise centralization 38
external costs 184, 193
external reference prices 361

fairness 362, 370
fast-paced innovation 188–90, 195
field pilots 157–9
final net price 141
financial service products 346–7, 349
financial statements (in due diligence process) 199–201
first-order factors 78–81
FMCGs (fast moving consumer goods) 361, 363
focus group 149
focus industries 165–7
Ford, Henry 6–7
free products 7–8
future market value 189–90, 193, 195
future of pricing 21, 403, 405–9

Gildert, Paula 236
Gossen, Hermann Heinrich 102
Gossen's Law 102–3

Harrex, Brendon 107
'hearts and minds' 339–40
'hiding' prices 357
higher margin 123
higher win rates 123–4
Human Accomplishment (book) 113
human resources 202
hybrid organizational design 30

ideal customer profiling 170–2, 175
IFI (Incremental Fit Index) 80–1
In Rainbows (album) 357
increased opportunities 124
increasing/decreasing prices 363–4
incremental costs 134–5
individualized pricing 9–10
information sharing/control 304
insurance products 346–7
internal costs 184–5, 193
internal reference prices 361
intuition 86
inventory management (in due diligence process) 202
investing in pricing systems 119–20, 124–6
invoice price 140
IP (intellectual property) 199, 202
IRR (internal rate of return) 214
irrelevant attributes 11–12
isolation of pricing 298

Jevons, William Stanley 102
JND (just noticeable difference) 363

Kennedy, Paul 106–7
Kierkegaard, Soren 112
KPIs (key performance indicators) 38, 138, 141–8, 321

labour 100–5
LACEY framework 109–13
language 138
language systems 305
large engineered solutions 346–7
large software deployments 346–7, 350
leadership (in LACEY framework) 109–11
life cycle of products 217, 219–20, 226, 229, 231–4
list price 140, 145
list/matrix pricing 288, 290, 291–2
LOI (Letter of Intent) 198

long cycle durable goods 346–7, 349
loss data 294
lowering prices 217–20, 223–6

M&A (mergers and acquisition): and pricing capabilities 197–8, 202–15; revised process 200–2; and target company information 197–8; typical process 198–200
margin reports 311–12
marginalism 102–3
market data (in WTP estimation) 292–3
market expansion 6–7
market offerings 331–5
market price 222–3, 226
market pricing intelligence 206–7
market research 35, 153–4, 157, 332–3
market-based pricing 133–4, 147
Marting, Elizabeth 3
Marx, Karl 101–2
'match-the-competitor' pricing 335
MATs (moving annual totals) 313
MDM (Master Data Management) 122
Menger, Carl 102
metrics 138–9
MFN (Most Favoured Nation) clause 124–5
Microsoft Windows 7 (operating system) 394–7
mid-market opportunities 408
mix effect 322
Moore's Law 222
MSV (maximum shared variance) 39
Murray, Charles 113
myths in pricing 217–27

net price 140–1
new metrics 5–6
NNFI (Non-Normed Fit Index) 80–1
non-market goods 369–70
non-response bias 76–7
normalization 293–4
NPI (new product introduction) 181
NPV (net present value) 214
NYOP (name your own price) 8, 357

observability 267
odd prices: and buyer behaviour 364–5; effectiveness of 386–8; origins of 376–7; and 'price illusion' 377–8; recommended research 389–90; research on 379–86
OEMs (original equipment manufacturers) 52–4, 57, 229–31, 236
operation phase (of asset lifecycle) 232

operations (in due diligence process) 199, 201
organization: barriers 47, 48, 50, 60–1; and CVMA 46–7; hybrid design 30; lack of research on 27; overview 14–16; practical variations 30–3, 42; research findings 35–41; research methodology 33–5; structure 28–9; theory of 28
organizational change 29–30
organizational variables 259–60
outcome risk perception 266–70
overall strategic clarity (in pricing capability assessment) 204–5
overall value equation 170–1

pay for performance pricing 5
PCBM (price endings and consumer behaviour model) 384
'pendulum swing' phenomenon 30
perceived value: and B2B companies 136–7; and buyer behaviour 359–60, 372; and market pricing 133; and value pricing 132–3; and VBP 186
personal win/risk factors 171–2
PLM (product lifecycle management) 298
PMO (project management office) 114
pocket price 322
'poker players' 221
polarization (in zero-based pricing strategies) 246–9, 251–2
portfolio price optimization 347, 350
power analysis 81–2
premium branding 348–9
prescriptive pricing 295–6
price band charts 311, 315–16
price-buyers 220–2, 226
price change versus previous period charts 311, 314
price comparison analyses 58
price elasticity 58, 217, 219–20, 310
price endings 11, 364–6; *see also* odd prices
price erosion 32, 189–90, 223, 243
price fences 159–60, 162
price floors 141–2, 144–5
'price illusion' 377–8
price indexing 318–19, 320
price–mix charts 311, 313–14
price performance measurement 209–10, 320–1
price point definition 35–7
price premium 212–14, 234, 237–8
price pressure 217, 222
price–quality perceptions 366–8, 382–3
price recall 368–9

price reduction 6–7
price reports 311–19
price–sales charts 311, 312–13
price snapshot reports 313–18
price tracking 310–22
price trends analysis 312–13
price–value graphs 143
price waterfall analysis 311, 319
'Priceberg' 232
pricing capabilities (PC): and championing 68, 72–4; and competitor pricing 190; and costs 184–5, 193; and due diligence process 197–8, 202–15; and M&A process 197–8, 202–15; measuring 75, 78–80, 89; model results 82–5; overview 10; and value assessment 186–7, 193; and value creation 183–4, 195
pricing clouds 147
pricing councils 180
pricing excellence 178–82
pricing explorer tool 147–8
pricing improvements 203, 207
pricing literature 68–71
pricing managers 142
Pricing Offices 321
pricing organizational alignment 210–12
pricing orientation 70–1, 73–5, 78–84, 87–8
pricing power 222–3
pricing process implementation 180
pricing skills 408
pricing tools 143–8
Principles of Economics (book) 102
procurement 259–62
product development 142
product utilization 346–7
Professional Pricing Society (PPS) 12, 21, 27, 33–4, 67, 109, 180–1, 321, 403, 408
professionalization of pricing function 406–7
profit leakages 120–1, 125
profitability 160–2
promotional pricing 288, 291–2
provenance 302
proving ROI 124–5
psychological benefits 257–8
psychology of pricing: behavioural aspects 357–72; and odd prices 376–89; overview 20–1; and software pricing 393–9

purchasing/vendors (in due diligence process) 201
PWYW (pay what you want) 8, 357

quality 366–8, 382–3
QUALY (quality-adjusted life year) 5

real versus target price charts 311, 317
rebates 218–20
recessionary strategies 241–6
'Recovery Killers' 243
redemption value 360
reduction of liability 124
reference prices 11, 361–2
reference value 186–7, 188–9, 192–3
relative performance 70–4, 76, 78–80, 82–4, 92
resource dedication 179–80
resource-based models 72, 85
revealed preference 369
revenue causality reports 311, 316–17
revenue growth 225, 227
revenue management 8–9
reviewing data (in zero-based pricing strategies) 249–50
RFP (Request for Proposal) 157, 242–3, 290
RG (revenue gain) 275–6, 279–81, 284–5
RMSEA (root-mean-square error of approximation) 80, 81–2
ROI (return on investment) 70, 119–26, 136
role specialization 37
'rules of thumb' 68, 73, 357

SaaS (Software as a Service) 300
sales and marketing (in due diligence process) 199, 201
sales and marketing alignment (in VBS) 328–9
sales channels strategy (in VBS) 337–8
sales effectiveness system 326–8
sales force management 46–7, 50
sales force price delegation 47, 50–61
sales force structure (in VBS) 337–8
sales managers performance assessment 311, 319
sales processes (in VBS) 335–7
sales promotions 363–4
sales tools (in VBS) 339–40
sales versus agreement tracking 311, 319
salience 381–4
scarcity 100
scatter charts 311, 314–15

Index

science (in pricing systems) 121–2
scientific decision-making 36
scope optimization 241–3, 244
second-order factors 81
security 302
segmentation: criteria of 131; effectiveness of 151–2; objectives of 154–6; and odd prices 386; overview 4–5; planning 156–60; and procurement 261; and sales strategies 160–2; and value 4–5, 152–4; and value chains 136–7; and VBS 329–30; and WTP 293–4
Segmentation Preparation Plan 155–6
self-esteem 110
SEM (structural equation modelling) 82
senior management commitment 179
Simon, Julian 112
SKUs (stock keeping units) 138–9, 206, 291, 320
smart pricing 241, 243–4
Smith, Adam 100, 104–5
'so what?' analysis 276–81, 283–4
social media 205, 299–300, 323, 368
software pricing 393–9, 406
Sowell, Thomas 103
SPAs (Special pricing agreements) 290
specialization of labour 104–5
spot pricing 288, 290
strategy: during recession 241–6; foundations of 137–42; and fundamental value factors 164–76; and integrating price 142–7; and M&A 197–216; and myths 217–27; overview of 16–18; and pricing excellence 178–82; and segmentation *see* segmentation; types of 132–5; and value creation 228–40; and zero-based pricing 245–52
subjective well-being 369–70
subscription pricing 288, 290–1
'supplier value' 324
surveys (in WTP estimation) 291
sustainable value-assessment 104–5

T&C (terms and conditions) tool 145–7
tactics: and communicating value 255–71; and cross-functional collaboration 298–307; overview 18–20; price tracking 310–22; and value triads 274–86; and WTP 288–97
TCO (total cost of ownership) 71, 132, 136, 141, 229–34
'teaching' customers 267, 269
technical benefits 257–8
technical buyers 258–9
technological advances 405
tenure of relationships 351
Thatcher, Margaret 111
The Journal of Professional Pricing (journal) 404
The Pricing Advisor (newsletter) 404
The Strategy and Tactics of Pricing (book) 300
thick/thin tails 347–9, 351–3
third party relationships 353
'three-legged race' collaboration 329
Tick-Tock model 189–90
time pacing 188–9
TMP (target market price) 141–2
top/bottom listing 311, 319
total cost-in-use components 325
transaction value 360–2
transactional pricing management 207–9
transparency 302, 305
traps 217–27
trialability 267
trust 302, 305, 306
turnover 139
turnover build-up graphs 143–4

under 'floor price' reports 311, 318
underestimation of price 383–4
unscientific decision-making 36
user buyers 258–9
utility 369–71

value: and B2B markets 11; and buyer behaviour 358, 360–3; and customer benefits 48–9, 153–4; defining 48–9, 100–3, 256–8, 273; fundamental factors 164–76; at organizational level 103–4; and price-buyers 220–2; quantifying 234–6; responsibility for 104–8; and segmentation 4–5, 152–4; and 'so what?' analysis 276–81, 283–4
value assessment 186–7, 193–4
value calculators 283–4
value chains 135–7, 147, 149–50, 191
value communication: in B2B markets 255–8, 270–1; and economic benefits 262–6; and economic buyers 258–62; and value perception 256, 270; strategies of 265–70
value councils 107, 110–11
value creation: in B2B companies 183–4, 187, 189–94; and CVOs 113–16; and pricing 228–9, 234–40; and response to price 358; and TCO 229–31; and VBS 325–6, 331, 333–5

value drivers 181, 276–81, 300–3, 305
'value in exchange' 100
'value in use' 100, 188, 360
value-informed pricing 70
value leakage 326
value management 71, 100, 116
value perception 256–7, 270
Value, Price and Profit (book) 101
'value-pricing thermometer' 366–7
value propositions 331–5
value quantification 181
value shop 191
value triads 274–86
variable pricing structures 349–51
VAT (value added tax) 149
VBP (value-based pricing): in B2B markets 132–3, 147; building 179–82; and centralized pricing function 38–9; and competitor pricing 123; and cross-functional collaboration 298–307; and customization 190–2; and CVMA 46–7, 53, 55–62; and CVOs 108; and dedicated pricing functions 38; and defining customer value 48–9; and economic crises 178–9; and expertise centralization 38–9; and marketing 38; and perceived value 186; and price point definition 35–6; and role specialization 37; and value assessment 186–7, 193–4; and value creation 228; and value factors 164; and VBS 335, 342–3

VBS (value-based selling): go-to-market strategy 329–38; implementation of 338–41; overview 323–6; and sales and marketing alignment 328–9; and sales effectiveness system 326–8; and VBP 335, 342–3
versioning (in software) 393–9
vertical markets 165–6
VOC (voice of the customer) studies 164, 167, 172–6
volume 134, 139, 144, 146–7

Walras, Leon 102
waterfall charts 122, 139–40, 144–5
Wealth of Nations (book) 100
web scraping 123
Wicksell, Knut 102
Wicksteed, Philip 102
window shopping 351
win-only data 294–6
workflow/business model studies 264–5
WTP (willingness-to-pay) 288–97, 351, 357–9, 362, 371

Young President Organization International (YPO) 74
youth (in LACEY framework) 112–13

zero-based pricing 7–8, 245–52

eBooks – at www.eBookstore.tandf.co.uk

A library at your fingertips!

eBooks are electronic versions of printed books. You can store them on your PC/laptop or browse them online.

They have advantages for anyone needing rapid access to a wide variety of published, copyright information.

eBooks can help your research by enabling you to bookmark chapters, annotate text and use instant searches to find specific words or phrases. Several eBook files would fit on even a small laptop or PDA.

NEW: Save money by eSubscribing: cheap, online access to any eBook for as long as you need it.

Annual subscription packages

We now offer special low-cost bulk subscriptions to packages of eBooks in certain subject areas. These are available to libraries or to individuals.

For more information please contact webmaster.ebooks@tandf.co.uk

We're continually developing the eBook concept, so keep up to date by visiting the website.

www.eBookstore.tandf.co.uk

CPSIA information can be obtained at www.ICGtesting.com
Printed in the USA
LVOW08s1928180914

404800LV00001B/1/P